Foreign Policy in Comparative Perspective

Foreign Policy in Comparative Perspective
Domestic and International Influences
on State Behavior

Edited by

Ryan K. Beasley, Juliet Kaarbo,
Jeffrey S. Lantis, and Michael T. Snarr

CQ PRESS

A Division of
Congressional Quarterly Inc.

CQ Press
A Division of Congressional Quarterly Inc.
1255 22nd Street, N.W., Suite 400
Washington, D.C. 20037

(202) 822-1475; (800) 638-1710

www.cqpress.com

♾ The paper used in this publication meets the minimum requirements of the American National Standard for Information Sciences—Permanence of Paper for Printed Library Materials, ANSIZ39.48-1992.

Cover design by Yasuyo Iguchi.

Printed and bound in the United States of America

05 04 03 02 01   5 4 3 2 1

Library of Congress Cataloging-in-Publication Data
Foreign policy in comparative perspective : domestic and international
influences on state behavior / edited by Ryan K. Beasley ... [et al.].
    p.   cm.
  Includes bibliographical references and index.
  ISBN 1-56802-626-9 (alk. paper)
  1. International relations. I. Beasley, Ryan K.

JZ1242 .F676 2001
327—dc21

                                                              2001004315

To Ellie, Joshua, Madison, Ty, and Isaiah

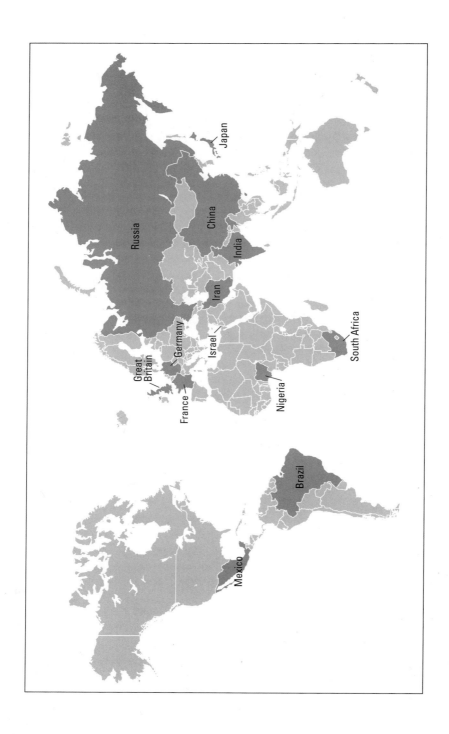

Contents

Contributors

Olufemi A. Babarinde is associate professor of international studies at Thunderbird, the American Graduate School of International Management in Arizona. His research areas and publications include African integration and regionalism, African enterprises, relations between the European Union and less-developed countries, European Union relations with the United States, the Economic and Monetary Union of the European Union, and Nigerian political economy. He currently serves on the editorial boards of *Africa Today* and *Thunderbird International Business Review*. Babarinde earned his Ph.D. from Miami University.

Ryan K. Beasley is assistant professor of political science at Baker University. His research and teaching interests include political psychology, group decision making, comparative foreign policy, and comparative politics. He has recently contributed articles and chapters to *Political Psychology; Research on Groups and Teams*, Volume 1; and *Problem Representation in Political Decision Making*. He has served on the Young Scholars Committee of the International Society of Political Psychology and is currently coeditor of the newsletter for that professional organization.

Paul D'Anieri is associate professor of political science and associate dean of international programs at the University of Kansas. His research focuses on international politics among the former Soviet states. Since earning his Ph.D. from Cornell University, D'Anieri has been visiting professor at the University of L'viv (Ukraine) and at Harvard University. His most recent book is *Politics and Society in Ukraine* (1999), written with Robert Kravchuk and Taras Kuzio.

Laura Drake is a Middle East scholar and consultant in Washington, D.C., and the Middle East, specializing in the region's political-military and strategic affairs. Presently she is adjunct professor in international relations at American University's School of International Service. She holds a Ph.D. in international relations from American University, School of International Service, as well as an M.A. in international affairs from Columbia University, School of International and Public Affairs. Her recent research and prior publications focus on the Arab-Israeli conflict and peace process, the Middle East peace process, the results of

U.S. containment strategies against Iraq and Iran, and unconventional weapons proliferation in the area.

Kenneth W. Grundy is the Marcus A. Hanna Professor of Political Science at Case Western Reserve University (CWRU) in Cleveland. He has served as visiting senior lecturer at Makerere University College (University of East Africa) in Uganda; as visiting scholar at the Institute of Social Studies (The Hague). He has published widely, including most recently *South Africa: Domestic Crisis and International Challenge* (1991). From 1998 to 2000 he was director of CWRU's Center for Policy Studies. He received his Ph.D. from Pennsylvania State University.

Paul D. Hoyt has taught international relations theory, decision-making theory, Middle Eastern politics, and post-Soviet foreign policy. His research has focused on international relations theory and foreign policy decision making. He has published articles on topics including group decision making and rogue states in journals such as *Political Psychology, Cooperation and Conflict, Global Society,* and the *Journal of Conflict Studies.*

Juliet Kaarbo is associate professor of political science at the University of Kansas. Her teaching and research interests include political psychology, leadership and decision making, group dynamics, foreign policy analysis, parliamentary political systems, and international negotiations. Her research has appeared in *International Studies Quarterly, European Journal of International Relations, Political Psychology, Cooperation and Conflict, International Interactions,* and *Leadership Quarterly.* She holds a Ph.D. from Ohio State University.

Steven Philip Kramer is professor of grand strategy at the Industrial College of the Armed Forces, National Defense University, in Washington, D.C. He is also senior policy adviser to the assistant secretary of state for European affairs, where he focuses on long-term issues and on issues related to France. His many published books include *Does France Still Count? The French Role in the New Europe* (1994) and *Trouble in Paradise: Europe in the 21st Century* (1996), cowritten with Irene Kyriakopoulos. Kramer received a Ph.D. in history from Princeton University.

Jeffrey S. Lantis is associate professor of political science and chair of the international relations program at the College of Wooster. He teaches courses on foreign policy analysis, international relations, and the politics of Europe and the United States. His major publications include "Rising to the Challenge: German Security Policy in the Post–Cold War Era," *German Politics and Society* (1996); *Domestic Constraints and the Breakdown of International Agreements* (1997); and *The New International Studies Classroom: Active Teaching, Active Learning* (2000), coedited with Lynn M. Kuzma and John Boehrer. He holds a Ph.D. in political science from Ohio State University.

Akitoshi Miyashita is assistant professor in the department of international relations at Tokyo International University. He is an author of *"Gaiatsu* and Japan's Foreign Aid: Rethinking the Reactive-Proactive Debate," *International Studies Quarterly* (1999), and a coeditor of *Japanese Foreign Policy in Asia and the Pacific: Domestic Interests, American Pressure, and Regional Integration* (forthcoming 2001). He received his Ph.D. from Columbia University.

Tinaz Pavri is assistant professor of political science at Spelman College in Atlanta. She teaches courses in comparative political systems, Japan in Asia, human rights and conflict resolution, and international organizations. Her research is in the areas of international negotiations, national identity, and the Indo-Pakistani conflict and has been published in such journals as *Negotiation Journal* and *Current World Leaders—International Issues.* She coauthored *Population Diversity and the U.S. Army,* published by the Strategic Studies Institute.

Brian Ripley received his Ph.D. in political science from Ohio State University. He was on the faculty of the University of Pittsburgh from 1989 to 1996 and spent 1994–1995 as visiting assistant professor at the University of Wisconsin. In 1993 he received the Chancellor's Distinguished Teaching Award at the University of Pittsburgh. He was selected as a 1994–1995 Pew Faculty Fellow in International Affairs (under the auspices of the John F. Kennedy School of Government at Harvard). In 1996 he joined the faculty of Mercyhurst College, where he teaches courses in American political institutions, international political economy, and Asian politics. He has published in the area of foreign policy decision making.

Michael T. Snarr is assistant professor of social and political studies at Wilmington College. His research focuses on Latin American foreign policy toward the United States, and he is coeditor of *Introducing Global Issues* (1998). His most recent publication is a chapter on empirical approaches to Global South foreign policy, to appear in *The Foreign Policy of the Global South: Seeking Conceptual Frameworks* (forthcoming). He has taught courses on Latin American politics, contemporary Mexico, U.S. foreign policy, and international organization, and he regularly takes students to Mexico on study tours.

Scott D. Tollefson is assistant professor of political science and director of the M.A. program in political science at Kansas State University. Previously, he taught at the Naval Postgraduate School in Monterey, California. He is the author of various articles and chapters on Brazil's foreign policy and on civil-military relations in Argentina, Brazil, and Chile.

Brian White is professor of international relations at Staffordshire University (United Kingdom) and currently is a visiting professor at Warwick University (United Kingdom) and the University of Toulouse (France). He has also been a visiting professor at Rhodes University (South Africa) and the University of Wales (Aberystwyth). He teaches and does research in foreign policy analysis and British and European foreign policies. His major publications include *British Foreign Policy: Tradition, Change, and Transformation; Understanding Foreign Policy; Britain, Détente and Changing East–West Relations;* and *Issues in World Politics.* His latest book is *Understanding European Foreign Policy* (2001).

Stephen Wright is professor of political science at Northern Arizona University. His research interests focus on African foreign policy and political economy. Among his more recent publications is *Nigeria: Struggle for Stability and Status* (1998). He was editor of *African Foreign Policies* (1999).

PREFACE

This book presents a look at foreign policy in comparative perspective by focusing on thirteen countries. Although many scholars have abandoned the term *comparative foreign policy* because of its past association with positivist, inductive, and quantitative approaches, we believe in the importance of theoretically driven comparison to gain a greater understanding of the nature and explanations of foreign policy in general. Comparisons of foreign policy behavior often reveal similarities and differences that are the building blocks of further social scientific exploration. To that end, the editors and contributors of this book met in Los Angeles at a workshop funded by the International Studies Association. This special opportunity enabled contributors to present chapter drafts, engage in critical dialogue, and bring consistency to the chapters.

Once Roy C. Macridis's long-running *Foreign Policy in World Politics* was out of print, we, like many others, were at a loss for well-written material that offered the historical background of states' foreign policies and discussed the contemporary issues they face in world politics. Moreover, we recognized the need for material that dealt with the major factors driving foreign policy. We expect this book to be used as a basic text for that purpose. The countries were chosen, as we discuss in the introductory and concluding chapters, to allow for meaningful comparisons relevant to the theories and issues that are current in foreign policy analysis. We also chose them because they tend to be the countries with which students are most familiar, as they are covered in many introductory comparative politics texts. In this book the countries are presented in the same order typically seen in such textbooks, with the more familiar states appearing first. Because the country chapters stand alone, however, instructors can easily modify the order of presentation. Chapters 2 through 14 each deal with a particular country and its foreign policy. We chose not to group countries into a single chapter, treating them as a particular region (such as Africa or Latin America). Although the country chapters in this book speak to common concerns shared by states within in a region, they also illustrate important variations.

The focus of each country chapter is the substance of its foreign policy. These chapters are divided into sections dealing with a country's foreign policy during the Cold War and the issues the country confronts in the post–Cold War period. Each country chapter contributes to the overall theme of the book—understanding domestic and international influences on foreign policy. For example, in the sections on external and internal factors, each country chapter looks at the international actors and forces that not only constrain but also provide opportunities for the state. Country chapters also discuss the domestic actors and processes that shape foreign policy.

Each chapter reminds the student of the theories and concepts presented in Chapter 1, which introduces various explanations of foreign policy derived from theories of international relations and research on its domestic sources. After defining the term *foreign policy* and discussing the nature of comparison and foreign policy analysis, Chapter 1 takes the student through many aspects of foreign policy, comparing them and pointing out which of the country chapters demonstrate application of the theories.

The book is designed primarily for undergraduate courses on comparative foreign policy, although the material is also useful for students in courses that involve role-playing simulations, such as international organization or model United Nations courses. Instructors can use this text to provide students with important information about the content of their countries' positions and give them a better understanding of their countries' priorities and dilemmas, at home and abroad. Finally, we know that many instructors search for different ways to teach introductory courses in international relations. This book is an alternative for those who choose a foreign policy or a country-by-country approach to international politics.

We have included several pedagogical features in this book to encourage students to think critically and connect the theoretical discussion of the first chapter to the material in the country chapters. Chapter 1 includes a list of questions for students to consider as they read the remaining chapters. Editors' introductions summarize the themes of each country chapter and compare the countries to others in the book at critical points. Each country chapter is organized consistently to include sections on internal and external factors. Finally, the concluding chapter brings together the important points of the country chapters and compares the foreign policies of several states, according to the theoretical expectations presented in Chapter 1. This approach may serve as the foundation for case teaching, in-depth comparative analysis assignments, role-playing simulations, or issue-area research projects. The chapter concludes with a discussion of the linkages between external and internal factors, as observed throughout the book, and the implications for future foreign policy and the study of foreign policy.

Acknowledgments

We express our appreciation to the editorial team at CQ Press, particularly Charisse Kiino, for making this book possible and for being such a pleasure to work with. We would also like to thank Michelle Tupper and Belinda Josey for their contributions to the production of this volume. The reviews of the proposal and the manuscript solicited by CQ Press helped us develop the text, and we thank Douglas A. Borer (Virginia Tech University), Marijke Breuning (Truman State University), Maurice A. East (George Washington University), Anthony

Gadzey (Auburn University), Joe Hagan (West Virginia University), Valerie Hudson (Brigham Young University), William H. Meyer (University of Delaware), and Robert Pastor (Emory University) for their careful reading and constructive comments and suggestions.

We also thank the International Studies Association for funding a conference held in March 2000 in Los Angeles, which brought together the editors and the contributors and proved invaluable in shaping this effort. The contributors deserve much credit, not only for their individual chapters but also for their ideas and lively discussions during the conference and throughout the process of developing this book. Their feedback was critical in molding the form of the book. We especially express our appreciation to Brian Ripley, who was present at the creation of the book and greatly contributed to our early discussions.

Finally, we thank our professors at Ohio State University graduate school who taught us how to study foreign policy. We particularly appreciate the efforts of Chuck Hermann and Peg Hermann, whose ideas have significantly influenced the way we teach, research, and think about foreign policy. Indeed, their invitation to a small conference on comparative foreign policy in 1989 in Jackson Hole, Wyoming, sparked not only our scholarly interest in foreign policy but also our friendship. That interest and that friendship are the foundations of this book.

R.K.B., J.K., J.S.L., and M.T.S.

CHAPTER I

The Analysis of Foreign Policy in Comparative Perspective

Juliet Kaarbo, Jeffrey S. Lantis, and Ryan K. Beasley

Recent and far-reaching changes in the world present a challenge to leaders charged with making foreign policy, as well as to those who study foreign policy. Consider the changes in global politics that have occurred just since the mid-1980s. The world suddenly transformed from one in which the two "superpowers," the United States and the Soviet Union, were the primary players in an international drama dominated by military tensions (with millions of soldiers and thousands of nuclear warheads), with subplots of political upheaval, alliance formation, human rights catastrophes, and proxy wars in developing countries. In the 1980s few could have predicted how this drama would play out. Some experts expected the Cold War to end with a bang—a global thermonuclear war; others suggested it would end with a whimper—the rapid decline of the U.S. role in world politics and the erosion of global order. Clearly, many of these predictions were off the mark.

The world has undergone a transition from Cold War bipolarity to something quite new and different. Citizens of the world witnessed the fall of the Berlin Wall in 1989, the disintegration of the Soviet Union into fifteen republics, real European economic integration, and the emergence of new powers in Africa, Asia, Latin America, and the Middle East. Meanwhile, the international system comprises more diverse actors—from nongovernmental organizations to ethnic nationalist groups seeking autonomy to bigger multinational corporations. New means of global interdependence have also emerged—from the Internet to satellite communications technology to global financial networks.

The changes that characterize contemporary politics include pressures for globalization and economic liberalization. As a result more economies are opening up and more parts of economies are being connected across country borders. Pressures for democratization are also sweeping the world. Inside of countries, new groups seek empowerment. Outside of countries, actors such as the United Nations, the International Monetary Fund, and Amnesty International, more than ever before, are arguing that a state's internal affairs and human rights records are legitimate concerns of the international community. Due to democratization, globalization, and demographic changes within many societies, new groups are demanding a voice in governance or are competing with governments to represent segments of society. Many of these groups are seeking independence as national self-determination reasserts itself in the world. Of course, the end of the Cold War brought about, or at least fueled, many of these changes. The rivalry between the United States and the Soviet Union affected nearly every aspect of international politics for most of the second half of the twentieth century. The end to this rivalry has given rise to changes and developments that are significantly transforming international relations and domestic politics.

In one way or another, virtually all of these developments are potential threats to states. Sovereign states are the primary way international politics has been organized for centuries. Yet today, more than ever, states have difficulty controlling politics within their borders and serving as the highest authority to represent their territory in international politics. In essence, the very notion of sovereignty is under challenge. Some states are fighting to retain their sovereignty. Others are adapting to these new challenges by devolving power to other groups within their territories or by transferring parts of their sovereignty to international organizations, such as regional economic coalitions. Indeed, regionalism has become a characteristic feature of contemporary international politics. In this way, states themselves are changing international relations and domestic politics.

States and their leaders today are facing a crisis, one whose resolution is still uncertain. Although significant changes are indeed altering the landscape of international politics and present a challenge to state sovereignty, states remain an important part of international and domestic politics. They continue to make decisions that shape the nature of international politics. These decisions—states' foreign policies in the context of contemporary internal and external developments—are the focus of this book.

Studying Foreign Policy in Comparative Perspective

It is precisely because states are experiencing challenges and transformations both internally and externally that the analysis of foreign policy is important. Foreign policy analysis as a distinct area of inquiry connects the study of international relations (the way states relate to each other in international politics) with the study of domestic politics (the functioning of governments and the relationships among individuals, groups, and governments). Because most theories of international relations are primarily concerned with state behavior, the study of international relations includes explanations of foreign policy. These theories, however, focus on the external environment as the primary or single explanation of why states do what they do in global affairs. Those who study foreign policy certainly draw on these theories, as will be discussed shortly, but they also look inside the state for further explanation. Theories of domestic politics, found in the study of U.S. politics and in the study of comparative politics, share this attention to internal factors. These theories, however, tend to explain the functioning of the state or political system and the domestic policies that are chosen—they rarely comment about the effects of internal politics on a state's foreign policies.

Thus, the study of foreign policy serves as a bridge by analyzing the impact of both external and internal politics on states' relations with each other. Contemporary analyses focus on the previously mentioned changes that states are facing. These changes are occurring at the level of international relations and at the level of domestic politics. Perhaps most interesting is that these changes are influencing the relationship between these two levels as well. In other words, the connections between domestic and international politics have taken on new forms. Leaders cannot effectively forge foreign policy without being aware of these connections; students cannot effectively evaluate foreign policy choices without recognizing these linkages.

Defining Foreign Policy

The first step in a comparative investigation of foreign policy is to define what we mean by the term. As you will see, a discussion of the definition of foreign policy also raises issues concerning how foreign policy is studied and how foreign policy may be changing. We begin with the first term: "foreign." We typically make the distinction between foreign policy and domestic policy. "Foreign" is meant to apply to policy toward the world outside states' territorial borders, and "domestic" is meant to apply to policy made for the internal political system. Going to war with another country, signing an international trade agreement, and aiding a rebel insurgency in another country are examples of foreign policy. Taxes, education standards, and civil rights are examples of domestic policy.

In the recent past, this distinction between foreign and domestic policy was easier to make than it is today. Contemporary politics has blurred the line between what is foreign and what is domestic. Consider, for example, a country that passes an environmental law that requires cars sold within its borders to reach minimum emission standards. This is a domestic issue in the sense that it aims to improve the air quality for its own citizens. But it also affects companies and economic conditions of countries outside its borders by requiring that all auto imports have additional features, which may be costly and affect foreign sales. Consider, also, a country that signs an international trade agreement in which it pledges to keep its government spending at a certain level. Because it is an agreement between states across borders, it is a foreign issue, but it also has implications for how much the government can spend domestically on education and welfare. These examples demonstrate that because of the increased interdependence binding countries together, most policies have consequences inside and outside state borders, and therefore concern both foreign and domestic issues.

This does not mean, however, that there is no longer a difference between foreign and domestic policy. Although the line may be blurred, scholars still tend to make the distinction, as do the chapters in this book. At the heart of this distinction is the intended target of the policy. If the primary target lies outside the country's borders, it is considered foreign policy, even if it has secondary consequences for politics inside the country. Similarly, if the primary target is inside the country, it is considered domestic policy, even if it affects others outside the country's borders. Building on the examples above, if the intention of an environmental law is to alter the trade balance with another country by placing restrictions on imports, we would consider that foreign policy. Many policies, of course, have multiple targets. The air quality for the domestic population and the effect on foreign automobile competitors might have been equally important in the design of the environmental policy, for example. In such cases, a single policy can be both foreign and domestic. It should be clear from our discussion that the targets of foreign policy are not limited to other countries. Foreign policy may be targeted at specific individuals (such as a particular leader), nonstate actors (such as international organizations, human rights groups working across borders, or multinational corporations), or international conditions (such as the international environment or the global economy).

Another difficulty in distinguishing foreign from domestic policy concerns the status of territorial borders. Many countries' borders are currently in dispute. Part of a country, for example, may be attempting to establish its independence and may have only partial control in running its own affairs. The rest of the country may be engaged in forceful suppression of its attempt at secession and independence. Is a country's policy toward a group seeking self-determination foreign or domestic policy? In some ways, it depends on your point of view. If you are part of the group claiming independence, you see the country acting across a border that you have defined (and may even control), and thus it is foreign policy. If you are the leader of the central government, you deny this independence and see the situation as a strictly internal, domestic affair. For such cases, we tend to rely on the judgment of the international community to distinguish foreign policy from domestic policy. If most other countries have recognized the breakaway region as independent, the relations between it and the country are foreign policy. Although in some cases it is clear what the judgment of the international community is, in others it is not. Furthermore, this issue of how much a country actually controls its borders is of extreme importance in states that are so weak internally that rival factions control different parts of the territory. Such "failed" countries, or countries that are sovereign only in international legal terms, have become part of the twenty-first-century international landscape and raise further questions regarding the distinction between foreign and domestic policy.[1]

Now that we have defined "foreign," let us further clarify the second part of the phrase "foreign policy." "Policy" is a fairly broad term, representing a whole range of activities. It can include specific decisions (to sign a weapons treaty, for example) and general guidelines (to support human rights, for example). Policy can include observable behaviors by countries (such as committing military forces to interventions) or verbal pronouncements that do not necessarily lead to follow-up action (such as declaring support for another leader or condemning the action of another government). As you can see, foreign policy is not limited to military or security policy. It also includes such areas as foreign economic policy, international environmental policy, and human rights policy.

Who makes policy? The answer to this question is also an important part of the definition of "foreign policy." Policies are typically thought of as the product of governments and thus governments are the "actors." There are other actors that take actions whose intended target is outside a country's borders and are therefore considered "foreign" actions. Businesses, for example, may market their products in other countries. Multinational corporations are businesses that are owned by interests in various countries or divide their production across country borders. International organizations, such as the United Nations, act across borders. You, yourself, may travel to foreign countries, supporting the economy of others outside your home country and interacting with persons in foreign lands. Although these actions are certainly "foreign," and are an increasingly significant part of international politics, we rarely consider them "policy." Instead, the term "policy" is typically reserved for the actions of governments, government institutions, and government officials. Hereafter, when we refer to "countries" or "states" in a discussion of foreign policy, we are referring to the governments or their officials that are acting in their name.

Comparing Foreign Policies

The approach taken in this book focuses on the analysis, or explanation of foreign policy. To begin such an inquiry, one need only ask the basic questions of why a state does what it does in foreign affairs and how the foreign policy may have developed. When analyzing foreign policy, we are searching for regular and understandable patterns—across time, space, and issues—and explanations of foreign policy. In other words, we assume that at least some of the same reasons behind Catherine the Great's Russian foreign policy in the eighteenth century can be behind Vladimir Putin's Russian foreign policy in the twenty-first century; that some of the motivations for India's border conflict with China can perhaps be found in Argentina's decision to start a war with Great Britain; and that some of the same explanations behind France's nuclear policy are useful for understanding French foreign policy toward Africa.

In the search for regular and identifiable patterns, the field of foreign policy analysis rejects the view that every event is completely unique, that there are no common explanations. Finding patterns is important to the end goal of a general understanding and an increased capability for prediction. In other words, we seek to explain the factors that influence state behavior generally, not just a specific policy, because general knowledge can be used to anticipate future action. If we know, for example, the factors that shape decisions for war, we are better able to predict, control, and possibly even prevent future international conflicts.

This is not to say that we assume that all states' foreign policies can be explained in exactly the same way. In order to discover similarities and differences across foreign policies, we use the "comparative method." The comparative method involves selecting what to examine (in this instance, states and their foreign policies) and determining patterns. It is "comparative" because it involves comparing two or more states or, in some cases, one state at different time periods to determine similarities and differences.

Selecting the countries to compare is a very important step in the comparative method. The countries selected are shown in Table 1-1, along with some demographic, political, and economic characteristics that give a bird's-eye view of their similarities and differences. The table includes the United States for a convenient comparison even though the United States is not included in the book. We chose to do this for several reasons, one of the most important being the fact that the United States is, in a very real sense, exceptional when compared with other countries of the world. The United States has the largest economy of any country in the world, has one of the largest and best-equipped militaries, is a nuclear power, is relatively isolated geographically and bordered by countries that do not represent a military threat, is the longest-standing presidential democracy in the world, and is arguably the economic hegemon of the world. To have included the United States among the countries examined in this book might have made comparison with other countries rather difficult—like comparing apples and oranges.

The countries chosen for this volume are some of the most central players on the global and regional stages today. In order to evaluate the different theories scholars have used to explain states' foreign policies, we tried to do two things when choosing the countries to examine. First, we included countries that have some factors or characteristics in common with other countries in order to facilitate comparison—like comparing red apples with green ones. For example, we have several economically strong countries that can be compared with one another (France, Germany, Great Britain, and Japan), and several developing countries (Brazil, India, Iran, and Mexico). We can also compare the foreign policies of states in the same region dealing with some of the same issues (such as the policies of France, Germany, and Great Britain toward the European Union).

Second, we chose countries that are diverse on some dimensions in order to generate some contrasts and to see how different theoretical perspectives fare in different settings. For example, some theories emphasize democracy and nondemocracy as being important determinants of how a state conducts itself internationally. Thus, we have included several democracies (such as Britain, India, Israel, and South Africa) and some nondemocracies (such as China and Iran). We have also chosen states with large militaries (such as China and Russia) and states with smaller militaries (such as Mexico and Nigeria). This choice allows us the opportunity to comment, albeit in a limited way, on observed differences in foreign policy between democracies and nondemocracies and between military giants and military dwarfs. Had we chosen only democracies, for example, we would not be able to say much about how well theories of foreign policy explain the behavior of nondemocracies.

Table 1-1 Characteristics of Countries

Country	Population (millions)	GNP (US$, billions)	GNP per capita (US$)	Military spending (US$, millions)	Armed forces	Human development index[a]	Government type	Freedom status
Great Britain[b]	59	1,338	22,640	31,180	218,000	0.918	Parliamentary	Free democracy
France	61	1,427	23,480	46,792	475,000	0.917	Semi-presidential	Free democracy
Germany	82	2,079	25,350	39,543	335,000	0.911	Parliamentary	Free democracy
Russia	147	333	2,270	22,400	1,300,000	0.771	Transitional	Partly free democracy
China	1,250	980	780	18,400	2,600,000	0.706	Authoritarian/ one-party state	Not free
Japan	127	4,079	32,230	51,184	250,000	0.924	Parliamentary	Free democracy
India	998	442	450	10,174	1,260,000	0.563	Parliamentary	Free democracy
Israel	6	104	17,450	8,364	185,000	0.883	Parliamentary	Free democracy
Iran	63	111	1,760	3,042	575,000	0.709	Authoritarian/ theocractic state	Not free
Nigeria	124	38	310	1,240	76,000	0.439	Transitional	Partly free democracy
South Africa	42	133	3,160	2,230	75,000	0.697	Parliamentary	Free democracy
Brazil	168	743	4,420	14,294	296,000	0.747	Presidential	Partly free democracy
Mexico	97	429	4,400	1,668	250,000	0.784	Presidential	Partly free democracy
United States	273	8,351	30,600	259,913	1,530,000	0.929	Presidential	Free democracy

Sources: Population, GNP, and GNP per capita: 1999 figures, World Bank, *World Development Indicators* database, http://www.worldbank.org/data/, August 2, 2000. Military spending: 1998 figures, Stockholm International Peace Research Institute, *SIPRI Yearbook 2000: Armaments, Disarmament, and International Security* (Oxford: Oxford University Press, 2000), except for Iran, 1994 figures, Annmarie Muth, ed., *Statistical Abstract of the World*, 3d ed. (Detroit: Gale Publishing, 1997). Armed forces: 1997 figures, U.S. Department of State Bureau of Verification and Compliance, *World Military Expenditures and Arms Transfers, 1998* (Washington, D.C.: U.S. Department of State, 2000); http://www.state.gov/www/global/arms/bureau_ac/wmeat98.html. Human development index: United Nations Development Programme, *Human Development Report 2000* (New York: Oxford University Press, 2000). Freedom status: 1999–2000 rankings, http://www.freedomhouse.org/ratings/, © 2000 Freedom House, 2000.

[a] Human development index based on life expectancy at birth; adult literacy; gross primary, secondary, and tertiary enrollment; and purchasing power parity in U.S. dollars.

[b] Data for the United Kingdom are presented for Great Britain.

Analyzing Foreign Policy

The analysis of foreign policy begins with theories that identify different factors—various forces that influence a state's foreign policy. Most analysts recognize that any explanation of foreign policy typically involves multiple factors. As you will see, there is no shortage of theories on what factors influence foreign policy. These multiple factors, however, can be grouped into two broad categories of explanations: those dealing with factors inside the state, and those dealing with factors outside the state. The first category points to the international environment as the explanation for countries' foreign policy. In other words, factors external to the state—how the international system is organized, the characteristics of contemporary international relations, and the actions of others—can lead the state to react in certain ways. The second category points to factors internal to the state. In other words, characteristics of the domestic political system—citizens and groups within that system, the government organizations, and the individual leaders—can be the source of a state's foreign policy. As previously noted, the study of foreign policy uniquely bridges the study of international relations and domestic politics by considering how both internal and external factors influence state behavior. We turn now to a discussion of these categories and the variety of theories associated with each.

External Factors in Contemporary Foreign Policy

All states, regardless of their type of political system, their history, or their culture, reside within an international system that limits the choices they can make. The worldwide distribution of economic wealth and military power and the actions of other powerful states, multinational corporations, and international organizations often mean that states cannot pursue their preferred option in foreign policy. Scholars of foreign policy have long recognized that to understand how states behave toward each other, it is important to understand the influence of the systemic factors and the external actors and conditions that are outside the control of policy makers. In fact, for a long time, many argued that states' foreign policies were solely a product of the international system—merely a reaction to external conditions and other actors. This is the expectation derived from such theories of international relations as realism and liberalism. Thus, foreign policy analysts often use perspectives on the international system to infer the actions that states are likely to take in their foreign policies.

Anarchy and Power in the International System

The lack of an overarching government in the international system is one of the most important external conditions that affect foreign policies. In fact, realist theory proposes that anarchy is the characteristic of the international environment that makes international politics so dramatically different from domestic politics. In domestic political systems, political actors (such as groups and individuals) can cooperate because there are rules governing behavior and a government to enforce those rules. In the international political system, conflict is more likely because the absence of an overall system of law and enforcement means that each political actor (almost 200 states in 2001) must look out for itself.[2]

What is the effect of anarchy on foreign policy? Without the protection of a legal system and an "international police force," states must look out for their own interests. The result is distrust, competition, and conflict among states. The driving force, then, behind foreign policies is the constant need to acquire and safeguard one's security and power. A state's foreign policy will be one that pursues various sources of power. For most realists, the key components of power are military in nature, because ultimately it is the goal of every state to survive and to protect its territorial integrity (if not its citizens as well). Several factors can contribute to military strength, including the size and sophistication of military forces, the economic wealth to purchase military strength, and good military and political leadership. Geopolitical factors, such as natural defenses and abundant resources, have also long figured into the calculation of military strength. If a state does not have much power, it must enter into an alliance with states that are more powerful and can protect them. Alliances and powerful allies, then, become additional external conditions that can constrain states.

This perspective leads to several specific expectations about foreign policy, based upon the power capabilities of a state and the potential threats to it. The foreign policies of states that are quite powerful militarily, such as China and Russia, will focus on preserving their power by maintaining a high profile in world affairs and balancing against other powerful states. Policies aimed at demonstrating military capabilities and securing spheres of influence are most important. If there is only one other major power in the international system, such as was true during the Cold War, competition for allies and possible conflict with the other power will likely dominate the foreign policy agenda.

For states that have some capabilities but are not global powers, such as Brazil and Great Britain, foreign policy often depends on the distribution of power in the international system (another systemic characteristic that realism sees as important). In a bipolar system, a middle power faces strong pressures to become a compliant alliance partner of one of the major powers and ultimately give up autonomy in its foreign policy for the sake of security. During the Cold War, Germany and Japan were arguably so dependent on their alliance with the United States that their potential as middle powers in the international system was largely constrained. Middle powers may instead try to maximize their influence by playing one major power off against the other (as India and France attempted to do at times during the Cold War), but this can be a risky business.[3]

In a multipolar system, middle powers often have the most autonomy and regional influence because there is greater choice in alliance partners when the major powers are competing. Middle powers often worry, however, that the great powers will cooperate and rule the international system like an "oligarchy," ignoring the interests of the middle and smaller states. In terms of military capabilities, the current international system is hegemonic, with the United States as the lone superpower. This presents new opportunities for middle powers. Although it is no match for the hegemonic state and must often follow its lead in areas of interest to the hegemon, a middle power may assert its influence regionally. Indeed, we are currently witnessing a resurgence of regional powers around the globe with states like Brazil, Nigeria, and South Africa, playing new, more independent roles in their regions.

States with little military capability of their own, like Mexico and Israel at the beginning of its statehood, are the most constrained. According to realism, they have little opportunity to forge an independent foreign policy, for they must satisfy their protector. Geographic vulnerability and regional threats made Israel's relationship with the United States, particularly U.S. aid to build up Israeli offensive and defensive capabilities, of utmost importance.

All states, according to the realist perspective, must be vigilant and react to potential threats, regardless of their military capability and their place in the international system. They constantly seek to attain a balance with the power of others. Thus, Russia and China must be wary of U.S. attempts to dominate the international system. France must be concerned about Germany's influence in the European monetary union. India must carefully watch and react to Pakistan's military capabilities, including its nuclear capability. And finally, Israel must prepare for, and even attempt to preempt, a war with its Arab neighbors.

Although realism captures an important aspect of states' foreign policies — the primacy of security interests and the drive for power among all states — it is often criticized for its excessive focus on military conflict at the expense of economic cooperation. Military capability supposedly gives a state influence in international politics — influence to deter others from attacking and influence to protect its allies, for example. But economic power, and not just economic wealth to purchase military capability, can also give a state influence in international politics. Even if a state does not use its wealth to build a strong military, it may be able to influence others through the use of economic sanctions or promises of an economically rewarding relationship. In other words, it may be able to "buy" its influence. Indeed, because of changes in the international system, economic power may be more significant in contemporary international relations. Military force, for example, is often ineffective at solving some problems (such as trade imbalances and global environmental threats) and may be more costly to a state than economic sanctions. Such problems are arguably more important in an era of increasing interdependence.

Interdependence and Dependence in the International System

Other theories of international relations focus more directly on the distribution of economic wealth as the primary characteristic of the international system that affects states' foreign policies. Liberalism, in particular, sees the world as markedly different from what it was fifty years ago. With the increase in global trade and financial relationships and the technological advances that have facilitated this increase, states have become more interdependent.[4] How is foreign policy affected by interdependence? According to liberalism, states find cooperation, rather than conflict, more in line with their interests. Arms control agreements, trade agreements, and cultural exchanges are examples of cooperation that can benefit states. Cooperating with other states, and building international institutions to facilitate that cooperation, allow states to further their goals of economic wealth. Indeed, economic liberalism argues that all states will be better off if they cooperate in a worldwide division of labor, with each state specializing in what it is relatively better at producing. Japan, for example, decided long ago that it was not possible to try to produce all that it needed to consume. Its experience in World War II of trying to control its access to resources through conflict was not successful in the end. Instead, it came to see participation in the post–World War II trading system as a more efficient way to generate wealth.

An increase in interdependence can have a downside. The more numerous the connections between states, the greater the opportunities for conflicts of interests. Japan and western European states, for example, are highly dependent on Middle East oil, and their economic interests have often diverged with Middle Eastern states' political and military interests. When states fail to resolve these differences through cooperation and compromise, states may resort to force to ensure access to resources on which they are dependent, as Japan and western European states did when they participated in the coalition against Iraq in the 1991 Persian Gulf War. More generally, when states become intertwined in one area, they often become concerned with one another's actions and reactions in other areas.

Interdependence also means that states can be fairly constrained in their foreign policy. Because the fortunes of one state are connected to the fortunes of another state, when one state harms another, it does so at its own peril. Going to war in an effort to gain power may make sense militarily, but in doing so, states in an interdependent world harm themselves by destroying potential trading partners and markets in which to sell their goods. After World War II France and Germany deliberately chose the path of interdependence and constraint, transforming a centuries-old relationship of distrust and rivalry into one of economic cooperation. Thus, for liberalism, economic interdependence is the key characteristic of the international environment that states must consider when they make foreign policy.

Some states are more dependent than others. Richer states, such as Japan and Great Britain, are very much affected by the actions of other states, but they can afford to sacrifice part of their economic wealth in order to pursue other goals. Their wealth and the centrality of their state in the world economy often give them a choice in trading partners, and they do not have to rely on others for economic assistance. Poor states that are in the periphery of the international economic system, such as India and Nigeria, enjoy no such luxury and, therefore, must be highly constrained in their foreign policy. Their very economic existence depends on their relationships with other states, as well as with nonstate actors such as multinational corporations and international financial organizations. Thus, they are often forced to comply with the foreign policy wishes of their benefactors. Furthermore, some suggest that the leaders of poor states often act in collusion with the rich states that exploit the poor states' cheap labor and abundant raw materials.[5]

Because there is no overarching authority to ensure cooperation, states may support international organizations that help coordinate cooperative efforts. What may be sacrificed in the short term, liberals believe, is offset by the long-term benefits of stability, efficiency, and greater wealth. Thus, many states' foreign policies are supportive of international agencies such as the United Nations and the World Trade Organization as forums for coordinating states' interests. However, with international cooperation in the form of international organizations and with the rise of multinational corporations as the engines of globalization, states have no choice but to deal with these nonstate actors and sometimes compete with them for influence in international politics. At times, states compete with nonstate actors for control over their own domestic politics. Nigeria, for example, continually faces pressure from the International Monetary Fund and Human Rights Watch.

Current globalization and liberalization pressures complicate the effects of interdependence in the early twenty-first century. Globalization connects more economies in worldwide financial and trading markets, but it has not done so evenly. Indeed, the gap between rich and poor states is ever widening. Poor states have little ability to resist pressures to open up their markets, even when they disagree with the liberal philosophy and risk political retribution when the gap between rich and poor becomes greater within their economies. Some states, such as Mexico, have changed their past positions and embraced some of the liberal economic philosophy, whereas others, such as Russia, continue to try to safeguard their autonomy.

One response to current globalization is regional economic integration. Both rich and poor states are engaging in agreements and dialogues to establish greater interdependence at the regional level. The European Union (EU) is the most successful effort, particularly with the establishment in 1999 of a common currency for most of its member states. Although the EU evolved over several decades from its 1951 origins in the European Coal and Steel Community, its current level of integration was achieved only through efforts in the last two decades. There have been other recent attempts at regional integration in response, in part, to globalization. Such attempts have become more possible now that the Cold War security structures are not complicating such efforts. This is particularly true for states in Latin America and southern Africa that are trying to replicate the benefits of regional cooperation seen in the EU. If these attempts are successful, states in southern Africa and Latin America may find themselves constrained by the new international organizations that they build—much as British, French, and German states are sometimes constrained by the political and economic structures of the EU. Thus, regional integration provides another layer of external factors that may affect states' foreign policies.

In sum, external factors focus on a presumed drive for self-interest in an anarchical international system. Realism proposes that this drive will result in the quest for military power, the creation of alliances, and the submission of states to more powerful actors. Liberalism suggests that an interdependent international system will result in more cooperation, support for organizations that help coordinate activities, and submission of economically weak states to the forces of the international marketplace. Proponents of each of these perspectives agree that foreign policies are a result of states' rank, status, and links to other states in the international pecking order.

Internal Factors in Contemporary Foreign Policy

Theories that focus on internal sources of foreign policy offer a rather different perspective and set of expectations. In contrast to the externally based theories, those who point to sources internal to the state expect differences across states' foreign policies, despite the similar international circumstances. For these analysts, the great diversity of political systems, cultures, and leaders point states in different directions, even though they are facing the same external forces. Furthermore, externally based theories often assume that the policies that states make are in response to their interests and the demands of the international system. Their response is "rational," or the most optimal decision given those interests and demands. Domestically oriented explanations, in contrast, argue that states sometimes make decisions that do not necessarily benefit them in international politics. These theories explain such "deviations from rationality" by pointing to the need of leaders to satisfy both domestic political goals and foreign policy interests, or by examining the imperfect nature of the decision-making process. Finally, those who point to external sources, particularly realists, tend to examine states as if they were "unitary actors" whose politicians and citizens put aside any differences they may have and act with one voice for the sake of national security. Conversely, those who point to domestic sources of foreign policy highlight the many different voices and conflicts over foreign policy. These many voices reside at several levels within countries—the public, societal groups, government organizations, and leaders.

The Public: Opinion and Culture

Public opinion concerns the attitudes people of a state have on particular foreign policy issues. The public may, for example, be for or against their state intervening militarily in another country, or signing a particular trade agreement, or interfering in other states' internal affairs based on human rights concerns. The public may agree on an issue or may be deeply divided. Scholars continue to debate the impact of public opinion on foreign policy, even in highly democratized states in which policy supposedly reflects "the will of the people." Based on numerous findings in research, the conventional wisdom is that the public simply does not influence foreign policy. The average person, for example, tends to know little and care little about his or her country's foreign affairs. Even if the public were knowledgeable about foreign policy issues, it is not clear that leaders would follow the public's opinion. They may instead lead the public to opinions that are in line with their preferences or ignore their opinion altogether.[6] Evidence suggests that many times leaders who do ignore the public are not held accountable at the polls, because elections typically revolve around domestic rather than foreign policy concerns. The media also play a role in this relationship as they too may influence public opinion on foreign policy. The information that the media provide the public may also be biased in favor of the government's policies.[7]

The question of public opinion and foreign policy may, however, be more complicated than this conventional wisdom implies.[8] Evidence suggests, for example, that there is some congruence between changes in public opinion and changes in foreign policy.[9] And in many specific cases of foreign policy decisions, we do know that leaders were quite sensitive to public reactions. Furthermore, although the public may not formulate specific stable opinions about foreign policy, it often expresses rather enduring "core values" or opinion "moods."[10] These refer to underlying beliefs — such as isolationism, anticommunism, nonappeasement, neutrality, and anti-imperialism — that the public holds and uses to judge foreign policy. In Germany and Japan, for example, the public has come to value multilateralism and antimilitarism. In post–Cold War Russia and in contemporary India, core values support the maintenance of a "great power" identity. "Moods" such as these do not necessarily suggest concrete foreign policy guidelines, but they do set boundaries within which leaders must remain or risk public opposition.

Thus far, most research on public opinion as a source of foreign policy has focused on democracies in which there are institutionalized channels for the public to hold leaders accountable for their decisions. The public is often assumed not to have any influence in the foreign policies of more authoritarian political systems. The views of society, however, may be just as important in these types of systems, although in an indirect fashion. As in democracies, core values held by the public may work to set boundaries. Indeed, authoritarian systems may be built on the foundation of such foreign policy orientations as self-determination and nationalism in Mexico, and anti-imperialism in China and Iran. Thus, despite the fact that nondemocracies may not be "of the people, by the people, and for the people," the people may still constrain the government in its foreign policy decisions.

Core values are connected to a society's political culture — the values, norms, and traditions that are widely shared by its people and are relatively enduring over time. These enduring cultural features may also set parameters for foreign policy. A country's culture may value, for example, individualism, collectivism, pragmatism, or moralism, and these culturally based values may affect foreign policy. Cultures that place a premium on morality over practicality, for example, may be more likely to pass moral judgment over the internal affairs and foreign policy behaviors of others.[11] Culture may also affect the way foreign policy is made. Cultures in which consensual decision making is the norm, for example, may take longer to make policy, because the process of consultation with many people may be just as important as the final decision.[12] Despite the general recognition that cultural particularities do affect foreign policy, scholars have experienced great difficulty in defining culture, which in turn makes assessing the impact of culture on foreign policy even more difficult.

Societal Groups: Links and Opposition

Leaders may be more likely to pay attention to and react to the opinions of specific, organized societal groups than to the society at large as they play the role of linking society to the state or of opposing and competing with the state. Interest groups articulate a particular societal sector's position and mobilize that sector to pressure and persuade the government. Interest groups come in a variety of forms. They may, for example, be based on a single issue, on ethnic identification, on religious affiliation, or on economics. Nongovernmental organizations focused on human rights are becoming increasingly visible in countries as different as France and Nigeria.

Economic interest groups can be an especially important societal source of foreign policy because they help to generate wealth, and economic welfare has become one of the primary functions of the modern state. Economic groups often have an interest in foreign relations as they seek to promote their foreign business adventures abroad or to protect markets from competitors at home.[13] Business groups in Japan have often been considered partners with the bureaucracy in foreign economic policy making, and a wide range of business, labor, financial, and trade groups quite actively attempt to influence foreign policy in South Africa.

An interest group's influence on foreign policy often depends on the particular issue, how organized the group is, and the relationship between the interest group and the government. Interest groups face an uphill struggle in attempting to influence a government that disagrees with their position. The government typically has greater resources to bring to bear on the issue and more control of the information that flows to the public. Depending on the political system, the government also has more diffuse political support from the public. Globalization and liberalization trends have certainly increased the number of economic groups that have an interest in their state's foreign policies, as can be seen in contemporary Nigeria. Such trends have also arguably strengthened the capability of these groups to influence foreign policy.

Political parties, although often part of the government, also play the role of linking societal opinion to political leadership.[14] In many ways, political parties function much like interest groups. In some countries, such as Iran, only one party exists or dominates the political system, and the party's ideology can be important in setting the boundaries for debate over foreign policy decisions and in providing rhetoric for leader's speeches. In such cases, parties become less important than factions, which often develop within political parties. Factions are also important in political systems in which one party holds a majority in parliament and rules alone. In these countries too, factions may disagree over the direction of the country's foreign policy, as have the pro- versus anti-European integration factions in the British Conservative Party. Party factions may seek to outmaneuver each other or they may be forced to compromise for the sake of party unity. Even if there is a consensus within the party, foreign policy might get captured by the intraparty fighting as factions compete with one another for party leadership. These dynamics internal to political parties can be seen in countries as different as China, Iran, and Japan.

Factions are also important in more fragmented multiparty political systems, but in such countries, the competition between parties becomes significant as well. In vying for the public's support, parties may attempt to distinguish themselves ideologically from each other, thus polarizing the debate over foreign policy, or they may rush to the center of the political spectrum to capture the moderates, who often decide elections. In some multiparty systems, such as Germany, India, and Israel, the political scene is so fragmented that parties must enter into coalitions and share the power to make policy. In such cases, each foreign policy decision can be a struggle between coalition partners, who must get along to keep the coalition together.[15]

A country's military is, of course, part of the government, but in many countries military leadership competes with civilian leadership for control over policy, as in China and Nigeria. At times, the military can be a powerful source of opposition to a government's foreign policy goals, especially if those goals concern national security issues or imply a cut in the military's resources. At other times, military groups might push leaders in expansionist directions to further self-interested goals of organizational growth and prestige.[16] Since a military that is not subordinate to civilian leaders controls the primary means of coercion, policy makers may be very sensitive to this opposition. If they are not, they risk a military coup.

Government Organization: Democracies and Bureaucracies

How a government is organized may also affect foreign policy. Two characteristics are particularly important: democratization and bureaucratization. The foreign policy process is quite different for democracies—decision-making authority tends to be diffused across democratic institutions, and thus more actors are involved. In contrast, authoritarian leaders often make decisions by themselves. Democratic leaders are also directly accountable to political parties and the public and thus must build a consensus for foreign policy. Authoritarian leaders do not face these constraints and may enjoy considerable latitude in choosing their own policies.

Liberal theory argues that because of these differences in government organization, democracies will behave more peacefully than will authoritarian systems.[17] The difficulty of building a consensus among a larger set of actors and mobilizing them for conflict constrains the war-making abilities of democratic leaders, the argument goes. These leaders are accountable to a public that is often more concerned with economic than military issues. Furthermore, democratic institutions are built on and create a political culture that is likely to emphasize the value of peaceful resolution. In a democracy, citizens learn that conflicts of interest can be resolved nonviolently (for example, through elections, through peaceful means of influence, in the courts), and they transfer that value to their relations with other states.

Despite these expectations, the proposition that democracies are generally more peaceful in their foreign policy is not supported by most evidence. Democracies and authoritarian governments, it seems, are both likely to be involved in and initiate conflict. Democratic constraints, for example, did not prevent British involvement in the Falklands War, French military interventions in Africa, India's conflicts with China and Pakistan, and Israel's participation in numerous Middle East conflicts. Democracies, however, rarely fight other democracies. Scholars continue to work on the answer to this puzzle, but many return to the ideas that democratic cultural values and institutional constraints make democratic foreign policy different, even if only when dealing with other democracies.

The differences between the making of foreign policy in democratic and authoritarian governments may, however, be exaggerated. First, actual decision-making authority may not be as diffuse or constrained in democracies as sometimes supposed. As noted earlier, citizens in a democracy are often not well informed, and their influence over foreign policy is debatable. Furthermore, foreign policy decisions, unlike most domestic policy decisions, are often highly centralized at the top of the government's hierarchy, as they typically are, for example, in France, Great Britain, and India.

Second, it is not always the case that authoritarian leaders act without constraint. These leaders often face considerable opposition from society, interest groups, party factions, and their own militaries and may consult frequently with these groups before making foreign policy decisions. Although citizens in authoritarian systems cannot vote their leaders out of office, they do have other means of holding leaders accountable, including forming or pledging allegiance to nongovernmental groups who oppose the authoritarian leader, backing a coup and change of government, assassinating a leader, and starting a revolution. Indeed, simply being voted out of office may pale in comparison.

Authoritarian regimes that are fairly new, face tremendous internal opposition, or are otherwise weak in their control of the country especially need to pay attention to public reaction to foreign policy. Countries such as India, Nigeria, and Russia have severe economic, religious, and ethnic internal divisions that detract from the legitimacy of the state. Leaders of such governments may use foreign policy to build national identity, demonstrate strong leadership, or divert attention away from internal problems.[18] Finally, in some authoritarian systems, no single leader controls foreign policy; decisions are made collectively, as they tend to be in the current Chinese Communist Party. Since there are considerable differences in the organization of authoritarian governments and democratic governments, it may be better to think of government organization in regard to how centralized decision-making authority is and how strong the government is in relation to societal opposition.[19]

A second feature of government organization that affects foreign policy concerns the bureaucracy, which is charged with gathering information, developing proposals, offering advice, implementing policy, and, at times, making foreign policy decisions. Because of the complexities involved in dealing with the many issues of international politics, governments organize themselves bureaucratically, assigning responsibility for different areas or jurisdictions of policy to separate agencies or departments. Separate agencies, for example, are responsible for diplomatic relations, for trade ties, and for different parts of the military.

Although such bureaucratic organization is necessary to deal with a complex world, it can create problems for foreign policy.[20] The different departments, for example, may come into conflict over what foreign policy should be adopted, partly because departments tend to develop their own sense of identity, or organizational mission. Bureaucratic conflict is a common problem, for example, in the process of making foreign policy in China and Japan. The conflict in viewpoints may create inconsistent foreign policy if departments are acting on their own, rather than in coordination. It may also result in compromises that are not necessarily in the best interests of the state.

These problems that stem from bureaucratic organization in the government are less likely under certain conditions. Although most states have some sort of bureaucracy, in some, a single leader or a single unifying force (such as one political party) can impose a decision on a reluctant or conflicted bureaucracy. On some issues, moreover, all agencies may share an overriding value that guides foreign policy, making inconsistencies and conflict less likely. Finally, in crisis situations, the top leadership often takes over, minimizing (but not always eliminating) the effects of bureaucratic politics.

Leaders: Personalities and Beliefs

At the top of government sits a leader, or leaders, who has the authority to make foreign policy. Since leaders are human, what they are like can have a profound effect on a state's foreign policy. Characteristics of leaders are generally more important when the situation is ambiguous, uncertain, and complex, and when the leader is involved in the actual decision making rather than delegating his or her authority to advisers.[21] Under these conditions, which occur frequently in foreign policy making, a leader's personality and beliefs may shape what the state does.

Leaders' decisions may be shaped by their own personal history. Their childhood or early political experiences, for example, may have taught them that certain values and ways of handling problems are important.[22] The revolutionary tendencies of the Chinese leader Mao Tse-tung, for example, can be traced back to when he was a child. Since every leader's personal history is unique, we might expect each individual to draw on a particular set of beliefs, values, and experiences in coping with foreign policy issues. The Ivy League education of the former Mexican president Carlos Salinas, for example, predisposed him toward opening up the Mexican economy and was an important factor in his decision to support the North American Free Trade Agreement.

Because as human beings we prefer to be consistent in the beliefs that are important to us, we often ignore or distort information that contradicts what we already believe. This is especially likely when we have strongly held "images" of other countries. Leaders who see another country as their enemy, for example, will often selectively attend to or perceive information about that country in a way that confirms their original belief. For this reason, images are extremely resistant to change, even if the "enemy" is making cooperative gestures.[23] Ayatollah Khomeini's image of Saddam Hussein, for example, was significant in his decisions during Iran's war with Iraq.

Leaders can also be categorized into types of personalities. Some leaders, for example, may be motivated by a need to dominate others and may thus be more conflictual in foreign policy, whereas others may be more concerned with being accepted, and may therefore be more cooperative. Some leaders are more nationalistic, more distrustful, and believe that the world is a conflictual place and that problems are solved through conflictual means, whereas others see themselves and their state as part of the world community that can be trusted and believe that problems are best solved multilaterally.[24]

Leaders' decision-making style or how they manage information and the people around them can also be important. Some leaders, like Brazil's Fernando Cardoso, choose to be quite active in foreign policy making, whereas others, like Brazil's Itamar Franco, tended to delegate the authority to make foreign policy decisions. Some leaders are "crusaders" who come to office with a foreign policy goal. They tend not to compromise on their vision and are less open to advice. Others are interested in keeping power or bridging conflicts. They tend to be sensitive to advice and are reluctant to make decisions without consultation and consensus.[25] India's Indira Gandhi, for example, tended to be an advocate for her own positions, whereas her father, Nehru, preferred to build a consensus among those around him.

Conclusion: Examination and Analysis

As noted earlier, we have chosen a variety of countries in which to examine the links between international and domestic politics and the various propositions presented above. The following chapters afford a look at these various theories, which expect states' foreign policies to differ according to their level of economic development, dependence, and military might. We gain insight by comparing, for example, Germany with Nigeria, Russia with Israel, and China with Mexico. We also assess other theories that point to countries that are very similar in their placement in the international security and economic system (such as Great Britain and France) but that choose different paths in their foreign policies, possibly because of internal factors. These countries also include a variety of different political systems, cultures, core values, historical experiences, societal opposition, degrees of centralization of political authority, and levels of bureaucratization, and they are led by leaders with their own beliefs and styles.

In addition, the countries represented in the chapters that follow provide an excellent opportunity to examine some of the recent changes in domestic and international politics and the effects these changes might have on foreign policy. Many of these states (such as Germany and Japan) were assumed to be significantly constrained by the Cold War international system. An examination of contemporary foreign policy allows us to assess how such states are coping with the post–Cold War world and its new security structures. Also of interest is how states, especially poorer states, are coping with globalization and pressures for liberalization, which may not be new but have intensified in the last decade. In internal matters, many of the states in this book (such as India and Israel) have experienced changes in leadership over the past few years; several states (such as Russia and South Africa) have experienced significant changes in the type of political system; and other states (such as Mexico and Iran) are facing significant pressures for reform. We examine how changes in domestic politics have influenced foreign policy in these states.

As you read the chapters that follow, we invite you to learn about contemporary politics (both domestic and global) of central actors in the world today. We also encourage you to apply the theories discussed in this chapter to an understanding of each country's foreign policy and to think critically about these theories as you compare the countries' experiences. As you go along, consider the questions presented in the box. In addition, try to assess which theories or group of factors are being emphasized as important for understanding the country's foreign policy. Each chapter presents a brief historical review of the country's foreign policy during the Cold War, an analysis of the most important external and internal factors in the country's foreign policy, and a discussion of contemporary foreign policy issues. At the beginning of each chapter, we include an introduction to the country and the themes stressed in the chapter. We also note which other chapters in this book contain similar themes and are particularly relevant for comparison. In the book's final chapter, we return to a discussion of thinking comparatively and analytically about contemporary foreign policies.

**Questions to Consider
When Analyzing Foreign Policy
in Comparative Perspective**

• Has the foreign policy behavior of most countries undergone fundamental change since the end of the Cold War? What theories best explain little or no change in other countries' foreign policy?

• Which theories of international constraints on state behavior are most important and for which countries? Overall, how do these perspectives help to account for the foreign policy behavior of countries in comparative perspective?

• How are states coping with globalization and the pressures for liberalization in contemporary international relations? Are there fundamental differences in how states deal with these challenges?

• Which theories of internal influences on state behavior are most important and for which countries? Overall, how do these perspectives help to account for the foreign policy behavior of various countries?

• Can external and internal factors be linked to better understand foreign policy in the twenty-first century? What type of conceptual framework would capture the interaction of these levels?

• What are the benefits of studying foreign policy in comparative perspective? What are the limitations?

Suggestions for Further Reading

Ayoob, Mohammed. *The Third World Security Predicament: State Making, Regional Conflict, and the International System.* Boulder: Lynne Rienner, 1995.

Clarke, Michael M., and Brian White, eds. *Understanding Foreign Policy: The Foreign Policy Systems Approach.* Aldershot, U.K.: Edward Elgar, 1989.

Goldmann, Kjell. *Change and Stability in Foreign Policy.* Princeton: Princeton University Press, 1988.

Hermann, Charles F., Charles W. Kegley Jr., and James N. Rosenau, eds. *New Directions in the Study of Foreign Policy.* Boston: Allen and Unwin, 1987.

Holsti, Kal J. *Why Nations Realign: Foreign Policy Restructuring in the Postwar World.* London: Allen and Unwin, 1982.

Hudson, Valerie, with Christopher S. Vore. "Foreign Policy Analysis Yesterday, Today, and Tomorrow." *Mershon International Studies Review* 39 (October 1995): 209–238.

Korany, Bahgat. *How Foreign Policy Decisions Are Made in the Third World: A Comparative Analysis.* Boulder: Westview Press, 1986.

Neack, Laura, Jeanne A. K. Hey, and Patrick J. Haney, eds. *Foreign Policy Analysis: Continuity and Change in Its Second Generation.* Englewood Cliffs, N.J.: Prentice Hall, 1995.

Rosati, Jerel A., Joe D. Hagan, and Martin W. Sampson III, eds. *Foreign Policy Restruc-*

turing: How Governments Respond to Global Change. Columbia: University of South Carolina Press, 1994.

Singer, Eric, and Valerie Hudson, eds. *Political Psychology and Foreign Policy.* Boulder: Westview Press, 1992.

Skidmore, David, and Valerie Hudson, eds. *The Limits of State Autonomy: Societal Groups and Foreign Policy Formulation.* Boulder: Westview Press, 1993.

Smith, Steve. "Theories of Foreign Policy: An Historical Overview." *Review of International Studies* 12 (1986): 13–29.

Notes

1. Robert Jackson, *Quasi-States: Sovereignty, International Relations, and the Third World* (Cambridge: Cambridge University Press, 1990); Stephen Wright, "The Changing Context of African Foreign Policies," in *African Foreign Policies,* ed. Stephen Wright (Boulder: Westview Press, 1999), 1–23.
2. Hans J. Morganthau, *Politics among Nations,* 3d ed. (New York: Knopf, 1960); Kenneth Waltz, *Theory of International Politics* (Reading, Mass.: Addison-Wesley, 1979).
3. Laura Neack, "Linking State Type with Foreign Policy Behavior," in *Foreign Policy Analysis: Continuity and Change in Its Second Generation,* ed. Laura Neack, Jeanne A. K. Hey, and Patrick J. Haney (Englewood Cliffs, N.J.: Prentice Hall, 1995), 215–228.
4. Robert O. Keohane and Joseph S. Nye, *Power and Interdependence* (Boston: Little, Brown, 1977).
5. Bruce Moon, "The Foreign Policy of the Dependent State," *International Studies Quarterly* 27 (1983): 315–340; Bruce Moon, "Consensus or Compliance? Foreign Policy Change and External Dependence," *International Organization* 39 (1985): 297–329; Neil R. Richardson, *Foreign Policy and Economic Dependence* (Austin: University of Texas Press, 1978).
6. Robert Shapiro and Lawrence Jacobs, "Who Leads and Who Follows? U.S. Presidents, Public Opinion, and Foreign Policy," in *Decisionmaking in a Glass House: Mass Media, Public Opinion, and American Foreign Policy in the 21st Century,* ed. Brigette L. Nacos, Robert Y. Shapiro, and Pierangelo Isernia (Lanham, Md.: Rowman and Littlefield, 2000), 223–245.
7. John Zaller and Dennis Chiu, "Government's Little Helper: U.S. Press Coverage of Foreign Policy Crises, 1946–1999," in Nacos, Shapiro, and Isernia, *Decisionmaking in a Glass House,* 61–91.
8. Ole R. Holsti, "Public Opinion and Foreign Policy: Challenges to the Almond-Lippmann Consensus," *International Studies Quarterly* 36 (1992): 439–466.
9. Shapiro and Jacobs, "Who Leads and Who Follows?"
10. Jon Hurwitz and Mark Peffley, "How Are Foreign Policy Attitudes Structured? A Hierarchical Model," *American Political Science Review* 81 (1987): 1099–1119.
11. Valerie M. Hudson, ed., *Culture and Foreign Policy* (Boulder: Lynne Rienner, 1997), 12.
12. Martin W. Sampson III, "Cultural Influences on Foreign Policy," in *New Directions in the Study of Foreign Policy,* ed. Charles F. Hermann, Charles W. Kegley Jr., and James N. Rosenau (Boston: Allen and Unwin, 1987), 384–405.
13. Stephen D. Krasner, *Defending the National Interest: Raw Materials Investments and U.S. Foreign Policy* (Princeton, N.J.: Princeton University Press, 1978); Jack Snyder, *Myths of Empire: Domestic Politics and International Ambition* (Ithaca: Cornell University Press, 1991); Helen Milner, "Resisting the Protectionist Temptation: Industry and the Making of Trade Policy in France and the United States during the 1970s," *International Organization* 41 (1987): 639–666.

14. Joe D. Hagan, *Political Opposition and Foreign Policy in Comparative Perspective* (Boulder, Colo.: Lynne Rienner, 1993); Thomas Risse-Kappen, "Public Opinion, Domestic Structure, and Foreign Policy in Liberal Democracies," *World Politics* 43 (1991): 479–512.
15. Juliet Kaarbo, "Power and Influence in Foreign Policy Decision Making: The Role of Junior Coalition Partners in German and Israeli Foreign Policy," *International Studies Quarterly* 40 (December 1996): 501–530.
16. Snyder, *Myths of Empire*.
17. See, for example, Zeev Maoz and Bruce Russett, "Normative and Structural Causes of Democratic Peace, 1946–1986," *American Political Science Review* 87 (1993): 624–638; James Lee Ray, *Democracy and International Conflict: An Evaluation of the Democratic Peace Proposition* (Columbia: University of South Carolina Press, 1995).
18. Hagan, *Political Opposition and Foreign Policy in Comparative Perspective*, 7. See also Adeed Dawisha, "Arab Regimes: Legitimacy and Foreign Policy," in *The Arab State*, ed. Giacomo Luciani (Berkeley: University of California Press, 1990), 284–299.
19. Hagan, *Political Opposition and Foreign Policy in Comparative Perspective*; Risse-Kappen, "Public Opinion, Domestic Structure, and Foreign Policy in Liberal Democracies"; Peter J. Katzenstein, "International Relations and Domestic Structures: Foreign Economic Policies of Advanced Industrial States," *International Organization* 30 (1976): 4–13.
20. Graham T. Allison, *Essence of Decision: Explaining the Cuban Missile Crisis* (Boston: Little, Brown, 1971); Morton H. Halperin, *Bureaucratic Politics and Foreign Policy* (Washington, D.C.: Brookings Institution, 1974); John D. Steinbruner, *The Cybernetic Theory of Decision* (Princeton: Princeton University Press, 1974).
21. Fred I. Greenstein, *Personality and Politics: Problems of Evidence, Inference, and Conceptualization* (New York: Norton, 1975).
22. See, for example, Alexander L. George and Juliette L. George, *Woodrow Wilson and Colonel House: A Personality Study* (New York: John Day, 1956).
23. Ole Holsti, "Cognitive Dynamics and Images of the Enemy," *Journal of International Affairs* 21 (1976): 16–39; Robert Jervis, *Perception and Misperception in International Politics* (Princeton: Princeton University Press, 1976); Yaacov Vertzberger, *The World in Their Minds* (Stanford: Stanford University Press, 1990).
24. Margaret G. Hermann, "Explaining Foreign Policy Behavior Using the Personal Characteristics of Political Leaders," *International Studies Quarterly* 24 (1980): 7–46.
25. Margaret G. Hermann, "Leaders and Foreign Policy Decision Making," in *Diplomacy, Force, and Leadership: Essays in Honor of Alexander George*, ed. Dan Caldwell and Timothy J. McKeown (Boulder: Westview Press, 1993), 77–94.

CHAPTER 2

British Foreign Policy: Continuity and Transformation

Brian White

This chapter marks the beginning of our analysis of foreign policy behavior in thirteen different countries. Brian White describes major developments in British foreign policy that represent both continuity and change. At the end of World War II, Winston Churchill provided his vision of Britain as a global power with global interests, at the center of three concentric circles of world politics (the British Empire/Commonwealth, the Atlantic community, and a united Europe). These circles defined British foreign policy to varying degrees through much of the Cold War. After joining the European Community in 1973, Britain became progressively enmeshed in integration and partnership with its neighbors. Prime Minister Tony Blair has described Britain today as a "pivotal power" to shape the world. This chapter illustrates the incredible complexity of challenges facing contemporary British foreign policy. Britain may be compared with a number of different countries examined in this volume. First, Britain's reluctance to participate fully in the European Union can be contrasted with the pro–European Union policies of France (Chapter 3) and Germany (Chapter 4). This reluctance stems in part from the British identity. The effects of identity as a core value can also be seen in the foreign policy of Russia (Chapter 5) and India (Chapter 8). The importance of alliances, particularly the "special relationship" between the United States and Britain, parallels the special relationship that Israel (Chapter 9) and Japan (Chapter 7) also have with the United States. Finally, Britain is confronting the role of human rights concerns in its post–Cold War foreign policy, as are France, Germany, and South Africa (Chapter 12).

Little appears to have changed in the rhetoric of British foreign policy since the late 1940s. In October 1948 Winston Churchill located Britain at the center of world politics in a famous statement on foreign policy: "Now if you think of the three interlinked circles ['British Commonwealth and Empire'; the 'English-speaking world'; a 'united Europe'] you will see that we are the only country which has a great part to play in every one of them. We stand, in fact, at the very point of conjunction, and here in this island at the center of the seaways and perhaps of airways also, we have the opportunity of joining them all together."[1] In November 1999 Prime Minister Tony Blair gave an important foreign policy speech in which he identified Britain as a pivotal power in world politics: "We have a new role — to use the strengths of our history to build a future not as a super power but as a pivotal power, as a power that is at the crux of the alliances and international politics which shape the world and its future."[2] Although Blair dismissed Churchill's "interlinked circles" vision in passing, his conception of Britain's role was of evident Churchill lineage even if he had changed the metaphor and chosen to focus on British history rather than geography. If nothing else, this comparison reminds us that the traditional role of foreign policy in helping to define national identity — who *we* are and how we relate to *others* — is undiminished.

But if we look behind a rhetoric that underlines the idea of continuity and try to analyze the substance as well as the sources of contemporary British foreign policy, we cannot but be struck by evidence of substantive change and also of transformed environments in which policy is made and implemented. The central dilemma that British political leaders face at the beginning of the twenty-first century is the need to adapt foreign policy to a rapidly changing global environment while at the same time giving the impression, at least to their various domestic audiences, that nothing fundamentally has changed with respect to sovereignty. The British state, led by its duly elected government, but accountable through Parliament to the British people, is nevertheless still able to make critical choices about policy with respect to other international actors, choices that both express and are legitimized by the sovereign will of the people.

This chapter is an attempt to make sense of contemporary British foreign policy and to establish a list of current problems faced by both the policy maker and the foreign policy analyst. To this end two key distinctions are drawn — one historical and the other analytical. The first distinction deals with the period between the late 1940s and 1990, generally known as the Cold War, and the period since 1991, still labeled rather unsatisfactorily the post–Cold War era. Comparing and contrasting different themes, issues, and problems over time can help us to make sense of change in British foreign policy. The second distinction, drawn for more overtly analytical reasons, involves the domestic and international settings of policy, particularly over the last thirty years or so. This analytical perspective will help us to understand the sources of policy and policy change. How has a changing international environment affected British foreign policy? To what extent is it now more appropriate to see British foreign policy as an extension of domestic politics, explaining policy in terms of domestic rather than international factors? More radically, what are the implications for our analysis if we accept the important point made in the first chapter that the distinction between internal and external environments has become increasingly blurred? Without that clear boundary, it might be argued, foreign policy itself now lacks distinctiveness.

British Foreign Policy during the Cold War

As the disturbing idea of a Cold War between East and West began to frame British foreign policy in the late 1940s, the distinctiveness and importance of foreign policy became clear.[3] With World War II still a very fresh memory, it is not surprising that political leaders were reflecting on Britain's role in an international environment that remained very threatening but was also obviously changing. When former prime minister Churchill addressed the annual Conservative Party conference on this theme in 1948, there were already important indicators of change, such as the ceding of independence the previous year to the Indian subcontinent—the "jewel" of the British Empire. Even as Churchill spoke, the first major crisis of the Cold War, over access to West Berlin, remained unresolved. What was significant about Churchill's three circles vision, however, was its prescriptiveness. In it he sought to establish the continuing "realities" that should guide British policy makers despite clear indications of significant change in the postwar international environment. Three key assumptions underpinned this powerful image. First, it depicted Britain as a global power with global interests to defend rather than a regional power pursuing essentially regional interests. Second, it raised pragmatism and flexibility almost to a guiding principle. The object of British foreign policy, Churchill implied, is to play a leading role in all three geographical arenas of activity but not to become committed to any one circle at the expense of the other two. Finally, Churchill's notion that the British "have the opportunity of joining them [the three circles] all together" provided an influential rationale for a freewheeling bridge-builder role for Britain. This self-image, as we shall see, has continued to be powerful throughout the postwar period.

But this image is also useful for analytical purposes and provides a convenient framework for us to characterize the major arenas of activity in Cold War British foreign policy—denoted here by the labels "globalism," "Atlanticism," and "Europeanism"—and to indicate from a policy maker's perspective the relationship between continuity and change.

Globalism

From an immediate postwar perspective, the assumption that Britain would and should continue to play a leading role in constructing a new international order needs little explanation. However ravaged the British economy was as a result of the war, all the trappings of being a great power remained ostensibly intact. As a key member of the victorious alliance against Hitler, Britain (together with the United States and the Soviet Union) was regarded as one of the postwar "Big Three." Britain had already played a leading role in setting up the Bretton Woods system (which established important international economic institutions like the World Bank and the International Monetary Fund) and the United Nations (UN) and was a permanent member of the UN Security Council. British military power still stretched throughout the world, and the Labour government of Prime Minister Clement Attlee was about to play a major role in setting up the North Atlantic Treaty Organization (NATO). It may well be, as Ritchie Ovendale argues, that "Britain's position at the conference tables of world diplomacy obscured the reality of Britain's diminished power," but this reality was not accepted by policy makers in the sense of requiring a radical reassessment of policy objectives.[4] The decisions of 1946–1947, to develop an independent atomic bomb capability, for example, were fundamentally shaped by the simple but continuing assumption that Britain as a great power with global interests should possess the very latest and most potent weapons system.

The 1947 decision to give independence to the Indian subcontinent, which may have accelerated the process of decolonization, might have been expected to prompt Britain to radically reassess its position. But, as David Sanders argues, until the Suez debacle in 1956 (discussed later) administered a great psychological shock to the British, retrenchment aimed at preventing any further erosion of influence, rather than withdrawal, best characterizes the British approach to the end of empire.[5] Indeed, the fact that India, Pakistan, and Sri Lanka (then "Ceylon") all chose to remain within the British Commonwealth after independence boosted hopes that this unique, multiracial organization might serve as an alternative vehicle for maintaining British influence at the global level.

With respect to the emerging bipolar structure of postwar international relations, Britain did play a leading role in establishing institutions (such as NATO) that effectively severed West from East. Less noted is the important role Britain also played in helping to establish a process of East-West diplomacy that was later to be called *détente*. In the decade after 1953, culminating in the signing of the Partial Test Ban Treaty in 1963, so persistent and eventually fruitful were efforts to build bridges between East and West on a range of issues that it is appropriate to regard Britain as an early catalyst of détente.[6] The symbols of power, such as membership in a still-exclusive nuclear club, close links with Washington, diplomatic skills, and a worldwide network of contacts, were all deployed successfully during this period as Britain played an influential mediation role between the superpowers.

The limits of this role, however, soon became apparent. After the Cuban missile crisis in 1962, British governments found it increasingly difficult to play a distinctive role in the process of détente. A weakening role in East-West relations coincided with a realization that hopes and expectations about the commonwealth were optimistic at best. By the early 1960s, policy makers recognized that Britain no longer possessed the military and economic capability to sustain what remained of the empire. It was also recognized that in the longer term a rapid withdrawal would be less painful than a long, drawn-out retreat. Thus, a second wave of decolonization in Africa and the Caribbean followed, and by 1966 the process was effectively complete.

If, by the 1970s, the global circle appeared to be redundant as a principal guideline for British foreign policy, any possibility of retrenchment or reorientation was swiftly countered by the election of the Conservative government under Prime Minister Margaret Thatcher in the 1980s. Thatcher was committed to restoring Britain to a position of international influence and prestige. An unexpected opportunity for an impressive display of national resolve came with Argentina's invasion of the Falkland Islands in April 1982. The repossession of these disputed islands by military force over the following three months did much to establish the international reputation of Thatcher as a tough leader who would not flinch from doing whatever was necessary to defend Britain's national interests. The Falklands conflict, however, was an aberration rather than an indication that the Thatcher government was seriously trying to stem the tide of imperial retreat. This was clearly shown by the almost immediate attempts to negotiate a settlement with China over the future of Hong Kong, another residual piece of empire, that led to an agreement for British withdrawal by 1997.

Where Britain was able to exercise some continuing influence at the global level was, once again, in the area of East-West relations. The second Thatcher government (1983–1987) made a significant contribution to the development of a less confrontational and more constructive relationship between the superpowers and helped to open up contacts with Eastern Europe. As a third party that enjoyed excellent relations with Washington and rapidly improving relations with Moscow and various members of the Soviet bloc, Britain was in a good position to play an influential role. Particularly important was the personal relationship between Thatcher, U.S. president Ronald Reagan, and the Soviet leader Mikhail Gorbachev, which enabled the prime minister to be an important intermediary between the two other leaders.

Once direct superpower contacts resumed, however, British influence again began to wane, and the opportunity to gain an even more authoritative position disappeared. Indeed, as changes in Europe took on a distinctly revolutionary look by the end of the 1980s, Thatcher began to appear more and more as an unreconstructed Cold Warrior, preoccupied with security, worried about the prospect of German reunification, and either unwilling or unable to adapt to the changing mood and ultimately the transformed face of East-West relations.

Atlanticism

In an important sense, the relationship between Britain and the United States during the Cold War was the key to relationships with the other two circles of activity. Not only was influence in Washington central to Britain's ability to influence East-West relations, but this relationship also helped to define the limits of Britain's interest in relations with Western Europe. A principal lesson learned from World War II was that U.S. intervention had rescued Britain from Hitler's clutches and that it was crucial to postwar British security to retain that relationship at the center of policy. Growing perceptions of a major Soviet threat only served to underline this imperative. In a less-well-known section of Churchill's 1946 "Iron Curtain" speech in Fulton, Missouri, he called for a special Anglo-American partnership (thereafter referred to as the "special relationship") in the face of a common Soviet threat.

But the fear that the United States would respond to isolationist pressures at home after the war necessitated some determined British diplomacy. Foreign Secretary Ernest Bevin developed a strategy designed to persuade the Americans to join a military alliance by demonstrating to a skeptical U.S. Congress that the West Europeans were prepared to stand on their own feet and organize themselves for collective security. Hence the signing of the Brussels Treaty with France, Belgium, the Netherlands, and Luxembourg in March 1948—in effect establishing an embryonic NATO—was crucial. Bevin was also a key player in organizing the West European response to the Marshall Plan through the creation of the Organization for European Economic Cooperation (OEEC) in 1948.

Successful though British efforts were to help create an Atlantic community in the late 1940s, significant costs were attached to this role. Fears during the Korean War about the reliability of the U.S. commitment to European security persuaded the Attlee government to undertake a massive rearmament program in 1950 that the weak British economy could scarcely afford. Similar fears saw the Churchill government commit a permanent British military presence to the European continent once it became clear that the French Assembly would not ratify the European Defense Community agreement in 1954. Both decisions contributed to an overcommitment to defense spending and an overextension of military forces, which, given the underlying weakness of the British economy, created serious problems for succeeding governments.

The fundamental weakness of the economy was dramatically highlighted by the Suez crisis in 1956. An Anglo-French invasion of Egypt, ostensibly to protect the integrity of the Suez Canal, was brought to a premature halt by a run on the British pound. The U.S. government made it clear that it would be prepared to support the pound only if Anglo-French forces were immediately withdrawn. The U.S. reaction was undoubtedly a humiliating shock and it led almost immediately to the retirement of the British prime minister, Anthony Eden. But what is striking is how little else changed, at least in the short term. Unlike the French, who drew the opposite conclusion, the British concluded that it was necessary to repair relations with Washington as soon as possible. This the Macmillan government did with some success. Indeed, by the beginning of the 1960s, Anglo-American relations looked to be in good shape.

By the mid-1960s, however, the relationship was beginning to look distinctly normal and the precipitating issue was Vietnam. In the wake of President Lyndon B. Johnson's decision to escalate that conflict, the United States issued urgent requests for support. The refusal of the British government to offer material or diplomatic support led to a sharp deterioration in relations. Another blow to Anglo-American relations came with the planned withdrawal of British forces from east of Suez and the concentration of defense efforts primarily in Western Europe. Withdrawal itself was bad enough from an American perspective—leaving U.S. forces to contain the Soviet Union alone, without British support—but the timing, coinciding as it did with Vietnam, only served to heighten its impact on the relationship. Further problems followed the election of the government of Edward Heath in 1970. Prime Minister Heath made it clear from the outset that his main priority was joining the European Economic Community (EEC) and establishing Britain's credentials as a "good European." He was not prepared to put this endeavor at risk by appearing to covet special links with Washington.

But if Anglo-American relations per se were equivocal at best from the mid-1960s up to the election of the Thatcher government in 1979, it is important to note that Atlanticism remained a dominant orientation of British foreign and defense policy during this period. This can be illustrated by the active role the British played in a NATO crisis. The French decision in 1966 to withdraw from the integrated military command structure of NATO threatened the cohesiveness of the alliance. Stepping into the breach left by the lack of leadership within the alliance at this critical time, the British, with some quiet but decisive diplomacy, helped to formulate a common response that effectively managed the crisis. A concern with alliance cohesion was also reflected in the leading role played by Britain in the establishment of a distinct European defense identity within NATO based on the Eurogroup. Initiated by the defense secretary, Dennis Healey, in 1968 as a forum for ministerial discussion, the Eurogroup spawned a number of subgroups in the early 1970s that dealt with practical areas of cooperation and contributed to transatlantic cohesion.

At the beginning of the 1980s, when East-West relations began a downturn, all the anticommunist instincts of Prime Minister Thatcher told her that a resolute approach abroad was necessary. Thus it was important to increase defense spending and move closer to the Americans. During her first year in office, decisions to purchase the American Trident missile, to support the NATO decision to increase defense spending, and to endorse the "dual track" approach to the deployment of cruise and Pershing II missiles all contributed to an image of strength as far as foreign and especially defense policy was concerned.[7] Underpinned by the close personal and ideological relationship between Thatcher and

Reagan and apparently evidenced by the extensive though largely covert assistance given to Britain during the Falklands War, the special nature of the Anglo-American relationship received greater emphasis in London than it had for twenty years.

After the Falklands War, however, the continuing assumption of special links with Washington began to appear increasingly obsolete. What appeared to many observers as an excessive willingness to underwrite American foreign policy in the mid-1980s highlighted the uncomfortable notion that dependence rather than specialness now characterized the relationship. As Reagan approached the end of his second term, the British also began to worry about the extent to which the relationship depended essentially upon the personal relationship between the two leaders. In fact, the incoming Bush administration did go to some lengths to avoid encouraging any lingering illusions about special transatlantic links and, following the dramatic changes in Europe, to press Britain to play a full role in the shaping of the new Europe. Now let us turn our attention to British policy toward Europe, the third of Churchill's three circles of activity.

Europeanism

At the end of a major speech to the House of Commons in May 1953, Churchill repeated a comment that he had made in various speeches since the 1930s, to the effect that the British are *with* but not *of* Europe. This formulation conveniently summarizes a distinctive British approach to Western Europe that is useful for understanding postwar British policy, certainly up to the late 1990s. The British had a keen interest in cooperating with the governments of Western Europe, particularly in the defense sphere. But the impression was also created that Britain might be interested in a relationship with Western Europe that went beyond intergovernmental cooperation. The sharp-eyed reader will already have noted that Churchill refers to a "united Europe" in his 1948 speech — undoubtedly a reference back to a speech he had made in Zurich in September 1946 in which he had talked about the need to construct a "United States of Europe." At the beginning of 1948 Bevin made some rather vague proposals in the House of Commons about a "Western Union," and Eden, as foreign secretary in the early 1950s, made encouraging noises about the possibility of Britain joining the proposed European Defence Community. In the end, however, Britain chose to remain aloof from the European integration movement at a critical time.

An explanation of this takes us back to some familiar themes. First, Britain was unwilling to forge closer links with Western Europe because a closer identification with the Continent was not consistent with the prevailing conception of Britain as a global power. Moreover, policy makers feared that it would damage relations with the empire/commonwealth. Second, the ambitious plans for European economic integration initially outlined by French foreign minister Robert Schuman in the 1950 Schuman Plan offended the pragmatic British approach to policy making. The plan called for France and West Germany to pool their coal and steel industries under joint management and eventually led to the European Coal and Steel Community (ECSC) and later to the EEC. Not only were the British instinctively suspicious of large conceptions and grand schemes but also they were convinced that these schemes simply would not work. Finally, Britain had a very different recent historical experience from the other six countries that eventually formed the EEC. Unlike countries either defeated or invaded in World War II, the British experience served to reinforce a continued faith in the nation-state as the basic unit of political organization. Thus, they were unwilling to contemplate giving up sovereignty to supranational institutions like the ECSC and missed an important opportunity through 1956–1957 to join the EEC.

By the early 1960s, nevertheless, the European circle was looking increasingly attractive if only because of growing problems with the other circles. But, significantly, Europe was not seen as an alternative to the other two circles. Britain had no special commitment to the European circle and certainly it did not convert overnight to the merits of European integration. From this perspective then, the first application to join the EEC in 1961 was not a radical shift away from the Churchillian prescriptions noted earlier. Politically, membership was seen as a useful way of augmenting power, of adding to the totality of political influence that Britain could exercise in world politics. The particular lure of the EEC, however, lay in the economic field. As evidence of Britain's poor economic performance mounted at the end of the 1950s, the attractions of being a member of a much larger domestic market grew. And, importantly, from the mid-1950s, the pattern of Britain's trade had begun to change dramatically, away from the empire/commonwealth and toward Europe.

But, after joining the EEC in 1973, successive British governments managed to give the impression that they were less than committed to their new European role. This was partly a result of specific issues such as the terms of entry and the question of Britain's contribution to the EEC's budget. More damaging was the continuing evidence of the "three circles" thinking that made Britain a rather awkward partner with a different perspective on EEC matters.[8] To some extent, this assertive stance can be explained by the need to take on the now established Franco-German alliance at the heart of the European Community. A consistently intergovernmental approach perhaps was never going to please the more federalist member states. But the prospects for harmony with EEC partners looked distinctly unpromising once Margaret Thatcher took office.

The early years of the Thatcher period looked like a rerun of the 1970s with a continuing preoccupation with the EEC budget. But another five years of often acrimonious negotiations about both the size and the equity of the British contribution soured relationships and it was to get worse. By the time Thatcher won her third successive election in 1987, questions about the future direction of the European Community in regard to extending the integration process to a wider range of issues had reached center stage. Having ratified the 1986 Single European Act, which, among other things, set a target date of 1992 for a single European market, the British government, like its partners, was now not just committed to harmonizing its foreign policy but also to working toward political and economic union.

The prime minister's response to this prospect came in a famous speech delivered in Bruges, Belgium, in September 1988—a speech that was to have a major impact both domestically and in the European Community. Thatcher took great care to establish her commitment to Europe as a continent—to a Europe that was both "open" and "free" in political and economic venues, as she later put it.[9] The prime minister could and did claim that her government had done much through its détente policy to speed up the process of change in central and Eastern Europe. The thrust of her speech, however, was an unprecedented attack on the European Community. In a section often quoted thereafter, Thatcher not only attacked the Brussels bureaucracy but integration theology as a whole: "We have not successfully rolled back the frontiers of the state in Britain, only to see them reimposed at a European level, with a European super-state exercising a new dominance from Brussels."[10]

Clearly, the prejudices of the prime minister against the EEC were given full vent in this speech. As a committed Atlanticist, Thatcher was predisposed to measure European cooperation in every sphere in terms of its contribution to the solidarity of transatlantic relations. In domestic political terms, her acceptance of the loss of a number of senior ministers from 1986 onward over Europe-related issues was testimony to the strength of her Atlanticist convictions. Unfortunately for her, the resignation of the last of these ministers, Foreign Secretary Sir Geoffrey Howe, triggered the crisis that led to her own resignation in November 1990. Thus, the end of the Thatcher era coincided with the end of the Cold War, and both events in significant ways provided a context for British foreign policy in the 1990s. But before we review developments in the post-Thatcher, post–Cold War era, for analytical purposes we should look more closely at important elements of change and transformation in both the international and the domestic environments, particularly since the 1970s.

External Factors

A narrative account of British foreign policy through the Cold War period constructed around Churchill's three circles offers instructive insights into a number of themes, issues, and problems—some of which continued through the 1990s and into the new millennium. But, as students of foreign policy, we need to remember that every story told about foreign policy is a particular story based on particular working assumptions. Stepping back from the narrative, we can see that the analysis presented so far in this chapter is based, albeit implicitly, on realist assumptions. If we examine the assumptions, we immediately find a state-centric world, with a focus clearly on states rather than other international actors. The British state is also analyzed as a unitary actor, either reified as Britain, or personified, usually by reference to a prime minister—the "Thatcher era," for example.

The process of policy making is also simplified in this realist account. The political leadership is clearly in control here, making more or less effective choices about policy and direction. The subject matter of elite decision making is similarly limited. Foreign policy is largely security policy, a particularly relevant agenda, perhaps, in a Cold War, but nevertheless restrictive. Finally, consistent with traditional realist assumptions, the international environment appears to be much more significant than the domestic in explaining policy.

In summary form, this is a story about British power, influence, and ultimately survival in a hostile world, where conflict rather than cooperation is the norm. The focus is on Britain as an archetypal "middle power" pursuing a traditional balancing or bridge-builder role. But we can challenge this analysis and start to outline other analytical approaches based on different assumptions by looking more closely at significant changes in the two policy environments, starting appropriately with the external one.

From Interdependence to Globalization

As Michael Clarke observes, "the Cold War itself did not end during the 1970s, but the world of the Cold War did."[11] By this he means that the characteristic structures and processes associated with the Cold War began to change, and consequently the whole context of foreign policy began to change. New structures and processes, a new cast of actors, and a broader agenda of issues emerged in their place. Significantly, not only did the bipolar world begin to change in the 1970s but international relations scholars also began to develop new ways of explaining that world. As discussed at length in the first chapter of this book, interdependence theorists like Robert O. Keohane and Joseph S. Nye began to draw upon a liberal rather than a realist tradition to highlight not just change in a state-centric realist world but what they claimed was a total transformation of world politics.[12] Steve Smith and Michael Smith offer a neat encapsulation of this transformationalist perspective: "In this view, states and their concerns are only a part of a much broader and diverse reality which encompasses a host of participants, issues and interactions, affecting and constraining states, but often neither controlled or even strongly influenced by them."[13]

Interdependence theorists clearly overstated the impact of change in the 1970s. The emergence of a *new* cold war in the 1980s powerfully suggested that states remained key actors in world politics and that the traditional security politics agenda had not been wholly replaced by a preoccupation with other types of issues. Interestingly, both liberals and realists began to revise their theories in the 1990s in an attempt to come to grips with a more complex world that defied any simple explanation. But, as globalization followed interdependence as a central organizing concept in new theories, it was also apparent that explaining foreign policy could not remain immune to these theoretical debates. In particular, it was clear that traditional state-centric realist assumptions were inadequate to capture the complex nature of a rapidly globalizing world in which states must implement their foreign policies. Insights derived from other theoretical accounts are needed to supplement realism.

We can draw first upon liberal theories here to outline a rather different analysis of British foreign policy, but this does not mean wholly rejecting the pervasive realist approach. The decision to join the EEC, for example, despite the continuing rhetoric of great power independence, suggests a different reality of Britain as a medium power with a fragile economy increasingly locked into an interdependent network of economic relationships. Changes in trade flows and the pressing need for a larger domestic market in which to sell British goods — rather than traditional security factors — were crucial to the decisions to move progressively closer to the European "circle." Rapid decolonization in the 1950s and 1960s and the withdrawal of British military forces from east of Suez in the 1970s are other illustrations of significant adaptations to change.

But, crucially, it was not simply a matter of British governments adapting to change by deciding to do some things differently while remaining essentially in control as independent, sovereign actors. The growth of interdependence, liberal theorists argue, must erode the independence and autonomy of even the most powerful states. This means that all governments operating in this new environment are much more constrained than before in the choices available to them. In regard to the new nonstate actors, new transnational processes, and new issues, they argue that governmental *control* of world politics is now much more contested. To illustrate the impact on British foreign policy of this structural challenge to governmental control, the next section looks at Britain's changing regional context and the process known as Europeanization.

From Europeanism to Europeanization

References to Europe in the earlier narrative are located within Churchill's European circle. The conventional story of Britain's postwar descent from power tells of the political elite initially choosing only limited involvement in Europe. Increasing involvement followed largely because of problems with the preferred global and Atlantic circles.[14] Europeanism, then, denotes the painful choice of joining the EEC and thus selecting Europe as a home of last resort as the other two circles became more and more problematic. Not surprisingly, given a continuing preference for a different policy orientation, elite attitudes toward Europe remained ambivalent at best.

The concept of "Europeanization," in contrast, suggests a process of regional integration over time in which the individual member governments of what is now the European Union (EU) have far less control over policy making. Premised upon the liberal imperative of cooperating with regional partners on a range of issues in order to achieve wider objectives in a global environment, the concept suggests that the ability of British and other member governments to make genuinely independent decisions is being progressively eroded in a multilateral policy environment. From this perspective, the EU has provided a radically new context for British foreign policy making—whether the political elite accepts this or not.[15]

The most obvious change—a genuine transformation indeed—immediately followed the signing in 1972 of the Treaty of Rome, which had established the European Economic Community in 1957. At that point, Britain, in common with all new member states, accepted the accumulated rules and obligations derived from European Community (EC) treaties, laws, and regulations. Even more significantly, Britain had signed on to a new system of international law— Community law—that, in the event of conflict, takes precedence over relevant national (English, Scottish, Northern Irish) systems of law. Although commentators continue to argue about the implications of this, most have accepted that if sovereignty is defined in legal terms, Britain, in common with other members, is no longer a sovereign state with the final court of appeal located within its territorial frontiers.

The real arguments that continue in Britain, however, are normally framed in terms of political rather than legal sovereignty, where "sovereignty" is a synonym for other symbolic values like independence or freedom. This perspective leaves room for different views about whether or not Britain as a member of the EU is, or is not, sovereign. Trade policy most obviously and aid policy to a lesser extent are made by Community institutions and through Community processes, rather than by member states, although states are an important part of that process through their membership in the European Council of Ministers. In contrast, the making of foreign and defense policy within the EU remains largely an intergovernmental process controlled by member states; pressure, however, is growing to integrate or "communitize" policy even in these areas.

A second area of dramatic change lies in the range of issues that now constitute the foreign policy agenda. This agenda has so blurred the boundaries between foreign policy and domestic politics that it raises the question of whether a distinctive area of British foreign policy exists any more. "In a sense," William Wallace has argued, "foreign policy has now disintegrated within the widening agenda of intergovernmental business."[16] Certainly, it is no longer appropriate to try to analyze Britain's policy toward its European partners as a foreign policy issue area only. Nevertheless, the demands posed by having to deal with a widening agenda of foreign policy issues have been felt within the foreign policy machinery, as we shall see in a later section of this chapter.

A transformed operational environment is the final area of change emanating from the European regional context. EU membership has transformed the nature of Britain's relations with other member states, nonmember states, and international organizations. An increasing range of issues has to be negotiated with partner states *and* with Community institutions. On a day-to-day basis, British representatives are locked into a complex, multilateral, and multilevel process of foreign policy making: the UK government with other member governments in bilateral and multilateral fora; the Foreign and Commonwealth Office and other government departments with their opposite numbers in state and Community institutions; the British ambassador with other permanent representatives and the relevant departments (called directorate-generals) of the European Commission; British embassies abroad with other member state embassies and the external representatives of the commission. Much of the operational side of European foreign policy, indeed, is now managed by the European Commission rather than by member states like Britain.

A key question that emerges from all this is whether membership overall has augmented the capabilities and policy instruments available to British policy makers or whether the costs (in regard to constraints) outweigh the benefits. Is Britain a more effective actor on an interdependent, global stage as a result of these regional arrangements? To date, the study done in 1992 by Simon Bulmer, Stephen George, and Andrew Scott has been the only extensive survey that addresses this question.[17] Their findings are nevertheless still broadly relevant. In regard to autonomy, they argue that British foreign economic policy has been most Europeanized, foreign policy less so, and defense policy least Europeanized. Overall, they conclude that the benefits of membership outweigh the costs, particularly given a general decline in independent British foreign policy capabilities in the postwar period.

But there is a continuing debate between realists and liberals about the impact of Europeanization on the member states of the EU. Realists insist that states and governments are still ultimately in control of the process of integration, particularly in the key areas of foreign and defense policy. Some argue, indeed, that the process of integration has rescued the nation-state by enabling it to adapt and survive in postwar Europe.[18] Other analysts are more impressed by the growing constraints upon state autonomy revealed by transnational and globalization theories. Whichever theoretical perspective is preferred, we can conclude this section by arguing that British foreign policy located within a transformed regional context is now a far less distinctive phenomenon than the earlier historical analysis would suggest. Further challenges to our narrative picture emerge from a review in the next section of the changing domestic context of British foreign policy.

Internal Factors

The Westminster Model of Policy Making

A central component of the realist perspective on international relations is a conception of foreign policy as a distinctive area of governmental activity. Separate from domestic politics it is nevertheless, realists argue, an area supported by a domestic consensus on at least the major principles of policy. The traditional account of British government, often referred to as either the "Westminster" or the constitutional model of policy making, fits neatly into this conceptual framework and therefore provides a useful starting point for a review of the changing domestic context of British foreign policy.[19] The traditional foreign policy context can be characterized first in constitutional terms, then by the nature of the policy process, and finally in terms of the relationship between domestic politics and foreign policy.

Constitutionally, British foreign policy is or at least was (never entirely clear in an unwritten constitution resting upon tradition and precedent) controlled by the monarchy. The importance historically of foreign policy is indicated both by the fact that it was the last area of government to be relinquished by the monarchy in the nineteenth century and that it was handed down not to Parliament but to the executive or, strictly speaking, to His or Her Majesty's ministers. Foreign policy has never been controlled by Parliament except in the indirect sense though crucial to the British concept of parliamentary democracy—that ministers are ultimately accountable to Parliament. As Clarke notes, British foreign policy "has always been directed from the center; whether that center has been expressed through royalty or through a powerful political executive."[20] The special location of foreign policy constitutionally at the heart of the machinery of state helps to explain why foreign policy traditionally has been so closely identified in symbolic terms with statehood and in particular with the concept of sovereignty and associated concepts of freedom, independence, and national identity.[21]

The assumed distinctiveness and centrality of foreign policy also links in highly prescriptive ways to other elements of the traditional British context. The policy process is expected to match the substance of this "high policy" arena in regard to unified, centralized control, which is at the heart of the Westminster model. If foreign policy is central to the fundamental concerns of the state, to its security in particular, then foreign policy is literally too important to be left to the cut and thrust of domestic politics. As David Vital puts it in a classic commentary, "foreign policy, then, is the business of the Executive and for almost all practical purposes the Executive is unfettered in its exercise of this function."[22] From this perspective, indeed, this conception of foreign policy requires the executive—formally the cabinet, which constitutionally shares collective responsibility for policy—to play a sort of gatekeeper role, policing the boundary between the state and the external environment. To ensure effective coordination of policy at the bureaucratic level, Vital suggests that the management of foreign policy also requires the traditional lead department in foreign policy, the Foreign and Commonwealth Office (FCO), to play a parallel gatekeeper role in Whitehall, the location of Britain's government in London.

The last element of the traditional context is the relationship between foreign policy and domestic politics. From the perspective of a Westminster model, it is already apparent that these areas are assumed to be distinctive and clearly differentiated. Moreover, for all the reasons touched upon here, there is an expectation that domestic politics will not undermine foreign policy, a prescription that is captured by the phrase "politics stops at the water's edge." Historically, bipartisanship has reinforced this view, with the two major political parties in Britain agreeing on the essentials of foreign policy. This in turn has underpinned a broader domestic consensus.

The Westminster model provides a powerful view of how British government works. But it is highly prescriptive and obscures the effect of change, particularly the changing domestic context of foreign policy. All the elements of this model can be challenged, and the idea of the Europeanization of policy making can again be used to illustrate the extent of change in the domestic environment. A better understanding of a transformed domestic context will also underline the relevance of other theories to an explanation of British foreign policy at the beginning of the twenty-first century.

The Europeanization of the Policy Process

Britain's foreign policy agenda has greatly expanded as a result of its membership in the European Union. This expansion has had a major impact on the nature of the foreign policy making process. Most obviously, it has drawn more domestic actors and institutional players into the process, making it much more difficult to identify a distinctive foreign policy process. Although some government departments have been closely involved with the European Community for many years, by the mid-1990s it could be said that *every* British government department was to a greater or lesser extent involved in networks of transnational and transgovernmental relations with other actors and institutions across the EU.[23]

It is apparent then that Europeanization now affects domestic politics as much as it does foreign policy. Equally clearly, the challenge for national policy systems is to devise effective systems of coordination and control across a widening range of actors. The vast increase in activity across EU borders poses particular challenges to traditional conceptions of the government and the FCO as gatekeepers. Three sets of actors in the Whitehall machine are important in coordinating all aspects of European policy—the small European Secretariat of the Cabinet Office, the FCO, and the British ambassador to the EU (or UKREP). The European Secretariat provides strategic coordination. This body coordinates the responses of Whitehall to European issues; resolves any conflicts between departments; and, through its close links with the prime minister's office, ensures that policy is in tune with wider governmental objectives. In contrast, the FCO and its external arm, UKREP, provide operational coordination. Any problems are dealt with at a weekly meeting between representatives of the three institutions.

But there is a debate between analysts of different theoretical persuasions about how effectively the process of Europeanization has been assimilated into the centralized Westminster model. Traditionalists argue that this system of coordination works well and that control is effectively retained at the center. Institutions have been skillfully and smoothly adapted over time rather than radically changed. Central control is effective but exercised with a light touch, with departments retaining much operational control of the policy process. The FCO, in particular, still plays a gatekeeper role. Europeanization has obviously occurred but, from this perspective, its impact on the policy process has been limited. There have been changes in the operation of the machinery, notably the introduction of Cabinet Office oversight, but these changes have taken place within a robust traditional system of central state administration.[24]

Some recent research, however, questions the assumptions that underpin these conclusions, and points to a rather different account of the impact of Europeanization on the policy process in Britain. Martin Smith explicitly challenges the traditional model from a policy networks perspective. He identifies two countervailing trends in the coordination of European policy: a centralizing trend that is consistent with the analysis above and strong centripetal forces based on departmental interests. Despite high levels of departmental satisfaction with coordination at the center and the continuing FCO belief that it alone controls contacts with UK representation in Brussels, the centripetal forces appear to be at least as significant in explaining the impact of the EU on the policy process. "The reality," Smith argues, "is that as EU business increases, the FCO and the Cabinet Office are losing control, and departments are increasingly conducting business with the Commission, and other states, *directly*."[25]

With central control apparently diluted at best, Smith goes on to reveal a differential pattern of coordination among departments. Some departments like the Ministry of Agriculture and Fisheries and the Department of Trade and Industry are at the highly Europeanized end of a spectrum, with a considerable degree of autonomy over their issue areas and actively geared up to exploit relevant transnational networks across the EU. At the other end of the spectrum are departments like the Home Office, which are much more ambivalent about the opportunities that EU policy networks offer to increase their role and autonomy. But if some departments at least are becoming more autonomous — and increasingly locked into networks that are difficult for the national government to control — this must challenge the traditional gatekeeper role of government in general and the FCO in particular.

The changing domestic context of foreign policy has increased the demands upon the FCO enormously. It is now the focus of a wide range of domestic as well as external pressures that emanate from a domestic political system that has itself been radically transformed by membership in the EU. Since the 1970s the issue of a multidimensional Europe has increasingly come to dominate domestic politics in Britain. This issue has created major fault lines within as well as across both the Conservative and the Labour Parties and, in its various manifestations, "Europe" remains a highly controversial issue for the general public. The clear absence of anything approaching a consensus on Europe means that policy making on a wide range of issues must take place within a domestic context that is fraught with difficulties for policy makers. From a theoretical perspective, assumptions that informed the traditional context about bipartisanship and a consensus with respect to foreign policy have thus been seriously undermined. This highlights the potential of explanations of British foreign policy derived from domestic political analysis.

One promising theoretical development from a broadly political culture perspective explores the role of popular attitudes toward Europe in foreign policy. Discourse analysts have taken a lead in exploring the importance of the images revealed by the language used by the British about Europe.[26] They have discovered that, in the absence of any serious domestic debate, the key elements within both the dominant elite and a wider popular discourse about Europe over the last forty years or so have remained remarkably consistent and reflect a persistent and strongly held conception of national identity. Critically, the concept of Europe has been and continues to be suffused with almost wholly negative connotations. To select some important elements: Europe is seen as a threat to independence, autonomy, and the very idea of "Britishness"; the idea of Britain-in-Europe is linked to ideas about decline and failure; Europe is regarded as an "optional extra" to be embraced—or not; Europe is seen as a business arrangement, an economic necessity even, but not as central to Britain's wider interests.[27]

Interestingly, Helen Wallace notes that initial British membership in the EEC was not accompanied by "a conversion to the concept or the symbolism of integration" and that membership over time has not been characterized—as might have been expected—by further adaptation to Europe through a process she calls "retarded Europeanization." But, significantly, Atlanticism continues to attract a strong, symbolic attachment in popular discourse. Compared with other member states, "the British pattern is quite different. The symbolic dimension to integration is either absent or negative for large sections of British opinion. Only a minority of the British feel strong symbolic attachment to European integration as defined by the EU, while NATO attracts positive symbolic resonance, as does Atlanticism. There persists a sense of a distinct British political identity and of distance from the European institutional framework."[28]

These findings clearly challenge the conventional assumption that domestic public opinion has little or no impact on a state's foreign policy. Wallace and other analysts have revealed certain core values and underlying beliefs of the British people that are not easily changed, at least in the short term, and must set boundaries for foreign policy makers. This further underlines the general point that an understanding of a radically changing domestic environment can improve our understanding of contemporary British foreign policy. Informed by a better understanding of changes in both internal and external policy settings, and alerted to theoretical possibilities beyond realism, we turn in the final section to a review of the most recent period of foreign policy.

Contemporary British Foreign Policy

As noted earlier, Thatcher's resignation as prime minister in November 1990 was closely linked, in regard to foreign policy, to her negative attitudes toward Europe. Despite the hostile rhetoric, Thatcher's tenure in office in fact coincided with an accelerating process of Europeanization in Britain. This is best illustrated by her support for the Single European Act (SEA) in 1986. This support led to considerable debate about what the fiercely intergovernmentalist Thatcher was doing supporting a crucial piece of legislation that introduced the idea of majority voting into European Community business. As Hugo Young puts it, the legislation constituted "the most practical advance towards the abolition of national frontiers and national powers that the Community had undertaken in the whole period of British membership."[29] One answer lies in the adaptations that were perceived to be necessary if Britain were to survive in a transformed international environment. The Thatcher government appears to have been focusing on supporting the prime objective of the SEA, the creation of a single European market that promised to make Europe and Britain much more competitive in a globalized economy, rather than studying the fine print of the act.

The Major Government and Europe

Thatcher's exit four years later at least spared her from the final stages of the ongoing negotiations with Community partners that led to the Treaty on European Union (or simply, the Maastricht Treaty) in 1991. Although Prime Minister John Major successfully negotiated "opt-outs" for Britain on both the common currency and new social provisions, he committed Britain to political and economic union and, as a result, to even deeper integration with the new European Union. The first foreign policy issue that Major had to deal with, however, was the Persian Gulf War, an issue that underlined the continuing resonance of both the Atlantic and the global "circles." But on Europe the rhetoric had clearly changed. Major's key statement on the subject came on a visit to Germany shortly after the Gulf War: "I want us to be where we belong. At the very heart of Europe. Working with our partners in building the future."[30] Although Major did eventually manage to get the Maastricht Treaty itself ratified in 1993, any desire to implement this objective on a wider canvas was destroyed by the 1992 election, which delivered a very small Conservative majority.

After the 1992 election, the European issue almost totally dominated British foreign policy. European policy in turn was very much an extension of domestic politics and can best be explained in regard to a transformed domestic political context. Given his slim parliamentary majority, Major was compelled to listen to backbench opinion (opinions of members of Parliament who do not hold positions within the government) and modify policy accordingly. Not only was his parliamentary majority small — a mere twenty-one seats — but ominously for a leader trying to ratify the Maastricht Treaty, 130 Conservative backbenchers, known as the Bruges Group, had joined an anti-EU faction after Thatcher's famous speech in which she was highly critical of the European community. A divided party infected the cabinet, which in turn also fractured on the European issue into so-called "Euro-skeptics" and "Euro-philes." An extremely hostile press, which increasingly took both an anti-EU and an anti-Major stance, completed the picture of a beleaguered prime minister who lacked authority as the head of a Conservative Party that, by the mid-1990s, had all but disintegrated.

A landslide defeat in the May 1997 election duly followed. Significantly, neither of the main political parties made Europe a key issue in that election because, less dramatically perhaps, the Labour Party was also split on this issue.

New Labour, New Foreign Policy?

Nevertheless, having won the sort of overall parliamentary majority that John Major could only have dreamed of (197 seats), the Labour government under the new prime minister, Tony Blair, appeared to be sufficiently detached from party constraints to succeed where Major had failed: in placing Britain at the heart of Europe. But this was only one aspect of foreign policy in which the Labour Party, out of office for eighteen years, sought to establish its much-heralded credentials as "New Labour." Two key areas of foreign policy quickly emerged, both of which suggested change if not transformation from the traditional foreign policy agenda. The first was an explicit attempt to introduce an ethical dimension into British foreign policy and to turn foreign policy making into a more open, transparent process. The second area was an attempt to establish a new international role and identity for Britain.

Ethics and Openness. The new liberal foreign policy agenda, sensitive to ethical concerns, focused on three issue areas: aid and development, human rights, and arms sales. The new Department of International Development speedily published the first official paper on aid and development in twenty years. This White Paper, as such reports are known, contained ambitious plans: to halve world poverty by 2015; to raise foreign aid to the UN target of 0.7 percent of gross national product; to delink aid subsidies from commercial objectives; and to advance debt relief. The promotion of human rights took various forms. At home, the European Convention on Human Rights was incorporated into British law. Abroad, a Human Rights Project Fund was established to promote human rights worldwide. Human rights were broadly conceived. The military intervention in Kosovo in 1999, for example, was defined as a "just war," with British participation legitimized by reference to what Blair later called "a new doctrine of international community, defined by common rights and shared responsibilities."[31] In line with these responsibilities, the Blair government undertook to reduce arms exports to countries where they would be used for internal repression or external aggression.

Making progress in all these areas rested in part at least on greater openness and transparency in foreign policy making. From this perspective, there were notable achievements. New annual reports on government efforts to promote human rights and on British arms exports were established and Britain's EU partners were persuaded to sign a European Code of Conduct for arms exports. Other indicators of progress included the promotion of a ban on land mines and torture equipment. On debt relief, Chancellor of the Exchequer Gordon Brown played a leading role in the International Monetary Fund and Group of Seven (G-7) decisions to finance massive debt relief to the most indebted countries. On arms sales, legislation was promised that would require British arms brokers to be licensed and would switch export guarantees away from arms exports and toward civilian projects.

But critics focused on unfulfilled expectations. In particular, continuing British arms sales to unsavory regimes with poor human rights records attracted the criticism of excessive secrecy and seriously challenged the credibility of claims to a more ethical foreign policy. In opposition, the Labour Party had acquired considerable political capital by accusing the Conservative government of failing to implement the recommendations of the judicial Scott Report on arms sales to Iraq (1996). The apparent unwillingness of the government to implement Sir Richard Scott's central recommendation—to enable Parliament to scrutinize arms exports more effectively—was highly damaging. Not only was it clear that a culture of secrecy was still deeply embedded in the British political culture, but the Blair government was widely accused of exacerbating the problem of secrecy by distorting information to the public through persistent "spin-doctoring." By the summer of 2000, recurrent criticisms of Labour's ethical foreign policy had taken their toll. The press strongly hinted that the Labour Party manifesto for the next election would contain no references to an ethical foreign policy.

Orientation and Identity. The most dramatic indication of a new European approach to foreign policy was the transformed British position on defense after 1998. The British view through the 1990s, initially supported by the Blair government, had been to oppose Franco-German attempts to promote a coordinated EU approach to defense. The objective was to avoid any policy that might weaken the American commitment to European security. But after a summit meeting with the French in December 1998, the Blair government sought, with the French, to take the lead in establishing a European defense force. The EU thereafter collectively decided to establish an integrated European force of 60,000 by 2003.

Whatever the practical problems to be faced in implementing these decisions, the new British position on European defense was certainly a radical shift away from an Atlanticist approach and appeared to herald a fundamental reorientation of British foreign policy toward Europe. However, the government was careful to locate defense and other elements of contemporary foreign policy within a traditional conception of Britain's role in the world. In particular, this government, like its predecessors, rejected the idea that there was any necessity to choose between Atlanticism and Europeanism. This position was clarified in the first major speech on foreign policy delivered by the prime minister at the London Guildhall in November 1999. Blair's central point, quoted at the beginning of this chapter, was to establish a role for Britain as a "pivotal power" in world politics. Thus positioned, Blair went on to argue that the British should not "continue to be mesmerized by the choice between the U.S. and Europe. It is a false choice. . . . My vision for Britain is as a bridge between the EU and the USA." From this rather familiar perspective, Blair sought to downplay the radical nature of the new British approach to European defense. The objective is to "shape European defense policy in a way designed to strengthen [the] Atlantic bond by making NATO a more balanced partnership, and by giving Europeans the capacity to act whenever the United States, for its own reasons, decides not to be involved."

This general approach encompasses two problems: its viability in regard to policy and its likely impact on the ingrained British attitudes toward Europe. The view that choices do not need to be made assumes a high degree of common interests and positions across the Atlantic that the evidence, particularly since the end of the Cold War, suggests is unlikely to be sustained. It may well be that Britain can, on certain issues at certain times, act effectively as a bridge builder with the United States. On other issues at other times, however, choices may need to be made. Defense, for example, may well become an increasingly problematic issue, particularly given the almost instinctive British predisposition to defer to and support the American line in crises (the wars in the Persian Gulf and Kosovo, for example). Will Britain's European partners trust Britain not to take a U.S. line on defense issues in the future? The election of George W. Bush suggests that choices on defense in particular may need to be made sooner rather than later. Dilemmas with respect to the proposed U.S. national missile defense system are likely to be compounded by the planned reorientation (following a review by Secretary of Defense Donald H. Rumsfeld) of U.S. defense policy toward the Pacific and the perceived Chinese threat.

From a more analytical perspective, continuing adherence to the bridge-builder image clearly understates the impact of Europeanization on British foreign policy. The new Blairite location of Britain is revealed to be very conservative, as if role and identity can be detached from a policy context and process that are increasingly Europeanized, as are the instruments and outputs. To this extent, it continues a tradition dating back at least to the 1960s whereby important decisions are taken with respect to Europe that produce major transformations over time. At the same time, however, the impression is created that nothing of great significance is actually changing.[32] But this approach does have significant consequences for domestic politics. Not only are the British people left in ignorance of the real extent of change but also they are led to believe that British governments are less constrained by the international environment and have more room to maneuver than is the case. Indeed, arguing persistently that no choices need to be made suggests that the parameters of choice are wider than in fact they are. Such an approach, it may be argued, is more likely to reinforce than to modify hostile domestic attitudes toward Europe.

The dilemmas of choice generated by the need to trade off competing demands and constraints from internal and external environments can be seen most starkly in the current debate about whether or not Britain should join the common European currency, the Euro. The position of the Blair government in the early months of 2001 was as follows. In principle, joining the Euro was accepted, but a decision would be deferred pending the meeting of certain criteria in regard to the convergence of the economies of EU members. If these criteria were met, the government would hold a referendum on the issue within two years of the next election. Meanwhile the Conservative opposition was opposed in principle to the Euro, and opinion polls unambiguously indicated that a popular vote would oppose membership—a position that may well be reinforced by the vote of no in the September 2000 Danish referendum on Euro membership.

Conclusion

The record of the Blair government on foreign policy to date neatly illustrates both the policy problems that confront the foreign policy maker and the analytical problems that confront the foreign policy analyst. The policy maker faces the dilemma of needing to adapt policy to change and transformation while also maintaining the position that states and governments as independent actors continue to make the critical choices about foreign policy on behalf of their citizens. Trying to resolve the tensions between continuity and transformation is the policy maker's problem. Trying to explain the nature of these tensions and their policy implications is the policy analyst's problem. These tensions have been explored here both historically and analytically, using a variety of theories to highlight the changing nature of the international and the domestic environments that provide the settings of foreign policy in order to understand the sources of policy and policy change in Britain.

Two general conclusions are appropriate in the British case, one substantive and the other theoretical. Both the internal and external environments of British foreign policy have changed dramatically in the postwar period generating a pattern of often-conflicting demands and constraints that continue to create major problems for foreign policy makers. We can conclude, however, that pressures for foreign policy change have come predominantly from transformations in the external environment, particularly from a dynamic regional context. Whereas the demands for change have come predominantly from the outside, the pressures for continuity and the resistance to change have come predominantly from the domestic environment. The importance of the domestic environment as constraint, however, has been significantly increased by developments, again largely at the regional level, that have effectively removed the boundary between foreign policy and domestic politics.

A second conclusion that can be drawn is the importance of applying theory to foreign policy. Although narrative historical descriptions are useful, they always contain, if only implicitly, particular sets of theoretical assumptions. To illustrate this important point, a narrative account of British foreign policy during the Cold War was constructed upon realist assumptions and then supplemented by a variety of other theoretical perspectives that highlight different dimensions of change and offer different explanations of policy. Some theories explain foreign policy as essentially an adaptation to a changing external environment, whereas others see foreign policy as an extension of domestic politics. An explanation of British foreign policy thus depends on the theoretical approach taken.

Suggestions for Further Reading

Clarke, Michael. *British External Policy-Making in the 1990s.* London: Macmillan, 1992.
George, Stephen. *An Awkward Partner: Britain in the European Community.* 3d ed. Oxford: Oxford University Press, 1998.
Larsen, Henrik. *Foreign Policy and Discourse Analysis: France, Britain, and Europe.* London: Routledge, 1997.
Smith, Martin. *The Core Executive in Britain.* London: Macmillan, 1999.
Smith, Michael, Steve Smith, and Brian White, eds. *British Foreign Policy: Tradition, Change and Transformation.* London: Unwin Hyman, 1988.
White, Brian. *Britain, Détente, and Changing Patterns of East-West Relations.* London: Routledge, 1992.
———. "British Foreign Policy: Tradition and Change." In *Foreign Policy in World Politics.* 8th ed. Ed. Roy Macridis. Englewood Cliffs, N.J.: Prentice Hall, 1992.
———. "The Europeanization of National Foreign Policies." In *Understanding European Foreign Policy.* London: Palgrave, 2001.
Young, Hugo. *This Blessed Plot: Britain and Europe from Churchill to Blair.* London: Macmillan, 1998.

Notes

1. The relevant parts of Churchill's speech are quoted in Avi Shlaim, "Britain's Quest for a World Role," *International Relations,* May 1974, 840–841.
2. Tony Blair, http://www.fco.gov.uk/text/news, November 1999.
3. This section draws upon Brian White, "British Foreign Policy: Tradition and Change," in *Foreign Policy in World Politics,* 8th ed., ed. Roy Macridis (Englewood Cliffs, N.J.: Prentice Hall, 1992).
4. Ritchie Ovendale, "Introduction," in *The Foreign Policy of the British Labour Governments, 1945–51,* ed. Ritchie Ovendale (Leicester: Leicester University Press, 1984), 3.
5. David Sanders, *Losing an Empire, Finding a Role: British Foreign Policy Since 1945* (London: Macmillan, 1990).
6. See Brian White, *Britain, Détente, and Changing Patterns of East-West Relations* (London: Routledge, 1992).
7. Michael Clarke, "The Soviet Union and Western Europe," in *British Foreign Policy under Thatcher,* ed. Peter Byrd (New York: St. Martin's Press, 1988), 62.
8. Stephen George, *An Awkward Partner: Britain in the European Community,* 3d ed. (Oxford: Oxford University Press, 1998).
9. Margaret Thatcher, "My Vision of Europe: Open and Free," *Financial Times,* November 19, 1990, 17.
10. Quoted in Hugo Young, *One of Us* (London: Pan, 1990), 169.
11. Michael Clarke, *British External Policy-Making in the 1990s* (London: Macmillan, 1992), 10.
12. Robert O. Keohane and Joseph S. Nye, eds., *Transnational Relations and World Politics* (Cambridge: Harvard University Press, 1972); Robert O. Keohane and Joseph S. Nye, *Power and Interdependence* (Boston: Little, Brown, 1977).
13. Steve Smith and Michael Smith, "The Analytical Background," in *British Foreign Policy: Tradition, Change, and Transformation,* ed. Michael Smith, Steve Smith, and Brian White (London: Unwin Hyman, 1988), 5.
14. See, for example, the classic textbook analysis in Fred Northedge, *Descent from Power: British Foreign Policy, 1945–1973* (London: Allen and Unwin, 1974).
15. Much of the analysis that follows draws upon Brian White, *Understanding European*

Foreign Policy (London: Palgrave, 2001), esp. chap. 6, "The Europeanization of National Foreign Policies: The Case of Britain," 118–141.

16. William Wallace, "The Nation State and Foreign Policy," in *French and British Foreign Policies in Transition,* ed. Françoise De La Serre, Jacques Leruez, and Helen Wallace (Oxford: Berg, 1990), 241.

17. Simon Bulmer, Stephen George, and Andrew Scott, eds., *The UK and EC Membership Evaluated* (London: Pinter, 1992).

18. See Alan Milward, *The European Rescue of the Nation State* (London: Routledge, 1992).

19. A very readable critique of the Westminster model of British parliamentary sovereignty from a policy networks perspective is contained in Martin Smith, *The Core Executive in Britain* (London: Macmillan, 1999).

20. Clarke, *British External Policy-Making in the 1990s,* 73.

21. A useful discussion that contrasts parliamentary sovereignty in Britain with other European conceptions of sovereignty through different histories of internal struggles for political authority, can be found in ibid., 5–8, 247–249.

22. David Vital, *The Making of British Foreign Policy* (London: Allen and Unwin, 1968), 49.

23. Martin Smith, *The Core Executive in Britain,* 232–233.

24. See, for example, David Allen, "United Kingdom. The Foreign and Commonwealth Office: 'Flexible, Responsive, and Proactive'?" in Brian Hocking, *Foreign Ministries: Change and Adaptation (Studies in Diplomacy)* (London: Macmillan), 207–225; Simon Bulmer and Martin Burch, "Organizing for Europe: Whitehall, the British State and European Union," *Public Administration* 76 (winter 1998): 601–628.

25. Martin Smith, *The Core Executive in Britain,* 234. My italics.

26. See, for example, Henrik Larsen, *Discourse Analysis and Foreign Policy: France, Britain, and Europe* (London: Routledge, 1997).

27. This illustrative list is compiled from a variety of sources, including ibid.; Hugo Young, *This Blessed Plot: Britain and Europe from Churchill to Blair* (London: Macmillan, 1998); William Wallace, "Foreign Policy and National Identity in the United Kingdom," *International Affairs* 67 (1991): 65–85; Christopher Tugendhat and William Wallace, *Options for British Foreign Policy in the 1990s* (London: Routledge, 1988).

28. Helen Wallace, "At Odds with Europe," *Political Studies* 45 (1997): 677–688.

29. Young, *This Blessed Plot,* 333.

30. Ibid., 424.

31. Tony Blair, speech in Chicago, April 1999.

32. See Young, *This Blessed Plot,* 129.

CHAPTER 3

French Foreign Policy: The Wager on Europe

Steven Philip Kramer

French foreign policy is the product of both deep historical traditions and geopolitical circumstances. Once one of the most powerful countries in Europe, France experienced military defeats by Germany in 1870 and 1940 that significantly limited its influence. French foreign policy during the Cold War was characterized by the drive for security and restoration of its great power status. Under the leadership of President Charles de Gaulle, France developed a nuclear deterrent, maintained neo-colonial ties to Africa, fostered a close Franco-German partnership, and served as an architect of European integration. Today, France continues its drive for global influence in the face of new and dynamic challenges.

French foreign policy may be compared with that of a number of different countries examined in this volume. French foreign policy toward the European Union, for example, shows some of the same patterns as other European states. Like Germany (Chapter 4), France has incorporated European integration as a cornerstone of its foreign policy, but like Great Britain (Chapter 2), it has shown concern about challenges to its sovereignty and independence in the EU framework. France can also be compared with other democracies. Although France is one of the world's oldest democracies, this chapter shows that its system of making foreign policy remains surprisingly centralized, more like policy making in the newer democracies of Russia (Chapter 5) and South Africa (Chapter 12). Also like Russia, France has struggled to be taken seriously as a great power—to still count in world politics. This is a theme French foreign policy also shares with the foreign policies of China (Chapter 6) and India (Chapter 8).

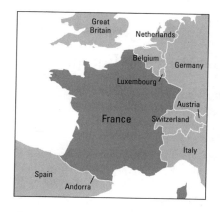

The basic goals of French foreign policy since 1870 have been to guarantee the security of France and to maintain France's status as a great power. That status was dramatically called into question by defeat in the Franco-Prussian War and once again by German occupation during World War II. Modern French foreign policy has thus been characterized by continuity of ends, if not means.

But there has been significant change as well. After World War II, French leaders slowly came to realize that only through cooperation with Germany could France's security be assured. Moreover, France alone, as a middle-sized power, could not play a global leadership role. Only as part of Europe—and in partnership with Germany—could it compete with the American superpower whose hegemony it resents. Consequently, French foreign policy is based both on a special Franco-German relationship and on a related "wager" on Europe, which it hopes will emerge as a global power in the long term. But it has been a wager on a certain kind of Europe, largely intergovernmental, which would not wrest too much power from the French nation-state. What makes this wager plausible, however, is the new strategic environment of the post–Cold War era, in which "for the first time in its history, France no longer faces a direct military threat near its frontiers."[1]

France has struggled to be taken seriously as a great power in the postwar era. Since 1958 there has been a resurgence, within limits, of French influence in the world. The causes for France's relative success include a broad consensus of the political elite on foreign policy and defense, a belief in the primacy of foreign policy, political institutions that enable France to effectively leverage its resources and national will for foreign policy purposes, a willingness and capacity to use military force, a relatively robust economic and social base, a long tradition of effective diplomacy, and the remarkable role of Charles de Gaulle.

France was the most powerful state on the European continent from the days of Louis XIV until the fall of Napoleon. It continued to see itself—and was perceived by others—as the greatest continental state until the humiliation of the Franco-Prussian War of 1870. In that war, Napoleon III's misfortune was facing an adversary with none of his shortcomings, a realist who understood power politics and who pursued his policies with cold rationality: Otto von Bismarck, chancellor of Prussia. Bismarck realized that for Prussia to unify Germany, he would have to defeat France, whose interests were threatened by the emergence of a powerful, united Germany. Ultimately, the German Reich was born of French defeat; it was proclaimed at Versailles, and included the French provinces of Alsace and Lorraine. A zero-sum game relationship was established between France and Germany. At the time, most European leaders did not grasp the dangers presented to European peace by these developments. They were only too glad to get rid of a troublesome French bully, and Bismarck made clear that Germany was a satisfied power. From 1870 to World War II, a period known as the Third Republic, France was a weak great power. Characterized by political instability, the period saw frequent changes in government but no civil wars and no insurrections. In the 1880s, leaders used education to create a sense of republican national identity, and they protected all major economic interests including the agrarian, commercial, and industrial sectors. The price of social peace, however, was a less-than-dynamic economy. Still, the Third Republic practiced foreign policy with far greater skill than had Napoleon III, and its army was far stronger than it had been decades earlier. The Republic also entered into a program of colonial expansion, in part as a means of propping up its self-image and creating the illusion of one hundred million Frenchmen. In World War I, unlike 1870, the French army held. France was on the abyss, but its enemies fell first. But after World War I, an increasingly divided France was faced with an insoluble German problem and the Republic began to unravel.

The Battle of France in 1940 killed the Third Republic just as the Franco-Prussian War had destroyed the Second Empire. But whereas the provisional government of 1870 had attempted to continue the war, the government of Marshal Philippe Pétain (called the Vichy regime because it was located in the town of Vichy), which had come to power following the military defeat in 1940, wrongly concluded that if France had lost the battle, the Allies had lost the war. The Vichy regime thus summarily abandoned them and sought a space for France in a German-dominated Europe. Some found a "divine surprise" in the opportunity presented to undo a century and a half of republicanism by means of an authoritarian national revolution. Vichy became an instrument of collaboration with Germany, not resistance.[2]

Before 1940 America perceived France as a great power. After the dramatic fall of France, American leaders no longer thought France deserved that status. France's eclipse corresponded with the rise of the United States as a dominant member of the wartime Allies and then as leader of the free world during the Cold War. Indeed, the fall of France was what obliged President Franklin Roosevelt of the United States to make an unprecedented open-ended commitment to the survival of Britain. Had there been no de Gaulle and no one but the Vichy government to speak for France, even with the existence of the resistance movement, postwar France would have had a government imposed by the Allies and would have lost its claim to sit on Allied councils and participate in the occupation of Germany. It would have been relegated to the sidelines of global politics, playing approximately the same minor role as postwar Italy. This did not happen because of the French general Charles de Gaulle.[3] The decisive role de Gaulle played supports theories of leadership in the development of foreign policy (noted in Chapter 1).

De Gaulle established "Free France" (an organization representing French national interests, which eventually claimed the status of a provisional government) during World War II and began a diplomatic campaign to gain legitimacy from Western allies. From the start, de Gaulle was a political general whose main goal was restoring France's status as a great power after the war, and he took on this mission when no major national figure was willing to take command of remaining French forces. De Gaulle was determined to assert France's role as a great power and to gain a place at the table after the war. Faced with bitter American hostility, de Gaulle drew the lesson that U.S. hegemony was a threat to France, and that Britain was part of the Anglo-Saxon team.

In the end Britain and the United States agreed to give France the trappings of great power status in the postwar settlement, including an occupation zone in Germany and permanent membership in the United Nations (UN) Security Council. At home, de Gaulle had hoped to endow a new republic with a strong executive. But his authoritarian style angered the political elite, which maneuvered him out of office and established the Fourth Republic in 1946, with a weak executive strangely reminiscent of the Third.

French Foreign Policy during the Cold War

At first glance the Fourth Republic (1946–1958) seems to be one of the low points in French history. France had not yet recovered from the destruction of World War II. Governed, if one can call it that, by a succession of weak and unstable governments, it was embroiled in two colonial wars, both of which ended in ignominious defeat. The Republic was brought down by the military, like some kind of banana republic. Yet, despite its notorious failures, the Fourth Republic laid the foundations for a modern France.

Profound and positive changes also occurred during the Fourth Republic. The French population began to grow again and the French economy took off, thanks to statesman Jean Monnet's formula for state planning. To be sure, rapid change brought about great social dislocation, and the French population, always ambivalent about authority, did not suffer change gladly. The result was political and social instability, swelling the ranks of protest parties and movements.

By the late 1940s France was faced with the onset of the Cold War and became a charter member of the North Atlantic Treaty Organization (NATO). The outbreak of war in Korea in 1950 convinced the United States of the need to create a robust European conventional force that included German troops (an idea attractive to no one, including many West Germans). Some French leaders, opposed to rearming Germany, suggested the creation of an integrated European army under the aegis of a European Defense Community. For four years the debate raged, but in 1954 the National Assembly rejected the plan. Germany was rearmed under the Western European Union (WEU), and NATO was born. Forty years later, the idea of a European Security and Defense Identity would reemerge, spearheaded by France.[4]

Enlightened statesmanship was bringing the cycle of conflict and war between France and Germany to an end and calling into existence a new Europe. Jean

Monnet proposed a way out of the zero-sum game relationship with Germany, which France had more or less mindlessly pursued after World War II. The Schuman Plan, authored by Monnet and presented by Foreign Minister Robert Schuman, made France and Germany into privileged partners. The European Coal and Steel Community (ECSC), which it created, placed coal and iron of all members under a supranational authority, ensuring equal access. It was situated in Brussels and designed as the nucleus of a potential United States of Europe. By 1957 the ECSC became the Common Market through the Treaty of Rome. France and Germany became the locomotive of Europe.[5]

The Fourth Republic's greatest failures lay in the colonial arena. Humiliated by its defeat in World War II, France still looked upon colonization as a sign of power and prestige but, in its effort to hold onto Indochina and Algeria, weakened both. France failed to reach a possible accord with the insurgent Vietnamese nationalist movement, the Viet Minh, in 1946 and instead faced an impossible war. It took seven years and the defeat at the French stronghold Dien Bien Phu in Vietnam to persuade the French to abandon Indochina (or at least part of it)— a humiliation the army was ill prepared to accept. The army—which in the process thought it had learned the lessons of counter-insurgency and revolutionary warfare—would not be willing to accept failure in the next great conflict, which began in Algeria on November 1, 1954, just after the Indochina War ended.

The Algerian War witnessed French military successes but could not be won politically (Algeria could be secure only through permanent and massive military occupation). Indications that a new French government might be willing to negotiate with the rebelling Algerian nationalists led to a first in French history—a military uprising in May 1958. Unable to suppress it, Fourth Republic leaders were forced to call upon their bogeyman, Charles de Gaulle, to save, not the institutions of the Fourth Republic, but democracy itself. The return of de Gaulle to power resulted in the demise of the Fourth Republic but ended the military insurrection. The Algerian War also led to one of the great fiascoes of the period, the Suez expedition. Convinced that Egypt was providing sanctuary for the Algerian insurgents, the French government joined Britain and Israel in a military invasion of Egypt in 1956 to stop President Gamal Abdel Nasser from nationalizing the Suez Canal. Although the operation was successful on the ground, the United States, which had not been consulted beforehand, and the Soviet Union, which had vested interests in the region, both opposed it. The result was highly significant. Britain never again embarked on a major foreign policy action without American clearance, whereas France looked for ways to regain its independence. It was understood that the price of independence was a nuclear capability; thus the Fourth Republic began its development.

In 1958 de Gaulle launched a new effort to reassert France's rank as a great power. De Gaulle and his supporters believed that this could be facilitated by domestic political reforms. They would create stable political institutions with increased power for the executive (so that national power could be leveraged in the pursuit of foreign policy), resolve the colonial dilemma (especially the urgent problem of Algeria), restore the military as a stable tool of the state, and create a nuclear capacity that would give France the standing to speak as a major power. Like other leaders before him, de Gaulle embarked on a reform of the state in order to create the conditions for France's exercise of a global role.

De Gaulle's first task was to quickly construct new political institutions that would constitute a synthesis between a strong executive and a parliamentary system. This new system of governance became known as the Fifth Republic. Second, de Gaulle had to deal with the continuing Algerian crisis, which had brought him to power but could easily bring him down (along with the framework of republican legality). De Gaulle ultimately opted for a negotiated settlement for Algerian independence while trying to avoid a successful military coup. He did so, surviving several uprisings and assassination attempts. Naturally, when the Algerian crisis was over, a priority was purging the army and creating an instrument that would be completely apolitical and compliant. De Gaulle gave other colonies independence, but close ties between France and these now independent states—especially their governing elites—were maintained. France's continued role in much of Africa gave credence to claims of being a global power.

De Gaulle's ultimate purpose was to restore France's role as a power of the highest rank.[6] For him, the nation-state was the basic unit of international politics, a viewpoint that was both descriptive and normative. He believed it was unnatural for countries to suppress national interest in the name of Cold War ideology. Although recognizing the necessity of Atlantic cooperation—especially at times of genuine military tension—he anticipated (and worked to create) the breakdown of both Eastern and Western blocs, a return to "normal" international conditions in which nations recovered their independence. Certainly, there was ample evidence of centrifugal forces at work in the Eastern bloc, above all the Sino-Soviet split. De Gaulle not only attempted to play on these tensions, but he also sought to increase tensions within the West.

Even if the bipolar political world turned into a multinational world, how would France retrieve its appropriate place? There was a basic ambiguity in de Gaulle's policies. Was the goal one of national grandeur or was it necessary for France to operate within a genuinely multilateral European framework? Manifestations of de Gaulle's international activism included a drive for French prestige; an active presence in international organizations, like the UN Security Council, of which France was a permanent member; special relations with French Africa and francophone nations in general; a "Russian policy" attempting to be a privileged interlocutor with the Soviet Union (or USSR); early recognition of the People's Republic of China; an "Arab policy" aimed at increasing the French role in the Middle East (even at the price of bad relations with Israel); opposition to the U.S. role in Vietnam; and a general support for Third World ambitions. Nuclear weapons were a *sine qua non* for being considered a major player.

The key to de Gaulle's ambitions remained Europe, and in particular, Germany. He sought to cement close relations with Germany both for their own sake and in order to create a Franco-German relationship that could constitute the core of Western Europe. By leveraging Germany, France could become the leader of Europe, thereby changing the balance of forces within the Atlantic community. De Gaulle developed a personal relationship with the German chancellor Konrad Adenauer (1949–1963), who strongly believed in the need to tie Germany firmly to France and Western Europe and who was both dependent on the United States for security and somewhat doubtful about the U.S. commitment. Germans were relieved that de Gaulle was not out to dismantle the Common Market, which he had opposed before but accepted when he returned to power for the sake of his policy toward the Federal Republic of Germany and for economic reasons.

Another key concern for de Gaulle and French foreign policy was the creation of an intergovernmental European Community. In this, his views differed from the French federalists (and from many Germans who were strongly federalist). De Gaulle opposed the extension of federalist principles but was Europeanist in wanting greater independence from the United States and a distinctive European role in foreign policy development. Wary that Britain would undermine the Common Market and that it might complicate the Franco-German relationship, de Gaulle vetoed Britain's application for membership in 1963. In the process, he offended many Europeans, including the Germans. De Gaulle pushed for close bilateral ties with Germany, which were embodied in the Franco-German Friendship Treaty of 1963, generally known as the Elysée Treaty. Among other things, it provides for periodic meetings of French and German leaders, including summits at the highest level, but his efforts to force Bonn to give its relationship with France priority over its relationship with Washington failed. De Gaulle further damaged relations with Germany and the other Common Market partners when he created a crisis by blocking majority voting in the Common Market (1965–1966) and vetoed Britain's second application for Common Market membership in 1967.

At the same time, de Gaulle was challenging the status quo in NATO. Convinced that NATO was being run by the Americans and British, de Gaulle wanted France to be an equal partner in its leadership. The United States was not prepared to accept de Gaulle's demands. Ultimately, de Gaulle decided to pull French forces out of the integrated military command and evict NATO from its headquarters in Fontainebleau in 1967. These actions severely damaged U.S.-French relations and were seen as a blow to common Western interests.

By the late 1960s de Gaulle had lost much of his support inside of France for his foreign policy agenda. Many opposition politicians criticized the general's positions on NATO, his opposition to European federalism, and his preoccupation with prestige that included the development of a French nuclear force. De Gaulle's actions and rhetoric reached a level of stridency that seemed counterproductive to French national interest—notably his strong anti-Israel line and his support for Quebec's independence from Canada. Continued veto of British membership in the Common Market and mediocre relations with Germany left France isolated and de Gaulle's policies at a dead end. The 1968 Soviet invasion of Czechoslovakia demonstrated that the disintegration of the blocs on which de Gaulle counted was not on the agenda for the foreseeable future. At home, the enormous growth and modernization of the French economy were profoundly dislocating. This was true not only for workers and the lower middle class but for students as well. Widespread student discontent ignited the vast social explosion of May 1968, which called into question de Gaulle's legitimacy. This forced de Gaulle to seek to renew his mandate in April 1969 with a referendum calling for the abolition of the Senate and greater administrative decentralization. When it was rejected, he left office and abandoned public life. Ultimately, a domestic crisis reinforced by a deteriorating international situation caused the collapse of de Gaulle's presidency.

Although there was basic continuity in the rhetoric and style of French policy from 1969 to 1981, this period was also one of transition. French leaders slowly came to realize that France alone as a middle-sized power was not in the same league as the two superpowers and that only through European integration could France effectively play a global role. Yet that implied relinquishing more power to the European Community, even if only by intergovernmental means. It also required restoring the primacy of the Franco-German relationship as the locomotive of Europe but on the basis of equality between the two countries.

The Franco-German relationship continued to be rough during the presidency of de Gaulle's successor, Georges Pompidou (1969–1974). Germany had once again become the economic and monetary powerhouse of Europe. Then, in late 1969, Germany also became a central foreign policy player under a new Social-Democratic leadership with its *Ostpolitik* (Eastern policy). As Bonn pursued a new relationship with Eastern Europe and the United States explored détente with the Soviet Union, France's role was less important. De Gaulle had hoped to broker the kind of negotiations taken up and pursued by the United States and Germany for reasons of their own. They needed no broker. France's role was quite marginal in the broad Ostpolitik and détente negotiations, and at the same time the French began to fear "condominium," that the two superpowers would try to run the world together. In this context, Pompidou decided to hedge his bets and allowed the United Kingdom to join the Common Market. Later, the French president Valéry Giscard d'Estaing (1974–1981) and the German chancellor Helmut Schmidt (1974–1982) restored the Franco-German partnership and relaunched European integration (including creation of the European Monetary System and direct election of the European parliament). Bilateral relations between France and Germany became characterized by what Dominique Moisi called "the balance of the bomb and the mark."[7] But the late 1970s also marked the end of a great period of economic prosperity and growth in Europe. In 1982 the Schmidt government fell and in the French presidential elections of 1981 the Socialist François Mitterrand defeated Giscard.

Mitterrand was elected president on a domestic agenda to restore prosperity, solve the problem of unemployment, and change the very essence of French life through socialist reforms. In these efforts he failed. Yet France changed in unexpected ways. Not only was doctrinaire socialism (but not the Socialist Party) discredited during this period, but communism was marginalized and much conservative thinking abandoned. By the end of Mitterrand's first term, a consensus of the political class emerged not only on foreign policy and defense but also on European policy and economics. This made the pursuit of foreign policy much easier. The only worm in the fruit was the emergence of the racist, xenophobic Front National as the major protest party in France.

During his two terms in office, Mitterrand dealt with two very different sets of problems. The first term took place during the Cold War. Mitterrand had to respond to what he perceived to be greater truculence on the part of the Soviets and a serious effort to undermine Western cohesion. Mitterrand was particularly concerned about any signs of neutralism in Germany. What looks today like the last gasp of a dying Soviet empire looked quite different in 1981, and the end of the USSR appeared far from inevitable.

French relations with Germany became especially close, as did the personal relations of Mitterrand and the German chancellor Helmut Kohl. The failure of Mitterrand's socialist project was perhaps not the cause of his rapprochement with Bonn and his growing commitment to Europe, but it was at least the catalyst. The legacy of Mitterrand's presidency is certainly France's commitment to Europe as the focus of its policy. Security cooperation with Germany was broadened with the belated application of the security provisions of the Elysée Treaty. Mitterrand and Kohl tried to revive the somnolent WEU, the only instrument of European security cooperation. The ambitious Single European Act was enacted to give greater reality to a common market of goods and services, and serious planning was underway to create monetary union.

During his second term, Mitterrand had to assess the implications of a new strategic situation brought about by the end of the Cold War and German unification. By the end of the era of Mikhail Gorbachev in the Soviet Union, there was no Eastern bloc or Soviet Union, but there was a united Germany. A Europe divided along the lines drawn at the Yalta summit in 1945 by British, American, and Soviet leaders—so long decried by de Gaulle and others—was over. But France was not satisfied. The end of the Cold War meant a disturbance in the "balance of the bomb and the mark," and some suggested that France would be the great loser of the Cold War. New kinds of international conflict soon emerged, including the Persian Gulf War and the conflict in the former Yugoslavia, for which France and Europe were ill prepared. And the end of the bipolar world did not produce a multipolar world but the apparent dominance of a U.S. superpower. The new international situation raised profound questions about European foreign policy and security. Mitterrand had begun the process of bringing France into the post–Cold War era, but cautiously.

External Factors

As the narrative of the history of French foreign policy clearly shows, the nature of the international system has been extremely important for the conduct of French foreign policy. Indeed, since the seventeenth century, France has been struggling to cope with the changes in the continental and global balances of power, as well as with changes inside the French polity that have contributed to the demise of its once-held great power status. Only the military defeat of the Franco-Prussian War, relative economic decline, demographic stagnation, and political instability served to end its regional primacy. Ultimately, the two world wars, combined with new rivals for global influence, limited French foreign policy in the Cold War era.

With France's loss of primacy, the drive for security shaped postwar French foreign policy. Although developments in the interwar period, the defeat in 1940, and the Vichy regime diminished French influence in the region, de Gaulle and other leaders resolved to reassert their country in postwar regional arrangements. Securing an occupation zone in Germany and a role in Allied councils was the first step in the drive to renewed primacy. France also gained momentum in its drive to regional security through European integration. French foreign policy toward Germany changed from balancing German power to embracing it, or harnessing it, in the Common Market. With changes in the international system due to the rise of the United States, cooperation with Germany and the European Community became the way France could balance against this new power in the Cold War era.

Given this historical narrative, one could argue that realism best explains French foreign policy decisions directed toward enhancing security (and maintaining primacy). After serving as tutor to Europe and the world through imperial drives, France learned some difficult lessons about *realpolitik* from three major wars with Germany in the nineteenth and twentieth centuries. French leaders like Charles de Gaulle clearly interpreted the lessons of the past as imperatives for French activism during the Cold War. Fifth Republic France, with strong centralized authority in the executive, was testament to the power of security in shaping state behavior. Over domestic opposition, de Gaulle ushered in a period of neocolonial interventionism and, of course, the development of a French nuclear deterrent.

But a closer look at French foreign policy suggests the limits of realism for interpretation of state behavior. Although French foreign policy was certainly constrained by the international system, in some ways it defied it. French leaders never accepted their new postwar status but, rather, continued to pursue great power policies long after it was clear that France's power had waned. In the bipolar world of the Cold War, they did not play the "good ally" to the United States; their foreign policy appeared less constrained by their dependence on the Western alliance than were the foreign policies of Great Britain and Germany, for example. France's desire to create an independent Europe through the Common

Market, its decision to pull out of the NATO command structure, its active involvement in international organizations, its overtures to the Soviet Union, and its continued involvement in Africa are all examples of its attempts to remain autonomous and a great power *despite* the international structure. Once again, this defiance of the international system during the Cold War can be traced largely to the leadership of de Gaulle and the domestic structures he created in the Fifth Republic.

European economic integration suggests a liberal challenge to the assumptions of realism. Short of regional primacy, France sought economic and political control of a new European entity. The new European Community would be intergovernmental in structure, allowing continued influence for the French government. Furthermore, this new integrated economic unit would have a Franco-German engine.

Taken together, these patterns in French foreign policy suggest major questions about the utility of classical realism for interpretation of state behavior. Both the defiance of international structure and economic interdependence in Europe highlight linkages between external and internal factors. In the post–Cold War era, profound questions have been raised about European security that once again push theoretical boundaries, including: Would the United States remain committed to Europe? If not, what would keep Germany from re-nationalizing its defense? One answer to these uncertainties was the drive to foster greater Franco-German security cooperation and to develop a European Security and Defense Identity (ESDI). This represented a response to both a fear and a wish: the need to prepare for a regrettable situation in which the United States returned to isolationism and the realization of France's ambition—realistic or not—to fashion Europe as a superpower, as a France writ large, for the twenty-first century.

Vast areas of what was once French foreign policy are now European issues. In part due to French efforts, many foreign policy and security issues are matters for European cooperation. A common European policy for security and defense is now being formed. Although much cooperation in foreign policy areas is intergovernmental, it nonetheless changes the nature of foreign policy making. The French state is also losing power to the regions, not only to regions within France but to regions that cut across several nations. French regional and local governments cooperate routinely with German, Italian, and Spanish regional authorities. In short, as a unified Europe increasingly becomes a reality, the nature of foreign policy making in any nation will change in ways that cannot yet be imagined.

Internal Factors

For those familiar with the making of United States foreign policy, the way in which French foreign policy is made must come as something of a shock. In the United States the foreign policy process involves struggles for influence within the executive branch and between the executive and Congress as well as the active involvement of civil society and special interest groups, including powerful business interests, nongovernmental organizations (NGOs), public interest groups, and foreign government lobbies. As noted in Chapter 1, pluralist models of foreign policy making allow ethnic groups, like the Irish, Greeks, Jews, and Armenians, to weigh in as well. There are profound ideological differences within and between the major political parties in the United States, and the media can also have a decisive influence on public perceptions.

In France, the situation is different. Foreign policy making is the preserve of the foreign minister, the president, and the prime minister and their staffs. Centralized authority in the making of French foreign policy is the result of a long history of a strong, unitary state and a weak civil society in which the influence of regional or local governments, or secondary associations between the state and the individual, has been discouraged. The state has traditionally defended the interests of society as it felt appropriate rather than being pressured by organized groups to act in their favor. There is a consensus on foreign policy and defense within the political class, and even cohabitation does not disrupt it. The political class is pretty homogeneous; most high officials and ministers are graduates of the same schools. The French National Assembly (parliament) is far weaker than most European counterparts and has little say in foreign policy. The Senate has even less. There are no hyphenated Frenchmen and no ethnic lobby groups. The military's views on political questions are not solicited, and the private sector still looks to the state for guidance as well.

Since 1962 the French president has been chosen by popular election. Under normal conditions, when supported by a parliamentary majority, he is all-powerful. Invariably, under these conditions presidents have maintained control over the broad lines of foreign policy and defense. Things are very different under "cohabitation," a situation in which the presidential majority and parliamentary majority (and therefore cabinet) are not the same. Cohabitation did not occur until 1986, but it has become common since then. Under cohabitation, the president loses control over domestic policy and is forced to share his authority in foreign affairs and defense with the cabinet.

French presidents are motivated by a wide range of considerations, ranging from realistic to idealistic. During the Cold War, de Gaulle, Pompidou, Giscard d'Estaing, and Mitterrand played important roles in guiding the country through difficult international waters. De Gaulle's challenge to Vichy France began even before World War II, when he alone understood that war of the future would be a war of mobility and had campaigned against the military strategy of the top brass. He had appealed over their heads to the politicians, but the political system was in such shambles that it could not respond. Of course, de Gaulle was contending against the immense prestige of generals who had won the Great War and the wonderful hope they offered of winning the next with a defensive posture and thus without loss of blood on the same scale. From this experience he would draw conclusions about the inability of a system based on parties to defend national interest. De Gaulle established Free France during World War II, and when no major national figure was willing to take command, granted himself the role of trustee for French national interest. His establishment of the Fifth Republic cemented the power of the president to rebuild French security and influence in the world.

In the 1970s Giscard d'Estaing developed a strong working relationship with the German chancellor Schmidt, ushering in a period of unprecedented cooperation. Franco-German initiatives, including the European Monetary System, would establish the institutional roots of the modern European Union (EU). Later, Mitterrand presided over France during a tumultuous period of world politics. In his first term, he benefited from the development of political consensus not only on foreign policy and defense but also on European policy and economics. This made the pursuit of foreign policy much easier, even during cohabitation. But Mitterrand, who had seemed such a master of strategy and tactics in his first term, hesitated and faltered in his second. His initial response to German unification was hardly enthusiastic, and this was duly noted by the Germans. Yet he soon returned to an updated version of the Schuman Plan of anchoring Germany, this time a larger and more powerful Germany, to Europe through monetary union, greater EU political cooperation, and eventually, the creation of the European Security and Defense Identity. The Maastricht Intergovernmental Conference of the EU set up the timetable and conditions for achieving the European Monetary Union (EMU) but also established difficult standards that had to be achieved and that required reducing budget deficits and government spending. The Maastricht conference also provided that the European Common Foreign and Security Policy (CFSP) "include all questions related to the security of the European Union, including the framing of a common defense policy, which might in time lead to common defense." This provided a constitutional basis for EU involvement in security and defense issues. Yet Mitterrand was reluctant to go along with German suggestions several years later that were intended to move toward a serious deepening of EU institutions by federalist means. He continued to prefer an intergovernmental approach. In addition, Mitterrand would not hurry to incorporate the states of Eastern Europe into the EU.

The traditional approach to French foreign policy development has been evolving with the rise of civil society. Public opinion (not just intellectuals, who historically counted for more in France than in many other countries) and NGOs play a larger role today and, for example, have strongly supported humanitarian interventions, like those in Kosovo in 1999. Many state-owned industries are being privatized, and in an information age, the private sector is growing more independent and assertive. We can assume that in the future foreign policy making in France will involve a larger role of nonstate actors.

The future of the EU is the issue that most profoundly divides the French today. On September 20, 1992, a referendum was held on the adoption of the Maastricht Treaty. It was the first and only time the French public was directly consulted on French policy toward Europe. Mitterrand had expected the referendum to produce a landslide victory for the treaty; instead it just squeaked by. The referendum campaign demonstrated that France was evenly split between a virtual "party of movement," which believed that France's future lay with Europe and that integration would mean a better future, and a virtual "party of order," which feared the consequences of the decline of the all-powerful French state. But these virtual parties did not correspond to any existing parties. With the exception of the Communist Party and Front National, both opposed to European integration, the mainstream parties were divided. But the elite that has governed France since the 1970s has represented the party of movement. That elite, however, must take into account the existence of a large part of the population that fears a united Europe — and now also fears globalization.

Contemporary French Foreign Policy

President Jacques Chirac (1995–present) has shown greater courage and willingness to reformulate French foreign policy than did his predecessor, François Mitterrand. But he has been far less successful in dealing with domestic politics. Chirac was elected by appealing to the "forgotten man" at a time when the French public was concerned about high unemployment and economic and social marginalization. Once elected, however, he seemed to lose sight of this populist orientation. His prime minister, Alain Juppé, was preoccupied with making the economic reforms necessary for France to qualify for EMU, which was made more difficult by the poor economic situation. Juppé showed little tact or empathy in his approach. When Chirac unwisely dissolved the National Assembly in 1997, the result was a victory for the left. France has experienced cohabitation between Chirac and the Socialist prime minister Lionel Jospin, and French foreign policy making has truly been based on a consensus of the left and right. The economic situation has improved since 1997 and with it the mood of the country.

Chirac tried to come to terms with the fact that the post–Cold War situation was really new. For the first time in its history, France no longer faced a direct military threat near its frontiers, but the world was still an unstable place. Chirac recognized that the end of the Cold War and globalization meant it was necessary to reform some of the instruments of French national power. One of the most significant reforms begun under the Chirac presidency was that of the French military. During the Cold War, nuclear deterrence against the Soviet Union was the key role of the armed forces. With the end of the Cold War, this role became less important. France was neither well prepared to fight a conventional war like the Persian Gulf War nor for participating in peacekeeping or peacemaking operations in the Balkans. The priority was now highly mobile conventional forces, equipped with high-tech weapons, modern systems of command and control, and effective lift. An army based largely on conscripts, or draftees, was not suitable for interventions outside of metropolitan France.

Chirac decided to move toward a professional army better equipped for these kinds of missions. The problem, however, was that it was hard to develop a state-of-the-art military dependent on expensive technologies at a time of declining military budgets, which made France's cooperation in a system of European defense all the more important. Chirac also realized the increased role of economics as an instrument of national power in an age of trade and economic competitiveness. Much of his considerable travel and much of the activity of the government was focused on promoting French economic interests abroad. French diplomacy, always an effective instrument of national power, was increasingly focused on European security cooperation and French trade.

Human Rights

Chirac injected a greater emphasis on human rights into French policy. He was the first French president with the courage to accept national responsibility for the Vichy government's collaboration with the enemy during World War II, including its role in developing its own anti-Semitic policy and facilitating the Holocaust. He also was far more willing to act decisively against international human rights abusers. This made him ready to support more energetic action against the Bosnian Serbs in 1995, which helped produce the Dayton Peace Accords, and later to act in concert with NATO against Yugoslavia as a result of the suppression and expulsion of the Albanian population of Kosovo by Serbia's President Slobodan Milosevic. Chirac also took the lead in developing a hard-line EU policy toward Austria when Georg Haider's Freedom Party, with its extremist rhetoric and occasional nostalgia for the Nazi past, entered the government in February 2000.

Human rights as well as a redefinition of French interests also led to a sharp break with France's African policy. In the past, France's role in Africa served the useful purpose of keeping the Soviets out of the region, maintaining France's claim to global leadership, and keeping the region as a preserve for French business (although it was unclear whether the expenses justified the investment). The French kept order, often through military intervention or the threat of it, but did little to encourage respect for law or democracy. Now that there was no Soviet Union, the French role was expensive not only in terms of money but morally: how could intervention to maintain dubious dictators be justified? And although the French fought often imaginary threats of poaching by the Americans and British, their focus on their former colonies cut them out of the more profitable markets of English-speaking Africa. Chirac thus began a policy of nonintervention in francophone Africa and refocused French interests to economic relations with the rest of Africa, especially countries like Nigeria. France was deeply concerned about the civil war that engulfed Algeria during the 1990s, but it was unable to have much effect on the crisis.

The Future of Europe and European Security

At the heart of French foreign policy in the post–Cold War era, the great issues remain: the future of the European Union and of European security, which are inseparable from the future of the Franco-German partnership, and France's relationship with the United States.

Recognizing that NATO was not going to disappear and that trying to create an ESDI outside of NATO posed serious problems for many European allies and antagonized the United States, Chirac undertook the perilous enterprise of rethinking France's relationship to NATO. France returned to several key committees of NATO that it had abandoned under de Gaulle and made it clear that it was willing to consider fully rejoining NATO if the alliance was sufficiently reformed. The reforms envisaged involved a greater European role within the organization and the possibilities of European-led operations under an alternative European command structure using NATO assets when the United States did not want to become involved directly. In this effort, it found support from Britain and Germany and, ultimately, acquiescence from the administration of President Bill Clinton. At that point in the discussion, France posed another condition: European control over one of NATO's southern commands. Unfortunately, subsequent negotiations led to a stalemate. Success would not have ended the debate over ESDI but might have facilitated a compromise between the United States and Europe and would have increased the likelihood that ESDI would be created within NATO and not outside it. For some time, it appeared that the failure to fully reintegrate France into NATO would marginalize France and weaken NATO reform and that the idea of ESDI outside of NATO was dead. Surprisingly enough, closer Anglo-French relations put that issue back on the agenda.

The experience of being together "in the trenches" in Bosnia in the early 1990s without the United States may have been the precipitating factor in Anglo-French rapprochement. The two nations had also worked toward a common nuclear doctrine. Under Prime Minister Tony Blair, Britain began to cooperate closely with France as the one other West European nation serious about projecting power globally. The British—who could not proceed quickly into EMU—also wanted to use the security domain, an area of their strength, as a means of establishing their credentials as good Europeans. The British concluded that Europe needed to have the military capacity to do more for itself and the political and diplomatic willingness to act. The British reversed their policy on the WEU, deciding to support its fusion with the EU in order to increase Europe's capacity to take military action without direct U.S. involvement, if necessary. Although preferring NATO-wide action when possible, it wanted a kind of insurance policy against what happened in Bosnia in 1991–1993. Because Britain had doubts about American dependability and fears about American unilateralism, it decided to hedge its bets. Blair thus revived what seemed to be a doomed French effort to create ESDI outside of NATO. The French saw this as a step toward greater European autonomy. The new Franco-British partnership was also based on the recognition that Germany was not likely to take the lead in creating a more robust European security system.

Franco-German Relations

It is difficult to predict the future of Franco-German relations at this point. Critics charged that Chirac was less pro-European than Mitterrand, that Chancellor Gerhard Schröder was less pro-European than Kohl, and that bilateral relations had deteriorated in the 1990s. Certainly relations were far from the ideal, but the relationship has rarely ever been ideal. The key to Franco-German relations is not that the two nations agree on everything, but that they seek compromises that can become the basis of a European consensus. Without Franco-German cooperation, Europe cannot find agreement, and there is still no alternative to the two countries' central role. Although Britain has become more involved in security issues within the European context, its relationship to the Continent is still ambiguous; its membership in EMU is far from certain.

There is certainly a difference between the French and German visions of the EU's future. In his speech of May 12, 2000, at Humboldt University in Berlin, the German foreign minister Joschka Fischer outlined a three-stage process of moving toward greater EU federalism. The first stage of a German proposal—reinforced cooperation—corresponded exactly with one of France's goals for the EU's intergovernmental conference (IGC) in Nice. Fischer recognized the permanent role of the nation-state within Europe and the need to clearly define the relationship of the nation-state to EU institutions by means of a constitutional compact. Proposals from the German government also allowed a significant role for national parliaments on the European level by creating a second chamber of the European parliament composed of their representatives. Soon Chancellor Schröder too became committed to European federalism. Chirac's response, in a speech to the German parliament on June 27, 2000, seemed to demonstrate willingness to reflect on long-term issues, such as a constitution for Europe, after the IGC. But Chirac and the French still bridle at federalism. The failure of France and Germany to agree to a common program of institutional reform for the EU—and France's inability to act as an honest broker during its six-month EU presidency before the Nice summit in December 2000—led to an unsuccessful EU summit conference and the recognition that the Franco-German relationship needed to be repaired.

Conclusion: Does France Still Count?

France continues to play a role in the world disproportionate to its size. The extent to which French foreign policy is capable of affecting debate (and disturbing policy makers) in Washington is testimony to the persistence of a French role. Will France continue to count in international councils? Part of the answer surely depends on the future of France's instruments of national power.

Will the French economy cope with globalization and remain a strong second to Germany? That it does so is crucial for several reasons. France needs a strong economic base to maintain social peace, to be able to project power, and to remain in the same league as Germany, lest the "balance of the bomb and the mark" become too distorted in Germany's favor. The current French government of Prime Minister Lionel Jospin has done a good job of trying to find a middle path on globalization. It has worked in favor of modernization and flexibility in the French economy while demanding international controls over a global free market. The Maastricht referendum demonstrated that France is evenly divided between those who see opportunity in a more united Europe and a global economy and those who imagine a threat. No French politician can fail to take that into account, but France is not unique in Europe in this respect.

Will France remain politically stable? Part of the answer to this question depends on the state of the economy. Because of France's long history of political instability, the most recent striking example of which is the near revolution of May 1968, few politicians will take for granted the political stability of the Fifth Republic and deal with social protest in a confrontational manner. The Jospin government, unlike its predecessor, has been able to maintain public confidence while pursuing a policy of gradual reform.

The most serious threat to political stability in France today is the collapse of the democratic right. Since the early 1980s a growing party of the extreme right, the Front National, has been attacking the democratic right with a program that is racist, xenophobic, and fascistic. By the late 1990s the Front National was regularly earning more than 15 percent of the vote in all elections, and unlike previous parties of the extreme right, had built up powerful local organizations as well. The national leadership of mainstream party organizations pursued a policy of zero tolerance toward the Front National, refusing any deals on the local level. In the parliamentary elections of 1997, the result was a Socialist Party victory. This defeat precipitated divisions on the democratic right, deepened by the willingness of some politicians to make a deal with the Front National in the 1998 cantonal and regional elections, leading to splits in both major party organizations. Even though the Front National Party has split as a result of conflicts between its two leaders, Jean-Marie Le Pen and Bruno Mégret, it has left the French right in shambles. The collapse of the democratic right will doubtless have long-term consequences on French political stability. It will also have an impact on the consensus of the political class. Leaders of mainstream parties have generally leaned far more toward a united Europe than their constituents. But will this be possible with a fragmented right? The foreign policy and defense consensus of the political class has been a major factor in France's ability to maximize its influence. Any change in this situation would certainly be harmful.

At the core of contemporary French policy is the steadfast determination to strive for a multipolar world in which a French-led Europe will assert itself as a major power and in which American hegemony will be brought to a close. To what end has never been clear. One can only assume that this is seen as an end in itself. The centerpiece of French policy thus is European security.

There are two plausible ways of looking at European security in the twenty-first century. The first is an "Atlanticist" thesis, strongly defended by the United States and historically by Great Britain as well. It represents a continuation of the Cold War leadership role of the United States into the post–Cold War epoch, with minimal modification. The world is still an unstable place and there is still value in the old NATO adage of "keeping the Americans in, the Germans down, and the Russians out." This thesis serves the American interest of remaining a European power and maintaining American leadership. It provides some degree of burden sharing, cooperation, and division of labor with Europe. NATO, appropriately enlarged, remains the basic instrument of security, collective defense, and common action, with an increasing emphasis on peacekeeping activities out-of-area. It presupposes that, within the NATO context, nations operate as individual entities, that there is no European bloc or caucus that comes to NATO councils with a decision already made; in short, a NATO of nations, rather than a NATO of two blocs or pillars.

France carries a disproportionate weight in European politics today because it acts as the defender of the antithesis (the idea that Europe has its own specific interests that are different and sometimes opposed to those of the United States). Europe must be Europe, and French leaders believe that this position is plausible for many reasons. First, with the Cold War over and the Soviet Union gone, Europe faces no great external security threat that should be beyond its means to cope with. Second, it seems bizarre that a continent that once dominated the world, whose major nations were all great powers, should be unable to exercise a powerful security influence in the world. Third, Europe has moved far toward integration in the last half-century. The European economies are increasingly unified, a common currency and a central bank exist, something the United States achieved only in 1912. However cumbersome, the embryo of European government exists. An effective common foreign policy and security and defense framework is a logical step. Fourth, Europe's security dependence on the United States not only weakens its freedom of action but reduces its bargaining position in other aspects of the relationship. Europeans are becoming more resentful at what they perceive as American tendencies toward hegemony and unilateralism.

European ambivalence has characterized the debate on European security since the end of the Cold War. There is an undeniable logic to both the American and French positions. Few countries wish to choose or to be pressured to choose. Nonetheless, the grounds of the debate have evolved in the direction of the French position. First of all, the Maastricht Treaty gave Europe the legal basis for developing a common security and defense policy. Increased forms of European military cooperation emerged, like the Eurocorps, composed primarily of French and German units, but also including Belgium, Italy, and Spain. A consensus developed that Europe should have the right and ability to take part in operations like peacekeeping on its own. From this developed the idea that, if the occasion arises in which Europe wishes to act but the United States does not, Europe should be able to use NATO assets and operate with a purely European chain of command.

The Kosovo war experience raises the question of how much the United States and Europe can count on each other. Europeans cannot fail to be struck by the way in which the U.S. grand strategy was driven by concern for force protection. The United States publicly and preemptively foreclosed strategic options, like use of ground forces, because of fears about the impact of casualties on public opinion and Congress, even though this attitude could only encourage Milosevic. Concern about American dependability necessarily increases the desire for ESDI. The United States too can ask the question of how much it can depend on Europe. After all, this was a conflict in Europe, so it would not have been strange if the Europeans had taken primary responsibility. But without the United States, could Europe have found sufficient political will and military clout to wage a war in Kosovo?

France's attempt to make Europe into a great power in a multipolar world raises several grave problems. First, there can be no solution to the quandary of U.S.-European security relations without a breakthrough in U.S.-French dialogue, yet nothing in the past indicates that such a breakthrough is probable. Thus, the future is likely to be similar to the past: conflict over doctrine, cooperation on concrete issues. Within that atmosphere, European capacity will grow slowly at best, but the future of ESDI will continue to be poisoned by the sempiternal, tortuous, and bootless debate between the United States and France. For its part, France should realize that, without a more constructive Franco-American security dialogue, France's EU partners can only go so far in seeing merit in French arguments.

Second, if the world really becomes more multipolar, as France seems to desire, it will mean more than just the emergence of an independent Europe as a major player. Other powers will also emerge. The question is whether these new powers will be benign. France should beware of getting what it wants. Balance of power politics was not always good for France. A multipolar world including potentially threatening and unsatisfied powers might once again make Europe dependent on the United States for security, but it is not a foregone conclusion that the United States would assume that role under different conditions. France and Europe might look back with longing on the mild Pax Americana (a beneficent period of American world dominance).

Third, a Europe that really moved toward becoming a United States of Europe with a federal government in charge of foreign policy, security, and defense should have the means to play the role of global superpower, maintaining a robust defense and military capacity. But here it is essential to point out that French plans for European cooperation presuppose a certain idea of Europe that is largely intergovernmental, not supranational. Today's EU structures generally reflect France's historic preferences. They give France as nation-state a fair amount of leverage in Brussels, the seat of the EU, and minimize loss of national sovereignty. But attempting to navigate between the ancient Gaullist concepts of retaining a maximum of national sovereignty while creating a Europe capable of countering U.S. hegemony has produced a French policy too clever by half—and a feckless Europe with too many telephone numbers.[8] If France is really interested in making Europe into an international actor, it will have to accept a United States of Europe, which will mean the end of France as a nation-state. There is no indication that this is what France really wants. France is still fundamentally ambivalent about a united Europe, but an ambivalent France will never create a united and powerful Europe. And it is by no means certain that even if France were fully committed to a federal Europe that the new Germany would go along with France and the rest of the EU would follow.

France is thus embarked on a course fraught with peril.

Suggestions for Further Reading

The Cambridge History of Modern France. New York: Cambridge University Press, 1983–2000.
Friend, Julius W. *The Long Presidency.* Boulder: Westview Press, 1998.
De Gaulle, Charles. *The Complete War Memoirs.* New York: Simon and Schuster, 1964.
Hoffman, Stanley, et al. *In Search of France.* Cambridge: Harvard University Press, 1963.
Kramer, Steven Philip. *Does France Still Count?* Westport, Conn.: Praeger, 1994.
Tiersky, Ronald. *France in the New Europe: Changing yet Steadfast.* Belmont, Calif.: Wadsworth, 1994.
Vedrine, Hubert. *Les Mondes de François Mitterrand.* Paris: Fayard, 1996.

Notes

I would like to thank Julius Friend and Josef Konvitz for reading a first draft of this manuscript, and Anton De Porte for his very detailed comments

1. *Livre Blanc sur la défense 1994* (Paris: Documentation française, 1994), 17.
2. For a classic account of why France fell, see Marc Bloch, *The Strange Defeat* (New York: Norton, 1968). On Vichy, Robert O. Paxton, *Vichy France, Old Guard and New Order, 1940–1944* (New York: Knopf, 1972).
3. On de Gaulle's conflicts with the United States, see Arthur Layton Funk, *Charles de Gaulle, the Crucial Years, 1943–1944* (Norman: University of Oklahoma Press, 1959).
4. Edward Fursdon, *The European Defence Community* (New York: St. Martin's Press, 1978).
5. See Frank Roy Willis, *France, Germany, and the New Europe, 1945–1967* (Stanford: Stanford University Press, 1968).
6. For a brief and astute summary of de Gaulle's policies, see Anton W. DePorte, *Europe between the Superpowers* (New Haven: Yale University Press, 1986).
7. Dominique Moisi, "Die Mark und die Bombe," *Die Zeit,* December 8, 1988, 4.
8. Henry Kissinger, secretary of state under President Richard Nixon, once claimed that Europe was weak because it had too many telephone numbers, that is, it consisted of many independent states.

CHAPTER 4

The Evolution of German Foreign Policy

Jeffrey S. Lantis

Germany, as a large country in the center of Europe with great power status in the nineteenth and early twentieth centuries, has historically played an important role in international relations. After World War II, however, its division into East and West Germany and its dependence on the Western alliance significantly diminished its freedom and status as an actor in world politics. After the end of the Cold War, many expected a reunified, economically powerful Germany to reassert itself on the world stage. This did not happen immediately and this chapter presents some answers to this puzzle. In his discussion of the development of Germany's new role, Jeffrey Lantis stresses the role of a political culture of restraint that developed in postwar Germany, the need to secure consensus among the political actors within Germany, and the nature of the issues facing Germany in the post–Cold War era as factors influencing German post–Cold War foreign policy.

Germany, like Japan (Chapter 7), was a state that depended on the United States for its security during the Cold War and has struggled with its new post–Cold War identity. Germany's involvement in European-based institutions like NATO, however, suggests that it experienced this security dependency differently from Japan. Indeed, Germany's overall orientation toward European affairs can be compared with that of Great Britain (Chapter 2) and France (Chapter 3). Germany's deep entrenchment as a central economic figure in the European Union differs dramatically from the French position, and German commitment to European economic integration contrasts with Britain's tepid approach to monetary union. As are the other democratic states in this book, Germany is an excellent country in which to examine public opinion, the political actors who seek to represent the public, and the effect these actors have on foreign policy. Germany has recently experienced a change of leadership and the effects of the new ruling coalition on contemporary German foreign policy can be compared with the consequences of the new leadership in Great Britain (Chapter 2), Russia (Chapter 5), and Mexico (Chapter 14).

Dramatic changes in world politics have produced a series of new and difficult foreign policy challenges for the Federal Republic of Germany. Unified in 1990, Germany emerged as a sovereign state with a unique opportunity to develop a post–Cold War identity that would guide its behavior into the new millennium. This chapter tells the story of continuity and change in German foreign policy. It examines the history of German foreign relations during the Cold War, the role of external and internal pressures on state behavior, and the evolution of contemporary foreign policy.

World War II ended in Europe in May 1945 with the defeat of Nazi Germany. The victorious Allies — the United States, Great Britain, the Soviet Union, and France — subsequently disarmed the country and divided it into occupation zones for more efficient postwar governance. The four powers also divided and occupied Berlin, the German capital. In 1949 the division of Germany became formalized through the establishment of the Federal Republic of Germany (West Germany) in the former occupation zones controlled by the United States, Great Britain, and France. Bonn, a tranquil university town along the Rhine, was selected as the capital of the new democratic state. The Soviet Union created the German Democratic Republic (East Germany) as a Communist proxy state, and East Berlin became its capital.

Postwar West German foreign policy was a product of the country's circumstances. Germany was divided by the "Iron Curtain" and located on the front lines of the Cold War superpower struggle that would last for forty-five years. At home, the polity was deeply affected by the weight of the past — by the guilt associated with having launched three, aggressive foreign wars, in 1870, 1914, and 1939; by twelve years of National Socialist Party control of the government and its affairs; by the tens of millions of casualties and incredible destruction in World War II; and by genocide in the Holocaust. Accordingly, West Germans adopted a new domestic political culture of restraint that emphasized core values, including democracy, consensus-building, gradualism in the policy process, and pacifism. These ideals became manifest in democratic institutions established in West Germany's Basic Law (or constitution)—including limitations on the development and use of German military force. For example, articles 24 and 87 of the Basic Law implied that Germany could develop an army only for a role in regional, collective security institutions. In such matters, Germany would "consent to such limitations upon its rights of sovereignty as will bring about and secure a peaceful and lasting order in Europe and among the nations of the world."[1]

The development of German foreign policy in response to challenges and opportunities in the past fifty years can best be explored through a series of case examples, informed by major theories of foreign policy analysis. Wolfram Hanrieder was one of the first scholars to explore the impact of external-internal linkages on German foreign policy. Hanrieder argued that analysts must examine the linkages between the "internal predispositions" of the country, including value systems and political culture, and conditions in the external environment in order to reach a comprehensive understanding of foreign policy. He said that foreign policy change ultimately hinges on compatibility, "the degrees of feasibility of various foreign policy goals, given the strictures and opportunities of the international system," and consensus, the amount of domestic political agreement on the ends and means of foreign policies.[2] This chapter juxtaposes changing international conditions, challenges, and opportunities with domestic political conditions and constraints to review the history of German foreign policy. Particular attention is paid to the role of elites, political parties, and the public in defining a postwar German political culture of restraint.

German Foreign Policy during the Cold War

German foreign policy was driven by three maxims in the Cold War: security, restoring German unity, and economic development. These priorities varied in intensity and relative importance over time, but together they shaped foreign relations from 1949 to 1990.

Security

German foreign policy during the Cold War was largely defined by international constraints. For decades, Germans feared that a Soviet-led invasion of Western Europe was imminent. When Konrad Adenauer became the first chancellor of West Germany through democratic elections in 1949, he determined that cooperation through international institutions would be the only way to ensure German security, restore its sovereignty and legitimacy, and achieve major foreign policy objectives in the aftermath of World War II. Adenauer aligned Germany with key Western countries, including the United States, Great Britain, and France, through a foreign policy program he termed *Westpolitik* (Western policy). These ties promoted German security, but they also created a great deal of foreign policy dependency between Germany and key allies like the United States.

In the wake of the Soviet blockade of land access routes to West Berlin (1948–1949), Europe and the United States entered into talks on creating a new Western military alliance. Leaders from Belgium, Canada, Denmark, France, Great Britain, Iceland, Italy, Luxembourg, the Netherlands, Norway, Portugal, and the United States established the North Atlantic Treaty Organization (NATO) in April 1949. In June 1950 the Korean War created new security concerns for Western Europe. Some allies believed that the war in Asia was just a feint by the Communist bloc to draw NATO's attention away from Europe before invading and occupying the region. U.S. leaders initiated a dialogue on whether to allow German rearmament and membership in the NATO alliance, given the urgent need for more troops on the Continent. The French government was opposed to the move, but the tensions of the Cold War only deepened.

Chancellor Adenauer responded positively to the idea of conditional German rearmament and NATO membership as a route toward greater sovereignty and legitimacy. He knew that European governments would demand that Germany renounce any future production of weapons of mass destruction in return for a greater role in regional affairs, and the chancellor made that formal pledge in 1954. But Adenauer faced a difficult domestic political battle for these policies that illustrated the clash between international pressures and the political culture of restraint. Many Germans opposed the idea of rearmament, given the horrors of the recent past. The opposition Social Democratic Party (SPD) led a public campaign against rearming and joining NATO in the early 1950s. Opponents believed that rearmament would be unconstitutional—and would be financially and morally too burdensome for the new Germany. After years of debate, however, Adenauer was able to establish a domestic coalition to allow German participation in militarized, regional collective security arrangements like NATO. Over time, this became an accepted *Verfassungswirklichkeit* (constitutional political reality) that a number of cabinet decisions confirmed during the Cold War.

On May 6, 1955, West Germany joined NATO, and the alliance moved troops into the country for a frontline defense against any Soviet bloc military action. The Federal Republic became the only member of the alliance to have all its 340,000 combat forces assigned to NATO (excluding two territorial divisions designated for protection of the heartland). In exchange, Western allies pledged to come to the aid of Germany in case of an attack, and the United States and Great Britain extended their "nuclear umbrella" to include the protection of German sovereignty. Any invasion of West Germany, they warned, would be met by swift retaliation on the Soviet Union.

West Germany and France also developed a special relationship during the Cold War. With memories of three wars between them in a seventy-year period, Franco-German relations were strained. But both Chancellor Adenauer and the French president Charles de Gaulle took steps toward cooperation in the 1960s. For de Gaulle, developing better relations with Germany would serve as leverage to lessen U.S. and British influence on the Continent (see Chapter 3). For Adenauer, Franco-German cooperation could serve as a bond for promoting German security, economic development, and even unification. In early 1963, leaders of France and Germany signed a treaty of reconciliation, and the two countries began to cooperate on a range of regional issues.

Germany's commitment to the conventional forces component of the NATO alliance remained relatively stable over time, but the question of nuclear weapons created a great deal of controversy for the government. In many ways, the question presented deep contradictions between Germany's commitment to foreign policy objectives and the domestic political culture of restraint. In the 1950s Chancellor Adenauer had to struggle to secure government support for the deployment of NATO nuclear weapons in West Germany to deter a Soviet-led invasion. In the late 1970s Chancellor Helmut Schmidt fought a bitter domestic political battle over plans by the United States to develop an Enhanced Radiation Weapon (ERW, also known as the "neutron bomb") that NATO sought to deploy in defense of Western Europe. When Schmidt authorized the modernization of intermediate-range nuclear weapons to be deployed in Germany in the early 1980s, the political left had had enough. From 1979 to 1983 Germans took to the streets to fight plans to cooperate with the modernization policy, and Schmidt's governing coalition eventually collapsed. The newly elected conservative chancellor, Helmut Kohl, championed modernization and successfully weathered challenges to the government from the political left to support the NATO alliance. Overall, the deployment of nuclear weapons in Germany during the Cold War clearly pushed the envelope of restraint in the name of multilateralism.

Finally, throughout the Cold War the West German government maintained a policy of noninvolvement in military challenges outside of the NATO area. Leaders accepted a common interpretation that the Basic Law prevented troop deployments elsewhere, and this reflected a political culture that eschewed the idea of a globalized foreign policy construct. The attitude of the West German political culture toward security concerns outside of the NATO area was probably best captured in a survey at the very end of the Cold War. When Germans were asked what country they most preferred to emulate in foreign policy, a majority chose Switzerland, a prosperous country that practiced military neutrality in global affairs.[3]

Reunification

The pursuit of West German security was integrally related to the goal of reunification. Adenauer and the German government refused to recognize the status quo of Germany's division throughout the 1940s and 1950s, and they withheld diplomatic recognition from any states that established formal relations with East Germany. In 1955 Adenauer made his first and only visit to Moscow, where he negotiated the future of Germany with the Soviet premier Nikita Khrushchev. Adenauer sought Soviet approval for a free all-German election as the basis for reunification, but the Soviets insisted that the Federal Republic recognize the legitimacy of East Germany and pledge complete military neutrality in the future. Adenauer refused and returned to Bonn resolved to continue the standoff over German reunification.

Problems in East-West relations in the late 1950s and early 1960s deepened the division of Germany. As tensions mounted between the superpowers, Khrushchev sought to place increasing pressure on West Germany through divided Berlin. Berlin had become a real problem for the Soviet bloc by the early

1960s. Millions of refugees had escaped to the West by crossing over to western occupation zones and never returning. On August 13, 1961, the East German government erected a wall across Berlin to stem the flow of refugees to the West. The Berlin Wall quickly became the most visible symbol of the Cold War division of Europe.

In 1969 a new German chancellor, Willy Brandt, proposed a different strategy to improve relations with East Germany and the Soviet Union. Brandt's *Ostpolitik* (Eastern policy) was significant because it marked a redirection of German foreign policy after twenty years of confrontation with the Soviet Union. In his first government declaration in October 1969, Brandt signaled a readiness to engage Soviet leaders in dialogue on the basis of the territorial status quo. The declaration recognized "two states in Germany." *Ostpolitik* saw almost immediate results. In 1970 Brandt and Soviet premier Leonid Brezhnev signed the Moscow Treaty, which called for the mutual renunciation of the use of force and the recognition of existing borders in Europe. This paved the way for historic openings between East and West Germany and East European neighbors, including Poland. Furthermore, these openings helped to sustain a period of détente between the Soviet Union and United States in the 1970s.

Economic Development

The West German government launched programs for reconstruction and economic development after World War II and received a great deal of assistance from the West. The Marshall Plan, sponsored by the United States, provided billions of dollars and resources for reconstruction to West Germany and other West European countries. At home, the German government, business leaders, labor groups, and the banking sector collaborated to build significant industrial capacity within a decade after the war. Germany's economic recovery in the 1950s was also a function of the newly designed social market economy, a system of regulated capitalism founded upon a broad social welfare network. Together, government and business leaders successfully promoted sound fiscal and monetary policy and held down inflationary pressures.

Germany's recovery was directly related to European regional economic cooperation in the production of raw materials and industrialization. In 1951 the governments of Belgium, France, Germany, Italy, Luxembourg, and the Netherlands created a European Coal and Steel Community (ECSC), and institutional cooperation in key economic sectors became a turning point for Europe. Building on the success of the ECSC, Germany entered into the European Economic Community, or Common Market, in 1957. Belgium, France, Germany, Italy, Luxembourg, and the Netherlands agreed to intensify regional policy coordination with the goal of fostering economic cooperation among member states in progress toward a common market. Brussels was chosen as the headquarters of the new European Community (EC, later known as the European Union), and member states coordinated economic policy in many sectors, including trade, raw materials production, industrial regulation, agriculture, and the environment in the decades that followed. With the support of member states, the EC developed into a standing structure of both consultative bodies and centralized bureaucracies that supported European economic integration.

External Factors

A survey of West German actions in the Cold War demonstrates how both external and internal factors have shaped foreign policy development. First, it is clear that the international and regional circumstances in which the Federal Republic of Germany found itself had a dramatic effect on foreign policy decision making. The old German state had been divided at the end of World War II. Militarily, Germany was an occupied country—a reluctant host to troops from Britain, France, the Soviet Union, and the United States who patrolled specific zones of occupation (witness the example of divided Berlin and "Checkpoint Charlie," a famous transit point between eastern and western zones). West Germany was soon on the front lines of the superpower confrontation. Its eastern border defined the Iron Curtain, and hundreds of thousands of NATO troops were deployed in West Germany in the 1950s to prevent a Soviet invasion of Western Europe. Politically, the Federal Republic was not fully sovereign. It was a "penetrated state," in which policy decisions were greatly affected by its allies. The level of penetration and compromised sovereignty did vary during the Cold War, but one can better understand German foreign policy decisions in this context. Economically, West Germany was also greatly dependent on assistance from its neighbors and friends. The Marshall Plan enabled postwar reconstruction, but it was trade and regional integration that truly fueled the West German economic recovery in the decades that followed.

Consistent with the predictions of realism, West German foreign policy during the Cold War was characterized by a preoccupation with security, reunification, and economic development. Each of these objectives would maximize state security in a competitive environment. Furthermore, realism seems to predict German acquiescence to allied wishes in a number of circumstances. Given its security dependence on the West, German leaders regularly bowed to pressure from NATO allies on controversial issues such as rearmament, support for the forward deployment of NATO troops in Germany, and endorsement of the modernization of nuclear forces for the defense of Western Europe.

A careful examination of the record of West German foreign policy in the Cold War does provide challenges to realism, however. First, the actions of this penetrated state sometimes surprised both its friends and its enemies. West German leaders occasionally practiced diplomacy designed to balance the concerns of East and West rather than simply to oppose the Soviet bloc. This seemed a recognition of the crucial geostrategic role that Germany played at the center of Europe (and a natural extension of the maxim of reunification). Chancellor Willy Brandt's *Ostpolitik* initiatives suggested a willingness on the part of the German government to improve relations with the East. These openings began in a period of deep Cold War hostility and continued to flourish through détente in the 1970s. In the wake of the Soviet invasion of Afghanistan in 1979, Chancellor Helmut Schmidt refused to go along with the Carter administration's embargo on the sale of grain to the Soviet Union and maintained relations with Eastern European countries in spite of superpower tensions in the 1980s.

An analysis of the timing, direction, and scope of West German foreign policy behavior during the Cold War suggests that realism alone is not sufficient to explain key developments. Even this brief survey has shown that the path from recognition of external pressures to the formulation of a foreign policy response was rarely simple, direct, or immediate. Rather, the story of West German foreign policy is better understood as fits and starts of uncertainty and hesitancy in policy development that sometimes stretched over a period of years. This hesitancy can be traced to the German political culture of restraint that was deeply embedded in the public psyche and in political institutions. When Adenauer led the Federal Republic toward rearmament in the 1950s in order to join NATO, the polity was highly resistant to this move and the legitimation process was quite slow. Later, Chancellor Schmidt was asked by NATO allies to support the development of the neutron bomb, but the incredible amount of domestic opposition to this move at the time slowed government responses to alliance pressures. Schmidt subsequently viewed the ERW debacle as the beginning of his own political demise.

Finally, the development of the European Economic Community supports liberal interpretations of state behavior over realism. Adenauer and other leaders of the Federal Republic actively supported the creation of the ECSC and the Common Market in recognition that economic interdependence could fuel greater political cooperation in Europe. Building on Jean Monnet's vision of integration in Europe, West German leaders endorsed federalism—the creation of a United States of Europe—surprisingly soon after World War II. To some extent, it could be argued that Germany found it much easier than other European countries to consider a future of compromised sovereignty for the benefit of all. But it is also important to recognize that German leaders embraced the idea that European integration would become the only way to achieve national and regional objectives. Chancellor Kohl and Foreign Minister Hans-Dietrich Genscher became leading voices for broadening and deepening European integration in the 1980s.

In summary, it is extremely important to recognize the external and internal factors that may shape the development of foreign policy over time. In particular, one sees manifestations of the German political culture of restraint in the diplomatic history noted above, as well as contemporary foreign policy maneuvering. The next section outlines the importance of domestic actors and institutions for foreign policy development.

Internal Factors

According to the Basic Law, West Germany holds periodic elections to a bicameral legislature based on a system of modified proportional representation. The chancellor is the elected head of the major party in government and possesses primary legal authority to determine domestic and foreign policy. The chancellor is responsible for selecting members to serve in the German cabinet, a central forum for the development of domestic and foreign policy. Generally, the distribution of ministry seats in the cabinet reflects powers and interests of the parties in government. Cabinet debates about key issues, based on the principles of "collegiality" and consensus stipulated by the Basic Law, have guaranteed a voice for all ministers in the decision-making process. Furthermore, most German cabinets have adopted a de facto principle of unanimity for major decisions.

As noted in Chapter 1, parliamentary governments often allow an important role for political parties and public opinion in the policy-making process. Since 1949 all West German cabinets have been composed of coalitions of party organizations, including major and junior parties. After every election coalition negotiations have occurred in which major parties consider the appropriate distribution of ministerial seats and general influence in coalition cabinets. These arrangements have allowed even junior parties to play pivotal roles in foreign policy development. For example, from 1974 to 1992, Genscher was both foreign minister and a key leader of the junior coalition partner, the Free Democratic Party. Genscher was able to moderate the policies of the major party in government during his tenure, working with both the Social Democratic Party and the Christian Democratic Union (CDU).

Political party organizations can also play a key role in the foreign policy making process. Before 1933, parties were only marginal actors in German politics, and most party organizations were weak and divided on a number of issues. After World War II the founders of the Federal Republic believed that party organizations could actually help to organize and control the new political life, and they institutionalized party behavior in the Basic Law. Thirty-six political parties competed for representation in the legislature in West Germany's first federal election in 1949. In the 1950s government leaders introduced new electoral laws requiring that parties receive at least 5 percent of the popular vote or three direct constituency seats to be represented in the legislature. German leaders passed a tighter set of federal laws regulating party activity and finances in 1967. These principles established a democratic principle of restraint within and among party organizations.

Three political parties regularly drew support from the electorate during the Cold War, whereas others have gained attention more recently. First, the Christian Democratic Union was a classic *Volkspartei,* or mass party organization, which represented conservative political ideals and eventually drew a great deal of support from both Catholic and Protestant voters in Germany. The CDU was the major party in government under the leadership of Chancellors Konrad Adenauer (1949–1963), Ludwig Erhard (1963–1966), Kurt Kiesinger (1966–1969), and Helmut Kohl (1982–1998). Second, the Social Democratic Party was another *Volkspartei*, which represented liberal social welfare and labor concerns. The SPD became the major party in government in the Federal Republic under the leadership of Chancellors Willy Brandt (1969–1974), Helmut Schmidt (1974–1982), and Gerhard Schröder (1998–present). Third, the Free Democratic Party (FDP, or Liberals) was established in 1948 to represent liberalism and alternative ideals, and the party drew steady support from a relatively narrow constituency of intellectuals and business leaders. Its leaders included two federal presidents and the long-time foreign minister Hans-Dietrich Genscher (1974–1992).

Two other party organizations emerged as political players in the Federal Republic of Germany in the 1980s and 1990s. The Green Party became a player at the federal level in 1980 as both a vehicle for protest against government policies and militarism and an advocacy group for environmental and feminist causes. In 1983 the Greens won 5.6 percent of the popular vote, and outspoken representatives, including Joschka Fischer, took party seats in the parliament and entered the public dialogue. Fischer, who wore sweatpants and tennis shoes to parliamentary debates, quickly gained a national reputation as an outspoken critic of the West German government. After the first unified German election in 1990, the Greens joined forces with another political organization, known as Alliance '90. Finally, the Party of Democratic Socialism (PDS) was established in 1990 as the successor organization to the Socialist Union Party, the communist party of East Germany. The PDS represented a new generation of socialism and emerged as a voice for the disaffected in zones of the former East Germany after unification.

The individual leaders of these parties have been important foreign policy players in their own right. Chancellors Adenauer and Brandt, for example, had very different beliefs about the best policy to follow to achieve reunification. Adenauer considered German commitments to Western allies and multilateral organizations (*Westpolitik*) to be the best direction for restoring his country's legitimacy on the road to reunification. But Brandt believed that a different path was needed for Germany ever to achieve that objective, and he embarked on a series of *Ostpolitik* initiatives to normalize relations with the Soviet bloc. Different leaders' management styles for their governments and party organizations also affected the development of German foreign policy. For example, Helmut Schmidt struggled constantly to build a foreign policy consensus between the left and moderate wings of the Social Democratic Party, and it was the breakdown of this consensus in the debate over modernization of NATO's intermediate-range nuclear forces that led to his political end. The new chancellor, Helmut Kohl, had witnessed Schmidt's demise firsthand, and he was determined to forge political consensus for his policy initiatives at all costs. Even foreign ministers, such as Genscher and Fischer (appointed to this cabinet post in 1998), have been significant leaders in foreign policy debates, and their styles and beliefs have affected

German foreign policy. Genscher's ideas about how Germany should balance itself between the United States and the Soviet Union in the 1980s even earned their own label "Genscherism," and recent developments suggest that Fischer will leave his own distinctive mark on German foreign policy in an era of globalization.

At the federal level, key institutions in the policy process include both houses of parliament, the *Bundestag* and the *Bundesrat*, and the Federal Constitutional Court. Parliamentary debates represent a forum for governance by consensus, and committee deliberations and public debates foster a policy-making process that is decidedly cumbersome and reticent. The Federal Constitutional Court, located in Karlsruhe, represents the highest level of judicial authority in Germany. The Court regularly reviews legal cases related to interpretation of the Basic Law, and it has become an important institution for rulings on the constitutionality of foreign policy initiatives. In the post–Cold War era, the Court played a significant role on the question of military involvement outside the NATO area, as will be discussed later in this chapter.

Finally, public opinion and attitudes influence German foreign policy by setting broad parameters for consideration of policy alternatives (referred to as "core values" in Chapter 1). Public opinion can affect the choices of top decision makers in relation to how foreign policy goals are prioritized, by limiting the range of available instruments of statecraft, and by winning concessions in changing political agendas. In other words, collective attitudes and perceptions of average citizens may shape the elite discourse by ruling certain initiatives "in" or "out" of political bounds. Political culture has consistently bounded German government behavior on issues like support for democracy, humanitarianism, opposing the development of weapons of mass destruction, and maintaining an aversion to the use of military force. These collective belief structures may be characterized as mass political culture, and several contemporary studies have linked political culture directly to continuity and change in German foreign policy.[4]

Contemporary German Foreign Policy

Germany's commitment to its foreign policy objectives paid off in the late 1980s, as Cold War tensions began to fade. In November 1989 the East German communist regime led by Erich Honecker collapsed, and Berliners danced atop the Wall that had become the most hated symbol of the Cold War. German leaders entered into negotiations with other countries on unification almost immediately, including the "Two-plus-Four Conferences" (East and West Germany, plus the four allied occupation powers). Chancellor Helmut Kohl negotiated a final deal with Soviet president Mikhail Gorbachev in August 1990 that paved the way for unification. On October 3, 1990, Germany was unified.

Unity and the end of the Cold War represented a grand strategic opportunity for Germans to reflect on their country's past, present, and future. In reality, Germany had achieved many of the objectives of its Cold War foreign policy programs, and the country was in a position it had never before enjoyed. Neo-realists predicted that given geopolitical changes Germany would soon normal-ize its foreign policy by taking on a more assertive foreign profile focused on strategic interests, backed by the threat of the use of force.[5] They argued that a modern European state like the Federal Republic would pursue a natural path toward military dominance.[6] Kenneth Waltz coyly suggested that "Germany may ultimately find that reunification and the renewed life of a great power are more invigorating than the struggles, complications, and compromises" of European integration.[7] According to Michael Stürmer, developments in Europe after the Cold War placed Germany at the *Bruchzone* (geostrategic crux) of the Continent, with "all the dangers that this situation always entailed, and always will entail."[8] This implied an "obligation to embrace realism, clarity of goals, and predictabil-ity of means."[9]

Political leaders were more cautious in this transition, however, and they assured the world (and their own citizens) that the new Federal Republic of Ger-many would behave much like the old. Foreign Minister Genscher pledged to maintain a commitment to foreign policy traditions and values that had brought the Federal Republic such success in the past. He argued that a "German foreign policy based on responsibility rather than power has remained unaffected by uni-fication. It is only through the continued adherence to these basic principles that a European Germany can secure the kind of influence in the future that it had acquired in the years up to 1989."[10] In 1992 the new foreign minister, Klaus Kinkel, proclaimed:

> Germany owes its unity and present status in the world to the trust we have built up with our consistent policy of conciliation and readiness for compromise. This trust is our greatest asset. We must not carelessly jeop-ardize it by committing ourselves to adventures which could reawaken dangerous misunderstandings among our friends and neighbors. Ger-many's policy will remain consistent and calculable. Our reluctance to use military force has been, and will continue to be, part of this calculability.[11]

Nevertheless, the Federal Republic was no longer the same political entity after the fall of the Berlin Wall, and the world began to undergo incredible polit-ical transformations in the years that followed. Put simply, Germany entered new geopolitical territory with the end of the Cold War. It faced no strategic threats for the first time in its history. Enemies of the past had become collaborators in projects like the promotion of international security and European integration. But new questions emerged all too soon about a proper German identity for the post–Cold War era, about sovereignty in an era of increasing interdependence, and about an emerging sense of German responsibility for the maintenance of international peace and security. Two key themes are examined to illustrate con-tinuity and change in German foreign policy in the post–Cold War era: the use of military force outside the NATO area, and European integration.

The Use of Force: From Kuwait to Kosovo

The Persian Gulf Crisis: Popping the Question. The crisis in the Persian Gulf that began on August 2, 1990, with the Iraqi invasion of Kuwait became the first serious foreign policy challenge for Germany in the post–Cold War era. Even before official unification, the crisis drew leaders into a debate about the country's proper role in the new international order. In August 1990 President George Bush personally requested that Chancellor Helmut Kohl consider the deployment of troops to join Operation Desert Shield—a multinational defense force assembling in the Persian Gulf. U.S. leaders urged Germany to make a significant contribution to the liberation of Kuwait and freedom in the Middle East. Recognizing that coalition operations in the Gulf would be expensive (some estimates at the time topped $100 billion), U.S. diplomats also proposed that countries like Germany, Japan, and Saudi Arabia share the financial burden of coalition operations.

German cabinet ministers agreed that their country had significant interests in the region that were threatened by Iraqi aggression and regional instability, including vital access to oil for Europe. However, they disagreed sharply on the proper response to this aggression, and German foreign policy activism was significantly constrained by serious domestic political disagreements about the crisis. To some extent, this struggle reflected a reckoning by German leaders and average citizens with the domestic political culture of restraint in a changing world.

At issue was the interpretation of Articles 24 and 87 of the Basic Law, limiting German military activity to participation in regional collective security defense. Conservative leaders suggested that they might allow a broader interpretation of the Basic Law for German participation in collective security operations and peacekeeping ("blue helmet") missions sponsored by the United Nations (UN). They could not garner support for this stance from junior party leaders, however, who said they were unwilling to support German military action in the Gulf region based on a strict interpretation of the Basic Law as barring Germany from military involvement outside of the NATO area. The only way to resolve these matters, junior party leaders argued, was for the government to make a change in the Basic Law. Any amendment would require a two-thirds majority in both houses of parliament, the Bundestag and the Bundesrat, but Chancellor Kohl was well aware that opposition leaders of the Social Democratic Party and Green Party would oppose any attempt to change the constitution to allow German troops to participate in combat operations outside the NATO area. Meanwhile, public opinion polls conducted in the fall of 1990 indicated that many Germans maintained a commitment to restraint in foreign policy. Although a majority supported a multilateral effort to evict Iraqi troops from Kuwait, an even stronger percentage opposed direct German participation in the operation.[12]

German leaders agreed to disagree on the use of military force and instead arrived at a workable compromise. They announced that Germany would provide economic assistance to those states most affected by the invasion and logistical and financial support for the military coalition aligned against Iraqi forces—but they would not deploy troops to the region. Germany followed the lead of other EC members in pledging $2 billion in nonmilitary assistance to countries in the Gulf region, including Egypt, Israel, Jordan, Syria, and Turkey. Turkey was granted about $1.2 billion in military assistance, and Israel received more than $500 million. In time, the government committed $11.5 billion to the coalition effort, about one-sixth of the total cost of the war.

The Humanitarian Crisis in Somalia: Defining New Roles. The humanitarian crisis in Somalia represented a different type of foreign policy challenge for Germany in the post–Cold War era. The United Nations Security Council voted in 1992 to create a militarized relief mission (UNOSOM II) to intervene in the civil war in Somalia and secure the delivery of humanitarian aid to those in need. UN officials lobbied Germany and other Western nations to help with relief operations by providing financial contributions and deploying soldiers to Somalia. In January 1993 the UN secretary general, Boutros Boutros-Ghali, visited Bonn and said that the world needed "Germany to be fully responsible and engaged in peacekeeping, peace enforcement, and peacemaking."[13]

In the face of continued violence in Somalia and international pressure on Germany for action, Chancellor Kohl announced that he wanted to deploy a battalion of 1,600 soldiers (mainly engineers, medical personnel, and telecommunications specialists) to Africa to participate in UNOSOM II. This commitment of troops to a peacekeeping mission would be possible if the chancellor could work out an agreement within the governing coalition to deploy the troops legally and under the existing constitution. But at the time it was by no means certain that the chancellor could actually assemble a political consensus to legitimate this action. Kohl's defense minister said at the time that the government should "take speedy, practical steps [because] Somalia cannot wait for the solution of our constitutional problems."[14] Meanwhile, junior party leaders in government demanded that an amendment to the Basic Law be considered as a precondition for German participation in such missions. Once again, the Social Democratic Party and Green Party took a firm public line against German participation in the Somalia mission, but behind closed doors the issue divided the party leadership. Some of the more moderate leaders of the opposition began to suggest that there might be room for compromise with the government on support for peacekeeping missions consistent with the UN charter.

Public attitudes were quite mixed during the debates over the proper course of action on Somalia. In the summer of 1993, for example, a majority of Germans said that they would support the Somalia mission, but an even larger number said that some sort of negotiated settlement between the government and the opposition to amend the Basic Law must occur before participating in UNOSOM II.[15] It is clear that the domestic political culture of restraint still pervaded popular sentiments about Germany's role in the world. Citizens saw a need for humanitarian action, but they resisted international pressure for German involvement in peace-building operations.

The German government responded to the crisis in Somalia and international appeals for support for the humanitarian relief operation at two levels. First, conservative leaders realized that they must appease domestic political opponents of any troop deployment to Somalia by entering into negotiations on amending the Basic Law. Although these talks soon collapsed, the negotiations were symbolic of the willingness of all party leaders to discuss a new constitutional consensus. Second, cabinet leaders moved forward with plans to deploy 1,600 soldiers to Somalia as part of the UNOSOM II relief mission, and the Bundestag authorized the deployment in April 1993. By the summer of 1993, 1,700 German soldiers were committed to the UNOSOM II operation. Troops helped with road and bridge repair projects and the reconstruction of schools, city buildings, and the Belet Uen hospital. The German mission to Somalia ended when the multinational force withdrew from the country in March 1994 in the wake of continued clan violence and attacks on UN peacekeepers. Nevertheless, German leaders had clearly established a new consensus in support of troop deployments for humanitarian operations, and the Somalia mission was considered a success for Germany's new foreign policy architecture in the post–Cold War era.

The German Constitutional Court Ruling of 1994. After years of uncertainty about German foreign policy, the government reached an important milestone in 1994 when the Federal Constitutional Court in Karlsruhe began considering the issue of out-of-area troop deployment. This review was actually prompted by court challenges to past government decisions about the deployment of troops abroad sponsored by the Social Democratic Party and Green Party. Justices would weigh the constitutionality of troop deployments and political requirements for such actions in the future, with the objective of establishing parameters for German foreign policy.

Formal hearings before the court were held in April 1994. Government leaders argued that Article 24 of the Basic Law allowed involvement in a system of mutual collective security (and that no constitutional change would be necessary for future troop deployments in that context). Experts on military affairs testified that the government was well within its rights to deploy troops in carefully controlled circumstances. Meanwhile, Social Democrats and Green Party leaders countered that participation in out-of-area operations was specifically forbidden by the Basic Law and represented a dangerous expansion of German policy.

On July 12, 1994, the Constitutional Court announced its ruling in favor of the government. The judges declared that Article 24 of the Basic Law offered the best guidance on the out-of-area question and that German participation in international military operations outside the territory of NATO would not violate the constitution. They said that the Basic Law provided a constitutional foundation for an assumption of responsibilities that are typically associated with collective security systems. Troops could be deployed in potential combat environments, so long as the government could secure a simple majority of support in the Bundestag for ratification of troop deployment plans. Government leaders interpreted this as the necessary legal authority for such missions that would pave the way for a change in the German political-military culture.

The Kosovo War: Latitude and Limits. Conflicts in the former Yugoslavia presented some of the most serious strategic dilemmas ever faced by leaders of the Federal Republic of Germany. In fact, some high-ranking German officials have contended that the Balkan wars of the 1990s were *the* primary catalyst for German foreign policy restructuring and changing domestic political alignments in the post–Cold War era. Germany's responses to the crisis in Kosovo, in the context of foreign policy compatibility and consensus, demonstrate the extent of this change.

In September 1998 Gerhard Schröder of the Social Democratic Party was elected chancellor in an overwhelming victory over Helmut Kohl. Schröder's new coalition cabinet included prominent SPD leaders from the left and right and members of the Green Party. Joschka Fischer of the Green Party was selected as foreign minister, and Social Democrat Rudolf Scharping became the new defense minister. Both had led their respective parties in the mid-1990s toward the acceptance of a stronger German foreign policy profile. As foreign minister, Fischer made it clear that the new German government would support NATO policy toward the crisis in Kosovo. When pressed on the possibility of war with Serbia over Kosovo in March 1999, Fischer said that Germany and the West had a "responsibility to stop Serbian aggression in Kosovo," and he rationalized the action in response to Serbian president Slobodan Milosevic's "direct attack against the security of Europe."[16]

The Kosovo crisis would be the first major foreign policy test for the new governing coalition. In early 1999 Chancellor Schröder set about building a consensus for German involvement in NATO efforts to stop the Serb crackdown in the province. He argued that the "fundamental values of freedom, democracy, and human rights" had been flouted in Kosovo, and he made it clear that he believed Germany had to respond to this crisis as a key member of the NATO alliance.[17] The chancellor believed that the new SPD-Green coalition had established a consensus for German action to stop ethnic cleansing and genocide in the wake of the war in Bosnia, and they knew that this support might be activated in the face of reports of atrocities from Kosovo. A majority in the Bundestag supported German participation in a NATO air war against Serbia, and top officials believed there to be latent public support for the operation as well. The only vocal opposition to German action came from a leader of the PDS, the far left former communist party, who denounced the government's participation by saying that "after what has happened this century, Germany above all has no right to drop bombs on Belgrade."[18] Cabinet deliberations led to a series of Bundestag resolutions that authorized the use of combat aircraft in NATO operations against Yugoslavia.

On March 24, 1999, German pilots joined with their allies in an opening round of air strikes on Serb targets in Kosovo. As the first offensive military action by German forces since World War II, this was a historic moment. German Tornado jets, their pilots, and ground crews were deployed to air bases in the theater, and they actively engaged in NATO operations throughout the war. At home, most Germans reacted calmly to these operations, and government decisions met surprisingly little opposition. German media experts said at the time that there was a general "kind of public emptiness" on the Kosovo question. Commenting on this silence, one columnist wrote that "the last victim of the fall of the wall was German pacifism."[19]

Unfortunately, NATO miscalculated the resolve of Milosevic and Serb forces in the spring of 1999, and the situation in Kosovo went from bad to worse. Instead of capitulating, Serbian security forces took almost full control of Kosovo on the ground in the opening ten days of the bombing and pushed more than 500,000 Kosovars across the border, creating a massive humanitarian crisis in Albania and Macedonia. Within weeks, 860,000 Kosovars had been expelled from the country and another 600,000 were internally displaced.

In April 1999 many observers of Operation Allied Force around the world began to question whether NATO was actually losing the war. The exploding refugee crisis, the resilience of the Serb military and civilian population under the daily pounding of NATO air strikes, and even mistaken attacks on civilian targets all contributed to the perception that things were going badly for the alliance. NATO leaders began to consider the use of ground troops for an invasion and occupation of Kosovo and Serbia. On the eve of the summit meeting in Washington in honor of NATO's fiftieth anniversary, British leaders began pressing allies to consider sending ground forces into Kosovo if a peace settlement was not achieved.

The question of support for ground troop operations in Kosovo became a highly charged issue in the Federal Republic that threatened to bring down the SPD-Green coalition. Although Chancellor Schröder and Defense Minister Scharping did conduct secret negotiations with their counterparts about changing NATO strategy, they were well aware that German participation in a ground war might be politically impossible. The Kosovo dilemma tested many assumptions that had guided the normalization of German foreign policy for the previous fifty years. German leaders faced an onslaught of concerns that extended from remaining a responsible member of the NATO alliance to German troops fighting a ground war in the Balkans, to standing up against ethnic cleansing, to popular concerns about becoming overrun by refugees from the Balkans (who might, in turn, feed tensions at home and contribute to right-wing extremism). In the Bundestag, conservatives reminded the government that the only mandate given by parliament was to achieve limited strategic objectives and peace for Kosovo—not to wage war in the Balkans.

The Green Party held an emergency conference meeting in early May 1999 to decide on the future of party support for cabinet initiatives on Kosovo. Foreign Minister Fischer approached the conference as a defining moment in the short history of the development of post–Cold War German foreign policy. Delegates to the meeting were presented with two competing resolutions: a left-wing resolution calling for an immediate and unconditional halt to NATO air strikes, and a more moderate statement urging a temporary cease-fire (backed by the party's governing committee). In a now-famous political speech, Fischer condemned the left-wing resolution on the grounds that it would send "the absolutely wrong signal" to Milosevic, and he made a personal appeal to delegates to "help me, to support me; not to cut the ground from under my feet."[20] He forged ahead in his speech in spite of a paint bomb attack that splattered him with red paint and punctured his eardrum and an interruption by an antiwar streaker. After tough negotiations and politicking, the governing committee's resolution won by a solid majority. Fischer had his victory, and the coalition government received a de facto endorsement by the Greens to continue the air war against Serbia. However, the opposition had sent a clear message about the limits of government latitude.

As party leaders wrangled over German involvement in the war in Kosovo, opinion polls charted a precipitous decline in popular support for the war. Once again, contingencies for a more assertive German role in regional security ran up against the limits of the evolving domestic political culture of restraint. In late April 1999 only 41 percent of Germans favored a continuation of the air strikes, whereas 34 percent supported a suspension of the bombing to allow diplomatic negotiations. Eighty percent said that they opposed sending German ground troops to Kosovo. Meanwhile, surveys showed a steady decline of voter support for the SPD-Green coalition as the war dragged on.[21]

Government leaders surveyed the domestic political climate on the question of ground troops and determined by late May that there was little support for intensifying German involvement in the war. They realized that they had taken Germany to the end of their domestic political tether and that continuing the air war and pressing for a diplomatic solution were the only viable paths to achieving NATO goals. Schröder and Fischer recognized that it was quite possible that serious consideration of sending ground troops would topple the coalition government and return their parties to the opposition. At the same time, both leaders were aware of the historical imperative of continued German support for the NATO alliance. They needed to find a diplomatic solution to avoid a catastrophe at home and abroad. One political adviser to the cabinet said at the time that "[b]y German standards, the change of policy has already been extensive and radical. We have come a huge distance in a short time, and managed to bring public opinion along. But for the government, ground troops would be too much at this stage."[22]

Schröder and Fischer decided on a two-pronged strategy to end the Kosovo War. First, Schröder became more vocal about German support for the continuation of the air campaign as the path to achieve NATO objectives—and more critical of a ground troops contingency. Schröder reminded the allies of the historical dilemmas that Germany faced in Kosovo (with persistent memories of Nazi Germany's occupation of the Balkans during World War II). Furthermore, he warned that even their participation in the bombing campaign stretched popular sensitivities. At a NATO summit, Schröder said unequivocally, "I am against any change of NATO strategy."[23] Second, Schröder and Fischer initiated a major diplomatic campaign to bring the Kosovo War to a close. They issued a peace plan of their own, and they began to try to draw Russia in to support the Western position on Kosovo. Bonn soon became the hub for diplomatic negotiations on the Kosovo crisis. In early May Russia joined with Western counterparts to issue the first joint statement on Kosovo. German leaders worked with regional envoys to develop provisions for a final diplomatic settlement, and Milosevic agreed to end the Kosovo War on June 2, 1999.

Germany celebrated the news of victory in the Kosovo War, and government leaders took credit for maintaining the delicate balance of coercive diplomacy to achieve peace. In private they breathed a sigh of relief that they had not been forced to confront much more serious challenges in the Kosovo War. Riding on this wave, the Bundestag approved a rotating deployment of 8,500 soldiers to participate in a peace enforcement operation in Kosovo.

Foreign Economic Policy and European Integration

The development of German foreign economic policy has been inextricably linked to the evolution of Europe from common market to monetary union. By the 1980s West Germany had emerged as the most powerful and influential economy in Europe, with a gross domestic product (GDP) exceeding $1.5 trillion. Germany's exports were the highest of any industrialized country in 1988. Thirty percent of all German GDP was generated through exports, and more than 70 percent of these exports were directed to EU markets. West Germany also became an exporter of capital and the leader in foreign direct investment in Europe. In 1990 German investment in eastern Europe reached unparalleled levels, exceeding $130 billion and accounting for more than 75 percent of total investments in the Czech Republic and Slovakia.[24]

The story of German unification and European integration were interwoven in the late 1980s and early 1990s. One month after the fall of the Berlin Wall, Chancellor Kohl proposed that the European Community support German reunification, but he faced a barrage of questions about Germany's long-term intentions in many policy areas. French president François Mitterrand, who had been supportive of Germany for many years, openly challenged Kohl on future multilateral commitments. After some deliberation, German and French diplomats announced a compromise: the European Community would support reunification in exchange for Kohl's pledge to support a special conference on a plan for European Monetary Union (EMU) to begin in the fall of 1990. In this pledge, the German government made a clear commitment to consider monetary union in the context of European support for reunification.

Negotiations on EMU began in December 1990, and the meetings soon became the central forum for consideration of ideas for intensifying European integration. In fact, negotiators went well beyond the blueprint for EMU and began drafting a comprehensive Treaty on European Union. This treaty would include three "pillars" of provisions for broad and deep integration: European Monetary Union, a Common Foreign and Security Policy (CFSP), and cooperation in Justice and Home Affairs. Plans for European Monetary Union included a three-stage process for cooperation on monetary policy, currency exchange, and the establishment of a European system of central banks. The third and most important stage of EMU would create a common single currency, the Euro. According to the plan, exchange rates among EU member state currencies would be "irrevocably fixed" in January 1999, and all national currencies would be replaced by the Euro in 2002.

European government representatives signed the Treaty on European Union at a special summit in Maastricht, the Netherlands, in December 1991. Helmut Kohl saw his commitment to deepening European integration as an extension of foreign policy multilateralism. He became comfortable with deepening integration as a payoff for German unification, and he believed that it would benefit all of Europe in the future. In an oft-quoted statement, Kohl proclaimed that the treaty signed at Maastricht was "proof that the united Germany assumes its responsibility in a united Europe actively, and remains committed to what we have always said, namely that German unity and European unity are two sides of the same coin."[25] In a speech before the Bundestag just days after the Maastricht summit, Kohl said that the progress toward union was now "irreversible . . . [T]he member states of the European Community are now ready to join together in an arrangement that will have no return."[26]

The chancellor enjoyed strong support for the Maastricht treaty from many of his cabinet ministers. Surveys of elite attitudes at the time found that more than 90 percent of leaders throughout Europe supported deepening economic and political union, but government leaders were rightly concerned that those numbers did not reflect the opinions of some party leaders or the public.

Opposition leaders generally favored the Treaty on European Union, but key sections of the treaty divided the Social Democratic Party along traditional ideological lines. Meanwhile, public attitudes toward German foreign economic policy and the Treaty on European Union were quite mixed in the 1990s. Surveys from the period measured a whole range of opinions from general disinterest to steadfast belief in the value of European integration, to serious concerns about the economic implications of the treaty. A majority of Germans offered their general support for the European Union in surveys in the 1980s and 1990s, but there was a gap between those generally favoring integration and those who actually expected positive benefits for Germany from the process. By 1996 German support for the EC bottomed out—with only 42 percent saying that they perceived real benefits from European integration.[27]

German leaders were nevertheless committed to building a consensus to ratify and implement the Treaty on European Union. Kohl set about the campaign to secure domestic support for ratification of the treaty by attempting to assure skeptics that it was the best possible outcome for Germany. The chancellor emphasized that the common currency plan, potentially the most salient and divisive short-term issue in the Maastricht treaty package, would only be implemented within a bounded realm of political and fiscal requirements. By conducting such a high-profile campaign in favor of ratification, Kohl was sending two messages: that he believed deeply in the treaty and supported its ratification, and that he was willing to stake his political future on the question. In a speech in Frankfurt in the fall of 1992 Kohl said: "The construction of a European house is a vital issue. My political fate is associated with it."[28] This would later prove to be a prophetic statement when the chancellor was held accountable in the 1998 elections for unstable economic conditions in Germany and the EU.

The German government formally ratified the Maastricht Treaty on European Union as a constitutional amendment on December 2, 1992. After dozens of special European Union negotiations and summit meetings, the German Bundestag joined with other governments in authorizing the adoption of the Euro as the common currency for Europe in 1998.

Conclusion: Evolution, Compatibility, and Consensus

German foreign policy has clearly evolved in response to a series of dilemmas and opportunities in the post–Cold War era, but this change has been gradual and moderated by a domestic political culture of restraint. It is clear that key domestic political actors and conditions have played a role in the restructuring of German foreign policy over time. This chapter seems to bear out Hanrieder's assertion that policy change was ultimately a function of compatibility and consensus. Time and time again the "degrees of feasibility" of various foreign policy goals and the amount of domestic political consensus shaped the evolution of German foreign policy.

An examination of a series of contemporary themes has helped to identify two additional conditions that shaped the evolution of contemporary German foreign policy: the evolution of perspectives on foreign policy responsibilities on the political left, and the actual nature of the strategic dilemmas and opportunities facing the Federal Republic in the post–Cold War era.

This chapter has shown the surprisingly important role of opposition parties in shaping the German foreign profile over time. In 1990 and 1991, for example, SPD leaders firmly rejected the possibility that Germany could deploy troops constitutionally to participate in Operations Desert Shield and Desert Storm. But as time wore on, many Social Democrats grew increasingly uncomfortable with opposing government plans that essentially meant voting against humanitarian operations. Televised images of starvation and unrest in Somalia moved many to reconsider the question of how and when German troops should be deployed abroad. The Balkan wars broadened the Social Democrats' perspective on German responsibility for regional security (especially the war in Bosnia), and it was Chancellor Gerhard Schröder who secured a coalition in support of German participation in the Kosovo War, the country's first offensive military action since World War II.

The story of the evolution of perspectives on German foreign policy in the Green Party in the post–Cold War era is even more intriguing. In the early 1990s many Greens became concerned by what they saw as a rapid progression from diplomatic solutions to a willingness to use the German military abroad. A vocal opponent of such moves at the time, the party challenged the government's latitude regularly on the floor of the Bundestag and in Federal Constitutional Court. Even as Greens spoke out against these actions, however, party members began internal debates over whether or not to support certain types of military action in response to humanitarian challenges. After a series of dramatic party conference meetings in the fall of 1995, half of the Green parliamentarians voted in favor of German troop deployment for the peacekeeping mission in Bosnia. In 1999 Foreign Minister Joschka Fischer of the Green Party not only supported Germany's involvement in the NATO war against Serbia, but he also fought to maintain party support for the coalition government's actions.

But how could the political left ever consider support for German military action? How could Germans overcome the sharply defined domestic political culture of restraint from the Cold War? These intriguing puzzles are answered in the actual nature of the strategic dilemmas and opportunities facing the Federal Republic in the post–Cold War era. In the 1990s the government and opposition parties were forced to confront humanitarian tragedies in the Balkans, the Middle East, and Somalia. In all cases, oppressive power groups were systematically targeting large groups of people, and genocide and ethnic cleansing occurred in a series of conflicts in the Balkans. Thus, the scale of these external shocks prompted a reexamination on all sides of the proper foreign policy response. Neither economic power nor diplomacy was sufficient to prevent these tragedies, and even pacifists were forced to consider the use of military force as the final option to end such conflicts. German domestic political culture had undergone a subtle but notable shift in the face of the tragedies of the 1990s.

Broadly speaking, Germany has emerged as a more powerful actor in regional and international affairs, but its foreign policy will continue to be based on multilateral cooperation and domestic consensus. European integration is an excellent case in point. In many ways, European integration and the evolution of German politics have reflected "two sides of the same coin" in past decades. The Treaty on European Union called for an entirely new level of political and economic integration, and this development demanded introspection on the part of member governments regarding the depth of multilateral commitments. With German support, Europe will establish daily use of a common currency in 2002. Europe is on the road to cooperation on a common foreign policy and a regional defense initiative, and European leaders have begun negotiations for a substantial enlargement of the EU in the next decade. But Germany's domestic political climate will continue to shape its involvement in European integration. The dramatic election victory of the Social Democratic Party set German policy

on a new middle course of domestic economic reform programs. The SPD-
Green coalition government has labored for the past three years to address internal problems, including unemployment, nuclear energy, immigration policy, tax
reform, labor policy, and social welfare reform. As in the past, the chancellor has
attempted to manage pressures for reform from all sides. Proposed government
solutions are expensive, and many Germans have expressed a commitment to
economic recovery at home before tackling any new regional programs.

The Federal Republic of Germany celebrated its fiftieth anniversary in 1999
as a nation proud of its stable democracy and achievements in economic, political, and humanitarian arenas. At the same time, changing geopolitical circumstances have allowed a gradual evolution of the domestic political culture of
restraint. This appears to be a natural transition in world politics and raises
important questions about the future of German foreign policy.

Suggestions for Further Reading

Ash, Timothy Garton. *In Europe's Name: Germany and the Divided Continent.* New York:
    Random House, 1994.
Banchoff, Thomas. *The German Problem Transformed: Institutions, Politics, and Foreign Pol-
    icy, 1945–1995.* Ann Arbor: University of Michigan Press, 1999.
Berger, Thomas U. *Cultures of Antimilitarism: National Security in Germany and Japan.* Bal-
    timore: Johns Hopkins University Press, 1998.
Conradt, David P. *The German Polity.* 7th ed. New York: Longman, 2000.
Duffield, John S. *World Power Forsaken: Political Culture, International Institutions, and
    German Security Policy after Unification.* Stanford: Stanford University Press, 1999.
Hanrieder, Wolfram. *Germany, America, and Europe: Forty Years of German Foreign Policy.*
    New Haven: Yale University Press, 1989.
Merkl, Peter. *German Unification in the European Context.* University Park: Pennsylvania
    State University Press, 1993.
Pond, Elizabeth. *The Rebirth of Europe.* Washington, D.C.: Brookings Institution Press,
    1999.
Pulzer, Peter. *German Politics, 1945–1995.* New York: Oxford University Press, 1995.
Verheyen, Dirk. *The German Question: A Cultural, Historical, and Geopolitical Exploration.*
    Boulder: Westview Press, 1999.

Notes

1. Hanns W. Maull, "Zivilmacht Bundesrepublik Deutschland," *Europa Archiv,* May 10,
   1992, 269–279.
2. See Wolfram F. Hanrieder, "Actor Objectives and International Systems," *Journal of
   Politics* 27 (February 1965): 109–132; Wolfram F. Hanrieder, "Compatibility and
   Consensus: A Proposal for the Conceptual Linkage of External and Internal Dimensions of Foreign Policy," *American Political Science Review* 61 (December 1967):
   971–982; Wolfram F. Hanrieder, *West German Foreign Policy, 1949–1963: International Pressure and Domestic Response* (Stanford: Stanford University Press, 1967).
3. Peter Meroth, "Deutschland 2000: Der Staat, den wir uns wünschen," *Süddeutsche
   Zeitung Magazin,* January 4, 1991, 8–15.

4. See John S. Duffield, "Political Culture and State Behavior: Why Germany Confounds Neorealism," *International Organization* 53 (autumn 1999): 765–803; see also John S. Duffield, *World Power Forsaken: Political Culture, International Institutions, and German Security Policy after Unification* (Stanford: Stanford University Press, 1998); Arthur Hoffmann and Kerry Longhurst, "German Strategic Culture in Action," *Contemporary Security Policy* 20 (August 1999): 31–49; Thomas Banchoff, *The German Problem Transformed: Institutions, Politics, and Foreign Policy, 1945–1995* (Ann Arbor: University of Michigan Press, 1999); Thomas U. Berger, *Cultures of Antimilitarism: National Security in Germany and Japan* (Baltimore: Johns Hopkins University Press, 1998).

5. See select chapters from *Deutschlands neue Aussenpolitik, Band 1: Grundlagen*, ed. Karl Kaiser and Hanns W. Maull (Munich: R. Oldenbourg Verlag, 1995), including: Christian Tomuschat, "Die Internationale Staatenwelt an der Schwelle des Dritten Jahrtausends"; Michael Stürmer, "Deutsche Interessen"; Norbert Kloten, "Die Bundesrepublik als Weltwirtschaftsmacht"; Hans-Peter Schwarz, "Das Deutsche Dilemma"; Ludger Kühnhardt, "Weltgrundlagen der Deutschen Aussenpolitik"; Helga Haftendorn, "Gulliver in der Mitte Europas: Internationale Verflechtung und Nationale Handlungsmöglichkeiten." See also Michael Brenner, Wolfgang F. Schlör, and Phil Williams, *German and American Foreign and Security Policies: Strategic Convergence or Divergence?* Internal Study, no. 98 (Saint Augustin, Germany: Konrad Adenauer Stiftung, 1994).

6. Kenneth N. Waltz, "The Emerging Structure of International Politics," *International Security* 18 (fall 1993): 66–67; see also Christopher Layne, "The Unipolar Illusion: Why New Great Powers Will Rise," *International Security* 17 (spring 1993): 5–51.

7. Waltz, "The Emerging Structure of International Politics," 71.

8. Michael Stürmer, *Die Grenzen der Macht: Begegnung der Deutschen mit der Geschichte* (Berlin: Siedler Verlag, 1992), 247.

9. Michael Stürmer, "Deutsche Interessen," in Kaiser and Maull, *Deutschlands neue Aussenpolitik*, 1–40. For a similar argument, see Hans-Peter Schwarz, *Die Zentralmacht Europas: Deutschlands Rückkehr auf die Weltbühne* (Berlin: Siedler Verlag, 1994).

10. Hans-Dietrich Genscher, *Erinnerungen* (Berlin: Siedler Verlag, 1995), 62.

11. Klaus Kinkel, "Peacekeeping Missions: Germany Can Now Play Its Part," *NATO Review*, October 1994, 7.

12. "Wir haben die Faust geballt," *Der Spiegel*, September 1990, 176–180; see also "Gezisch am Nachmittag," *Der Spiegel*, December 1990, 29–31.

13. "Wörner Urges FRG Role in Peacekeeping Missions," *Berlin DDP,* January 8, 1993; reprinted in *Foreign Broadcast Information Service—Western Europe* 93 (January 11, 1993): 10.

14. "Eine regelrechte Psychose," *Der Spiegel*, December 21, 1992, 18–19.

15. "INFAS-Umfrage zum Einsatz der Bundeswehr in Somalia sowie zur allgemeinen Beteiligung an UN-Einsätzen," television broadcast on Rückspiegel, MDR 3, May 15, 1993.

16. Lally Weymouth, "We Have to Win This," *Newsweek*, April 19, 1999, 30.

17. Roger Cohen, "Half a Century after Hitler, German Jets Join the Attack," *New York Times*, March 26, 1999, A10.

18. *Deutschland Nachrichten*, March 12, 1999, 1.

19. Stephan Speicher, *Berliner Zeitung*, March 25, 1999, 6.

20. When put to a vote, the government committee's resolution out-polled the left wing by 444 to 318; see "Greens Back Fischer on Kosovo, Urge Temporary Cease-Fire," *This Week in Germany*, May 14, 1999, 2.

21. As quoted in Caroline King, "The New German Government and the Kosovo Conflict: A Painful Awakening," *Politik* (summer 1999): 4–5.

22. Roger Cohen, "Schroder's Blunt 'No' to Ground Troops in Kosovo Reflects Depth of German Sensitivities," *New York Times,* May 20, 1999, A1.
23. Ibid.
24. Deutsche Bundesbank, "Exchange Rate Movements within the European Monetary System: Experience after Ten Years," monthly report, July 1993.
25. Speech before the Bundestag, reprinted in *Stenographischer Bericht,* December 13, 1991, Plenarprotokoll 12, 5705.
26. Helmut Kohl, "Erklärung der Bundesregierung zu den ergebnissen des europäischen Rates in Maastricht," 68. Sitzung des Deutschen Bundestages, December 13, 1991, reprinted in *Bulletin,* December 17, 1991, 1153–1159.
27. European Commission, *Eurobarometer 44* (Luxembourg: European Communities, 1996); European Commission 1994, 89–97, and 1996, 17; see also Christian Deubner, *Deutsche Europapolitik: von Maastricht nach Kerneuropa?* (Baden-Baden: Nomos Verlag, 1995).
28. Ralph Atkins, "Kohl Links His Political Fate to a United Europe," *Financial Times,* November 24, 1992, 2.

CHAPTER 5

Russian Foreign Policy: Continuity, Revolution, and the Search for Status

Paul D'Anieri

The disintegration of the Soviet Union in 1991 marked the end of the Cold War and the beginning of a global transformation. This survey of Soviet and Russian foreign policy, however, presents some startling similarities in behavior patterns over time. Paul D'Anieri argues that Soviet foreign policy during the Cold War was shaped by the superpower standoff and the personalities of dominant leaders. Since the disintegration of the Soviet Union, Russian foreign policy has been heavily influenced by a perceived loss of great power status and a drive to restore Russia's rightful place in world politics. Ironically, although Russia has undergone domestic changes in the past decade, foreign policy patterns have remained fairly consistent and the decision-making process rather centralized. Today, Russia faces many complex foreign policy challenges, including unstable relations with the United States, the evolution of ties to the nearby states that were part of the Soviet Union, and NATO enlargement, but D'Anieri argues that these concerns actually serve as unifying factors in the Russian polity in the twenty-first century.

Many interesting comparisons can be made between Russian foreign policy and that of other countries. One important connection can be found between Russia's drive for great power status in the latter part of the twentieth century and that of Britain (Chapter 2), China (Chapter 6), and France (Chapter 3). In this context, D'Anieri describes Russian foreign policy as "more about symbolism than about substance." Significant comparisons also can be drawn with other countries that seek influence within their geographic region, including Brazil (Chapter 13), Israel (Chapter 9), Nigeria (Chapter 11), and South Africa (Chapter 12). The end of the Cold War marked the beginning of a gradual transition to capitalism and democracy in Russia. Other countries experiencing dramatic transitions in the post–Cold War era include China and South Africa. The relative centralization of the foreign policy process and the powers of the president in Russia can be compared with similar systems in France, Iran (Chapter 10), and Mexico (Chapter 14). Like China, Iran, and South Africa, Russia must also confront the role of human rights concerns in post–Cold War foreign policy.

Since 1991, when the Soviet Union collapsed and Russia discarded communism, Russia has been involved in a tumultuous process of internal transformation. Almost everything in the domestic affairs of the state has changed, even its borders and territory. Yet, in some ways, as we move away from 1991, Russian foreign policy looks more and more like pre-1991 Soviet foreign policy, without the Soviet rhetoric. There is a reemergence of acrimony with the United States in particular and the West in general. From Iraq to Yugoslavia, the United States and Russia appear to be on opposite sides of major issues.

Post-Soviet Russian foreign policy raises serious questions about certain domestic-level theories of foreign policy determinants. Although Russian foreign policy has evolved in significant ways since 1991, the degree of change in foreign policy has not matched the revolutionary changes in domestic politics. Not only have the overall nature of the regime and its constitution changed, but the everyday bureaucratic process of foreign policy making has also changed. Moreover, the economic system has been destroyed and is in the process (one hopes) of being rebuilt. Even the population has changed. A country of roughly 300 million in 1991, roughly half of whom were ethnic Russians, has been truncated by the secession of the fourteen non-Russian republics of the Soviet Union such that today's Russia has fewer than 150 million inhabitants, some 80 percent of whom consider themselves Russians.[1] In light of this disconnection between drastic change in Russia's domestic life and substantial (though not complete) continuity in foreign policy, it appears that we must look to other, more continuous factors, to explain Russia's foreign policy today. And the continuities are not trivial. First among them is continuity in key personnel. Russia's president from 1991 through 1999, Boris Yeltsin, was a member of the Politburo of the Communist Party of the Soviet Union before becoming a "democrat." His successor, Vladimir Putin, came up through the ranks in the Soviet KGB. Russia therefore better supports a domestic explanation based on personnel and institutions than one based on the overall nature of the political regime. More broadly, one might argue that although smaller in territory and population, in international terms Russia was what the Soviet Union was, a large state in an anarchic world, and could be expected to behave that way. Geopolitically, Russia inhabits essentially the same landmass that it has for centuries, and to the extent that geography provides imperatives in foreign policy, is subject to the same motives as in the past.

The incongruities between change of regime and continuity of foreign policy frame this chapter. Viewing Russia's foreign policy in this way forces us to scrutinize some of the things we commonly take for granted about Russia's post-

Soviet transformation. Continuity in Russian foreign policy occurs not in spite of, but because of, Russia's domestic transformation. With Russian domestic politics in turmoil, foreign policy provides a sense of familiarity and continuity and a crucial area of consensus in the country. In the next section, I review the evolution of Russian foreign policy since World War II and the external factors that have shaped it. I then assess the process of foreign policy making in Russia by asking who, or what, makes Russian foreign policy. This leads into a section focusing on national identity issues and their influence on Russian foreign policy. That discussion will help resolve the disconnection between domestic change and international continuity. After surveying the major issues in Russian foreign policy today, I attempt to summarize how Russia's domestic transformation is linked to its foreign policy.

Soviet Foreign Policy during the Cold War

At the end of World War II, the Soviet Union was in some respects at the peak of its power, having crushed Germany and occupied most of central and eastern Europe, but it was also in a situation of insecurity.[2] Russia bore the brunt of defeating Germany. By the time of the Normandy invasion in 1944, Soviet forces had already broken the back of the German army at Stalingrad and pushed it out of the Soviet Union and to the outskirts of Warsaw. Whereas World War II left the United States with few battle deaths and industrially empowered, it left the Soviet Union with twenty million dead and the country's economy in ruins. Internationally, the Soviet leadership felt insecure due to its ongoing isolation and the U.S. monopoly on the atomic bomb. The often heinous policies of the Soviet regime in occupied Eastern Europe only increased Soviet isolation internationally.

Russia had been a European great power since 1709, when Peter the Great defeated Charles XII of Sweden at the Battle of Poltava. Russia's defeat of Napoleon in 1812 further enhanced this status. World War II transformed the international system, creating a bipolar world from a multipolar one, and elevating the Soviet Union, along with the United States, above the other traditional European great powers to superpower status. What had previously been primarily a European foreign policy agenda became a global agenda over the next few decades, such that no significant issue in the world was seen as resolvable without Soviet input, and such that the Soviets sought strategic victories on every continent.

Postwar Soviet foreign and domestic policies can be divided into four periods corresponding to the country's leaders (that we can do so indicates that the supreme leader in the Soviet system had immense personal control over foreign policy making, although the exact extent is debated). Under the rule of Josef Stalin, until 1953, the Soviet Union extended its totalitarian form of government to most of the territory it conquered in World War II. When Mao Zedong's communists succeeded in taking over China in 1949, communism seemed to be ascendant, and the Cold War reached the peak of its intensity in the Korean War from 1950 to 1953.

Following Stalin's death, the period of Nikita Khrushchev (1953–1964) was characterized more by decreased tension than by the blustery statements for which Khrushchev became famous. His replacement of Stalin resulted immediately in the end of the Korean War and, more gradually, in a denunciation of Stalin and the release of many political prisoners. Internationally, Khrushchev sought a decrease in tensions with the West, figuring that as long as nuclear war was avoided, communism would inevitably triumph. To this end, he made economic productivity a primary domestic goal. He took Soviet foreign policy more actively into developing countries, where he believed it would naturally thrive. But beginning in 1958, with a series of threats concerning the status of Berlin, and culminating in the Cuban missile crisis in 1962, Khrushchev became increasingly confrontational in foreign affairs, in part perhaps to make up for his domestic failures. Chief among those failures was his inability to accelerate economic productivity while at the same time retaining the authoritarian system of rule, a problem that recurs in Russian history from the reign of Peter the Great through the presidency of Mikhail Gorbachev. A combination of foreign policy and domestic failures prompted a group led by Leonid Brezhnev to remove Khrushchev in a peaceful Kremlin coup in 1964.

Brezhnev came to power seeking to restore the stability and predictability that had waned with Khrushchev's bold policies. Eventually, Brezhnev's tenure became known as the "period of stagnation" for the utter lack of domestic innovation, but the period from 1964 through 1974 fundamentally changed the conduct of the Cold War. The sting of the Soviet humiliation in the Cuban missile crisis, when Khrushchev had been forced by the United States to remove Russian missiles from Cuba, prompted Brezhnev to sponsor a massive nuclear arms buildup that finally made the Soviet arsenal comparable to that of the United States. Beginning in the late sixties, and culminating with the Strategic Arms Limitation Treaties of 1972, the United States and the Soviet Union engaged in détente, which promised reduced likelihood of war and less confrontational behavior.[3] The two sides never really had compatible motives in the process. The Soviet Union saw détente as an opportunity to increase support for communist regimes in developing countries without having to fear a nuclear showdown, whereas the administration of Richard Nixon saw it as a way of ending such support. Détente eroded quickly, beginning with the Soviet-sponsored intervention in Angola in 1975, and finally with the Soviet invasion of Afghanistan in 1979. By the early 1980s the Cold War had returned as Brezhnev's health failed and the Soviet economy continued to stagnate.

After the brief reigns of Yuri Andropov and Konstantin Chernenko, Mikhail Gorbachev came to power in 1985. He perceived a need to revamp the economy domestically and to restore some degree of stability internationally. His goal of reducing tensions with the United States proved difficult to achieve, in part because Ronald Reagan's administration was so profoundly distrustful of the

Soviet Union. But by encouraging the Eastern European satellites to break away from Soviet control in 1989, Gorbachev removed the original bone of contention in the Cold War.[4] Domestically, Gorbachev was much less successful. When he confronted the old Russian tension between improving economic performance and maintaining political control, he found that every measure of political liberalization led to calls for even more. He did not realize until it was too late that he was one of the few people in the Soviet Union who really believed in socialism, and that many of the citizens of the non-Russian Soviet republics considered the Russians colonizers, just as did the Poles, Czechs, and Hungarians.

Ironically, when the USSR finally collapsed and Russia and the other Soviet republics became independent states, the administration of George H. W. Bush regretted it, because the United States had finally believed in the reality of Soviet change and found the post-1989 Gorbachev government a partner with which it could work.[5] That the relationship had been fundamentally transformed was demonstrated in the Persian Gulf War in 1991. A few years earlier, it would have been unimaginable that the Soviet Union would have stood by and allowed the United States to attain such a victory. The Cold War was over, and the Soviet Union was gone, but no one inside or outside Russia knew what to expect next.

External Factors

There has always been considerable debate about the relative weight of internal and external factors in Russian foreign policy. Concerning the czarist era, one prominent interpretation was that the autocratic nature of the Russian regime made expansion necessary to control domestic tensions. A different domestic factor that received much attention was the tight bond between the czars and the Russian Orthodox Church, which allegedly gave Russian policy a "messianic" mission. At the same time, however, a compelling case was (and is) made that czarist foreign policy was driven primarily by geopolitical imperatives. These imperatives could be distilled down simply to the need to control a warm-water port to allow naval access to the world. In the nineteenth century, for example, British thinkers attributed Russian activity in Afghanistan to a drive toward the Persian Gulf and activity in the Balkans to a drive toward Istanbul and the Turkish Straits. A broader geopolitical view pointed out that there were few natural barriers on the Russian landmass, opening up Russia to repeated invasions, and enticing Russia to continuously push its frontiers outward in order to protect itself.

Under communism, two factors prompted many analysts to look even harder at the domestic level. First, Soviet ideology explicitly promised to bring a new perspective to foreign affairs, and the early diplomacy of the Bolshevik regime was colored by ideology. The first Bolshevik foreign policy decision upon coming to power in World War I, for example, was to withdraw from the war and to foment revolution in Germany and Austria to end the war. Given the Marxist notion that revolution, when it came, would be an international revolution, this approach made sense. Very quickly, however, it became clear that the German masses were not going to overthrow the regime and that communist ideology would not protect the country from German invasion. Thus the Bolsheviks adopted a much more practical policy.

A second domestic factor that appeared important during the Soviet era was the Soviet form of government. Highly autocratic, highly centralized, and extremely secretive, the Soviet form of rule was so different from that found elsewhere in the world that foreign policy analysts believed that it must somehow influence foreign policy. In a general sense, the old notion that Russian foreign policy was driven by the needs of an illegitimate and autocratic regime was revived in the Soviet era, most influentially by the American statesman and scholar George F. Kennan. One of the most visible influences of the Soviet system of government was the complete lack of preparedness of the country to face the German invasion in 1941. In the late 1930s Stalin had initiated a massive purge of the top military staff in order to ensure the complete loyalty of his officers. Roughly three-quarters of the general staff was eliminated (and, in most cases, executed). Russia thus went into the war with its military leadership in complete turmoil.

But regardless of these domestic influences there is much evidence that the same sort of international factors that drive the foreign policy of other countries also drove Soviet foreign policy. Despite the Bolsheviks' ideological pretensions, the Soviet government from the earliest days found that in order to preserve the state, certain imperatives could not be avoided. Thus when the Bolshevik revolution failed to halt World War I, a large army was quickly rebuilt, in part using former czarist officers. Russia attended the diplomatic conferences of the 1920s and 1930s and made what deals it could with whomever served its interest. When, in the 1930s, its interest was served by cooperating with ardently anticommunist Germany, it did so, and it cooperated with the equally anticommunist United States and Great Britain during World War II when that was necessary.

In the Cold War, most of the policies of the Soviet Union look analogous to those of the other superpower, the United States. The Soviet Union built a massive nuclear arsenal, closely controlled its allies in Europe, and spent vast sums of money seeking allies around the world. All these policies can be attributed to balance-of-power politics without much reference to the internal nature of the Soviet Union. For example, the imbalance in strategic nuclear forces that had emerged between the two superpowers easily explains the Soviet Union's decision to place missiles in Cuba in 1962, which touched off the most dangerous crisis of the Cold War. Similarly, the alleged ideological affinity between the Soviet Union and China in no way moderated the conflict between them that emerged in the 1960s, caused by the obvious security threat that the two countries posed to one another. Indeed, by the early 1970s, Soviet leaders considered China a more immediate security threat than the United States.

There is considerable debate concerning the relative weight of internal and external factors in motivating the changes that Mikhail Gorbachev adopted beginning in 1985.[6] There can be little doubt that his effort to end the Cold War was in part motivated by his desire to redirect resources toward the domestic economy. But the extent to which retrenchment from international affairs was forced on him is not clear. The failure of the invasion of Afghanistan to install a pro-Soviet leader, the challenge to Communist authority in Poland by the Solidarity trade union movement, and the massive U.S. military buildup all put pressure on the Soviet ability to maintain the status quo. However, it is not clear that Gorbachev had to react by making concessions. His immediate predecessors, Chernenko and Andropov, had reached the opposite conclusion and had withdrawn the Soviet Union from arms control negotiations with the United States. It seems clear that Gorbachev and his circle of advisers regarded his "new thinking" in foreign policy to be the needed response to international circumstances, but it is equally clear that had someone else come to power in 1985, a very different conclusion might have been reached. Indeed, one of the dominant undercurrents in post-Soviet Russian foreign policy is the belief that Gorbachev made too many concessions to the West and allowed the Soviet Union to collapse.

As Russia's international power has diminished, it has been less able to alter the international system and has been more constrained by it. But the degree of constraint Russia feels varies along two axes. The first is geographical. In contrast to the Soviet era, when the Soviet Union played a key role in Africa, Asia, and Latin America, Russia today lacks the resources to shape the international system far from its borders. In contrast, the last decade has seen an increasing ability of the United States and its allies to shape Russia's choices. This has been most obvious in the Balkans, where Russia has been reduced from a key player to a spoiler, able to frustrate the plans of other actors but unable to achieve its own policy, and in some cases an irrelevance. However, within its immediate region (the former Soviet states), Russia finds itself dominant. It is able to influence not only the international constraints its neighbors face, but in many cases the domestic constraints as well.

More significantly, perhaps, external influences vary according to issue. In the military-strategic realm, Russia is still a force to be reckoned with. Russia's nuclear arsenal provides it a core level of security from invasion. Although its conventional military power and political leverage have been reduced—as shown by the U.S. ability to unilaterally force a reconsideration of the 1972 Treaty on Anti-Ballistic Missile Systems (ABM treaty) and by the expansion of the North Atlantic Treaty Organization (NATO)—Russia's nuclear status and militarism still allow it a prominent voice in world politics. In the economic realm, however, Russia is largely at the mercy of international forces. In the early 1990s Russia was forced to ask other countries for aid and for foreign investment, requests that most Russians found humiliating. After the crash of the Russian economy, foreign lending and investment dwindled, which created short-term problems but was welcomed by many in Russia. But the way in which Russia's economy crashed in 1998 showed how much external factors influenced it. Essentially, a financial panic that started in Southeast Asia caused many investors to withdraw from all emerging markets, including Russia. Russia caught the "Asian flu" through no immediate fault of its own (although the underlying problems were massive). More broadly, Russia has had to confront difficult problems in maintaining its influence in the world. As international influence seems increasingly determined by economic rather than military might, Russia's weaknesses seem emphasized and its strengths devalued.

Internal Factors

The process of contemporary Russian foreign policy making has been characterized as informal and uninstitutionalized. In other words, bureaucratic procedures for making and implementing policies are not well defined and are fluid, such that the process that takes place in one decision may not characterize another decision. Because the president dominates foreign policy making in Russia, the process itself can change as the president changes his mind about how he wants to do things, or as new actors gain or lose influence within the Kremlin. This fluidity makes Russian foreign policy difficult to study in two ways. First, there is little transparency. We often know very little about the procedure that went into a given policy. Second, there is frequent change over time, so even when we learn something about how a decision was made, we have little confidence that the next decision will be made the same way.

The President

As in the United States, the Russian constitution gives the president primary authority over foreign policy.[7] Most significant decisions are made at the level of the president and his advisers. Unlike the system of governance in the United States, the Russian legislature has little ability to make specific foreign policy due to the lack of separation of powers, the unequal distribution of power between the executive and the legislature, and the general absence of a strong rule of law in Russia. Because the Russian president has considerable decree authority, he can pass legislation without having to get parliament's approval.[8] Not only can he make foreign policy in that way, but more broadly, he has much less incentive to compromise, because parliament has little ability to punish him on other issues. Even in a case where a unified parliament negates a presidential decree, there is little in Russia to prevent him from doing what he wants anyway.[9] He controls the executive branch, and if the executive does something that is technically illegal, the legislature can do almost nothing about it. The standard recourse in most Western states, a lawsuit, is difficult if not impossible to undertake in the atrophied Russian legal system. Moreover, the executive branch has a variety of economic instruments it can use to win legislators' support, most notably control over many of the best apartments in Moscow.

Boris Yeltsin defined the Russian presidency, both literally and figuratively. The constitution drafted by Yeltsin's advisers in 1993 was designed to give him the prerogatives he saw as necessary. Yeltsin's rather impulsive style of leadership led to constant efforts by various political actors to get him to change his mind on one policy or another. Additionally, Yeltsin's ill health, especially from 1995 on, tended to sideline him for considerable periods of time. During these periods, access to him was more jealously guarded than usual, which complicated the struggle of those beneath him to win his favor.

Although the laws defining the Russian presidency have not changed with the ascension of Vladimir Putin, his style appears to be vastly different from Yeltsin's (although we must caution that the evidence on policy making in Putin's Kremlin remains limited at this writing). Whereas Yeltsin's rule was based on charisma, emotion, spontaneity, and barely controlled chaos, Putin has succeeded in building a much more orderly and controlled governing style. He appears to value control and order above all else and so shuns some of the theatrics or surprises in which Yeltsin seemed to revel. In his first year of office, his only significant public misstep occurred when he remained on vacation after hearing the news of the sinking of the submarine *Kursk*. It appears that he has taken steps to reduce the amount of bureaucratic infighting among those beneath him, but it is unclear whether this has genuinely changed or is simply being conducted less publicly. The bureaucratic game remains the same (try to get the president to adopt your policy), but Putin controls it much more tightly. Because Putin gives the impression that he deliberates carefully before making a decision, and then sticks with it, there is less opportunity for him to be lobbied into a quick decision or to be lobbied out of it later.

The first year of the presidency of Vladimir Putin indicated that Russian goals are largely stable, although the tactics used in pursuing them can change. From the outset of his administration, Putin pursued Russia's objectives more actively while still emphasizing the basic goal of ensuring Russia's status as a great power. One of his first moves was to force ratification of the second Strategic Arms Reduction Treaty (START II) by the Russian parliament, where it had languished for several years under Yeltsin. By attaining ratification of START II, Putin was able to show that Russia was forging ahead with arms control, and that the United States, with its plans for missile defense, was now the obstacle. In the battle for the support of western European states, Putin achieved this significant tactical victory for Russia at little cost. Similarly, when Putin went to the G-7 plus Russia (the group of seven leading economies plus Russia) summit meeting in Japan in July 2000, he stopped in North Korea on the way and came away with a new proposal to end that country's nuclear weapons program (a key aim of U.S. and Western policy). He thus arrived in Japan with a major benefit to offer the other states, rather than with more requests for financial aid. He became the focus of the summit, and by the time it was over, many predicted that the question of whether Russia would become a full member of what would become the G-8 was now resolved in Russia's favor.[10]

There is some debate among scholars concerning how the process works below the level of the president.[11] The best evidence that we have indicates that the key body is the National Security and Defense Council, which is headed by the president and brings key ministers together to make policy. The National Security and Defense Council is charged with working out the broad directions of Russian foreign policy. This body, for example, developed and adopted the new "Foreign Policy Doctrine" adopted in 2000. However, it does not appear that this body plays the same crucial management and coordination function as that of the similarly named body in the United States. It is not responsible for the day-to-day flow of information to the president or for coordinating policy implementation. And it is not clear who, if anyone, is. In time, Putin or some successor may develop a foreign policy process within the presidential administration that is more structured than the one left by Yeltsin.

The Bureaucracy

The obvious place to look for the bureaucratic roots of foreign policy is the foreign ministry. Clearly, on the whole array of low-level issues entrusted to the foreign ministry, it plays the paramount role. But some argue that there is a disconnection between the experts making recommendations on a particular policy and the higher-level decision makers.[12] Research and advice, in this view, work their way up the chain at the foreign ministry but at some point get cut off before they can play a role in actual decisions. The key circle of trusted advisers to the president does not necessarily include anyone who is an expert on specific issues. This somewhat informal system leads to intense competition for access to the president, and to political infighting in place of policy debate.[13]

A related problem is that the lack of institutionalization in Russian foreign policy leads to instability in policy.[14] There is little mechanism to create closure, to declare that a policy decision is final. Because it is relatively easy to reverse a decision once made, dissatisfied actors have an incentive to reopen decisions endlessly. Again, this leads elites to focus more on gaining access to the president than on working out policy differences. To the extent that Boris Yeltsin often seemed erratic in his policies, the lack of institutionalization of policy, and the instability thus engendered, might have been partly to blame. The problem plagues the military apparatus as well as the foreign policy bureaucracy.[15] Two examples illustrate the problem. In 1992 the foreign ministry had been conducting negotiations with Japan to plan a visit by Yeltsin to Tokyo. After the foreign minister, Andrei Kozyrev, reached an agreement with the Japanese for Yeltsin to visit Japan, others in the Security Council persuaded Yeltsin not to go.[16] This backtracking, besides causing a furor within the Russian foreign policy establishment, presented Russia publicly as an unreliable negotiating partner and probably did more damage to the relationship with Japan than a clear and simple decision not to make the trip would have done. This is the type of infighting and inconsistency that Putin has tried to reign in, but even he could not avoid it in the summer of 2000 when the defense secretary and the chief of the general staff announced contradictory plans for revamping the role of the strategic nuclear forces. Neither Russians nor foreign governments have been able to be confident that Russia's announced policies would have "staying" power.

Over time, the problem of lack of institutionalization has been moderating for two reasons. First, after the initial chaos following the collapse of the Soviet Union and the setting up of separate Russian governmental institutions, normal routines have slowly been establishing themselves. This is likely to continue under Putin. Second, after the highly polarized foreign policy debates that characterized the early Yeltsin years, a considerable consensus has emerged on the basic goals and problems in Russian foreign policy. Because there is now less to fight about, there are fewer situations in which the institutional shortcomings of the system can be exposed.

The Media and Public Opinion

The media in Russia often attempt to take an active role in promoting certain policies, and the most powerful actors in the country control most of the media outlets. The state still controls much of television and radio, and large financial-industrial groups tied either to the government or the opposition control most major newspapers. Thus there are few "independent" media in Russia. In the late 1990s, media in Russia became considerably less independent of the government, and correspondingly less critical of government policies. When Russian forces invaded Chechnya in 1994, critical media coverage of the botched assault on Grozny was an important factor in the immense unpopularity of the war, and perhaps in the eventual Russian withdrawal. But when Russia invaded again in late 1999, coverage was much more constrained and was much more supportive of the government. In a polity driven at least partly by elections, the media have become tools of political influence, and the state has increased its control over these key levers.

As in most countries, we see in Russia a reciprocal relationship in which public opinion influences politicians, and politicians seek to influence public opinion in directions they find convenient. Russia is far from a perfect democracy, but elections are not completely fixed. In Yeltsin's 1996 election campaign and again in Putin's 2000 campaign, the presidential administration was able to use its direct control of much of the media to promote the incumbent's candidacy and keep challengers in the background. Public opinion therefore matters, but it is susceptible to manipulation by the government. In the shift away from a pro-Western foreign policy, it seems clear that public opinion mattered because politicians anticipated that a pro-Western policy would hurt its supporters at the polls. There seems to be some benefit, and little cost, to aggressive declarations such as those made by Moscow mayor Yuri Luzhkov in support of Russia's retaking control of the city of Sevastopol in Ukraine. At the same time, however, Yeltsin showed his ability to go against public opinion when he signed treaties with Ukraine acknowledging Ukrainian sovereignty over the city.

Interest Groups

A separate potential source of influence is Russia's notorious circle of "oligarchs."[17] The oligarchs are wealthy individuals who control diversified business, financial, and media empires; they seek political power both for its own sake and to use it to benefit their business interests. One such figure, Boris Berezovsky, in addition to being Russia's wealthiest individual, controls several major newspapers and for a time served as deputy secretary of the National Security Council. His leading positions in business, media, and government indicate just how heavily concentrated power is in Russia today. Because of the lack of transparency in Russian decision making, it is difficult to know exactly what role oligarchs such as Berezovsky play. We know that these oligarchs provided massive financial support to Yeltsin's 1996 reelection campaign and that they profited immensely from the privatization of state property. And although it is widely believed that some of the oligarchs were highly influential with Yeltsin and his closest advisers, it is impossible to know exactly how this influence manifested itself in foreign policy.

Similarly, there have been close connections between many of Russia's largest firms and the government.[18] For example, the Gazprom, the largest natural gas company in the world, was built from the formerly state-owned gas monopoly and is still largely controlled by the state.[19] Certain aspects of Russian foreign policy, notably an assertive role in the Caspian Sea region, indicate that the government is pursuing the firm's interests. The fact that Viktor Chernomyrdin, prime minister for five years (1993–1998), was formerly head of Gazprom and was reputed to hold a sizable amount of the firm's stock seemed to reinforce that connection. But there is also evidence that influence flows in the opposite direction, that the government uses the firm as a foreign policy tool. In its disagreements with states in the "near abroad" (Russia's special category for those neighboring states that were part of the Soviet Union), the Russian government has frequently threatened recalcitrant states with a gas cutoff or offered the inducement of cancellation of gas-related debts, moves that could only be made if the government controlled the firm. The state continues to hold nearly a majority interest in the company, and it appoints several members to the board, which has often included sitting cabinet ministers. Probably there is some merit in both perspectives: the government and Gazprom seem to find a good deal of mutual interest and to engage in informal deals in which one side expending capital for the benefit of the other is expected to be repaid in some way.

National Identity and Russian Foreign Policy

One reason why it is so difficult to identify which actors influence Russian foreign policy is that there is agreement on many of the basic questions. It is crucial to understand that, although Russian domestic politics is divided by sharp debates in which little compromise seems possible, Russian foreign policy is an area of general consensus. Foreign policy, therefore, has become something of a tonic used by the Russian leadership to build some overall consensus in the Russian polity. And this role that foreign policy plays helps explain why it does not look as different from Soviet or even czarist policy as we might have expected.

A fundamental political problem in Russia today concerns the idea of what Russia is, and what it means to be Russian. Russia has this national identity crisis because, as pointed out earlier, it has changed fundamentally in the last decade. Russia today is something that it has never been before, a nation-state. As Russia's former ambassador to the United States put it: "The starting point for any discussion about the interests of Russia has to be a discussion about Russia itself. What kind of country are we talking about—territorially, politically, ideologically?"[20] One of the key roles, therefore, of Russian foreign policy has been to help define how Russians (and others) perceive Russia. "The practice of our foreign policy . . . will help Russia become Russia."[21]

It is this need, not any immutable factor in global politics, that engenders policies that recall the Russia of the past. Russian foreign policy is not driven by the same forces as in the past, but it is aimed at acquiring much of the status and prestige of the past, even as its content changes. In order to achieve this status, Russia has sought to regain what it perceives as its pre-1991 level status. Thus there is little desire to create pro-Russian regimes around the world, as was the case during the Cold War, or for territorial expansion, as there was in czarist times. But there is a desire to regain the influence that Russia/the Soviet Union possessed in both those periods. As a result, we see Russia asserting rights and exercising power in a way that increasingly looks like revanchism, that is, that it is following policies to reclaim its former status, but the sources of these policies are different from what they were and therefore have different implications.

Russia was never a nation-state before 1991. Prior to 1917, it was a multinational empire, and identified itself as such. From 1917 until 1991, the Soviet Union behaved in fact like a multinational empire but rejected that designation. As a result, although ethnic Russians dominated the Soviet Union, the Russian nationality as a whole was submerged into the Soviet nationality, in policy as well as in reality. For, example, Soviet nationality policy broke up the Soviet Union into fifteen republics. All except Russia had highly developed republic-level governments, such as the Ukrainian republic in Kiev or the Georgian republic in Tbilisi. There was no Russian republic government for most of the period, in a strange recognition that Russia in fact ran the whole Soviet Union. Because there was no distinction between Russian and Soviet identities, a void was created when the Soviet Union collapsed. Now, for the first time in centuries, the state run from Moscow has a large majority of ethnic Russians and is not an empire (although Chechens might disagree with that assessment).

The issue is manifested most clearly in Russia's relations with Ukraine.[22] Russian history books teach that the society that became Russia was founded in Kiev in the tenth century, when Vladimir the Great had his people baptized into Christendom. Kiev is therefore known as the Mother of Russian Cities. The greatest military triumphs of Peter the Great (Poltava) and Catherine the Great

(Crimea) took place in territory that today lies in Ukraine, and many see those regions as having been consecrated as Russian territory by the blood spilled in expelling foreign invaders. Similarly, Russian tradition and government policy always saw Ukrainians as simply a variety of Russians.[23] When Ukraine seceded in 1991, emphasizing that the legacy of medieval Kiev belonged to Ukraine, and not to Russia, and that Ukraine and Russia were not only two separate states but two separate nationalities, it left Russia and the Russians with the question of what was left. The result has been a great deal of agonizing by leading Russian intellectuals such as Aleksandr Solzhenitsyn over both the loss of Ukraine and the search for "the Russian idea."

The political changes within Russia that took place in 1991 heightened this discontinuity in the past. Yeltsin's policies of democratization, liberalization, and internationalization, flawed as they were, essentially rejected everything that Russia had been. Combined with the changes mentioned above, Russia found itself in an identity crisis. Perhaps the greatest aspect of that crisis was directly linked to foreign policy: the question of Russia's status in the world. Although it was obvious to many in the West after 1991 that Russia was no longer a great power but a third world country with nuclear weapons, this loss in status has been understandably hard to swallow in Russia. Being a great power was a fundamental attribute of Russia, and being a resident of a great power was a fundamental attribute of Russian citizens. This concept was now being thrown out along with everything else. Thus great power status, viewed both as an established fact and as a desirable trait, has become a core value in Russian identity — and hence has a powerful influence on Russian foreign policy.

If it were possible to recover any of the other now-missing aspects of Russian identity, or any of the relative stability of Soviet days, the Russian government surely pursued the available ways. But economic reform went off course, and most have accepted that territorially Russia is more or less fixed. Foreign policy, however, is one area in which symbolic battles can be won in the absence of material resources, and much of Russia's foreign policy has therefore focused on these symbolic issues. For that reason Leon Aron has characterized post-Soviet Russian foreign policy as "Gaullist," in that it seeks to use foreign policy to prop up a self-image that is no longer supported by reality.[24] Much of contemporary Russian foreign policy can be understood as an attempt to get others to acknowledge Russians' image of their country. Although more concrete interests remain relevant, symbolic issues are an equal source of increasing tensions with the West.

The national identity goals of Russian foreign policy can be summarized simply by two basic interests: to be recognized as first among equals among the post-Soviet states, and to maintain its status as a great power in the world at large. Achieving the first goal means getting the states in the region to accept a certain Russian authority, including perhaps the right to intervene to quell trouble in the other states.[25] Related to this is a notion that Russia should be accorded this right because in fact the other post-Soviet states are essentially Russian, historically if not ethnically. It also means getting states outside the region to accept Russia's primacy in the region and not oppose Russia's taking the steps it sees fit.

To achieve the second goal specifically means denying the notion that the United States occupies a preeminent place in the world, either in actual power or in authority.[26] Russian leaders, in acknowledgment of Russia's decline, have given up entirely on the notion of bipolarity that Soviet leaders accepted during the Cold War. But they strongly oppose the notion of unipolarity and hence seek recognition that the world is multipolar. Russian leaders are adamantly against the existence or acknowledgment of a U.S.-led unipolarity or hegemony. It is debatable whether, empirically speaking, the world is multipolar, but Russia's wariness of American hegemony is shared by many in other aspiring great powers such as France and China. Thus in January 2000, when Putin, as acting president after Yeltsin's resignation, revised Russia's "National Security Concept," one of the main thrusts was neutralizing threats to the multipolar constellation in the world.[27] This leads to the Russian policy of paying close attention to any act that would imply that the United States has some right to action in the world that others do not (which is exactly what Russia seeks for itself in the near abroad).

It is tempting to say, therefore, that Russian foreign policy is more about symbolism than about substance, but it would be more accurate to say that in Russian politics and foreign policy, symbolism is substance. For a country whose most fundamental mission is to redefine itself politically and socially, the role that the international system gives to Russia has important consequences in how Russia does so. As discussed in Chapter 1, for states that are weak internally, a successful foreign policy and the recognition of the international community can be an important factor in establishing the legitimacy of the state.[28] Gaining the approval of the international system for Russia's vision of itself is of crucial importance for Russia, which has lost much of its historic territory, has had to fight to keep Chechnya, and is hobbled by the weakness of the state.

Contemporary Russian Foreign Policy

Since 1991 Russia has been in immense flux socially, economically, and governmentally, and the foreign policy arena has been no exception. With the demise of the Soviet state, there has been a fundamental reassessment of the basic goals of foreign policy, the interests of the state, the means of achieving goals, and the policy process. We can see an evolution of policies over time that can be broken into three periods, a period of pro-Western policy from 1991 until late 1993, a period of reassessment beginning in late 1993 and lasting until 1995, and a period of reassertion of Russian interests after 1995.

Following the collapse of the Soviet Union in late 1991 and the formation of an independent Russia headed by Boris Yeltsin, the warming of East-West relations that had occurred in the late Gorbachev years continued and even accelerated. Indeed, becoming part of the West was at this point the guiding goal of Russian foreign policy. This notion was driven by several overlapping domestic and international, political, and economic motivations. In part, the goal of becoming a "normal" Western state was one of national identity—of erasing the notion that Russia was fundamentally distinct. Looking to western Europe and North America, Yeltsin and the Russian liberals saw what they wanted Russia to be, both in regard to liberal democracy and in regard to a market economy. More prosaically, only through good relations with the West could Russia acquire the investment, market access, and aid needed to undo the damage done to its economy by Soviet rule. In retrospect, these views seem naive, but in the afterglow of the miraculous collapse of communism, they seemed natural and not especially ambitious.

This liberal, or Western-oriented, view of Russian foreign policy came under attack in early 1993, in part because of some conspicuous failures to produce results, in part because of the regrouping of leftist and nationalist forces in Russia, and in part because of the difficulties involved in Russia's domestic transition. Most Russians valued liberalization primarily as a route to greater prosperity. As reform came to be associated with lower standards of living and a shredded social safety net, the domestic and foreign policies of liberalization came into question. But at the same time certain concrete foreign policy issues were influential in causing the shift to more conservative views. Aid from the West, which was supposed to cushion the transition to the market, was minuscule in proportion to the size of the Russian economy. The new "Marshall Plan" never arrived, causing disillusion among Russian liberals and suspicion among many others.[29] A series of events beginning in late 1993 began to undermine faith in Russian liberalization and in the notion that Russia and the West had no major conflicts of interest. Most notable from the Russian perspective, perhaps, were attempts to shut Russia out of negotiations concerning the Yugoslav wars, increasing Western support for newly independent Ukraine against Russia, American unilateral actions in Iraq, and a nascent competition for control of the vast and lucrative oil reserves of the Caspian Sea basin.

While some of this opposition was harshly nationalist, the more credible and ultimately victorious criticism came from a "great power" school of thought.[30] This view held that Russia was a great power, and that its foreign policies should be driven by national interest, as in other great powers.[31] In this view, conflicts of interest with other great powers were natural. The great power view was a reaction against the sense that Russia's interests were being undermined and its pride destroyed by efforts to get along with the West. That the United States in particular seemed to believe that Russian input was no longer needed on global issues was especially insulting. With the Russian economy faltering, legislative elections due in 1995, and presidential elections coming in 1996, Yeltsin's team could not afford to ignore these views. The Yeltsin administration could not fix the economy, but it could change foreign policy, and it increasingly used foreign policy to build consensus, which was so elusive for domestic issues.

The shift in policy was made official in January 1996 with the resignation of Foreign Minister Andrei Kozyrev and his replacement by career KGB officer

Yevgeni Primakov. Even at this point, however, both the West and Russia were striving to limit the damage to the pro-Western view in Russia. Subsequent events have re-created the sense of rivalry and opposition that existed in the Cold War, although with lower levels of danger and hostility. Disagreement over Iraqi and Russian assertiveness in the near abroad propelled this tendency, but disagreement over Kosovo in 1999 finalized it and made it irreparable.

Along with that evolution in overall foreign policy orientation, two key facets of it have remained continuous since 1991. First, unlike Soviet foreign policy, post-Soviet Russian foreign policy has been limited geographically.[32] The global aspirations that characterized late Soviet foreign policy have largely been jettisoned. Russia's foreign policy focuses above all on its neighboring countries and into central and southeastern Europe and Iran and Iraq. Latin America, Africa, and Southeast Asia, three places the Soviet Union was successful in expanding its influence, are now minor priorities. Similarly, Russia's role in the Arab-Israeli conflict is much diminished. This geographical emphasis fits well with the more traditional notion of great power politics predominant in Russia, recalling as it does the notion of "spheres of interest." In the view of Russian leaders, other countries should leave the near abroad to its influence, and in turn Russia will leave other regions to other great powers. One of Yeltsin's advisers compared this view to the American Monroe Doctrine, which sought to exclude the involvement of European powers in Latin America.[33]

Second, Russia has consistently sought a dominant role in its own immediate region. Russian society has only very slowly come to accept that the territorial truncation of the traditional Russia in 1991 is permanent. Russia claims certain rights as a great power to influence the affairs of its neighbors, and since most of them are highly dependent on Russian markets, energy supplies, or both, Russia has considerable means to promote that interest. The high degree of interdependence in what was not long ago a single economy gives the former Soviet states a powerful economic interest in some sort of integrative arrangement, such as a free trade area or even a common currency. Russia has generally promoted this notion, both with incentives and threats, and the other states have varied in their willingness to go along. Belarus, Armenia, Kazakhstan, Kyrgyzstan, and Tajikistan have been amenable to a high degree of Russian leadership, for various reasons. But a group known as GUAM (Georgia, Ukraine, Azerbaijan, and Moldova; since joined also by Uzbekistan) has formed a somewhat informal strategic alliance of solidarity against Russian influence.

Both symbolically and practically, many other countries have been reluctant to acknowledge Russia as a great power in the traditional sense. It would be an oversimplification to state that all the issues between Russia and other countries concern status, but those issues do come up across the board. Whether we discuss Russia's immediate neighbors, or the states of NATO, or China, very concrete issues are at stake. For both sides, however, the handling of those issues is complicated by this overarching question of Russia's role in the world and Russia's rights in the world.

Russia and the "Near Abroad"

Russia's quest for recognition of special status is most evident in the near abroad, as discussed earlier. Because the states in this region are also new and have their own need to establish clear national identities and state legitimacies, the identity issues have become more complicated and also more hotly contested. The "Russian Monroe Doctrine" in this region seems old-fashioned and heavy-handed to many in the West, but for the states subject to it, each weak in its own way, it is perceived as a question of survival. There is also a plethora of concrete issues, big and small, that keeps diplomats busy. The fifteen constituent republics of the Soviet Union were more heavily integrated economically than the states of the European Union, and the dismantling of the Soviet Union, along with the subsequent creation of various impediments to trade, provided a shock to the economies of the region quite distinct from that created by the dismantling of state planning. There are powerful incentives for continued trade cooperation in the region, but the goal of each state to assert its independence and separateness (as well as the enormous profits that a few were able to reap from new trade barriers) have made cooperation difficult. The willingness to accept Russian leadership and dominance of a new trade grouping varies within the region, but even Kazakhstan, one of the most willing, has found the terms of cooperation too injurious to its independence.

Because there is so much consensus among Russian elites concerning goals in the near abroad, there is not much controversy within Russia on this policy, which in turn makes it more difficult to assess who the most influential actors are. The mid-1990s saw some discussion of whether Russia should pursue reintegration by offering incentives (use of the ruble as a stable currency, subsidized energy, military aid) or by using threats (cutting off energy supplies, support for insurgent movements). Both strategies have been used. In fact, all the major actors in Russian foreign policy are pursuing reintegration of the Soviet Union in their own way.

Most controversial has been the military. Russian military forces remained present and active in many of the successor states after 1991. They played a key role in arming separatist movements in Moldova and Georgia, raising a troubling dilemma. It remains unclear whether the Russian military was intervening on orders from the political leadership in Moscow or on its own initiative. Either possibility was ominous, but in different ways. Because Moldova and Georgia are new, small, impoverished states with limited military means, relatively minor assistance to separatist movements by the Russian military can turn the tide against the government. In the case of Georgia, military aid to rebels in Abkhazia seems to have been coordinated with diplomatic strategy. When the Georgian government with great reluctance agreed to base Russian troops on its soil and join the Commonwealth of Independent States, Russia enforced a cease-fire among the rebels.

The foreign ministry has equally pursued reintegration along different avenues. Above all, diplomacy has focused on trade agreements that reintegrate the economic space of the former Soviet Union. Again, both positive and negative incentives have been used. Access to the Russian market and to Russian suppliers is essential to firms across the region, giving Russia a powerful lever.

Russian firms (many of which continue to have close contacts with the government) are also engaged in reintegrating the former Soviet Union through economic means. Some of these also seem a bit coercive, such as Gazprom's effort to gain control of energy facilities throughout the region by forcing states delinquent on their gas bills to sell it pipelines and other facilities. It is doubtful that there is any "master plan" coordinating all these vectors of Russian policy in the former Soviet Union. Rather the degree of complementarity we see in various actors' policies reflects a common set of goals and common understanding that various means reinforce one another.

Russian Relations with the United States

It is not clear how Russia can remain equal to the United States while at the same time being a supplicant for Western aid. Compared with the postwar Marshall Plan or with what the Federal Republic of Germany has spent in aid to the former East Germany, Western aid to Russia has been quite limited. It has probably had only a marginal effect on the overall performance of the Russian economy. Nonetheless, individual leaders have seen it as important because it signals the West's commitment to that leader and to Russia. To many in the West, the fact that Russia desperately needs economic aid indicates that the underlying basis for its power has eroded. Thus Russia's position at the International Monetary Fund is that of a developing country. Russia has sought to combat this image by insisting that it gain membership in G-7.

In security affairs, Russia completely rejects the role of supplicant but finds that in practice it is often ignored or overruled in ways that the Soviet Union never was. Two issues have most bitterly brought home to Russia the nature of its current position, and a third one threatens to reinforce that notion. Russia strenuously opposed NATO expansion and NATO policy in Yugoslavia, but lost decisively on both issues. These issues have led Putin to place regaining Russia's international position at the top of the foreign policy agenda.

NATO Expansion

The expansion of NATO in March 1999 irked Russia for several reasons.[34] Although it was little acknowledged in the West, the expansion of NATO violated at least the spirit of the agreement struck in 1990 to allow the reunification of Germany. At that time, it was agreed that NATO forces would not expand into the former East Germany, and the decision to go even further east seemed to many Russians to indicate that by then Russia was so weak that the West did not have to obey its commitments. Carrying NATO into lands that the Soviet

Union had won at the cost of millions of lives during World War II was also insulting. Those in Russia most supportive of the West, moreover, feared that NATO expansion would lead to Russia's isolation from western Europe.

Most important, Russians could not understand why NATO needed to expand if Russia was not aggressive. After all, the alliance was formed to combat the Soviet Union, which no longer existed, and to guard against Soviet troops in Eastern Europe, which also were long gone. All along, however, Russia stated a willingness to acquiesce in NATO expansion if Russia was given a de facto veto in the alliance's activities in the region. Some Russians asserted that the alliance simply could not expand without Russian permission. The politics of the United States' presidential campaign in 1996 meant that NATO's expansion was announced before the necessary diplomacy was conducted. By negotiating a special bilateral "NATO - Russia" charter, NATO was able to take some of the sting out of expansion, but it was clear to all that Russia had objected and that NATO could and did proceed over Russian objections. In the end, the timing of the official entrance of the new members confirmed the worst Russian fears: the new members joined the alliance in March 1999, and within weeks NATO was bombing Kosovo, using Hungary as a base. The juxtaposition of events seemed to prove that NATO expansion was indeed aggressive.

The problem of NATO enlargement emphasizes the role of the system in constraining Russian foreign policy. On this key issue, one cannot really evaluate the Russian policy process because none of the key decisions were made in Russia or by Russia. There was widespread consensus in Russia that NATO expansion was undesirable, and this was communicated to the alliance repeatedly and often stridently. Russia offered a variety of "compromises," and NATO eventually came up with a plan for a somewhat meaningless mechanism for increased consultation. Russia could accept either this, or nothing, but it had no ability to form its own strategy for negotiating with NATO because it was simply powerless to stop the alliance expansion.

A New Battleground: Russian versus U.S. Interests in the Balkans

The war in Bosnia was one of several issues souring Russia's relations with the West in general and the United States in particular in 1993 to 1995. Russia was defending a traditional ally (Serbia) in a region it had traditionally influenced.[35] It was also standing up for the principles of state sovereignty and nonintervention. Russia also stood up for the principle that there could be no intervention against Serbia without a United Nations (UN) Security Council resolution, where Russia had a veto. Russia was not alone in this position, being supported at times by both France and China. Within Russia itself, none of this was controversial. There was little debate over what Russia should do and a fair amount of anguish and anger at U.S. and NATO policy. On this issue as well as NATO expansion, Russia found that the key decisions were made outside its borders, and increasingly against its wishes.

The foreign ministry led Russian policy on the Balkans during the war in Bosnia. Institutionally this made sense, because the key negotiations took place at the UN or in the "Contact Group" of great powers that convened to try to work out a solution. The foreign ministry was dominant in part because it was successful: Deputy Prime Minister Vitaly Churkin successfully negotiated a deal in early 1994 that temporarily headed off NATO military interventions. The deal was seen as a substantial coup for Russia, by showing that it had taken the initiative in the region and by foiling NATO's desire to move to military action.

Crucially, however, the NATO states limited themselves to actions that were approved by the Security Council. For Western powers who sought to stop the war, notably Great Britain and the United States, Russia's position was extremely frustrating and amounted essentially to using the Security Council veto to aid Slobodan Milosevic's aggression. After the Dayton Peace Agreement in 1995, however, Russian forces worked within the NATO-led peacekeeping force in Bosnia with little problem.

When the situation in Kosovo came to a head in early 1999, the Bosnia scenario, which many in NATO saw as a failure, seemed to be repeating itself. Again, Russian policy was based in the foreign ministry, because the primary mission was one of negotiating with NATO and the UN Security Council, and again there was little discernible debate within Russia. For Russia, NATO intervention over the Yugoslav treatment of Kosovo was even more problematical than the intervention in Bosnia. Bosnia was, at least in theory, an independent state. Kosovo was a province of Yugoslavia and hence was an "internal problem." Intervention here, in Russia's view, would create a precedent that was especially frightening to a country that had its own separatist conflict in Chechnya. If NATO could intervene in Kosovo, why not in Chechnya?

For this reason, Russia continued to oppose intervention and to use its veto in the Security Council to prevent adoption of resolutions to use force. Frustrated, NATO initiated hostilities without Security Council approval, rejecting the previous precedent. This move infuriated Russia. After ten years of foreign policy concessions, Russia had only one place left where it was still seen as the equal of the other great powers: the UN Security Council. The NATO decision to bomb Serbia without a Security Council resolution meant that the United Nations did not bind NATO. By showing the West's willingness and ability to ignore Russia's wishes, Kosovo was a disaster for Russian foreign policy. Again, however, there was little Russia could do, so it had to settle for a minor moral victory. Following the negotiation of a deal for NATO and Russian forces to occupy Kosovo, Russian forces in Bosnia sent a detachment overland to take control of the airport in Pristina before NATO forces arrived. NATO forces were infuriated, and Russian public opinion delighted, but this small symbolic jab did not obscure the extent to which Russia had become impotent in a region relatively close to its borders and where Russia had been involved for more than a century.

Ballistic Missile Defense

A similar scenario is now playing out between the United States and Russia over U.S. plans to construct a ballistic missile defense (BMD) system. For years U.S. policy makers considered such a system destabilizing, and in 1972, U.S. and Soviet leaders agreed to sharply limit such systems (an agreement that Russia took over as successor to the Soviet Union). Today, with improved technology and perceived threats from "rogue states," many in the United States seek to build such a system. Doing so would require modification or abrogation of the 1972 ABM treaty. At a time when Russia's conventional forces are deteriorating, Russia is relying increasingly on its nuclear arsenal to guarantee its defense. In this context, for the United States to be able to neutralize that deterrent is profoundly threatening to Russian strategists. Russia therefore has insisted on maintaining the treaty in its current form, to which the United States responded that if Russia did not renegotiate the treaty, the United States would simply abrogate it. From the Russian perspective, this is another case in which the United States and the West more broadly are using Russia's current weakness to roll back the equality that Russia had achieved in czarist and Soviet times.

Again, there is consensus within Russia. Although there is deep division concerning the relative importance of nuclear and conventional forces in Russia's defense mission, no part of the Russian elite sees a U.S. BMD program as anything other than a huge problem. Indeed, those who hope to shift resources away from the nuclear arsenal have the most to lose, because Russia will almost certainly see a need to augment its nuclear forces if the United States builds a ballistic missile defense. The consensus on this issue that exists at the time of this writing might well erode as negotiations between the United States and Russia continue. Although all agree that a BMD threatens Russia, there is probably disagreement concerning what sort of compromise would be acceptable to Russia, and there may also be disagreement about how to respond to a U.S. decision to build such a system.

Conclusion: Aspirations and Realities

All these episodes raise the question of whether Russia is becoming an aggrieved defeated power, as Germany became between the two world wars. There are doubtless some similarities. Today, Russia sees itself, not as having been defeated, but as having ended the Cold War voluntarily. Because the prevailing worldview counters this perception, Russians have more to be resentful about. The point, however, is not the parallel with the past, but the implications for the future. What are the implications for a Russia that economically and politically looks like a developing country but continues to have the foreign policy aspirations of a great power?

One fears, but certainly cannot predict, that a government seeking to attain a high level of influence with few resources might be more acceptant of risk. A hint of this was provided at the end of the war in Kosovo when Russian forces hurried into Pristina Airport ahead of NATO forces. After being humiliated repeatedly by NATO, Russian forces were able to make a move that irked NATO leaders, much to the delight of the Russian elite and public. A dangerous encounter between NATO and Russian troops was avoided only when a British general disregarded an order to beat the Russians to Pristina. It remains to be seen whether Russian foreign policy will be risk-acceptant in the future, but the logical conditions for that certainly are in place.

In this chapter I have sought to review the historical antecedents of contemporary Russian policy and to consider the forces motivating Russian foreign policy today and into the foreseeable future. Since the end of the Cold War, Russian foreign policy has been heavily conditioned by Russia's perceived loss of status, which has undermined the country's fragile notion of its national identity. The whole range of grand and small foreign policy issues, both economic and security, are viewed in Russia in light of a broader mission to reestablish Russia's notion of itself as a great power. In a society that is badly divided on almost every political issue, there is an astonishing degree of consensus on this basic goal. Foreign policy therefore is and will be one of the major unifying factors in Russian politics, even though (or perhaps because) it is not the highest priority on the agendas of most Russians. The symbolic politics of regaining Russia's acknowledged greatness will continue to influence Russian foreign policy in the foreseeable future.

Although the process of foreign policy making in Russia seems both inconsistent and exceptional, it must be studied with the same tools we use to study other states' foreign policies, as outlined in the introduction to this volume. Those factors may combine in unique ways in Russia, but the list of factors to be considered and the basic questions raised about them are no different for Russia than for other states.

However, we know far too little about the process by which Russian foreign policy is made to be able to make any serious predictions. Beginning with the rise to power of Mikhail Gorbachev in 1985, Soviet and Russian politics have continually surprised even the most careful observers. Most recently, Russia has seen the surprise resignation of Boris Yeltsin and the elevation to the presidency of the virtually unknown Vladimir Putin. Even if scholars of Russian foreign policy understood the process under Yeltsin, they now have to ask whether and how it has changed, and how it might change further in the future.

The fact that the process of Russian foreign policy is unstructured does not mean that this process is unimportant. It means that the process by which Russian foreign policy is made is opaque and perhaps even inconsistent. As a result, a high degree of latitude remains in the hands of the president of Russia. This explains why so much effort was expended trying to assess the health and competence of Boris Yeltsin and why, after Yeltsin's resignation, there was so much searching to glean the motives and attitudes of Vladimir Putin. Saying that Russia's foreign policy is conditioned by the goal of asserting Russia's great power status does not tell us how that will be done.

Some factors in Russian foreign policy transcend the politics of individual leaders. National identity, a factor important in Russian foreign policy, does not get much attention in the study of foreign policy in Western countries. Nevertheless, national identity variables will continue to influence foreign policy goals and the perceptions of leaders regardless of who is president. By forcing us to look more closely at that factor, the Russian case may prompt us to examine the role of national identity in other countries' foreign policies as well.

This chapter began with a paradox: Russia's domestic system has changed dramatically, but its foreign policy has not. Indeed, as Russia gets further away from the Soviet era, its foreign policy, both in substance and rhetoric, increasingly resembles Soviet policy. In part, the continuity in foreign policy stems from a continuity in geopolitical imperatives, and in part it stems from something that post-Soviet Russia inherited from the Soviet Union: the aspiration to be a great power. Even though post-Soviet Russia has scaled back its ambitions from superpower status to great power status, the same sorts of issues arise in the pursuit of that goal. The importance of Russia's great power aspirations explains why, despite the lack of structure in Russia's foreign policy making process, there is some consistency in policy. Nonetheless, much remains in flux, from the survival of Russia's current political institutions to the state of its economy. Even as we seek to understand Russian foreign policy today, we must be ready for it to change tomorrow.

Suggestions for Further Reading

Aron, Leon, and Kenneth M. Jensen, eds. *The Emergence of Russian Foreign Policy.* Washington, D.C.: United States Institute of Peace, 1994.

Black, J. L. *Russia Faces NATO Expansion: Bearing Gifts or Bearing Arms?* Lanham, Md.: Rowman and Littlefield, 2000.

D'Anieri, Paul. *Economic Interdependence in Ukrainian-Russian Relations.* Albany: State University of New York Press, 1999.

Dawisha, Adeed, and Karen Dawisha, eds. *The Making of Foreign Policy in Russia and the New States of Eurasia.* Armonk, N.Y.: M. E. Sharpe, 1995.

Donaldson, Robert H., and Joseph L. Nogee. *The Foreign Policy of Russia: Changing Systems, Enduring Interests.* Armonk, N.Y.: M. E. Sharpe, 1998.

Jonson, Lena, and Clive Archer, eds. *Peacekeeping and the Role of Russia in Eurasia.* Boulder: Westview Press, 1996.

LeDonne, John P. *The Russian Empire and the World, 1700–1917: The Geopolitics of Expansion and Containment.* New York: Oxford University Press, 1997.

Mandelbaum, Michael, ed. *The New Russian Foreign Policy.* New York: Council on Foreign Relations, 1998.

Nation, R. Craig. *Black Earth, Red Star: A History of Soviet Security Policy, 1917–1991.* Ithaca: Cornell University Press, 1992.

Sestanovich, Stephen, ed. *Rethinking Russia's National Interests.* Washington, D.C.: Center for Strategic and International Studies, 1994.

Wallander, Celeste A., ed. *The Sources of Russian Foreign Policy after the Cold War.* Boulder: Westview Press, 1996.

White, Stephen. *Russia's New Politics: The Management of a Postcommunist Society*. Cambridge: Cambridge University Press, 2000.

Notes

1. See the statistics in Dmitri Simes, *After the Collapse: Russia Seeks Its Place as a Great Power* (New York: Simon and Schuster, 1999), 10–13.
2. During the Soviet era, an immense literature on Soviet foreign policy emerged. For an overview, see R. Craig Nation, *Black Earth, Red Star: A History of Soviet Security Policy, 1917–1991* (Ithaca: Cornell University Press, 1992).
3. For excellent coverage of the détente period, see Raymond L. Garthoff, *Détente and Confrontation: American-Soviet Relations from Nixon to Reagan*, rev. ed. (Washington, D.C.: Brookings Institution, 1994).
4. On Soviet foreign policy under Gorbachev, see Michael MccGwire, *Perestroika and Soviet National Security* (Washington, D.C.: Brookings Institution, 1991).
5. Simes, *After the Collapse*, 16.
6. See MccGwire, *Perestroika and Soviet National Security*, chap. 10.
7. On the power of the Russian president, see Eugene Huskey, *Presidential Power in Russia* (Armonk, N.Y.: M. E. Sharpe, 1999), esp. chap. 5.
8. See Stephen White, *Russia's New Politics: The Management of a Postcommunist Society* (Cambridge: Cambridge University Press, 2000), 95–106.
9. On "superpresidentialism" in Russia, see M. Steven Fish, "The Executive Deception: Superpresidentialism and the Degradation of Russian Politics," in *Building the Russian State: Institutional Crisis and the Quest for Democratic Governance*, ed. Valerie Sperling (Boulder: Westview Press, 2000), 177–192.
10. *The Guardian* (London), July 24, 2000.
11. See Mikhail E. Bezrukov, "Institutional Mechanisms of Russian Foreign Policy," in *The Emergence of Russian Foreign Policy*, ed. Leon Aron and Kenneth M. Jensen (Washington, D.C.: United States Institute of Peace, 1994), 67–77.
12. Nodari A. Simonia, "Priorities of Russian Foreign Policy and the Way It Works," in *The Making of Foreign Policy in Russia and the New States of Eurasia*, ed. Adeed Dawisha and Karen Dawisha (Armonk, N.Y.: M. E. Sharpe, 1995), 25–29.
13. Jeffrey Checkel, "Structure, Institutions, and Power: Russia's Changing Foreign Policy," in Dawisha and Dawisha, *The Making of Foreign Policy in Russia*, 42–65.
14. Celeste A. Wallander, "Ideas, Interests, and Institutions in Russian Foreign Policy," in *The Sources of Russian Foreign Policy after the Cold War*, ed. Celeste A. Wallander (Boulder: Westview Press, 1996).
15. Eva Buzsa, "State Dysfunctionality, Institutional Decay, and the Russian Military," in Sperling, *Building the Russian State*, 113–136.
16. Huskey, *Presidential Power in Russia*, 126–127.
17. See David Lane, "The Russian Oil Elite," in *The Political Economy of Russian Oil*, ed. David Lane (Lanham, Md.: Rowman and Littlefield, 1999), 75–96.
18. This paragraph is based on Paul D'Anieri, *Economic Interdependence in Ukrainian-Russian Relations* (Albany: State University of New York Press, 1999), 75–77.
19. The influence of the energy industry on Russian foreign policy is detailed by Peter Rutland, "Oil, Politics, and Foreign Policy," and by Jean-Christophe Peuch, "Russian Interference in the Caspian Sea Region: Diplomacy Adrift," both in Lane, *The Political Economy of Russian Oil*.
20. Vladimir Lukin, "Russia and Its Interests," in *Rethinking Russia's National Interests*, ed. Stephen Sestanovich (Washington, D.C.: Center for Strategic and International Studies, 1994), 106.

21. Vladimir Lukin, quoted in James Richter, "Russian Foreign Policy and the Politics of National Identity," in Wallander, *The Sources of Russian Foreign Policy,* 69.
22. See Paul D'Anieri, "Nationalism and International Politics: Identity and Sovereignty in the Russian-Ukrainian Conflict," *Nationalism and Ethnic Politics* 3 (summer 1997): 1–28.
23. Jaroslaw Pelenski, "The Contest for the 'Kievan Inheritance' in Russian-Ukrainian Relations: The Origins and Early Ramifications," in *Ukraine and Russia in Their Historical Encounter,* ed. Peter J. Potichnij et al. (Edmonton: Canadian Institute for Ukrainian Studies, 1992), 3–19.
24. Leon Aron, "The Foreign Policy Doctrine of Postcommunist Russia and Its Domestic Context," in *The New Russian Foreign Policy,* ed. Michael Mandelbaum (New York: Council on Foreign Relations, 1998), 31. The word "Gaullist" refers to French policy under Charles DeGaulle, who sought to retain France's great power status after the decline of its power and the loss of its empire.
25. Alexander A. Pikayev, "The Russian Domestic Debate on Policy toward the Near Abroad," in *Peacekeeping and the Role of Russia in Eurasia,* ed. Lena Jonson and Clive Archer (Boulder: Westview Press, 1996); and Scott Parrish, "Will the Union Be Reborn?" *Transition,* July 26, 1996.
26. Aron, "Foreign Policy Doctrine," 31.
27. *Newsline* (bulletin of Radio Free Europe/Radio Liberty), Part I, January 7, 2000.
28. Robert H. Jackson and Carl G. Rosberg, "Why Africa's Weak States Persist: The Empirical and Juridical in Statehood," *World Politics* 35 (October 1982): 1–24.
29. Jeffrey Sachs, "Betrayal," *New Republic,* January 31, 1994, 14–16.
30. See Leon Aron, "The Emergent Priorities of Russian Foreign Policy," in Aron and Jensen, *The Emergence of Russian Foreign Policy,* 30–32.
31. Alexei G. Arbatov, "Russia's Foreign Policy Alternatives," *International Security* 18 (fall 1993): 5–43.
32. Peter V. Gladkov, "Superpowers No More: The United States and Russia in Post–Cold War Europe," in *From Rivalry to Cooperation: Russian and American Perspectives on the Post–Cold War Era,* ed. Manus I. Midlarsky, John A. Vasquez, and Peter V. Gladkov (New York: HarperCollins, 1994), 200.
33. The Russian "Monroe Doctrine" was first elaborated by Yevgenii Ambartsumov, chair of the Russian parliament's Committee on Foreign Affairs and Foreign Economic Relations, in 1992. See *Izvestiia,* August 7, 1992.
34. See J. L. Black, *Russia Faces NATO Expansion: Bearing Gifts or Bearing Arms?* (Lanham, Md.: Rowman and Littlefield, 2000).
35. This is one of many respects in which Russian foreign policy today seems to have more in common with czarism than with Soviet foreign policy. Serbia was an ally of czarist Russia, but Yugoslavia broke away from the Soviet bloc shortly after World War II, much to Stalin's displeasure.

CHAPTER 6

China: Defining Its Role in the Global Community

Brian Ripley

*The most populous country in the world and a nuclear power, China also is a promi-
nent and potent regional actor in the heart of Asia. Moreover, its efforts to gradually
liberalize its economy and its desire to attain membership in the World Trade Organization (WTO) have increasingly propelled it onto the world stage. Yet the communist
leadership of China has historically defended its sovereignty, attempted to chart an
independent course, and emphasized noninterference by outside forces in its internal
affairs. Indeed, after a period of pro-Soviet leanings, China broke with the Soviet
Union in the 1950s and pursued its own course of both communism and foreign policy. This development ultimately resulted in what Brian Ripley calls a "strategic triangle" comprising the United States, the Soviet Union, and China. Today, China is faced
with both internal and external pressures for political reform.*

*As one of the nondemocracies examined in this book, China might profitably be com-
pared with Iran (Chapter 10). Although very different regimes, the extent to which citizens and interest groups can directly influence foreign policy in those countries is somewhat similar. China also can be compared with states with fairly strong militaries such
as Britain (Chapter 2), France (Chapter 3), Russia (Chapter 5), and even Israel
(Chapter 9). Unlike the countries of Europe, however, China has a foreign policy that
is relatively unconstrained by alliances and organizational commitments, although its
efforts to join the WTO, if successful, will undoubtedly introduce important external
pressures and restrictions.*

*China currently is the most enduring communist country in the world. Its "one-
party" state does not have to grapple with the challenges of coalition government so frequent in Germany (Chapter 4), India (Chapter 8), and Israel (Chapter 9), but various factions within China's leadership can be potent sources of foreign policy friction.
Indeed, Ripley emphasizes the importance of leadership in shaping foreign policy, and
the relative impact of Mao Zedong and Deng Xiaopeng, for example, might be compared with the influence of France's Charles De Gaulle (Chapter 3), India's Jawaharlal Nehru (Chapter 8), or Iran's Ayatollah Khomeini (Chapter 10).*

The People's Republic of China (PRC) has all the attributes of a great power in world affairs. Its large population, growing economy, substantial army, high-tech military arsenal, and pivotal location in central Asia are all ingredients in the classic geopolitical recipe for active international involvement. Yet the great powers of the twenty-first century find themselves playing in an arena increasingly defined by globalization. International institutions, formal rules, informal norms, and a web of political and economic interdependence prevent states—even powerful ones—from acting with complete autonomy in world politics.

The era of globalization places China's deep commitment to sovereignty in peril. State security remains paramount in Chinese foreign policy.[1] Yet the Chinese government's desire to reap the benefits of the global economy and play an active role in world affairs makes it nearly impossible to maintain a clear distinction between internal and external politics. The Tiananmen Square episode of 1989 illustrates China's fundamental foreign policy dilemma. What was ostensibly a domestic policy decision—to impose order in the face of threats to the political establishment—was immediately transformed into a foreign policy crisis whose consequences are still being felt more than a decade later in, for example, the debates over whether China should join the World Trade Organization and whether China should achieve its goal of hosting the 2004 Summer Olympics.

Chinese Foreign Policy during the Cold War

Since World War II, China's foreign policy has undergone a substantial transformation. Once the source of a revolutionary, strident foreign policy, Chinese leaders now seem more committed to the country's greater integration into the global community. Like that of the other countries examined in this volume, China's foreign policy behavior during the Cold War period, including the shift in direction, stemmed from a combination of internal and external factors. The structure of the international system provided China, like most powerful states, with a set of opportunities and constraints.

Anyone undertaking a simple geopolitical analysis might assume history and geography would make China primarily a defensive power; after all, China has been surrounded by powerful neighbors for most of its modern history. Indeed, many of the foreign policy actions taken by China since World War II appear to be the behavior of a defensive state attempting to secure its borders and protect its own sovereignty.[2] One author characterizes Chinese foreign policy during the twentieth century as employing "strategies of weakness" because of its position in an international system dominated by the United States and Soviet Union.[3]

Yet China's postwar foreign policy also must be viewed as an extension of significant internal forces. The personality and aspirations of strong leaders such as Mao Zedong and Deng Xiaopeng, the role of ideology and nationalism in defining China's place in the world, and, at times, the effort to divert attention from domestic problems through deeper involvement abroad have all shaped Chinese foreign policy behavior. In some respects, Chinese foreign policy makers were challenged to overcome the "century of humiliation," when, prior to the 1949 revolution, the nineteenth-century great powers practiced imperialism.[4] These legacies from the past, perhaps exacerbated by the desire to overcome a perception of "backwardness," reinforced a sense of vulnerability, suspicion of outside powers, and strong nationalist sentiment.[5] As Nathan and Ross observe, "In contrast to the self-confident American nationalism of manifest destiny, Chinese nationalism is powered by feelings of national humiliation and pride. . . . Many Chinese see themselves as a nation beleaguered, unstable at home because insecure abroad, and vulnerable abroad because weak at home."[6]

Revolutionary Period (1949–1970)

The Chinese revolution of 1949 ended a decades-long struggle for power between the nationalist forces (the Kuomintang, or KMT) and the communist insurgents led by Mao Zedong. The communist victory allowed the imposition of order and an era of nation building after a prolonged period of war, foreign occupation, and internal instability. But the communist rise to power also ushered in the existence of a one-party state committed to implementing society-wide changes based on the Marxist-Leninist ideology, accompanied by an austere, often brutal governing style. China's foreign policy during this period reflected an odd mixture of grandiose ambition, ideological fervor, and deep-seated security concerns.

In the immediate aftermath of the 1949 revolution, the Chinese government was preoccupied with postwar recovery and reconstruction. The combined impact of civil war, Japanese occupation during World War II, and years of internal disarray provided strong incentives to look inward. Yet events around the world posed a combination of threats and opportunities that soon drew China into active involvement in foreign affairs.

Fundamental concerns about border security and maintaining relations with the Soviet Union dominated the foreign policy agenda of China's new leadership.[7] China's battle-hardened leaders under Mao issued tough rhetoric about exporting socialist revolution, but would likely have preferred the opportunity to set their domestic affairs in order. The dawning of the Cold War and the outbreak of the Korean War forced China to take on an even more ambitious foreign policy.

The Korean War was an unwelcome, even "agonizing" challenge for Chinese leaders given the vital domestic needs of their country.[8] In June 1950, North Korean troops crossed the border into South Korea. The United States soon entered the war (along with other UN forces) and fought to repel the North Korean military. Under the leadership of Gen. Douglas MacArthur, the UN forces were able to push the North Korean military back beyond the thirty-eighth parallel. Ignoring warnings from Zhou Enlai, China's top foreign policy official, MacArthur continued to press northward.[9]

China was not an influential player in the initial phases of the Korean War. The Soviet Union, rather than China, worked closely with the North Korean communist government (despite the proximity of the Korean peninsula to the Chinese border). The world community's response to the Korean War came from the United Nations (influenced heavily by the United States). The PRC had been denied membership in the new international organization; Taiwan (also known as "Formosa" during this period) had been given the "China seat" at the UN.[10]

The expansion of the Korean War to China's doorstep made involvement inevitable. Just as the Korean War was a defining moment in the U.S. strategy of containment under the Truman administration,[11] the war also placed a direct foreign policy challenge in the lap of the new Chinese leaders. For them, the proximity of U.S. troops to China would be both an embarrassment and an ongoing security threat. Thus, despite some opposition among top advisers, Mao's views prevailed and the Chinese entered the war in behalf of North Korea.[12] By the time the war ended in 1953 with an uneasy truce, the creation of a "demilitarized zone," and the more or less permanent presence of U.S. forces in South Korea, it was clear that China was bound to remain a player in world politics.

Already aligned with the Soviets on ideological grounds, the new Chinese government was quite logically pushed by these world events toward the Soviet camp. The early pro-Soviet tilt by the PRC was borne mostly of economic and military vulnerability. Despite sharing a border and an ideology, Soviet leaders failed to treat China as an equal partner in promoting worldwide socialism. Instead, the Soviets practiced what might be considered a form of imperialism toward their neighbor by extracting resources, establishing security and intelligence outposts, and generally treating the Chinese as backward cousins. Economic aid from the Soviets came with strings attached. Moreover, the Soviets expected full and prompt repayment of the $2 billion in military aid given to China during the Korean War.[13] A shared concern about the U.S. security threat, including ongoing American support for Taiwan and the rehabilitation of Japan, helped to maintain Chinese-Soviet unity for a time. Eventually, however, the strains in the relationship became overwhelming.

During this era, China also was a highly visible supporter of the "nonaligned movement"[14] and competed with countries such as Gamal Nasser's Egypt and Nehru's India for leadership of the developing world (see Chapter 8). The PRC, clearly motivated by Mao's ideological preferences, attempted to unite and mobilize nationalist forces in Asia and Africa to create an alternative to alignment with either Cold War superpower. It backed up its effort with both economic and rhetorical support for wars of national liberation, but no military intervention.[15]

By the late 1950s, a significant rift had developed between China and the Soviet Union. Clearly chafing under Soviet tutelage and eager to strike an independent course, Mao began openly criticizing the Soviets and expelled many Russian economic and technical advisers. Much to the dismay of Chinese leaders, Soviet leader Nikita Khrushchev continued to attend summit meetings with the United States, raising the possibility of closer U.S.-Soviet cooperation. Khrushchev also cancelled an agreement to help China develop its own atomic arsenal. (China eventually developed its own atomic bomb in 1964, without direct Soviet assistance.) Finally, Soviet leaders openly courted India and supplied it with economic aid and diplomatic support despite China's history of border disputes with the Indian military.[16]

Strategic Triangle (1970s)

By the 1970s, growing Chinese resentment and distrust of the Soviet Union, combined with a realpolitik agenda of pursuing national interests, created an opportunity for closer ties between China and the United States. In a remarkable turn of events, the Soviet Union had gone from one of China's strongest allies during the 1950s to one of its biggest antagonists. But the reality of the growing Sino-Soviet conflict was still not apparent to many U.S. foreign policy makers who persisted in their view of "monolithic communism"—that is, that all communist regimes pursued similar foreign policies and maintained cordial relationships with one another.

At one level, China's rift with the Soviet Union was fundamentally about ideology; Chinese leaders accused the Soviets of straying from orthodox Marxist-Leninist thought. But the conflict also may have been the natural outgrowth of two powerful states sharing a long border. In fact, tensions between the Soviet Union and China led to border clashes in 1969 along the Ussuri River. Nervous authorities in China's capital city of Beijing went so far as to begin the construction of fallout shelters in anticipation of a potential Soviet nuclear strike.[17] By 1969, Mao had concluded that the Soviets rather than the United States posed the greater threat to Chinese security.

The dramatic U.S. "opening" to China in 1972 by the Nixon administration and the formal recognition of China in 1978 by the Carter administration established a framework for Chinese cooperation with the West. President Richard Nixon's bold move to establish relations with China was part of a larger strategy involving a balance of power between the United States, Soviet Union, and China; the gradual withdrawal of U.S. troops from Vietnam; and the relaxation of Cold War hostility via a new policy of détente. The domestic political benefits that Nixon gained from this historic trip to China, complete with extensive media coverage of the president-as-statesman, were no doubt part of the equation as well.

For their part, Chinese leaders saw numerous opportunities in the U.S. initiative. Potential economic benefits and a counterweight to Soviet threats were accompanied by a face-saving means of reducing support for communist forces in Vietnam. Although the Chinese had been supplying military aid and rhetorical support for North Vietnam and the Viet Cong guerrilla forces in the south, a history of ethnic antagonism between China and Vietnam robbed the relationship of much enthusiasm.[18]

In many respects, the Sino-American rapprochement of the 1970s represents a classic case of foreign policy realism: great powers putting aside their profound ideological differences in order to pursue vital national interests. Yet even the mutual gains that brought China and the United States together did not eliminate problems such as differences over Taiwan. Diplomats in the Nixon administration sought to bridge differences with China by establishing a somewhat ambiguous stance toward Taiwan's status. Ultimately, however, the Carter administration was forced to be more explicit in its choice of Beijing over Taipei and agreed to allow the U.S.-Taiwan defense treaty to expire.[19]

Open Door Policy (1980s)

Under the reform leadership of Deng, China entered the global economy in a more fundamental fashion. The 1980s represented a hiatus for Chinese foreign policy to some extent, with peace and prosperity as the watchwords and no significant examples of Chinese military intervention. Deng was committed to the "Four Modernizations" (industry, agriculture, science, and defense) during this period as a way to mobilize resources for maintenance in areas that had been allowed to languish during the upheavals of the 1960s and 1970s. (The suggestion by dissident Wei Jingsheng in 1978 that democracy be included as the "Fifth Modernization" earned him a spot in Chinese prisons for nearly two decades, followed by surveillance, detention, and harassment until his release to the United States in 1997.)[20] Military modernization was actually the lowest priority of the "Four Modernizations" as attention was focused on more pressing domestic needs.

The Soviet commitment to internal reforms and opening to the West in the late 1980s also had consequences for Sino-Soviet relations. As Soviet leader Mikhail Gorbachev began to reduce troops and weapons in Soviet Asia, the Soviet Union and China began to thaw their relations.[21] It appeared that the two countries were following remarkably parallel courses of economic reform, political liberalization, and greater moderation in foreign policy.

Then came Tiananmen. On June 3–4, 1989, troops loyal to China's top leadership were ordered to clear pro-democracy protestors from Tiananmen Square in Beijing. The protests, led initially by students but later joined by a variety of pro-reform groups, had gone on for several weeks. Hunger strikes, antigovernment speeches and slogans, revolutionary songs from rock musicians, and the erection of a "Goddess of Liberty" statue (patterned, to some extent, on the U.S. Statue of Liberty) helped to maintain enthusiasm for the protests and drew larger crowds.

Nervous government officials, unwilling to compromise and convinced that the protests presented a threat to the very existence of the regime, imposed martial law. As troops implemented their orders, events began to spiral out of control. Military vehicles were blocked, and in some cases were overturned and set ablaze by angry protestors. Rocks were thrown by the crowds and troops responded with sporadic gunfire. As the violence escalated, dozens of troops and hundreds of protestors ultimately perished in what has become known around the world as the "Tiananmen massacre." Thus China ushered in the post–Cold War era with an act of bloodshed that raised significant doubts about its capacity to function as a responsible member of the global community.

External Factors

The international system has, as theorist Ken Waltz argues, the capacity to "shape and shove" the choices made by foreign policy decision makers.[22] Yet as Chapter 1 of this volume points out, no consensus exists within international relations theory on the precise nature of the system. The debate includes realists, who depict a world of security-driven, "self-help" states operating under anarchy, and liberals, who emphasize the role of institutions in establishing rules and norms of international behavior. Both can make a compelling case about Chinese foreign policy.

The realist view of an anarchic global system with its concerns about power distribution, sovereignty, and use of force is certainly relevant to China. For all practical purposes, Chinese foreign policy makers devoted much of the Cold War period to challenging the bipolar distribution of power. Lacking sufficient resources and reputation to be considered a superpower on a par with the United States and Soviet Union, the Chinese nonetheless took advantage of opportunities to join the power game. Indeed, the nonaligned movement was, in essence, an attempt by China and a host of other developing world middle powers to balance U.S. and Soviet domination. During the 1970s, the Chinese elevated the balancing technique to a high art form, successfully gaining concessions by playing to the worst fears of the superpowers.

In more recent times, tensions with the United States demonstrate the continuing relevance of realist explanations. In a 1995–1996 confrontation involving the United States and Taiwan, all the classic concepts associated with realpolitik (deterrence, coercive diplomacy, brinkmanship) were on display. In the spring of 2001, the Chinese downing of an American spy plane conducting surveillance off the southern coast of China garnered international headlines. Although the U.S. crew was ultimately released after tense negotiations, the episode resulted in an exchange of heated rhetoric and harsh accusations between the two governments. When it comes to defending against threats to its territorial integrity, China clearly operates as a self-help state in an anarchic world.

At first blush, the liberal world of interdependence, idealism, and institutions appears unlikely to apply to Chinese foreign policy. China is a tough customer, not predisposed to embrace warm and fuzzy commitments to cooperation, collaborative decision-making procedures, or global ethical norms. Yet aside from the sensitive issue of territorial integrity, China's post–Cold War foreign policy has been surprisingly accommodating to liberal institutionalism, and China's membership in international organizations has expanded significantly in the post–Cold War era.[23] Indeed, China has demonstrated an interest in becoming part of the global community.

Liberals use terms such as *institutionalism* and *global governance* to describe the phenomenon of cooperation among sovereign states as they monitor, regulate, and enforce the international system.[24] But why should a powerful state such as China submit to rules made by international organizations?[25] The answer is that China has a variety of pragmatic, even self-interested reasons for institutional cooperation. First, participation in an international institution can be a condition for receiving benefits. For example, if China wishes to receive financial support from the International Monetary Fund or World Bank, membership is required. Thus China joined both organizations in 1980 and has since become the World Bank's largest borrower.[26] Second, because international organizations have become more central to a range of significant policy issues (including security), it is only natural that China would seek to exercise its power in these forums if only to block the influence of other states such as the United States. China has played a decidedly more prominent role in the UN Security Council since the end of the Cold War, in part to help discourage collective security measures that violate national sovereignty. As the old adage goes, only those who play the game get to make the rules. Finally, institutional participation can be used to deflect criticism. How can China be accused of insensitivity to human rights, for example, when it is party to such a significant number of human rights institutions, treaties, and covenants?

Of course, the flip side of institutional participation is that once in, it is difficult to remain free from commitments or entanglements. Chinese diplomats are forced to defend their country's issue positions in a variety of formal and informal institutions. Although China is perfectly willing and able to reject some institutional demands (for example, it frequently abstains in UN Security Council votes to signal "principled opposition"), the sheer force of constant involvement leads to compromises and agreements.[27] Institutional involvement also places greater decision-making latitude in the hands of China's growing foreign policy bureaucracy rather than restricting it to a few top-level leaders.[28] As much as Chinese decision makers might prefer unilateral action and bilateral diplomacy (and to exercise these options when possible), multilateralism has become a dominant feature of the post–Cold War world.

Internal Factors

Few political systems operate in the tidy fashion outlined in their written constitutions or organizational hierarchies. China is no exception. In principle, Chinese foreign policy has been the result of the collective leadership operating in formal institutions such as the Politburo, the policy-making body of China's Communist Party. In practice, however, China's foreign policy has been driven by strong-willed individual leaders, compromises among party factions, battles between various bureaucratic entities, or a combination of these factors.

Leadership Beliefs

The role of the "paramount leader" was significant in Chinese foreign policy under Mao and Deng. These strong-willed leaders were able to think in strategic terms about the Chinese role in world affairs and could initiate rather substantial shifts in policy without extensive resistance from either the party elite or the general public. Although quite different in their personalities and ideological commitments, both Mao and Deng played a dominant role in foreign policy making not likely to be seen again in China's political system.

One of the towering historical figures of the twentieth century, Mao is the classic example of a revolutionary leader who, upon gaining power, must make a transition to the role of a more orthodox political leader. Mao's life as a rebel began early. In contrast to the norms of Confucian respect for elders, he was a rebellious child who often confronted his father and frequently ran away from home. One of the founders of the Chinese Communist Party, Mao spent his early years organizing support for the party among the peasants, outlining an ideological blueprint for the future of socialism in China, living underground with his fellow revolutionaries, and helping lead the communists to victory in 1949. Restless in the role of day-to-day management of Chinese policy, he spent much of his time redefining the governing ideology, rooting out political enemies (real or imagined), and punishing them.

Philosophically committed to the idea of a permanent, ongoing revolution, Mao was responsible for initiating drastic (and often destabilizing) shifts in domestic policy. The Great Leap Forward, intended to boost industry and agricultural production in the 1950s, and the Cultural Revolution of the late 1960s and early 1970s, intended to rekindle the spirit of the revolution of 1949, were both also aimed at producing a dramatic restructuring of political and economic power in China. But both were undertaken at tremendous cost to the ordinary citizens as well as the policy elite of China. The Great Leap Forward, for example, involved radical experimentation in agricultural production and resulted in a devastating famine that cost millions of Chinese lives.[29]

Relying on his charisma and ability to mobilize public support from the masses, Mao often cast himself in the role of the outsider doing battle with entrenched bureaucrats and outmoded policies. The Great Proletarian Cultural Revolution of the late 1960s and early 1970s was one such example of his efforts to abolish all vestiges of orthodoxy. Aligning himself with the nation's most ideologically zealous youth (the "Red Guard"), Mao initiated a campaign of criticism against high-ranking party officials. The punishment inflicted on the Communist Party elite during the Cultural Revolution included personal humiliation, loss of job and status, torture, imprisonment, and death. Deng Xiaopeng, who ultimately emerged as China's paramount leader after Mao's death, was among the targets of the Cultural Revolution. Like many other top-ranking officials, Deng was stripped of his formal title and sentenced to hard labor in the countryside. Later, however, he was "rehabilitated" when the ideological pendulum swung back in his direction.

The precise impact of Mao's beliefs and personality on Chinese foreign policy is difficult to gauge. It is clear, though, that Mao's personal animosity and ideological differences with Soviet leaders contributed to the Sino-Soviet split, and that his own more radical version of Marxism led to official Chinese support for revolutionary movements throughout the developing world. The internal chaos resulting from his periodic campaigns reinforced suspicions about China in the eyes of other world leaders and no doubt discouraged some from greater cooperation. Yet Mao's stature and remarkable political authority allowed him to shift Chinese foreign policy toward cooperation with the United States after his historic meeting with Richard Nixon.

Compared with Mao, Deng "saw the international system as a source of more opportunity than danger, and he was more inclined toward cooperation than confrontation in pursuing national interests."[30] Although Deng, like Mao, participated directly in the 1949 revolution, he was a younger, more pragmatic politician. Lacking Mao's capacity for rousing the masses, Deng managed instead to become a more adept negotiator and coalition builder within the party and government bureaucracy.[31]

Deng never abandoned Marxist ideology (and, in fact, relied on it heavily to justify the maintenance of a party-driven political system), but he was willing to put it aside from time to time in the interest of results-oriented reform. A famous observation attributed to Deng is that "it does not matter if the cat is black or white, as long as it catches mice." His pragmatism clearly appealed to foreign leaders interested in improving relations with China. Deng's personal commitment to economic reform also helped to propel China further into active participation in world affairs.

The dominant personality and influence of "paramount leaders" such as Mao and Deng have begun to disappear from the scene as more technocratic leaders such as today's Jiang Zemin have assumed leadership. In some respects a protégé of Deng, Jiang rose to political power as mayor of Shanghai, one of China's largest and most cosmopolitan cities. Like most of his counterparts within the top echelon of Chinese leadership, Jiang received a technical education (in his case a degree in electrical engineering). He devoted most of his career to the practical realm of factory management and public administration rather than the study of political philosophy.[32]

Party and State

In contrast to countries such as Germany and India where coalition building in a multiparty system is a key phase of foreign policy making, Chinese leaders deal with only one party. The Chinese Communist Party (CCP) has had a monopoly on power for decades. Traditionally, the multilayered institutions of the CCP have been interconnected with the various levels of government institutions in a relationship sometimes called "vertical and dual rule." In China, the foreign policy battles take place *within* the party rather than *between* parties.

The familiar pattern of the past few decades has been that few government decisions are made without the approval of the CCP hierarchy (many of whom occupy prominent positions in both party and government). The relationship between the military and party leadership, for example, has until recent years been reinforced by an officer corps made up of party members whose loyalty is supposed to be to the party rather than to the military as an institution.[33]

The contemporary debate about foreign policy within China's leadership circle is conducted over a limited spectrum. At one end are hard-line conservatives who are concerned about excessive political and economic reforms. They fear the effects of increased globalization and the unwelcome side effects of consumerism and exposure to Western ideals. At the other end are moderates who see advantages in global markets but are nonetheless hesitant to support political liberalization.[34] Thus even within the party hierarchy differences exist and are played out among the various coalitions and informal groups that emerge around significant foreign policy issues.[35]

In an era of rapid economic modernization and incremental political reforms, the CCP is struggling to remain relevant. Party theoreticians are straining to incorporate new social and economic phenomena (such as a rising middle class that includes profit-driven young professionals) into the traditional language of socialist ideology.[36] Ultimately, the role of party ideologues may be reduced in favor of technocrats and specialists. The long-running tension in Chinese elite politics between "reds" (doctrinaire party loyalists) and "experts" (technically trained specialists who are often more pragmatic in their political views) extends to foreign policy. Deng's push for military modernization during the 1980s, for example, placed more emphasis on technical competence than on ideological commitment. Thus after the People's Liberation Army (PLA) opened itself to study other military organizations around the world, the professional officer corps that emerged in China had a more apolitical view of the military's mission. The PLA's initial reluctance to use lethal force against the Tiananmen Square demonstrators made some officers subject to investigation and punishment for perceived disloyalty to the party.[37]

The role, strength, and vitality of the Chinese Communist Party also may be changing. A top-level insider offers this rather sobering assessment:

[The CCP] is now a melange of factions with diverse goals and differing ideologies. The differences between radicals and conservatives in the Party are now sharper than those between the Party and its traditional rival the Kuomintang. The Chinese Communist Party resembles the Communist Party of the Soviet Union around 1989. What looks on the outside like a solid structure can break into pieces overnight.[38]

The truth of such a claim is difficult to assess from outside the Chinese system. Yet, if valid, it illustrates the sensitive nature of foreign policy making for China's elite. A controversial foreign policy challenge, such as dealing with Taiwan, has the potential to unite members of various factions around a common purpose, or it may exacerbate intraparty conflicts to the point where the continued existence of the CCP is threatened.

Bureaucratic Politics

When Chinese decision makers do not agree on the substance or direction of foreign policy, those disagreements often play themselves out within the foreign policy bureaucracy. Competition for turf and influence by rival bureaucracies appears to pervade the Chinese foreign policy system.

Two trends have placed more emphasis on bureaucratic politics in Chinese foreign policy over the past decade. First, foreign policy issues have become more complex and numerous. Thus as China joins more institutions, expresses more formal opinions on significant world issues, and finds itself increasingly challenged to defend itself in more international forums, it requires an expanding staff of foreign policy experts to meet its needs. Second, the absence of a paramount leader with the stature of Mao or Deng opens up the possibility for more open clashes between various bureaucratic rivals.[39]

Especially noteworthy is the history of clashes between the Ministry of Foreign Affairs (MFA) and the People's Liberation Army over the direction of China's strategic doctrine as well as its more day-to-day tactical policy decisions. In recent years, the PLA has emerged as a more independent voice in establishing security policy. The PLA owes its independence in part to the fact that fewer high-ranking military leaders than in the early days can trace their roots to the revolutionary struggle.[40] Moreover, organizational affiliation influences policy preferences. As defenders of China's security, for example, the PLA is more likely to take a hard line on issues such as Taiwan or other territorial disputes.[41]

The contemporary foreign policy and national security process of the PRC is not highly integrated or systematic. Lower-level operations with highly routine structures are frequently conducted on "automatic pilot" by those closest to the operation. Yet many senior-level decision makers work on the basis of personal relationships (known as *guanxi*), various overlapping small groups, and (where present) the dominant voice of a paramount leader.[42]

Contemporary Chinese Foreign Policy

The end of the Cold War coincided with the Tiananmen Square episode, but it is difficult to say which event had more profound short-term consequences for Chinese foreign policy. The Tiananmen Square massacre was an abrupt interruption to increasingly normalized relations with the West. The event elevated the more conservative leadership domestically and caused a return to limited isolation in foreign policy. Yet, once again, the politics of self-interest among great powers appears to have trumped concerns about ideology or human rights. China's profound importance as a trading partner and its necessary inclusion on issues such as arms control and multilateral intervention made most governments eager to move past the Tiananmen episode. President Bill Clinton, for example, once a strong opponent of China's human rights policy, steadfastly refused to impose U.S. economic sanctions on China once he assumed office. By the mid-1990s, China had taken steps to produce a more engaged, moderate foreign policy and repair some of the damage done by the Tiananmen affair.

The end of the Cold War has proved to have more lasting consequences for China than the Tiananmen Square massacre. The collapse of communism in the Soviet Union and Eastern Europe diminished the utility of any "strategic triangle" diplomacy by Beijing and also minimized Chinese fears of a Soviet threat. Furthermore, the end of the Cold War reduced the potential of a major war for China, but increased the potential of limited wars near its border or in other areas that would demand a Chinese response.[43] The Persian Gulf War provided an opportunity for China to demonstrate a neutral (and even constructive, cooperative) role in international diplomacy. China did not, in fact, utilize its UN Security Council veto power to disrupt the functioning of the Gulf War coalition. The Chinese government seems to have warmed to multilateral diplomatic cooperation in more recent international disputes as well, although it remains concerned about setting dangerous precedents in UN-sponsored interventions that violate state sovereignty.[44] China's vocal opposition to the UN sanctions policy toward Iraq (a position shared by Russia and France, among others) indicates a willingness to challenge the United States in multilateral forums.[45]

Weapons Proliferation

China is a significant player in the realm of international weapons proliferation and arms control by virtue of several factors. China is a member of the Permanent Five of the UN Security Council, a declared nuclear state, and a producer of equipment, materials, and technology for nuclear and chemical weapons. Moreover, China has been active in the global sales of weapons-related technology to enhance the nuclear programs of countries such as Pakistan.

Possessing weapons of mass destruction helps China to maintain its reputation as a global and regional power. Yet China's regional neighbors include three declared nuclear powers (Russia, India, and Pakistan), a country widely suspected of having an active nuclear program (North Korea), and two close allies of the United States (Japan and South Korea, protected by the U.S. "nuclear umbrella"), making China's status as a nuclear power hardly unique. Nevertheless, the lack of transparency in Chinese decision making gives pause to the global arms control community. As Swaine and Johnston point out, "Officially, China states that it does not possess chemical or biological weapons, that its nuclear weapons are entirely for self-defense, and that its efforts to improve its nuclear weapons are focused entirely on improvements in warhead safety, reliability, and survivability."[46]

China's involvement in arms control institutions is inconsistent. Not surprisingly, the government prefers "free riding"—that is, supporting reductions in the arsenals of other states while successfully resisting actual reductions in its own arsenal.[47] Nevertheless, the Chinese position on arms control has evolved in ways that bring its policy closer to the norms established by other major powers. Once a harsh critic of the Nuclear Non-proliferation Treaty (NPT) on the grounds that it discriminated against small states at the expense of larger nuclear powers, China switched its policy in 1991.[48]

Although China is clearly a contributor to global arms proliferation, it could be argued that China is merely playing by the great-power "rules of the game" for the post–Cold War era. China's arms sales to Pakistan illustrate this point. Its transfer of M-11 missiles to Pakistan came after a controversial U.S. sale of F-16 fighter jets to Taiwan.[49] But China's efforts to strengthen its relationship with Pakistan make sense when viewed as a balance-of-power policy toward India with whom the PRC shares a 2,500-mile border and history of tension.[50] China also has strong commercial incentives to participate in the global arms market. Its willingness to sell weapons to unsavory regimes such as Myanmar has earned it few friends in the international arms control community, but has earned it some export revenue.

The Global Economy

Since the Deng era of economic reform in the late 1970s, China has taken steps to become more integrated in the global economy. Chinese leaders learned a lesson from the disintegration of their Soviet neighbor and vowed to focus primarily on economic competition in pursuing their post–Cold War foreign policy. National strength is increasingly measured in terms of economic growth and technological advancement.[51]

Deng's immediate challenge upon assuming power was to search for a means of moving China away from its reliance on Soviet-style, state-run heavy industry characterized by gross inefficiency and disconnection from market forces. Inevitably, economic reform also required moving beyond China's borders to become connected with global economic activity. At first, Chinese leaders intentionally limited outward expansion. For example, Deng established "special economic zones" in 1979 to attract foreign direct investment, but only in China's coastal regions (and by extension prominent commercial cities such as Shanghai) and not in the rural interior of the country. Opening to the West also meant sending some of China's best and brightest students abroad, often to study at American universities. Exposure to international commerce and education had immediate social consequences. The appearance on the streets of Chinese cities of women with makeup, young men in blue jeans, and teenagers of both genders with a taste for rock music, drugs, premarital sex, and other "Western" practices clashed with the puritanical ethic of Maoism that still prevailed despite the revolutionary economic innovations of the eighties.[52]

Deng's political opponents frequently cited such examples of "spiritual pollution" when attempting to restrict or reduce Chinese participation in global economic affairs. Although never a member of the General Agreement on Tariffs and Trade (GATT), China was allowed to benefit from the liberal trade policies of countries such as the United States through "most-favored nation" status.[53] China's desire to become a member of GATT's successor, the World Trade Organization (WTO), created in 1994, would seem to mark its full-fledged commitment to the magic of the global marketplace. China has sought membership in GATT/WTO since at least 1986. Yet thorny issues such as the domestic political and economic costs of liberalization (for example, massive unemployment resulting from the privatization of former state-owned industries), long-running disputes over intellectual property, and the potentially intrusive demands of transparency associated with WTO membership have not been fully resolved.[54]

The success of China's involvement in the global economy creates political risks for the country's leadership. For example, increased contact between China's outer provinces and the rest of the world weakens the central authority of Beijing.[55] The presence of foreign-owned multinational corporations in China brings with it a host of decision-making practices that run counter to party doctrine and domestic political institutions. For example, the leadership practices, habits of information sharing, and emphasis on merit-based hiring and promotion within multinational corporations might spill over into China's social and political realm. The creation of a "meritocracy cadre" (that is, a new social class of young Chinese leaders whose success is based on their own efforts and skills rather than obedience to party officials) could have profound implications for democracy and personal liberty in China.[56]

The internal debates over meeting the conditions for membership in international economic institutions have provided opportunities for savvy domestic reformers. For example, the arduous negotiations between China and the United States over the permanent normalization of trade relations (a necessary step toward Chinese entry into the World Trade Organization) led to a sharp internal debate between pro-reform and anti-reform factions of the Chinese leadership. Prime Minister Zhu Rongji, considered one of the strongest advocates of economic liberalization, represented China during most of the bilateral negotiations with the United States in 1999. Although Zhu had the blessing of President Jiang Zemin, he nonetheless faced harsh opposition from opponents of lib-eralization such as National People's Congress chairman Li Peng. Indeed, during the most difficult phases of the negotiations, Zhu was being pressed for economic concessions by the American team, while also facing tough criticism at home. He was privately rebuked by high-ranking party foes and publicly castigated in the government-controlled press. As he pushed for greater concessions to meet U.S. demands, Zhu even found himself being compared to the Chinese puppet gov-ernments that collaborated with Japanese imperialists in the early twentieth cen-tury.[57]

Yet Prime Minister Zhu ultimately prevailed over his domestic rivals in a way that illustrates the concept of "two-level games."[58] Negotiators who move between domestic and international arenas often find they can play one group off against another. When confronted by tough demands from the U.S. negotiators (for example, for major concessions on trade in agricultural goods), Zhu could emphasize the formidable nature of his domestic opposition on this point. Yet when bargaining with his bureaucratic rivals in China, Zhu could feign sympa-thy but note the intractable nature of trade rules emanating from global institu-tions. China's desperate need for access to global markets gave Zhu leverage to hasten the pace of privatization of state-owned industries, a move he favored anyway. In short, international institutions can sometimes serve as a convenient excuse for making tough domestic changes.

Human Rights

China's human rights record remains the target of intense international scrutiny and criticism. Unlike its progress in the economic arena, China's formal participation in international institutions has produced little in the way of signif-icant human rights reform in China. Accounts by high-profile dissidents such as Wei Jingsheng (author of the memoir *The Courage to Stand Alone*) have helped to publicize the unsavory practices of the Chinese government. Religious persecu-tion, the significant use of prison "education through labor" programs for dissi-dents, the lack of due process in the criminal justice system, and the periodic crackdowns on democratic reform movements (such as the recent response of the government to efforts to organize an opposition political party and to the spiri-tual group Falun Gong) are among the most notable human rights problems.

China's troubled history with Tibet is perhaps the most widely known human rights issue, thanks to the activities of nongovernmental human rights organiza-tions around the world. The Tibetan Autonomous Region (TAR) is located in the remote mountainous area of southwestern China bordering India and Nepal. This area is the historical and cultural home of Tibetan Buddhism and represents the most visible example of China's poor relationship with its various minority (that is, non-Han) populations. Soon after the communists came to power in China, Tibet was occupied by the Chinese military and forced to sign the infa-mous "Seventeen Point Agreement" in which considerable power was ceded to the Chinese government. An attempted rebellion in 1959 led to a brutal government response by the People's Liberation Army. Thousands of Tibetan rebels were killed, and several thousand more (including the spiritual leader, the Dalai Lama) fled to India to escape death or imprisonment.[59]

The decades since then have seen periodic bouts of state violence against Tibetan citizens, the destruction of religious sites, the forced migration of non-Tibetan ethnic groups into the region, and a concerted effort by the PRC to erase Tibet's cultural identity. The Tibetan exile community has successfully garnered the sympathy and support of human rights activists around the world. Chinese leaders, on the other hand, have compounded the negative international reaction to the Tibetan situation by repeatedly framing their government's actions in terms of "liberation" of a backward feudal society. During a highly publicized trip to the United States in 1997, Jiang Zemin compared China's actions in Tibet to Abraham Lincoln's freeing of the slaves during the American Civil War.[60]

Why does Tibet remain important to China? It constitutes a buffer zone between China and India, it is a source of natural resources, and it represents a dangerous precedent. If Tibet is granted independence, some of the other fifty-five ethnic minority groups within China might press for the same rights.[61]

Although China is actively involved in the global human rights regime through institutions such as the UN Human Rights Commission, it is unclear how willing the Chinese are to compromise in this most sensitive area of national sovereignty. In addition to disputes about sovereignty, the debate has often hinged on competing definitions of human rights — that is, do "Asian values" allow for a different interpretation of rights than those promoted by Western critics?

Regional Relationships

China figures centrally in any discussion of security in the Asia-Pacific region. China's size, military arsenal, and economic prowess make a compelling case for nominating it the regional leader. Indeed, because of its central location, China has territorial interests that coincide directly with those of twenty-four other governments.[62]

As in other issue domains, China utilizes a combination of bilateral and multilateral diplomacy in pursuing regional interests. It places high value on the mutual relationships among China, the United States, and Japan (sometimes referred to as the "new triangle") and tends to pursue these relationships through bilateral means. On a multilateral level, after the Cold War, China strengthened its ties to ASEAN (Association of Southeast Asian Nations), the most prominent regional organization, by moving from consultative/observer status to full participation in annual summits. China also participated in the complicated effort to sort out Cambodia's security and political situation during the 1990s. It cooperated with the United Nations Transitional Authority in Cambodia (UNTAC), providing political and economic support as well as a small engineering battalion as part of the peacekeeping operation.[63]

The most significant regional issue involves China's history of territorial disputes. Since the transfer of Hong Kong from British to Chinese rule in 1997, the world community has monitored China closely for signs of its willingness to abide by treaty obligations and international norms when incorporating territory. Every British government since that of Prime Minister Margaret Thatcher had signaled its willingness to follow through with the transfer (see Chapter 2 on Britain). The years leading up to 1997 were filled with a flurry of diplomatic activity to ensure that the freedoms gained by Hong Kong citizens under the last few years of British rule would be maintained by the PRC. Although promises were made, ultimately no iron-clad guarantees were established. The transfer was heralded with much celebration by PRC officials (and even many in Hong Kong) who viewed it as a long overdue end to British colonial rule. Christopher Patten, the last British governor of the territory, described the situation less optimistically by noting that Hong Kong was "the only example of decolonization deliberately accompanied by less democracy and a weaker protection of civil liberties. This was a cause for profound regret, especially for the departing colonial power. But it was China's doing and China's decision."[64]

The long-simmering debate over Taiwan (and the "one-China" policy) appears less amenable to peaceful resolution given the PRC's belligerency and Taiwan's feisty independence. Because of its recent strides in economic development and democratization, Taiwan is now in a better position, compared with that in the early years after the revolution on the mainland, to call for national self-determination.[65]

Taiwan is, by any objective measure, an independent sovereign state. As noted earlier, leaders of the Chinese nationalist forces (KMT) fled to the island of Taiwan following their defeat in the Chinese civil war of the late 1940s. In the decades that followed, Taiwan emerged as an "Asian Tiger" with the quintessential combination of a high-growth economy and an authoritarian political structure. During the 1990s, Taiwan underwent a gradual transition to multiparty popular elections and can now rightfully claim to be the more democratic and prosperous of the two Chinas.

To the PRC, however, Taiwan remains a wayward province destined to return home to its mother country but for the continued interference by outside powers. All states that wish to maintain a working relationship with China must accept this version of Taiwan's status or risk conflict. A March 1996 confrontation between China and Taiwan demonstrated how quickly differences can escalate in the "cross-straits" dispute. In an attempt to influence the outcome of Taiwanese elections, the PRC engaged in a series of military threats involving naval exercises (such as a simulated amphibious assault on Taiwan) and missile tests. The action provoked an immediate response by both Taiwan (which engaged in its own series of military exercises) and the United States (which deployed two aircraft carriers to the region).[66]

The relationship between China and the two Koreas is complicated by the fact that great-power interests collide in northeast Asia. Although China remains one of North Korea's only true allies, it is clear that Chinese leaders have some contempt for the regime and fear the consequences of an active North Korean nuclear program.[67] Militancy and aggression by North Korea toward South Korea, for example, could easily escalate into a great-power conflict involving Japan, Russia, and the United States.[68] China seems to want no part of this, but it is unclear how much control it can exert over its erstwhile communist ally North Korea.

As for other areas of Asia, China remains vigilant about threats to territory and sovereignty. Indochina poses no immediate threat to Chinese security in the post–Cold War world, but instability there could produce long-term negative consequences. As Nathan and Ross observe, "Geography forces China to see the region much as America sees Latin America or Russia sees Eastern Europe."[69] Both China and Russia, for example, have a common interest in preventing the spread of Islamic fundamentalism from Central Asia.[70]

In some ways, China's preoccupation with territorial disputes , such as the one with Taiwan over the Spratley Islands, seems misplaced. Why does one of the world's largest countries care about a few square miles of island territory with little economic value? Quite clearly the explanation involves precedent: compromise on small territorial issues might reduce China's credibility for driving a hard bargain when it comes to larger claims.[71] In the case of Taiwan, the stakes are obviously higher than the Spratley Islands, yet fear of setting a bad example continues to guide Chinese decision makers. If the Taiwan issue were settled in favor of complete independence, it would be difficult to stop the momentum for a similar deal in places such as Tibet or Inner Mongolia.[72]

Conclusion

Few of China's most significant national goals, whether economic prosperity or military security, can be achieved without active participation in world affairs. Absolute isolation is not a viable option in Chinese foreign policy. Involvement in world affairs, however, can be undertaken with various levels of enthusiasm, commitment, and sincerity. Is China truly interested in a full-fledged partnership with other active members of the community of nations?

The Chinese case tests scholarly assumptions about the power and influence of international institutions. Once China is entangled in global trade agreements, human rights covenants, or arms control treaties, is it inevitable that its autonomy in foreign policy will be eroded? Can global institutions shape Chinese foreign policy behavior, or will they be influenced (and perhaps stymied) by an assertive China seeking exceptions and loopholes?

China's willingness to become more integrated within the global community of nations coincides with Chinese leaders' insistence on maintaining a somewhat iconoclastic role in international affairs. More than likely, the country's foreign policy leadership will endeavor to have the best of both worlds for as long as such a strategy is feasible.

Suggestions for Further Reading

Economy, Elizabeth, and Michel Oksenberg, eds. *China Joins the World: Progress and Prospects.* New York: Council on Foreign Relations, 1999.

Gilley, Bruce. *Tiger on the Brink: Jiang Zemin and China's New Elite.* Berkeley: University of California Press, 1998.

Hung-mao Tien and Yun-han Chu. *China under Jiang Zemin.* Boulder: Lynne Rienner, 2000.

Nathan, Andrew J., and Robert S. Ross. *The Great Wall and the Empty Fortress: China's Search for Security.* New York: Norton, 1997.

Patten, Christopher. *East and West: China, Power, and the Future of Asia.* New York: Times Books/Random House, 1999.

Roy, Denny. *China's Foreign Relations.* Lanham, Md.: Rowman and Littlefield, 1998.

Wei Jingsheng. *The Courage to Stand Alone: Letters from Prison and Other Writings.* New York: Penguin Books, 1998.

Yong Deng and Fei-Ling Wang, eds. *In the Eyes of the Dragon: China Views the World.* Lanham, Md.: Rowman and Littlefield, 1999.

Zhang Liang, Andrew Nathan, and Perry Link, eds. *The Tiananmen Papers.* New York: Public Affairs, 2001.

Notes

1. Wu Xinbo, "China: Security Practice of a Modernizing and Ascending Power," in *Asian Security Practice: Material and Ideational Influences,* ed. Muthiah Alagappa (Stanford: Stanford University Press, 1998), 123–124.
2. Andrew J. Nathan and Robert S. Ross, *The Great Wall and the Empty Fortress: China's Search for Security* (New York: Norton, 1997), 16. See Chapter 1 of this book for a classic geopolitical assessment of China's foreign policy situation since World War II.
3. Michael Mandelbaum, *The Fate of Nations: The Search for National Security in the Nineteenth and Twentieth Centuries* (Cambridge: Cambridge University Press, 1988).
4. Michel Oksenberg, "China: A Tortuous Path onto the World's Stage," in *A Century's Journey,* ed. Robert A. Pastor (New York: Basic Books, 1999), 295–298.
5. Wu Xinbo, "China"; and Nathan and Ross, *Great Wall and the Empty Fortress,* 26–34.
6. Nathan and Ross, *Great Wall and the Empty Fortress,* 34.
7. Chi Wang, "Maoist China," in *China: A Nation in Transition,* ed. Deborah E. Soled (Washington, D.C.: CQ Press, 1995), 79.
8. Denny Roy, *China's Foreign Relations* (Lanham, Md.: Rowman and Littlefield, 1998), 18–19.
9. William R. Keylor, *The Twentieth-Century World,* 4th ed. (New York: Oxford University Press, 2001), 357.
10. Taiwan, known formally as the Republic of China, was established in 1949, when two million Kuomintang supporters fled mainland China during the civil war. Taiwan's status as the "other China" is described more fully later in this chapter.
11. During the years immediately after World War II, the Truman administration gradually adopted a strategic doctrine known as containment. The essence of containment was to stop communist (primarily Soviet) expansion in Europe and Asia through use of diplomacy, economic leverage, and military force if necessary. The Korean War in 1950 provided a major test of the U.S. commitment to this strategy.
12. Chi Wang, "Maoist China," 79.
13. Keylor, *Twentieth-Century World,* 361.
14. The nonaligned movement emerged in the 1950s through the support of nationalist leaders from newly decolonized nations such as India, Indonesia, and Egypt. Osten-

sibly, countries sought through nonalignment to adopt an independent foreign policy and avoid joining either the U.S.-led Western or Soviet-led Eastern camps of the Cold War. The nonaligned movement also provided a source of solidarity for developing countries in expressing their concerns about the global economic policy and the remnants of colonialism.

15. Wu Xinbo, "China," 119; and Roy, *China's Foreign Relations*, 20–21.
16. Keylor, *Twentieth-Century World*, 364–365.
17. Ibid., 378.
18. Ibid., 376–377.
19. Nathan and Ross, *Great Wall and the Empty Fortress*, 66–67.
20. Wei Jingsheng, "Democracy: The Fifth Modernization," reprinted in Wei Jingsheng, *The Courage to Stand Alone: Letters from Prison and Other Writings* (New York: Penguin Books, 2000).
21. Keylor, *Twentieth-Century World*, 444.
22. Kenneth N. Waltz, "Reflections on *Theory of International Politics*: A Response to My Critics," in *Neorealism and Its Critics*, ed. Robert O. Keohane (New York: Columbia University Press, 1986).
23. Samuel S. Kim, "China and the United Nations," in *China Joins the World: Progress and Prospects*, ed. Elizabeth Economy and Michel Oksenberg (New York: Council on Foreign Relations Press, 1999).
24. See, for example, Lisa A. Martin and Beth A. Simmons, "Theories and Empirical Studies of International Institutions," *International Organization* 52 (1998): 729–757; and Oran R. Young, *Governance in World Affairs* (Ithaca: Cornell University Press, 1999).
25. For one answer, see Kenneth W. Abbott and Duncan Snidal, "Why States Act through Formal International Organizations," *Journal of Conflict Resolution* 42 (1998): 3–32.
26. Nicholas R. Lardy, "China and the International Financial System," in *China Joins the World: Progress and Prospects*, ed. Elizabeth Economy and Michel Oksenberg (New York: Council on Foreign Relations Press, 1999), 206.
27. See Kim, "China and the United Nations."
28. Oksenberg, "China."
29. Jasper Becker, *Hungry Ghosts: Mao's Secret Famine* (New York: Free Press, 1996).
30. Wu Xinbo, "China," 122.
31. Lowell Dittmer, "Informal Politics among the Chinese Communist Party Elite," in *Informal Politics in East Asia*, ed. Lowell Dittmer, Haruhiro Fukui, and Peter N. S. Lee (Cambridge: Cambridge University Press, 2000), 128.
32. See, for example, his biography by Bruce Gilley, *Tiger on the Brink: Jiang Zemin and China's New Elite* (Berkeley: University of California Press, 1998).
33. Paul H. B. Godwin, "Party-Military Relations," in *The Paradox of China's Post-Mao Reforms*, ed. Merle Goldman and Roderick MacFarquar (Cambridge: Harvard University Press, 1999), 76–99.
34. Roy, *China's Foreign Relations*, 67–68.
35. Susan V. Lawrence, "Three Cheers for the Party," *Far Eastern Economic Review*, October 26, 2000, 32–35.
36. See, for example, the contributions to the edited volume *Informal Politics in East Asia* (New York: Cambridge University Press, 2000) for a discussion of the variety of ways informal relationships and small groups emerge within elite policy-making circles across Asia.
37. Godwin, "Party-Military Relations," 81–82.
38. Zhang Liang, "Preface," in *The Tiananmen Papers*, ed. Andrew J. Nathan and Perry Link (New York: Public Affairs, 2001), xiii.

39. See Michael D. Swaine, *The Role of the Chinese Military in National Security Policy-making*, rev. ed. (Santa Monica, Calif.: Rand Corporation, 1998), for an overview of the foreign policy process especially as it relates to national security.
40. Godwin, "Party-Military Relations," 77; and Wu Xinbo, "China," 139.
41. Wu Xinbo, "China," 139.
42. Swaine, *Role of the Chinese Military*, 73.
43. Wu Xinbo, "China," 135.
44. Jianwei Wang, "Managing Conflict: Chinese Perspectives on Multilateral Diplomacy and Collective Security," in *In the Eyes of the Dragon: China Views the World*, ed. Yong Deng and Fei-Ling Wang (Lanham, Md.: Rowman and Littlefield, 1999).
45. See, for example, Richard Butler's account of Chinese diplomacy and arms inspections of Iraq in *The Greatest Threat* (New York: Public Affairs, 2000), 165–167.
46. Michael D. Swaine and Alastair Iain Johnston, "China and Arms Control Institutions," in *China Joins the World: Progress and Prospects*, ed. Elizabeth Economy and Michel Oksenberg (New York: Council on Foreign Relations Press, 1999), 96.
47. Ibid., 118–119.
48. Weixing Hu, "Nuclear Nonproliferation," in *The Eyes of the Dragon: China Views the World*, ed. Yong Deng and Fei-Ling Wang (Lanham, Md.: Rowman and Littlefield, 1999). The author makes the case that Chinese elites may have experienced "learning" within the realm of nonproliferation, thus bolstering an internal or decision-making explanation of foreign policy.
49. Nathan and Ross, *Great Wall and the Empty Fortress*, 75.
50. Ibid., 118.
51. Wu Xinbo, "China. "
52. Keylor, *Twentieth-Century World*, 442.
53. Under the rules of GATT, member countries such as the United States could elect to treat nonmember countries (such as China) as if they were GATT members, thus exempting China from a variety of tariffs. The effect was to open up U.S. markets to Chinese-produced goods. The term *most-favored nation* was something of a misnomer, because it merely meant treating China the same as other GATT members. The periodic decision by the U.S. president and Congress about whether to extend most-favored-nation status to China was the occasion for internal debates in the United States about Chinese human rights abuses and arms control violations, because threatening to withhold MFN status was a bargaining chip with the Chinese government.
54. Dan Biers, "On Second Thought . . . ," *Far Eastern Economic Review*, February 22, 2001, 48–50.
55. Roy, *China's Foreign Relations*.
56. Michael A. Santoro, "Global Capitalism and the Road to Chinese Democracy," *Current History* (September 2000): 263–267.
57. Joseph Fewsmith, "The Politics of China's Accession to the WTO," *Current History* (September 2000): 268–273.
58. Robert D. Putnam, "Diplomacy and Domestic Politics: The Logic of Two-Level Games," *International Organization* 42 (summer 1988).
59. Melvyn C. Goldstein, *The Snow Dragon and the Dragon: China, Tibet, and the Dalai Lama* (Berkeley: University of California Press, 1997).
60. Matt Forney, "Hoist with His Own Petard," *Far Eastern Economic Review*, November 13, 1997, 16–20.
61. Roy, *China's Foreign Relations*, 44–45.
62. Nathan and Ross, *Great Wall and the Empty Fortress*, 9.
63. Jainwei Wang, "Managing Conflict."
64. Christopher Patten, *East and West: China, Power, and the Future of Asia* (New York: Random House, 1998), 70.

65. Wu Xinbo, "China."
66. Michael O'Hanlon, "Why China Cannot Conquer Taiwan," *International Security,* vol. 25, no. 2 (2000): 51–86; and Robert S. Ross, "The 1995–96 Taiwan Strait Confrontation: Coercion, Credibility, and the Use of Force," *International Security,* vol. 25, no. 2 (2000): 87–123.
67. Nathan and Ross, *Great Wall and the Empty Fortress,* 96.
68. Ibid., 98–99.
69. Ibid., 101.
70. Roy, *China's Foreign Relations,* 51–54.
71. Nathan and Ross, *Great Wall and the Empty Fortress,* 115–117.
72. Wu Xinbo, "China," 131.

CHAPTER 7

Japanese Foreign Policy:
The International-Domestic Nexus

Akitoshi Miyashita

The growth of Japan's economy after its recovery from defeat in World War II created an economic giant in the international economic system. Yet despite its strong economy, as well as its rather large military defense force, Japan is often considered a political dwarf, with a low profile in world politics and little influence on the global stage. In this chapter, Akitoshi Miyashita argues that Japan's foreign policy can be explained best by the interaction of domestic and international forces. During the Cold War, these forces included Japan's alliance with the United States, which allowed Japan to concentrate on economic growth but constrained it in its relations with other states, particularly with China. Internally, a domestic consensus on the primacy of economics eventually emerged, and the insulation of Japan's "strong state" from many domestic political pressures allowed an active bureaucracy, in partnership with Japanese business, to concentrate on foreign economic policy and to adopt an export-led, neomercantilist strategy. The end of the Cold War has presented Japan with new challenges. Externally, these include increased tensions in Asia and international demands for greater participation in UN peacekeeping. Internally, the realignment of major political parties and gradual changes in the culture of antimilitarism are challenges as well.

The post–Cold War challenges facing Japan today are in many ways parallel to those facing Germany (Chapter 4). Like Germany, Japan has reinterpreted its constitution to allow participation in peacekeeping missions; it is a major economic player in the international system; and it has seen policy shifts in parties that were once a source of vocal support for pacifist policies. Although Japan is not involved in an organization that is as integrating as the European Union, it too faces the opportunities and dilemmas associated with high levels of interdependence, particular with the United States and more recently with other Asian-Pacific economies. Japan can also be compared with states like Russia (Chapter 5), China (Chapter 6), and India (Chapter 8) that are also struggling to define their post–Cold War identity and role in international politics. This struggle is taking place as Japan's government faces new societal pressures to consider the adverse effects of its foreign economic strategy and to open up its policy making. In this way, Japan's centralized way of making foreign policy is facing challenges similar to those of France (Chapter 3), Nigeria (Chapter 11), and South Africa (Chapter 12).

To many students of international relations, Japan appears an enigma. Despite its status as the second largest economy in the world, Japan has been reluctant to translate its wealth into political influence. Although it currently ranks third in the world in the absolute amount of defense spending, after the United States and Russia, the relative size of Japan's defense budget measured in relation to gross domestic product (GDP) is one of the smallest among the advanced industrial nations. Despite its changing status in the international system, Japan has taken a low-profile stance on strategic issues and remains highly dependent on the United States for defense. Today, more than five decades after the end of World War II, Japan is still reluctant to assume a larger military responsibility for the peace and stability of the world. The international criticism of Japan's failure to go beyond its monetary contribution during the Persian Gulf War of 1991 forced Tokyo to pass a bill allowing the Japanese Self-Defense Forces (SDF) to participate in United Nations (UN) peacekeeping operations. Nonetheless, the bill allows Japanese forces to engage only in noncombatant activities.

Because it fails to act as expected in light of its position in the international system, Japan is also considered an anomaly, to which Western theories of international relations are not applicable.[1] In fact, Japanese foreign policy is neither an enigma nor an anomaly. Like most other countries, it is a product of interaction between international and domestic forces. If one carefully observes the external and internal contexts within which Japanese decision makers formulate policies, Japanese behavior makes much sense. This is not to say that Japan acts in the same way that other advanced industrial nations do: Japan does behave differently. But the Japanese "anomaly" stems not so much from its unique culture or peculiar political system but rather naturally from certain objective conditions that are unique to Japan. The purpose of this chapter is to reveal these conditions. Only by so doing can we make better sense of why Japan acts the way it does.

Japanese Foreign Policy during the Cold War

In many respects, the bipolar international structure and the alliance with the United States set the parameters of Japanese foreign policy during the Cold War. Japan's defeat in World War II was followed by seven years of Allied (virtually American) occupation intended to demilitarize and democratize Japan through various political, economic, and social reforms so that the nation would not again menace the peace of the world. But the emerging rivalry between the United States and the Soviet Union led the United States to change its policy toward

145

Japan from reform to recovery. The communist revolution in China in 1949 and the Korean War the following year reaffirmed policy makers in Washington in their view that Japan's strategic location and potential role as the workshop of Asia were of crucial importance to America's Cold War strategy in the Far East. Japan thus became an important ally to be protected instead of a defeated enemy to be punished.[2]

Alliance with the United States

The alliance with the United States benefited Japan in at least two important ways. First, it provided Japan with necessary military protection. Japan had been demilitarized by the occupation forces, and it had only the national police reserve of 75,000 men when it regained independence in 1952. The continued presence of American forces in Japan served to fill the void created by the new constitution, which prohibited Japan from possessing any war potential.[3] Moreover, this American military protection allowed postwar Japan to stay lightly armed while putting major efforts and resources into economic recovery. Inside what Donald Hellmann called the "American greenhouse," Japan enjoyed an unprecedented level of prosperity.[4] Although scholars debate how much the light rearmament contributed to Japan's postwar economic growth,[5] it is undeniable that it helped reduce budgetary pressure on the government, allowing it to spend more on social and economic infrastructure.

Second, the alliance with the United States provided Japan with access to American markets, technology, and foreign aid. These economic "carrots" were used to keep Japan from becoming neutral or "defecting" to the communist camp. Policy makers in Washington felt that the major source of threat to Japan was internal rather than external. George F. Kennan, then director of the policy planning staff in the State Department, noted: "If economic distress and insecurity prevail, this will provide greatly added incentive and assistance to communist efforts."[6] Indeed, during the 1950s the leftist–progressive movement was gaining momentum in Japan, and there was a possibility that Japan might fall to the socialists, who wanted to abolish the U.S.-Japan security treaty and close American bases. To counter this possibility, the United States provided campaign funds to Japan's Liberal Democratic Party (LDP) through the Central Intelligence Agency to strengthen the conservative and pro-American government in Japan. Notwithstanding the political reasons behind them, these "carrots" were enormously beneficial to the Japanese economy as a catalyst for growth. At the same time, however, they helped deepen Japan's economic dependence on American markets and thereby planted the seeds of the future trade friction between the two countries.

It must be noted that although the alliance with the United States provided domestic economic opportunities, it constrained Japan's postwar foreign policy by depriving the country of its diplomatic freedom. By allying with the United States and joining the Western camp, Japan was necessarily restricted in its foreign relations with communist countries. The highest price Japan paid was the delay in normalizing its relationship with China. The Japanese government felt it essential to regain access to China's market and raw materials to achieve post-war economic recovery and growth. China had been Japan's largest trading part-ner in the prewar period, and many Japanese officials, including Prime Minister Shigeru Yoshida, believed that Chinese communists were first and foremost nationalists and therefore not a major threat to Japan. But the United States rec-ognized only the nationalist regime in Taiwan as the legitimate government of China. It restricted Japan's trade with mainland China, fearing that economic dependence on China would make Japan vulnerable to communist influence. It was only after President Richard Nixon visited Beijing in 1972 that Japan was able to establish diplomatic ties with communist China.

Economic Growth

On the domestic front, the pro-U.S. prime minister Shigeru Yoshida played a key role in setting the basic orientation of Japan's postwar foreign policy in the late 1940s and early 1950s. Later known as the "Yoshida doctrine," his policy line contained three essential elements: (1) dependence on U.S. security guarantees, (2) a limited rearmament, and (3) focus on economic development.[7] Yoshida believed that the first national priority of postwar Japan was to put the economy back on its own feet. He strongly opposed heavy rearmament, thinking that it would drain resources from Japan's industry and international commerce. He felt that the alliance with the United States was indispensable not only to ensure the security of demilitarized Japan but also to save it from spending heavily on defense. In the eyes of Yoshida and other moderates, dependence on U.S. mili-tary protection, limited rearmament, and focus on economic development were closely linked as policy objectives.

The Japanese economy in the postwar period grew at a phenomenal speed. By the mid-1950s it had passed its prewar peak and then for the next two decades kept a growth rate of almost 10 percent a year in real terms. Between 1952 and 1974 its gross national product (GNP) grew six and a half times, making Japan the third largest economy in the world, after the United States and the Soviet Union. Much of this growth was driven by foreign exports. Between 1960 and 1970 the annual growth rate of Japanese exports was 16.9 percent, compared with the world average of 9.3 percent. Between 1955 and 1974 Japan's share of world exports more than tripled from 2 percent to 6.2 percent. This increase made Japan the third largest exporter in the world, behind the United States and West Germany.[8]

Following the national consensus on economic development, Japan pursued a strategy that emphasized foreign export as a way of promoting domestic growth. Specifically, it restricted foreign capital and imports while assisting exports through various means, including subsidies and control of the exchange rate. This export strategy was sustained by Japan's conservative coalition, consisting of the state bureaucracy, big business, and the ruling Liberal Democratic Party.[9] The powerful and efficient bureaucracy was crucial. Japan's economic bureaucrats played a major role in planning and guiding the national economy, often in close coordination with the business community. The LDP's one-party rule provided long-term political stability, and under the bureaucracy's guidance, Japan's key industries outperformed many of the foreign competitors. These industries ranged from steel and petrochemicals to automobiles and semiconductors.[10]

Japan's mercantilist export strategy was consistent with its domestic structure, often characterized as "strong state and weak society."[11] The Japanese state showed remarkable independence from various societal pressures, and the government was able to mobilize domestic resources for efficient and effective use. Unlike most other advanced industrial nations, the Japanese state actively intervened in the market and created comparative advantages in targeted industries to enhance the nation's international competitiveness.

The historical roots of Japan's strong state go back to the nineteenth century, when Japan entered the world scene as a late industrializer. Because of high entry costs into the more advanced world economy, where there already are many competitors and the capital requirements for industries are high, late industrializers need greater collective mobilization, which in turn requires greater central coordination to catch up with early industrializers.[12] In addition to the timing of Japan's industrialization, the threat of Western imperialism at that time made it a matter of life and death for Japan to develop a powerful industrial base upon which it could quickly build a modern army. The need for rapid industrialization, in turn, required great mobilization of society. As Chalmers Johnson puts it,

> the most important thing about contemporary Japan is that it was, like Germany, a late developer. It was not one of the original beneficiaries of the Industrial Revolution, and industrialism in Japan owes nothing to the 'invisible hand' of Adam Smith. Industrialization in Japan was introduced from above, for political and not economic reasons, in order to counter the threat of Western imperialism.[13]

Rise of Japan's Economic Power

Japan's strategy to emphasize exports was successful in large part because the post–World War II international economic order remained relatively open and stable, thanks to the hegemonic leadership of the United States. According to hegemonic stability theory, free trade is more likely to prevail when there is a predominant state, which is both willing and able to sustain the costs of maintaining a liberal international order.[14] As the world's wealthiest and most powerful nation after World War II, the United States took on the role of organizing and managing the world economic system by supplying capital, defining the rules for international trade, and having the dollar operate as a key currency. The United States also bore a disproportionate burden of sustaining peace in the Western alliance by contributing a higher percentage of its GNP for defense than did its allies. Japan and other U.S. allies enjoyed the fruits of the free trade system maintained by American hegemony without sharing a proportionate amount of the burden. Indeed, the military security and economic prosperity of American allies — including Japan and Germany — would have been difficult to achieve in the absence of the international order and stability provided by the U.S. postwar hegemony.

America's predominance in the global political economy, however, began to crumble in the late 1960s and early 1970s. The prolonged military struggle in Vietnam drained the U.S. economy by causing a chronic balance of payments problem. This led President Nixon to suspend the dollar's convertibility into gold and impose a temporary 10 percent surcharge on imports in 1971 in order to strengthen the U.S. trade standing. The Bretton Woods economic system, which provided postwar international economic stability by fixing exchange rates, eventually collapsed as the United States adopted the system of flexible exchange rates in which overvalued currencies would fall and undervalued currencies would rise to their real value. America's relative position in the world economy further declined in the 1980s. During President Ronald Reagan's tenure in the White House, America's budget and trade deficits soared. In 1985 the United States became the world's largest debtor nation, borrowing more than $100 billion from abroad to finance its budget deficit and other financial shortages.[15]

Meanwhile, the Japanese economy kept growing. Although Japan's phenomenal economic growth ended after the 1973 oil crisis caused by the Arab-Israeli conflict, its economy continued to grow faster than any other major industrial democracy. Japan started to enjoy favorable trade balances after the mid-1960s, and by the late 1980s Japanese trade surpluses amounted to $100 billion annually, more than half of which was with the United States. This trade surplus, combined with the 50 percent appreciation of the yen after 1985, gave Japan immense financial power. By 1986 Japan's net assets abroad reached $129.8 billion, making it the world's largest creditor nation. In 1988 Japan's per capita GNP of $19,200, measured in official exchange rates, surpassed that of the United States for the first time. The following year, Japan displaced the United States as the world's largest donor of official development assistance (foreign aid).

The rise of Japan's trade and financial power caused much friction between it and the United States. For one thing, the penetration of Japanese manufactured products and capital into the United States was so symbolic that it caused strong resentment among some Americans. For another, Japan's continued reluctance to open its domestic markets fully to foreign producers and investors, and its unwillingness to spend more than 1 percent of its GDP on defense, gave rise to criticism that Japan was not paying its fair share of sustaining the existing international order from which it benefited enormously. Japan increasingly was seen as a state that was undermining the free trade system and as a major threat that needed to be contained before it further undermined the U.S. economy.[16] The Japanese government rebutted these concerns by saying that tariffs in Japan were lower than those of most advanced industrial nations, including the United States. It also contended that Japan was indeed sharing the burden of sustaining the existing international order by using nonmilitary means, such as taking initiatives in resolving Third World debt problems and contributing a large sum of money to international organizations such as the United Nations and the World Bank.

Trade disputes between the United States and Japan often became fierce and even emotional as each side came to attack the other's culture and business practices. But the disputes also reflected the growing interdependence of the two largest economies in the world. The United States remained the largest export market for Japan, absorbing 30 percent of Japan's total exports. This, along with the dependence on American military protection, was an important reason behind Japan's purchase of a large amount of U.S. Treasury bills in the 1980s. Japan's purchase of Treasury bills in turn helped to sustain America's global hegemony by allowing the Reagan administration to pursue expansionist economic policies without cutting the defense budget drastically or raising domestic interest rates.[17] In trade, this practice saved Japanese manufacturers from suffering a sharp decline in exports to the United States. In defense, Japan's subsidization of America's hegemony helped sustain American commitment to global security, including the U.S.-Japan alliance. Thus, despite the sometimes contentious rhetoric, the bilateral trade dispute and the narrowing gap in economic power drew the two economies closer together.

The end of the Cold War did not bring us "back to the future" of the old multipolar world that existed before World War II.[18] Nor did it prove the oft-heard claim, "the Cold War is over; Japan won." Japan's deep economic recession in the 1990s, coupled with the long-lasting American economic boom, rendered unwarranted many pessimistic predictions made in the late 1980s about the decline of American hegemony. Instead, the demise of Soviet empire and Japan's slow economic growth in the 1990s made the United States the sole superpower in the world, and the new international political structure is best characterized as "unipolar," or renewed American hegemony. Moreover, for reasons discussed below, the U.S.-Japan security treaty continues to exist today despite the demise of the Soviet threat. This means that there is a degree of continuity in Japanese foreign policy after the Cold War.

At the same time, however, since 1991 there have been many changes in Japan's international and domestic environments. Some of those changes were brought about by the end of the Cold War; others had already started but were accelerated by its end. Even American hegemony today is not the same as it was in the late 1940s and 1950s. The following section will review these changes and examine their impact on Japanese foreign policy.

External Factors

Among the many changes that have taken place at the international level, two are particularly important in terms of their effect on Japanese foreign policy. One is the growing instability in Asia's security environment.[19] The end of the Cold War brought more uncertainty to the region, rather than less. There was China's rapid increase in military spending; North Korea's ambition for acquiring weapons of mass destruction (although temporarily muted after the 1994 agreement) and for developing long-range missiles; the military crisis between the Unites States and China over the Taiwan straits; the offshore territorial disputes between North and South Korea, South Korea and Japan, and China and Japan; and the nuclear confrontation between India and Pakistan. Defense expenditures in the region grew 25 percent in real terms between 1985 and 1998. With military expenses of $150 billion a year, Asia is one of the most heavily armed regions in the world.

Part of the problem is the lack of trust among countries in the region. There exist historically based mistrust and animosity among regional actors. As a result, measures taken by one state to increase its own security are likely to be seen by its neighbors as reducing theirs, forcing them to take countermeasures. This leads to spirals of tension and an arms race, making all feel less secure than they originally were. Thus China's aggressive modernization of its weapons system, facilitated after the Persian Gulf War of 1991, made Japan feel uneasy. Conversely, Japan's decision to join U.S. theater missile defense research in 1998—after North Korea's long-range missile testing—sent an alarming signal to Beijing. One of the reasons the United States took the leading role in dissuading North Korea from acquiring nuclear weapons in the fall of 1994 was to preempt a possible nuclear arms race in northeast Asia that might involve South Korea, Japan, China, Taiwan, and possibly others. The end of the Cold War intensified this security dilemma in Asia.[20]

Growing instability is the main reason the United States retains its military presence in Asia. The end of the Cold War eliminated the Soviet threat, but the historically rooted mistrust and animosity among Asian countries die hard, preventing them from creating a regional security institution like NATO. Asia needs a stabilizer or a reassuring force that would help ameliorate the security dilemma. U.S. military bases in Japan and South Korea served that function during the Cold War, and they are expected to continue performing that function in the post–Cold War era. As Thomas Christensen notes, "By reassuring both Japan and its potential rivals, the United States reduces the likelihood of divisive security dilemma scenarios and spiral model dynamics in the region."[21] Indeed, support among the regional actors for the retention of American forces in Asia is stronger today than it was during the Cold War.

Another major change at the international level is the growing economic interdependence among countries in the Asia-Pacific region. In sharp contrast to the fragmented and potentially unstable security environment, the Asian economy is moving toward greater conversion and integration. The volume of intra-Asian trade rose significantly in the 1980s and 1990s. Although the United States is the largest export market for many Asian economies, intraregional trade in recent years grew four times faster than Asian exports to the United States, and more than two-fifths of Asian trade today takes place within the region. The financial crisis of 1997 slowed down the Asian economy, but the trend toward greater interdependence seems irreversible.

Behind the growing integration of the Asian economy is the rise of Japan's foreign direct investment within the region. The appreciation of the Japanese yen after the 1985 Plaza accord by the Group of Five advanced industrial nations accelerated relocation of Japanese production abroad.[22] Although much of Japanese investment went to the United States, roughly one-fourth went to the rest of Asia. To cut rising labor costs at home, Japanese manufacturing firms, especially those in the consumer electronics and automobile industries, went offshore and engaged in an expanded, intra-industry division of labor throughout the Asian region. They started with the newly industrializing economies of South Korea, Taiwan, Singapore, and Hong Kong, then moved to Southeast Asia and to China. This facilitated integration of the Japanese economy into the region. In 1991 the volume of Japanese exports to other Asian countries exceeded the volume of Japanese exports to the United States. In 1995 Japan became the largest or second-largest export market for Australia, China, Indonesia, and South Korea and the largest source of imports for South Korea, Taiwan, Singapore, Indonesia, Thailand, Malaysia, and the Philippines.[23]

The increase in Japan's foreign direct investment in Asia was spurred primarily by the rise in the value of the Japanese yen. But the end of the Cold War created a favorable political environment under which Japanese investment expanded. The demise of the Soviet Union led many communist regimes in Asia to begin adopting market mechanisms and to seek Western capital to rebuild their economy. This created an economic opportunity for Japanese business to increase its presence in those nations, especially in Vietnam, Laos, and Cambodia. For its part, the Japanese government extended official development assistance to those countries to help reconstruct their economic infrastructures. This in turn removed some economic barriers and facilitated further private sector investment.[24]

The growing regional economic interdependence has affected Japanese foreign policy in at least two important ways. First, business has come to play a more important role in shaping Japan's foreign policy. As Kaarbo, Lantis, and Beasley note in Chapter 1, globalization and interdependence have led to a relative decline of government and subsequent rise of private actors in foreign policy making. This is particularly true in the case of Japan's foreign policy toward Asia, where Japan is building a dominant position largely through market forces.

Second, as Japan's stakes in Asia increased as a result of growing regional interdependence, some Japanese came to advocate a shift in foreign policy orientation. For example, Yotaro Kobayashi, chairman of Fuji Xerox, urged the "re-Asianization of Japan" by developing stronger ties with Asian neighbors while distancing itself from the United States.[25] A former Foreign Ministry official is quoted as saying, "Until now, Japan has often listened to American voices and persuaded Asians. From now, Japan needs to listen to more Asian voices and persuade Americans."[26] As Japan's presence in this region expanded, Washington and Tokyo increasingly found themselves at odds with each other on a number of issues, ranging from the suppression of human rights and the speed of market liberalization to the nature of a regional financial institution and the role of government in development.

Changes in the international environment in both security and economics have posed a challenge to the basic foreign policy line pursued by the Japanese government since the end of World War II. Under attack are two of the three components of the Yoshida doctrine — limited armament and export-led economic growth. In security, the regional uncertainty and the need to share a larger burden of the U.S.-Japan alliance require Japan to possess a defense capability commensurate with its economic power and to assume a greater military responsibility for the stability of the region. Indeed, Japan has been under pressure since the 1980s to alter its minimalist security posture, and it has abandoned or relaxed some of its self-imposed restrictions on defense, such as the commitment to military expenditures of no more than 1 percent of GNP, the limit on dispatching its Self-Defense Forces abroad, and the ban on arms exports. In economics, regional integration and the chronic friction with the United States over trade are forcing Japan to alter its neomercantilist trade policy and to undertake further liberalization and deregulation of its economic system. These changes are not easy to make, however, as they face strong political resistance at home. The following section examines how Japan has responded to the new realities created by the changing international environment.

Internal Factors

Japanese politics has gone through major changes since the end of the Cold War. Among them is the loss of the Liberal Democratic Party's parliamentary majority in 1993. The end of the single-party rule that lasted for thirty-eight years was certainly a significant event. Yet its impact on Japanese politics and foreign policy should not be overstated. To begin with, the end of the LDP's dominance came not so much from a decline in the party's popularity as from an internal split and the resulting defection of a group of LDP politicians, who formed the Japanese Renewal Party. Moreover, after a short interval, the LDP regained power in 1994 by forging an alliance with the Socialists, its long-time political opponent.[27] Perhaps more important than the LDP's loss of parliamentary majority was the fall of the Japan Socialist Party (JSP), the largest opposition party in Japan.[28] The number of seats the JSP gained in elections in the lower house declined from 136 in 1990 to 70 in 1993, and then to 15 in 1996. The JSP (since 1996, the Social Democratic Party) rebounded a bit in the 2000 election with 19 seats, but it was no longer a major force in the Diet, the Japanese parliament.

The virtual collapse of the JSP meant that Japanese politics no longer revolved around ideological competition between capitalism and socialism. With the demise of the JSP, a major controversy about Japan's postwar national security also ended. During the Cold War, the Socialists strongly opposed the U.S.-Japan security treaty. They argued that such an alliance would invite, rather than deter, a military attack on Japan from abroad and increase the likelihood of Japan's involvement in an unwanted war. In addition, they felt that an indefinite stationing of American forces made Japan's independence after the American occupation only nominal and would seriously impair Japan's ability to pursue an autonomous foreign policy. According to the Socialists, the best way to guarantee Japan's security and independence was to distance itself from either superpower and to adopt unarmed neutrality.[29]

The pacifist appeal of the JSP's foreign policy attracted many Japanese in the early postwar years, especially intellectuals and blue-collar workers. Over time, however, their plea to abolish the U.S.-Japan security treaty lost much support. The Japanese people came to realize that, instead of getting Japan involved in a war of American making, the alliance with the United States provided for Japanese security and saved the nation from undertaking substantial rearmament. This contributed to the gradual acceptance of the security treaty in Japan, along with the growing recognition that the alliance with the United States benefited Japan economically in the form of capital, technology, and export markets.

Despite the changes in the public's attitudes, the Socialists continued to oppose the U.S.-Japan security treaty. The party also sustained its attack on the constitutionality of Japan's Self-Defense Forces, even though they had been in existence for more than thirty years and had been accepted by the majority of the Japanese. A major turning point came in 1994, when the birth of the LDP–JSP coalition government under Socialist prime minister Tomiichi Murayama forced the JSP to modify its position on those issues.[30] The coalition was a political marriage of convenience. Once in power, the Socialists took a more realistic policy stance. Soon after his inauguration, Murayama announced that the U.S.-Japan security treaty was indispensable for the peace and prosperity of the Asia-Pacific region and that Japan's Self-Defense Forces were constitutional. The Socialist prime minister also acknowledged that "unarmed neutrality" as a policy goal had lost its significance in the post–Cold War era.[31]

The major decline of the JSP and its policy shift have reduced domestic political constraints on Japan's larger military role. In 1997 Tokyo's new defense guidelines for the U.S.-Japan alliance stipulated its commitment to increased logistics and rear-area support roles that included intelligence gathering, surveillance, and minesweeping missions. In the following year, Japan agreed to research theater missile defense jointly with the United States. Although external threats—the 1995–1996 Taiwan straits crisis between China and the United States in the case of the new defense guidelines and North Korea's long-range missile testing in 1998 in the case of the theater missile defense—provided Japan with direct motives for seeking these measures, the absence of strong opposition at home made it easier for the Japanese government to depart from its passive stance on defense.

Pacifist sentiment continues to exist in Japan, as evidenced by Japan's reluctance to join the U.S.-led coalition forces during the Persian Gulf War of 1991. As will be discussed later in this chapter, it was only after a lengthy debate that the Japanese Diet passed the UN Peacekeeping Operations Bill, which enabled the Japanese military to be dispatched abroad. But the bill is highly restrictive. It allows Japanese troops to participate only in noncombative peacekeeping activities sponsored by the United Nations. In other words, under current law Japan is unable to join the kind of coalition forces that fought the war against Iraq in 1991. As Chapter 1 points out, public opinion can affect foreign policy by providing "core values" or opinion "moods" that set parameters within which decision makers must operate. Japan's pacifism, or the culture of antimilitarism, constitutes such a core value and has since 1945 constantly set boundaries for state action in the realm of national defense.[32]

Another major change in domestic sources of Japanese foreign policy is the gradual erosion of the strong state. As mentioned earlier, Japan's mercantile trade policy was sustained by the strong bureaucracy allied with big business and the ruling LDP. During the high-speed economic growth of the late 1950s and 1960s, Japanese bureaucrats played a key role in promoting and protecting domestic industries by measures ranging from high tariffs and quotas to subsidies and tight control on the exchange rate. The government also imposed controls on domestic consumption and encouraged personal savings in order to accumulate investment capital for use by domestic industries. Cartels were tolerated, even encouraged, to reduce the "excessive competition" among Japanese manufacturers. Although Japanese society was made to serve the interests of producers rather than consumers, the people were largely satisfied as the fruits of economic growth were distributed relatively equally among them.

The strong state was maintained under the national consensus that economic growth was the top priority of postwar Japan. That consensus no longer exists today. Although the rapid economic growth brought Japan much wealth, it also created many quality-of-life problems, such as pollution, inadequate health care, poor housing and social infrastructure, and inequality in the workplace. The more affluent the Japanese became, the more attention they paid to the cost of growth. Economic growth also facilitated urbanization and higher education in Japan. As a result, Japanese society today is more pluralistic than in the past.

Moreover, as Japanese firms became internationally competitive, they required less protection by and guidance from the bureaucracy. A number of Japanese manufacturing companies today are multinational in nature. Unlike in the 1950s and 1960s, they raise much of their needed capital through bonds rather than by borrowing from the main banks, which were under tight control of the Ministry of Finance. Consequently, their successes and failures depend less on state control and more on exchange rates, bond markets, and other factors determined by market forces. Moreover, internationally competitive firms are likely to resist protectionism at home in order to avert foreign retaliation.[33] They thus apply pressure on the government for deregulation and liberalization of the domestic market.

Meanwhile, Japan's once efficient and effective bureaucratic system began to show signs of fatigue in the 1990s. A series of bureaucratic corruption scandals involving many high-ranking officials from various ministries planted in the Japanese people the seeds of deep distrust of the nation's professional elite bureaucracy. Public criticism of the Ministry of Finance was particularly keen. The ministry was not only at the center of scandals but it also mismanaged the economy. Many observers claim that the Ministry of Finance's interest rate policy led to a significant hike in real estate and stock market prices in the late 1980s, causing a "bubble economy" to develop, unsupported by economic fundamentals, while its decision to raise the consumption tax after the bubble burst delayed Japan's economic recovery.

Japan's economic recessions in the 1990s accelerated the erosion of the strong state. The banking system became paralyzed with a mountain of bad loans; the national debt as measured in terms of the percentage of GNP was higher in Japan than in almost any other industrialized country; the national budget was deeply in the red; the unemployment rate reached its highest point; and productivity in manufacturing industries was stagnant for several years. Persistently low economic growth intensified the potential for change. It became obvious to many Japanese that the neomercantilist policies could not continue in the face of severe economic realities. The result of these trends was increased pressure to deregulate the Japanese economy, demands to open the system to foreign (low-priced) products, and the decreasing ability of Japanese bureaucrats to manage the economy.

Contemporary Japanese Foreign Policy

This section deals with Japan's foreign policy today. First, it briefly reviews two recent major foreign policy problems currently facing Japan—a territorial dispute with Russia and the Asian financial crisis. Second, it provides a detailed analysis of Japan's response to the Persian Gulf War, the first major foreign policy challenge to Japan in the post–Cold War era. These case studies are designed to illuminate some of the general themes on Japanese foreign policy discussed earlier in this chapter.

Territorial Dispute with Russia

One of the major foreign policy issues facing Japan today is a long-standing territorial dispute with Russia. The Japanese government has claimed that the Northern Territories (the four islands north of Hokkaido) were seized by the Soviet Union at the end of World War II and therefore should revert to Japan. Moscow has refused to allow that, insisting that the islands became part of Soviet territory under the Yalta agreement signed by the United States, Britain, and the Soviet Union in February 1945.[34] The dispute has prevented the two countries from signing a peace treaty for more than fifty years, although Tokyo and Moscow established diplomatic ties in 1956.[35]

During the Cold War, Japan pursued a linkage policy toward the Soviet Union, whereby provision of Japan's economic assistance to the Soviet Union was made conditional upon the reversion of the four islands.[36] The end of the Cold War and the fall of the Soviet Union, however, changed the international environment within which Japan's linkage policy was pursued. Western nations, especially Germany and the United States, became enthusiastic supporters of Russia's transition to democracy and a market economy, and they put pressure on Japan to provide large-scale assistance to Moscow. Japan initially refused, but as voices for extending aid to Russia grew louder, it gradually modified its position, first by providing humanitarian aid and then by extending financial aid through multilateral institutions such as the International Monetary Fund (IMF) and the World Bank. In 1993 Japan pledged to offer $1.8 billion in bilateral aid to Moscow.

Meanwhile, Russia mitigated the tough position held by the Soviet Union on the territorial issue. Soviet leaders used to maintain that no territorial dispute ever existed between the two countries and refused to negotiate the issue with the Japanese government. During his visit to Japan in 1993, Russian president Boris Yeltsin acknowledged the existence of the territorial dispute and agreed to begin negotiations on a peace treaty through the resolution of the territorial issue. In 1997 Yeltsin went further to pledge that his government would make every effort to conclude a peace treaty with Japan by 2000.

Yeltsin's pledges, however, were little more than a way to pacify Japan in order to draw more concessions on economic cooperation, and they by no means reflected a serious commitment on his part to resolving the territorial dispute. Bilateral peace talks began, but Tokyo soon discovered that Yeltsin was not prepared to allow the islands to revert to Japan. The Russian president wanted to conclude a peace treaty while leaving the territorial issue unresolved. By that time, the territorial issue had become deeply entangled in Russia's domestic politics. Nationalists fiercely opposed any territorial concession to Japan, and conservative legislators in the Russian Congress tried to exploit the issue to undermine Yeltsin's political power. With neither side willing to concede on the attribution of the four islands, the year 2000 deadline was not met.

Although negotiations on the peace treaty continue, the gap between Tokyo and Moscow remains wide. It will probably take many years of confidence and trust building and strong leadership on both sides before the two can finally resolve the territorial dispute.

The 1997 Asian Financial Crisis

A financial crisis swept through East Asia in the summer of 1997. It began with a sudden currency devaluation in Thailand (more than 48 percent of the currency's value), causing a sharp downturn in Thai assets and growth. The devaluation was triggered by a massive selling of Thai baht by foreign hedge funds in the wake of rising trade deficits in Thailand. The currency crisis soon spread to neighboring countries, including Indonesia, Malaysia, Singapore, the

Philippines, and South Korea. Each was faced with a swift outflow of foreign capital, significant downfall in their exchange rates, and sharp decline in their stock markets.[37] Japan took a leading role in helping the economies hit by the sudden devaluation. In 1997 alone it provided more than $37 billion in bilateral aid, an amount far larger than any other bilateral contribution made in the aftermath of the crisis.

Japan's leadership was natural given its high stakes in the Asian economy. As noted earlier, the rising value of the yen in the 1980s and early 1990s led many Japanese manufacturing firms to expand their production facilities in Asia in order to cut high labor costs at home. The increase in Japanese foreign direct investment was accompanied by an increase in lending operations by Japanese banks. In 1996, a year before the financial crisis erupted, 53 percent of foreign loans made to Thailand came from Japanese sources. Japan's share in foreign loans made to Hong Kong, Indonesia, and South Korea respectively was 42.2 percent, 39.6 percent, and 24.3 percent.[38]

In September 1997 Japan proposed to establish a $100 billion Asian Monetary Fund (AMF) to provide emergency liquidity to regional economies faced with balance of payment problems. The AMF plan was initiated and strongly backed by Japan's Ministry of Finance, which felt that rescue packages prepared by the International Monetary Fund imposed conditions that often were too harsh and even counterproductive. The Ministry of Finance maintained that at a time of financial crisis providing quick and ample liquidity was more important than strict implementation of economic reforms and other stabilization policies that are insensitive to national differences.[39]

Japan's AMF plan, however, met with fierce opposition from abroad. The strongest criticism came from the United States. U.S. Treasury secretary Robert Rubin and deputy secretary Lawrence H. Summers saw the plan posing a potential threat to the IMF and the underlying American power and interests as it would divert resources and authority from Washington to Tokyo. IMF officials were also worried that the AMF could impair the consistency and effectiveness of IMF programs and undermine their legitimacy.[40] In Asia, China expressed strong opposition to the plan for fear that it would allow Japan to establish a dominant position in regional financial matters.[41]

There was domestic opposition as well. The Ministry of Finance, the most powerful ministry in Japan, was under attack for a series of scandals that involved acceptance of gifts and entertainment from businesses. The ministry was also being criticized for the introduction of an ill-timed raise in the sales tax in May 1997, the act that was said to have had adverse effects on Japan's already sluggish economy. Moreover, in November 1997, Hokkaido Takushoku Bank (the tenth largest city bank in Japan) and Yamaichi Securities (the fourth largest brokerage firm in Japan) went bankrupt. The incidents severely undermined the popular perception held after World War II that Japan's financial institutions were "uncollapsable." In short, the Ministry of Finance was pursuing the AMF plan on the international front at a time when it was quickly losing credibility at home. Given Japan's decade-long recession triggered by the burst of the bubble in the early 1990s, critics argued that the ministry's AMF proposal was a financial rescue plan made for foreign countries at the expense of Japanese taxpayers. In light of the strong international and domestic criticism, Japan backed down.[42]

In November 1998 Japan made a much more modest proposal for an Asian rescue plan in which it committed to provide $10 billion in assistance but sought no institutionalization of an Asian Monetary Fund. The United States quickly supported the new proposal. Earlier, U.S. president Bill Clinton and Prime Minister Keizo Obuchi of Japan had agreed that the two countries would cooperate closely in formulating financial packages to assist countries experiencing economic crisis. Although its high stakes in the Asian economy led Japan to play an active role in regional rescue plans, Japan's leadership was constrained by American power and interests. The aborted AMF proposal demonstrates that Japan's global leadership rests on a precarious balance between Japan's own agenda and the need to maintain a stable relationship with the United States.

The Persian Gulf War

As in the case of Germany, the Persian Gulf War posed the first major foreign policy challenge to Japan in the post–Cold War era. Although the Middle East is geographically remote, Japan's dependence on the import of foreign oil made the stability of the region of critical importance to Japan's economic security. Japan provided $10.7 billion in support of the U.S.-led multilateral forces in the war against Iraq, or roughly 20 percent of the total costs of operations "Desert Shield" and "Desert Storm." This made Japan one of the leading contributors to the war efforts. The comparable figure for Germany was $6.6 billion.[43]

And yet Japan's contribution was often criticized as "too little, too late." The lack of expertise in crisis management in the central government caused many of the slow and erratic moves Tokyo made during the crisis. But also at stake was Japan's reluctance to deploy the Self-Defense Forces beyond its national borders. Tokyo had long maintained that Article 9 of the Japanese constitution prohibited the government from dispatching military personnel overseas. During the Persian Gulf crisis, that position became seriously contested.

The issue was first brought up by the United States within a few weeks of the Iraqi invasion of Kuwait. In a telephone conversation with Japan's prime minister, Toshiki Kaifu, U.S. president George Bush mildly requested that Japan send minesweepers and refueling ships to the Arabian Ocean.[44] This led to some intensive discussion within the Japanese government. In the end, the Kaifu cabinet decided that it was premature to send Japan's military forces abroad. Instead, on August 29 it pledged a $1 billion financial aid package. Included in this package was a plan to dispatch 100 volunteer doctors and nurses to nonbelligerent countries in the region that were adversely affected by the sanctions—a measure designed to dodge the international criticism that Japan's contributions were only financial. To the government's embarrassment, however, only seventeen people actually volunteered. This number was in sharp contrast to the 170,000 American troops that had been sent to the region by that time.[45]

American pressure increased, rather than decreased, after Japan made the $1 billion financial aid pledge. In early September, U.S. Treasury secretary Nicholas Brady visited Tokyo and urged the Japanese government to make an additional contribution of $1 billion to the multilateral forces deployed in the Gulf region. U.S. ambassador to Japan Michael Armacost spent much time telling government officials and business leaders in Tokyo that Japan needed to play a greater role, including the provision of military assistance.[46] Meanwhile, frustrated by Japan's "minimal" contributions to the Persian Gulf War efforts, the U.S. House of Representatives sought to pass a bill calling for Japan to bear the full costs of U.S. military bases in Japan or the United States would withdraw 5,000 troops a year.[47] The White House and the State Department told the Japanese government that immediate and concrete actions in support of the multilateral forces in the war against Iraq would be necessary to dissuade Congress from passing the bill. Japan, however, failed to act quickly, and the bill passed on September 12. Two days later, the Japanese government announced that it would offer a new financial aid package of $3 billion.[48]

By that time, the view was growing within the Japanese government that Japan should move beyond financial contributions. Even those who initially were opposed to the dispatch of the Self-Defense Forces abroad now felt that such a measure would be necessary to keep the government from promising an even larger amount of financial assistance. In early September the Japanese government secretly launched a study seeking possible ways in which the SDF could be dispatched to the Middle East. High-ranking officials from key ministries were gathered to form a task force to draft a "United Nations peace cooperation bill."[49] The main idea was to allow the government to establish a Japanese version of a peace corps consisting mainly of the SDF.

However, the bill was met with fierce opposition in the Japanese Diet. At issue was inclusion of the SDF in Japan's peace corps to be established under the proposed law. Some members of the opposition parties supported the idea that Japan should contribute personnel to UN peacekeeping activities but only on the condition that the SDF would not be part of it. Among the opposition parties, only the Democratic Socialist Party (DSP) was willing to join the ruling LDP in voting in favor of the bill, but DSP support alone was insufficient to override opposition in the upper house, where the LDP had lost its majority after the summer election in 1989.[50] The rest of the opposition parties resisted any attempt to alter the existing status of the SDF. Memories of World War II continue to shape Japanese thinking on defense in such a way that the citizenry opposes anything that might suggest a resurgence of the militarism of the 1930s and 1940s.

Indeed, public opinion was opposed to sending the SDF overseas. According to one poll, 58 percent of the respondents opposed the bill, while 21 percent supported it. Even among supporters of the LDP, only 30 percent remained supportive, while 48 percent were opposed to the bill.[51] Moreover, during Diet deliberations, the government revealed that the SDF could be used not only for UN peacekeeping operations but also in support of multilateral forces then deployed in the Persian Gulf. This raised the question of "impartiality" and "legitimacy" of Japan's overseas mission, making the bill even harder for the Japanese public to accept.[52]

Finally, the fate of the bill was affected by the bureaucratic politics in the central government. The SDF was under the jurisdiction of the Japan Defense Agency (JDA). But the JDA often found itself excluded from the inner circle of decision making in the government. The Ministry of Foreign Affairs, in its attempts to retain control over Japan's foreign policy formation, persistently sought to block the JDA's involvement in Middle East decisions during the crisis. Although the Ministry of Foreign Affairs in general was in favor of Japan's participation in UN peacekeeping activities, its top officials were hesitant to dispatch the SDF abroad for that purpose. In the meantime, the legal affairs bureau in the prime minister's office suggested that the government would not be able to dispatch the SDF abroad unless revisions to the constitution were made.[53] After three weeks of lobbying, the government failed to obtain enough domestic support for the bill. On November 8 the bill died without coming to a vote in the Diet.

Three months later a war broke out between the U.S.-led multinational coalition forces and the Iraqi military. Japan soon promised to offer $9 billion in financial assistance to the war effort. Although the amount was significant by international standards and in comparison with Japan's past contributions, Japan was criticized for failing to go beyond monetary contributions. Japan, it was said, was engaged in "checkbook diplomacy," trying to resolve any foreign policy issue with cash. After the war ended, the Kuwaiti government placed a full-page advertisement in the *New York Times* thanking those countries that provided assistance during the crisis. To the embarrassment of the Japanese government, Japan was not mentioned in the ad.

Strong international criticism forced Japan to reconsider its gun-shy diplomacy. In April 1991 the government decided to send SDF minesweepers to the Gulf. It maintained that the existing law allowed deployment of SDF minesweepers abroad as long as they operated exclusively in shipping lanes used by Japanese vessels.[54] With minor protests, the opposition parties remained quiet this time. That the war by then had well ended certainly contributed to the relative absence of parliamentary opposition to the government action.

Moreover, by that time public opinion had become more sympathetic to deployment of the SDF abroad. In a poll conducted after the war broke out in January 1991, 43 percent of respondents said they would support the idea of dispatching the SDF to move refugees out of Jordan by plane, while 48 percent opposed it.[55] Once the minesweepers were sent to the Gulf, an opinion poll found that 65 percent of the Japanese supported the government's decision and 74 percent supported the SDF's participation in UN peacekeeping activities in general.[56]

In 1992 Japan took a further step. In response to proposed UN peacekeeping operations in Cambodia, the Japanese government submitted to the Diet a new bill allowing deployment of the SDF overseas. The bill was strongly backed by the Ministry of Foreign Affairs. The ministry had been involved in diplomatic negotiations of the Cambodian peace settlement, and it felt that Japan should play a leading role in postconflict peacekeeping activities once an agreement was reached to end the civil war there. Officials in the Ministry of Foreign Affairs regarded a transition by Cambodia and other Indo-Chinese countries to democracy and a market economy to be vital to the peace and stability of Southeast Asia as a whole. Japan has a high stake in the region, which has been a major source of raw material imports and an export market for Japan. It is also a strategic location for Japan as it stands on Japan's "sea lanes"—the shipping route for crude oil originating in the Middle East. In particular, safe and undisrupted tanker passage through the Straits of Malacca is of vital importance.

In addition, the Ministry of Foreign Affairs was eager to see Japan obtain a permanent seat in the UN Security Council. The end of the Cold War had opened discussions on increasing the number of permanent members in the UN Security Council to reflect changes in the international system. Japan was the second largest contributor to the United Nations, but was often excluded from key decisions because of the lack of access to Security Council meetings. The Ministry of Foreign Affairs felt that Japan's participation in the UN peacekeeping operations would strengthen its bid for the permanent membership in the Security Council, as it could demonstrate to the world that Japan was both willing and able to assume its responsibility for global peace and security.[57]

The government and ruling LDP were determined to prevent the legislation from once again falling victim to domestic politics. They accepted several modifications to the 1992 bill to make it more acceptable to Komeito (Clean Government Party) and other centrist parties, whose support was essential for its passage. For example, it was made clear that the SDF's overseas missions would be restricted to participation in UN peacekeeping operations and humanitarian rescue operations—the old bill permitted the SDF to take part in UN-endorsed military activities, such as the U.S.-led multilateral coalition forces that fought the war against Iraq. The SDF would be allowed to operate only when belligerent parties agreed on a cease-fire and accepted UN and Japanese participation in peacekeeping operations. Moreover, the bill allowed Japanese forces to engage only in noncombatant activities. That meant that a major function of the SDF would remain in building roads, repairing bridges, providing transportation services, and the like.

Those restrictions, according to one observer, made the SDF's role little more than that of "construction workers."[58] They were nonetheless necessary to establish legal authorization for deployment of the Japanese military overseas for the first time in Japan's post–World War II history. After those restrictions were made, the Clean Government Party agreed to support the bill.

In June 1992 the UN peacekeeping operations bill passed both houses of the

Japanese Diet. The first SDF mission was sent to Cambodia in 1993. Since then the SDF has been deployed in Mozambique (1993–1995), Zaire (1994), and the Golan Heights (1996)—all as part of UN peacekeeping operations. Those missions have been received favorably at home and aroused no major criticism abroad. The future prospects of the SDF's overseas deployment, however, remain unclear. The issue is still politically sensitive in Japan, and the Diet continues to impose severe restrictions on the SDF's activities abroad. Nonetheless, the trend toward Japan's larger military role seems irreversible. In this sense, the Persian Gulf War was a major catalyst for a change in Japan's postwar defense policy.

Conclusion

Michael Blaker, a long-time observer of Japan's foreign relations, once noted, "Throughout the post–World War II era, the task of balancing U.S. demands and domestic Japanese constraints has become perhaps the thorniest task facing any Japanese prime minister."[59] That task seems to remain largely unchanged in the post–Cold War era. Japan is under pressure to alter its passive, minimalist stance on defense and its mercantilist attitude on trade—major components of the Yoshida doctrine that brought remarkable success to postwar Japan. International pressure is particularly strong for Japan to adopt a foreign policy that fits the new realities created by the end of the Cold War.

To do so, however, often requires costly changes in Japan's domestic structure, thereby inviting strong resistance at home. On defense, the Japanese are still uncomfortable with the idea of the nation assuming a larger military role beyond protection of their own land. On trade, powerful pressure groups and industries resist deregulation and liberalization of the Japanese economy. In the end, Japan's new foreign policy will be a product of dynamic interaction between international and domestic forces.

The emergence of Junichiro Koizumi as the new prime minister in the spring of 2001 signaled a possible change in Japanese politics and foreign policy. Koizumi came to power as the result of overwhelming popular support, winning a landslide victory in the LDP presidential election at the local level throughout Japan, not by the usual behind-the-scene politics of a handful of influential LDP politicians that had produced Japan's prime ministers in the past. He successfully established his image as a reformer, both willing and able to introduce various measures of deregulation to Japan's once competent but now inefficient political economy.

The prospects for his reform program, however, are uncertain. Although Koizumi enjoys an approval rating of nearly 80 percent, he lacks a firm base in his own party. That his political power derives almost entirely from his popularity among Japanese voters puts him in a difficult position. On the one hand, if his reform program goes too far, he will face strong resistance in his own party. On the other hand, if he makes too many concessions to interest groups and bends under pressure, he will appear weak in the eyes of the Japanese people and might quickly lose popularity. Thus Koizumi must walk a fine line, seeking to maintain a precarious balance between the conflicting forces of reform.

Some observers of Japan are rather pessimistic about the future. They hold that Japan's domestic political structure is such that a major change in Japan's foreign policy will be slow and incremental at best. For example, Kent Calder argues that bureaucratic turf battles, the medium-sized electoral district system (choosing more than one legislator from one district—a practice that lasted until 1995),[60] and weak political leadership (and control over the bureaucracy), among others, have made Japan slow to realize changes in the international environment and slow to take appropriate measures to cope with the new realities.[61] Calder conceptualizes Japan as a "reactive state" because the government is crippled by these domestic constraints, and, as a result, "impetus to policy change is typically supplied by outside pressure."[62]

Others contend that the passive, low-profile character of Japanese postwar foreign policy has become a thing of the past. They point to recent instances in which Japan exercised leadership and demonstrated greater activism, such as in the Asia Pacific Economic Cooperation, Asian Development Bank, and the new Asian Industrial Development plan, and they claim that "proactivism" better captures Japan's foreign policy stance today.[63]

Whether Japan is reactive or proactive is in part a matter of definition and interpretation and in part a matter of which case one examines.[64] Perhaps more important, there is a critical structural factor, aside from domestic politics, that is likely to constrain Japanese foreign policy in the future as it did in the past. That factor is Japan's dependence on the United States for export markets and defense. Japan's survival as a trading state depends on access to external markets and a peaceful security environment. And Japan depends on the United States for provision of these "goods" to a significant extent. This dependent relationship, a product of the Cold War, has constrained Japan's foreign policy autonomy and initiatives. It discouraged Tokyo from assuming a larger military responsibility and made Japan's defense policy largely an issue of burden sharing. Indeed, Japan's postwar government has operated under the strategy that "Japan should increase its defense capability only just enough so as not to worsen the U.S.-Japan relationship, since the nation's security depends on a favorable mood in this relationship."[65]

Shall the dependent relationship continue? Although some people on both sides of the Pacific have become increasingly frustrated about the bilateral relationship, both Washington and Tokyo have managed to sustain this relationship rather than fundamentally alter it. For Japan's part, no other nation is likely to replace the United States as the largest market for Japan in the near future, and pursuing autonomy in defense (including possession of nuclear weapons) is politically and diplomatically too costly for Japan. As for the United States, the existing security alliance with Japan is certainly unequal in terms of capability and commitment. But as the volume of trans-Pacific trade well exceeds that of trans-Atlantic trade today, the United States has high stakes in maintaining political stability in East Asia. Given the fact that Tokyo pays almost all the yen-based costs of the 50,000 American forces, or roughly 70 percent of the troops' overall costs, maintaining military bases in Japan has become increasingly cost-effective for the United States.

To be sure, the asymmetric exchange in trade and security has created much strain in bilateral relations, and the two governments have constantly sought to build a more "equal" partnership. Yet what they have actually done is largely to renegotiate the price Japan has to pay to maintain this asymmetric exchange rather than changing the asymmetric nature of the bilateral exchange itself. How long this arrangement can continue to exist is difficult to predict. What seems clear, however, is that it is this structure of asymmetric dependence that defines the parameters of Japanese foreign policy.

Suggestions for Further Reading

Calder, Kent E. "Japanese Foreign Economic Policy Formation: Explaining the 'Reactive State.'" *World Politics* 40 (July 1988): 517–541.

Christensen, Thomas J. "China, the U.S.-Japan Alliance, and the Security Dilemma in East Asia." *International Security* 23 (spring 1999).

Dower, John W. *Japan in War and Peace.* New York: Free Press, 1993.

Hatch, Walter, and Kozo Yamamura. *Asia in Japan's Embrace: Building a Regional Production Alliance.* New York: Cambridge University Press, 1996.

Inoguchi, Takashi, and Daniel I. Okimoto, eds. *The Political Economy of Japan.* Vol. 2, *The Changing International Context.* Stanford: Stanford University Press, 1988.

Johnson, Chalmers. *MITI and the Japanese Miracle: The Growth of Industrial Policy, 1925–1975.* Stanford: Stanford University Press, 1982.

Katzenstein, Peter J. *Cultural Norms and National Security: Police and Military in Postwar Japan.* Ithaca: Cornell University Press, 1996.

Katzenstein, Peter J., and Takashi Shiraishi, eds. *Network Power: Japan and Asia.* Ithaca: Cornell University Press, 1997.

Newland, Kathleen, ed. *The International Relations of Japan.* London: Macmillan, 1990.

Pempel, T. J. "Japanese Foreign Economic Policy: The Domestic Bases for International Behavior." In *Between Power and Plenty: Foreign Economic Policies of Advanced Industrial States.* Ed. Peter J. Katzenstein. Madison: University of Wisconsin Press, 1978.

Pyle, Kenneth B. *The Japanese Question: Power and Purpose in a New Era.* Washington, D.C.: AEI Press, 1992.

Scalapino, Robert A., ed. *The Foreign Policy of Modern Japan.* Berkeley: University of California Press, 1977.

Notes

I would like to thank the editors of this book for their insightful comments and Tokyo International University for financial assistance.

1. See, for example, Robert Gilpin, "Where Does Japan Fit In?" in *The International Relations of Japan,* ed. Kathleen Newland (London: Macmillan, 1990), 5–22.

2. John Lewis Gaddis, *Strategies of Containment: A Critical Appraisal of Postwar American National Security Policy* (New York: Oxford University Press, 1982), 89–126; John W. Dower, *Empire and the Aftermath: Yoshida Shigeru and the Japanese Experience,*

1878–1954 (Cambridge: Harvard University Press, 1980); Dower, *Embracing Defeat: Japan in the Wake of World War II* (New York: Norton, 1999); Michael Schaller, *The American Occupation of Japan: The Origins of the Cold War in Asia* (New York: Oxford University Press, 1985); Richard B. Finn, *Winners in Peace: MacArthur, Yoshida, and Postwar Japan* (Berkeley: University of California Press, 1992).

3. Article 9 of the Japanese constitution states that "the Japanese people forever renounce war as a sovereign right of the nation and the threat or use of force as means of settling international disputes" and that "land, sea, and air forces, as well as other war potential, will never be maintained."

4. Donald C. Hellmann, "Japanese Politics and Foreign Policy: Elitist Democracy within an American Greenhouse," in *The Political Economy of Japan*, Vol. 2, *The Changing International Context*, ed. Takashi Inoguchi and Daniel I. Okimoto (Stanford: Stanford University Press, 1988), 345–378.

5. Chalmers Johnson, *MITI and the Japanese Miracle: The Growth of Industrial Policy, 1925–1975* (Stanford: Stanford University Press, 1982), 15–16; John H. Makin and Donald C. Hellmann, eds., *Sharing World Leadership? A New Era for America and Japan* (Washington, D.C.: American Enterprise Institute, 1989).

6. *Foreign Relations of the United States, 1947*, vol. VI, 541.

7. On Yoshida's foreign policy stance, see Kenneth B. Pyle, *The Japanese Question: Power and Purpose in a New Era* (Washington, D.C.: AEI Press, 1992), chap. 3.

8. T. J. Pempel, "Japanese Foreign Economic Policy: The Domestic Bases for International Behavior," in *Between Power and Plenty: Foreign Economic Policies of Advanced Industrial States*, ed. Peter J. Katzenstein (Madison: University of Wisconsin Press, 1978), 169.

9. On Japan's conservative coalition, see Pempel, "Japanese Foreign Economic Power," "Japanese Foreign Economic Policy," 139–190; Michio Muramatsu and Ellis S. Krauss, "The Conservative Policy Line and the Development of Patterned Pluralism," in *The Political Economy of Japan*, vol. 1, *The Domestic Transformation*, ed. Kozo Yamamura and Yasukichi Yasuba (Stanford: Stanford University Press, 1987), 516–554.

10. For a major study analyzing the role the bureaucrats played in Japan's postwar economic miracle, see Johnson, *MITI and the Japanese Miracle*. It must be noted that the bureaucracy was not the sole reason for Japan's postwar economic success. There were cases where government intervention failed to produce the intended results and cases where firms succeeded without governmental assistance. See Steven R. Reed, *Making Common Sense of Japan* (Pittsburgh: University of Pittsburgh Press, 1993), chap. 5. For critique of the bureaucratic dominance thesis, see, for example, J. Mark Ramseyer and Frances McCall Rosenbluth, *Japan's Political Marketplace* (Cambridge: Harvard University Press, 1993); and Robert M. Uriu, *Troubled Industries: Confronting Economic Challenge in Japan* (Ithaca: Cornell University Press, 1996).

11. On the relationship between the state strength and the type of foreign economic policy, see Katzenstein, ed., *Between Power and Plenty*, chap. 9.

12. Alexander Gerschenkron, *Economic Backwardness in Historical Perspective* (Cambridge: Harvard University Press, 1962). For a discussion of Japan from this perspective, see William W. Lockwood, *The Economic Development of Japan* (Princeton: Princeton University Press, 1954).

13. Chalmers Johnson, "The People Who Invented the Mechanical Nightingale," *Daedalus* 119 (summer 1991): 72.

14. On the hegemonic stability theory, see, for example, Charles P. Kindleberger, *The World in Depression, 1929–1939* (Berkeley: University of California Press, 1973); Robert O. Keohane, "The Theory of Hegemonic Stability and Changes in International Economic Regimes," in *Change in the International System*, ed. Ole R. Holsti, Randolph M. Siverson, and Alexander L. George (Boulder: Westview Press, 1980);

and Robert Gilpin, *The Political Economy of International Relations* (Princeton: Princeton University Press, 1987).

15. Gilpin, *The Political Economy of International Relations*, 330–331; Joseph S. Nye, *Bound to Lead: The Changing Nature of American Power* (New York: Basic Books, 1990), 2.

16. See James Fallows, "Containing Japan," *Atlantic* 263 (1989): 40–48.

17. Gilpin, *The Political Economy of International Relations*, 328–336.

18. John Mearsheimer, "Back to the Future: Instability in Europe after the Cold War," *International Security* 15 (summer 1990): 5–56.

19. Aaron L. Friedberg, "Ripe for Rivalry: Prospects for Peace in a Multipolar Asia," *International Security* 18 (winter 1993–1994): 5–33; Richard K. Betts, "Wealth, Power, and Instability: East Asia and the United States after the Cold War," *International Security* 18 (winter 1993–1994): 34–77; Thomas J. Christensen, "China, the U.S.-Japan Alliance, and the Security Dilemma in East Asia," *International Security* 23 (spring 1999): 49–80.

20. For a discussion of the security dilemma, see Robert Jervis, "Cooperation under the Security Dilemma," *World Politics* 30 (January 1978): 186–214.

21. Christensen, "China, the U.S.-Japan Alliance, and the Security Dilemma in East Asia," 80.

22. In September 1985, finance ministers of the Group of Five advanced industrial nations (the United States, the United Kingdom, France, West Germany, and Japan) gathered at the Plaza Hotel in New York City and agreed to lower the value of the dollar against the other major currencies, especially the Japanese yen, in an attempt to reduce America's growing trade deficit.

23. For figures and analysis of the economic integration of Asia, see T. J. Pempel, "Transpacific Torii: Japan and the Emerging Asian Regionalism," in *Network Power: Japan and Asia*, ed. Peter J. Katzenstein and Takashi Shiraishi (Ithaca: Cornell University Press, 1997), 47–82.

24. David Arase, *Buying Power: The Political Economy of Japan's Foreign Aid* (Boulder: Lynne Rienner, 1995).

25. Yoichi Funabashi, *Asia Pacific Fusion: Japan's Role in APEC* (Washington, D.C.: Institute for International Economics, 1995), 223.

26. *Asahi Shimbun*, December 4, 1994.

27. For a good chronology and analysis of Japanese politics in the 1990s, see Gerald L. Curtis, *The Logic of Japanese Politics: Leaders, Institutions, and the Limits of Change* (New York: Columbia University Press, 1999).

28. The Japan Socialist Party changed its name to the Social Democratic Party in 1996. To avoid confusion, the former will be used throughout this article.

29. The Socialists, however, were divided on the timing of the peace treaty. In protest of the U.S. decision to retain its military bases in Japan after the occupation, the Soviet Union and its allies chose not to sign a peace treaty with Japan. As a result, Japan concluded a peace treaty mostly with those nations that were members of, or sympathetic to, the Western alliance (the "partial peace"). The leftists in the party argued that Japan should not conclude a peace treaty until all of the belligerents, including the communist countries, were ready and invited to sign (the "comprehensive peace"). The rightists maintained that the comprehensive peace was not pragmatic and would only delay Japan's independence. They insisted that Japan should sign a peace treaty with whichever countries wanted to conclude a peace with Japan.

30. The coalition government also included Sakigake, a small splinter party of former LDP members.

31. In April 2001 the Socialist Party modified its position held by the Murayama government. It now maintains that the U.S.-Japan security treaty has lost its significance

in today's world and that the treaty should be replaced by a friendship and economic treaty.

32. On the impact of shared norms on Japan's postwar defense policy, see Peter J. Katzenstein, *Cultural Norms and National Security: Police and Military in Postwar Japan* (Ithaca: Cornell University Press, 1996); Thomas U. Berger, *Cultures of Antimilitarism: National Security in Germany and Japan* (Baltimore: Johns Hopkins University Press, 1998).

33. Helen V. Milner, *Resisting Protectionism: Global Industries and the Politics of International Trade* (Princeton: Princeton University Press, 1988).

34. The main agenda of the Yalta conference was how to deal with a defeated Germany, but Roosevelt, Churchill, and Stalin also discussed the situation in the Far East. The agreement on the islands was secretly made in exchange for Soviet participation in the war against Japan.

35. On the territorial dispute, see for example Tsuyoshi Hasegawa, *The Northern Territories Dispute and Russo-Japanese Relations,* 2 vols. (Berkeley: University of California International and Area Studies Publications, 1998); Kimie Hara, *Japanese-Soviet/Russian Relations since 1945: A Difficult Peace* (New York: Routledge, 1998); Harry Gelman, *Russo-Japanese Relations and the Future of the U.S.-Japan Alliance* (Santa Monica: Rand, 1993); Lonney E. Carlile, "The Changing Political Economy of Japan's Economic Relations with Russia: The Rise and Fall of *Seikei Fukabun,*" *Pacific Affairs* 67, 411–432.

36. The 1973 oil crisis and the emerging need to diversify sources of raw material imports prompted the Ministry of International Trade and Industry to stimulate joint ventures in the Soviet energy sector by providing trade insurance and export credits to Japanese firms. Nonetheless, the Soviet Union never accounted for more than 2 percent of Japan's total trade throughout the postwar period, and the cumulative figure for Japan's direct investment in the country from 1951 to 1989 amounted to only $222 million, or 0.09 percent of Japan's total foreign direct investment during that period.

37. On the Asian financial crisis, see, for example, T. J. Pempel, ed., *The Politics of the Asian Economic Crisis* (Ithaca: Cornell University Press, 1999); Robert Wade, "The Asian Crisis and the Global Economy: Causes, Consequences, and Cure," *Current History* (October 1998): 1–15.

38. Saori N. Katada, "Determining Factors of Japan's Cooperation and Non-cooperation with the United States: The Case of Asian Financial Crisis Management, 1997–1999" (paper presented at the annual meeting of the International Studies Association, Los Angeles, March 14–18, 2000), 23.

39. Katada, "Determining Factors of Japan's Cooperation and Non-cooperation with the United States," 8.

40. *New York Times,* February 17, 1999; Katada, "Determining Factors of Japan's Cooperation and Non-cooperation with the United States," 12.

41. T. J. Pempel, "Conclusion," in *The Politics of the Asian Economic Crisis,* ed. Pempel, 230.

42. On the domestic impact of the AMF plan, see Katada, "Determining Factors of Japan's Cooperation and Non-cooperation with the United States," 8–12.

43. Stephen Daggett and Gary J. Pagliano, "Persian Gulf War: U.S. Costs and Allied Financial Contributions," *CRS Issue Brief,* March 26, 1991, Congressional Research Service, Library of Congress, 9, 13.

44. Akio Watanabe, "Japan's Foreign Policy-Making in Crisis: China (1989–90) and Kuwait (1990–91)," Working Papers, No. 34, Department of Social and International Relations, University of Tokyo, April 1993, 26; Edward J. Lincoln, *Japan's New Global Role* (Washington, D.C.: Brookings Institution, 1993), 224.

45. Watanabe, "Japan's Foreign Policy-Making in Crisis," 24.
46. Ibid., 24, 28; Lincoln, *Japan's New Global Role,* 225.
47. *New York Times,* September 30, 1990.
48. Michael Blaker, "Evaluating Japan's Diplomatic Performance," in *Japan's Foreign Policy after the Cold War: Coping with Change,* ed. Gerald Curtis (Armonk, N.Y.: M. E. Sharpe, 1993), 18–21; Lincoln, *Japan's New Global Role,* 224.
49. Watanabe, "Japan's Foreign Policy-Making in Crisis," 28.
50. The bill could still pass without the approval in the upper house. But to do so required the LDP to secure two-thirds of votes in the lower house, which was unlikely to happen.
51. *Asahi Shimbun,* November 6, 1990.
52. The weak public support was reflected by individual LDP politicians. According to a telephone survey of LDP Diet members conducted by a major daily in Japan, only 64 percent of those responded said they would support the bill. The remaining 35 percent were either opposed or undecided (*Asahi Shimbun,* November 1, 1990).
53. Watanabe, "Japan's Foreign Policy-Making in Crisis," 31.
54. *Nihon Keizai Shimbun,* April 25, 1991.
55. *Nihon Keizai Shimbun,* February 2, 1991.
56. *Asahi Shimbun,* June 19, 1991.
57. L. William Heinrich Jr., Akiho Shibata, and Yoshihide Soeya, *United Nations Peacekeeping Operations: A Guide to Japanese Policies* (New York: United Nations University Press, 1999), 20.
58. Takao Takahara, "Japan's Peacekeeping Experience." Unpublished ms., Ithaca, Peace Studies Program, Cornell University, n.d., quoted in *Cultural Norms and National Security: Police and Military in Postwar Japan,* ed. Peter J. Katzenstein, 128.
59. Blaker, "Evaluating Japan's Diplomatic Performance," 23.
60. Starting in the 1996 general election, Japan replaced the medium-sized electoral districts with a combination of single-member districts (electing 300 seats) and proportional representation (electing 200 seats) in the lower house. This change provides an interesting test for Calder's argument that the medium-sized electoral districts make politicians more concerned with parochial interests of their constituencies over broad foreign policy questions. The results so far seem to indicate that Japanese politicians have become more, rather than less, parochial in the new system than in the old one. See Hideo Otake, ed., *How Electoral Reform Boomeranged: Continuity in Japanese Campaigning Style* (Tokyo: Japan Center for International Exchange, 1998).
61. Kent E. Calder, "Japanese Foreign Economic Policy Formation: Explaining the 'Reactive State.'" *World Politics* 40 (July 1988): 517–541.
62. Ibid., 518.
63. See, for example, Dennis T. Yasutomo, *The New Multilateralism in Japan's Foreign Policy* (New York: St. Martin's Press, 1995); Stephen J. Anderson, "Japan as an Activist State in the Pacific Basin: Japan and Regional Organizations," *Journal of East Asian Studies* 7 (1993): 498–544.
64. On the reactive–proactive debate, see Akitoshi Miyashita, "*Gaiatsu* and Japan's Foreign Aid: Rethinking the Reactive–Proactive Debate," *International Studies Quarterly* 43 (December 1999): 695–732.
65. Richard Solomon and Masataka Kosaka, *The Soviet Far East Military Buildup* (Dover, Mass.: Auburn House, 1986), 137.

CHAPTER 8

Indian Foreign Policy: From Consensus to Disarray

Tinaz Pavri

Forged through nonviolent resistance to British colonial rule, the largest democracy in the world has ironically embraced force and the threat of force as central elements of its foreign policy. Tinaz Pavri argues that, indeed, a trend toward realism is evident in India as it attempts to establish itself as a powerful regional and international actor.

During the Cold War, India, like China (Chapter 6) and to some extent France (Chapter 3), attempted to chart a "third course," striving for autonomy and international recognition in a bipolar system. Although nominally nonaligned through much of the Cold War, India's pro-Soviet leanings and anti-Western sentiment left it with an uncertain post–Cold War vision. Moreover, its postcolonial partition into the dominions of India and Pakistan continues to occupy a significant portion of its foreign policy attention in the form of struggles to deal simultaneously with territorial issues in Kashmir and with the potential threats of two regional nuclear powers, Pakistan and China. India's regional threats frequently result in violence and warfare, much like those in China (Chapter 6) and Israel (Chapter 9). As a result, India's relevant foreign policies have frequently come under harsh international scrutiny. Overall, India's desire for international stature, foreign investment, and regional security, together with its ethnically diverse and politically fractured domestic landscape, offer numerous intriguing foreign policy challenges.

Domestically, like the decline of the Institutional Revolutionary Party (PRI) in Mexico (Chapter 14), India's long-dominant Congress Party recently gave way to a variety of other political forces. Indeed, like in Germany (Chapter 4) and Israel (Chapter 9), India's parliamentary democracy has moved toward coalition rule.

Finally, India is a land of contrasts. It is relatively poor economically and, like South Africa (Chapter 12), Brazil (Chapter 13), and Mexico (Chapter 14), is in need of foreign investment. Yet at the same time India is technologically advanced and possesses nuclear weapons, like Britain (Chapter 2) and France (Chapter 3).

Since receiving its independence from Great Britain in 1947, India has come into its own as an important player in Asian and world politics. However, much to its chagrin, it cannot seem to shake the global perception, a perception sometimes shared at home, that most of its potential has remained unrealized even after a half-century of independence. Much has been written about the potential strengths of India's emerging middle class, the brain power of its literate population (the impact of which has yet to be fully felt), its economic possibilities, its natural resources, its historical and cultural legacies, and its richness in so many respects. Scholars, students, and those interested in India, including Indians themselves, agree that the country is characterized by possibilities that might someday be realized but that have not been so far. In the spirit of one of Prime Minister Jawaharlal Nehru's favorite poems by Robert Frost, India still has "miles to go before [it] sleep[s]."[1]

This chapter examines Indian foreign policy within this larger context of unrealized potential. It traces the promising early evolution of India's foreign policy from its basis in Mohandas Gandhi's tenets of nonviolence and peaceful settlement of disputes and Jawaharlal Nehru's ideals of positive nonalignment to its current apparent lack of direction as it faces a region of escalating hostility and instability with a foreign policy characterized by a growing moral ambiguity. The chapter also describes the historical background from which Indian foreign policy has emerged and the regional and international setting that has prompted (and in some measure has been a result of) India's actions. It examines as well the domestic political context in India, which has changed dramatically since the days of the Cold War, with important consequences for foreign policy issues. And it offers some thoughts on future challenges facing India in the foreign policy sphere.

Indian Foreign Policy during the Cold War

Like many other countries that threw off the yoke of colonial rule in the post–World War II years, India was understandably anxious to overturn its subordinate position in relation to Britain in particular and the West in general. India's foreign policy thus had something of a homespun quality in those days, although the nuts and bolts of its bureaucratic component, the Indian Administrative Service (IAS) which includes the Indian Foreign Service (IFS), continued almost unchanged from the days of the British Indian Civil Service (ICS).

Jawaharlal Nehru, independent India's first prime minister, envisaged close and trusted relations among Asian countries, bound as many of them were by the common experience of colonialism. This closeness, he imagined, would produce shared strength and power for the region, a natural alliance against any attempts at domination by the West. This illusion, among others, was rudely shattered when China, which India and Nehru had assiduously cultivated with the slogan *Hindi-Chini bhai bhai* ("Indians and Chinese are brothers"), launched an attack on disputed Indian territory along the border in 1962. The Chinese claimed the territory to be rightly theirs, alleging that Britain had illegally incorporated it into British India, but India, of course, never accepted what it called China's territorial aggression. After that war, the two countries for the most part put this territorial issue and the troubling issue of China's occupation of Tibet on India's northern border on the back burner while they cautiously explored other areas of cooperation. Old tensions rose to the surface, however, after India's 1998 nuclear tests. These issues are further explored in other parts of this chapter.

The Chinese debacle notwithstanding, Nehru continued to nurture images of fraternal relations among the countries of the developing world, relations based on liberal notions of cooperation and shared values. As we shall see, these early aspirations have today largely evaporated as India confronts a quite different reality in the region and the world, a reality in which the rhetoric of oneness might still play a role but where action belies rhetoric.

1947: "India Awakes to Life and Freedom"

In his eloquent 1947 speech in New Delhi on the occasion of Britain's formal turnover of sovereignty to India, Nehru famously predicted that "at the stroke of the midnight hour, when the world sleeps, India will awake to life and freedom." Many scholars of India and of democratization have argued that the transition to independence was a relatively smooth one for India, especially when compared with the violent upheavals that characterized decolonization in many African and Asian countries. It is true that the party that led India to independence, Nehru's and Mohandas (Mahatma) Gandhi's Indian National Congress (INC) was already fielding candidates for local elections decades prior to independence and was by 1947 a relatively well-established and well-organized national political party.[2] This party and the independence elite that served it provided the Indian political landscape with much-needed stability in the years after independence. Nehru, Mohandas Gandhi, and other independence elite had worked with Louis Mountbatten, the last British viceroy to India, to negotiate a smooth transition.

Although the fight for independence was relatively nonviolent, independence itself brought with it an enormous loss of life when British India formally split into two sovereign countries, India and Pakistan. Until the last moments, Mohandas Gandhi and Nehru had strongly opposed the partition of the country, pleading with Mohammed Ali Jinnah, leader of the Muslim League (another independence party that primarily spoke to and for Indian Muslims), to remain within independent India. When it became clear that a compromise was not possible and partition became inevitable, the plans for separation were drawn up involving negotiators on all sides, including the British. Almost immediately, millions of Hindus fled the new state of Pakistan for India where they would feel safer, and Muslims fled India to settle in Pakistan. In the chaos that ensued, innumerable people lost their lives, homes, and property when sectarian violence broke out between the two communities during this large-scale human migration.[3] Thus the physical act of partition itself and the tragedy it produced fueled the Hindu-Muslim and Indian-Pakistani hostility and mistrust that have characterized relations between the leaders, and often the peoples, of the two states since that time.

Foundations of a Modern Crisis: Kashmir

Pakistan and Kashmir preoccupy Indian foreign policy making more than any other issue. Born out of the partition of the subcontinent when the British left in 1947, Kashmir has become the basis of the continued hostilities between India and Pakistan. From the beginning of the negotiations over the division of the subcontinent into a Hindu-majority India and a Muslim-majority Pakistan, Jinnah, the head of the Muslim League, would accept no alternative other than two separate states created out of one. His rationale was that Muslims needed their own country and that Hindu-dominated India would not be sympathetic to these needs. Jinnah himself, however, was never a religious man and has been criticized for playing the "religion card" in order to become the first prime minister of independent Pakistan.

Partition required that guidelines be drawn up for the division of government property, assets, and the armed forces, taking into account the expected movement of masses of people across the newly drawn borders. The some five hundred princely states that existed in British India also posed a problem: Should they be independent? Would they align with India or with Pakistan? And on what conditions would alignment be permitted? The option for independence was not a viable one as most of them lay well inside either country. Thus efforts were directed toward ascertaining how they would join India or Pakistan. The criteria finally agreed on were mainly the states' geographic location and the religious identity of the majority of their subjects. Many of the states in the geographic interior of India chose freely to join it. For the princely state of Kashmir, the decision was complicated by the fact that its ruler was a Hindu while the majority of its inhabitants were Muslim. Furthermore, it shared borders with both India and Pakistan. As the king vacillated, the stakes increased for India and Pakistan to claim Kashmir: for India, Kashmir constituted the proof of its policy of secularism; for Pakistan, Kashmiris were quite simply Muslim brethren.

While the decision-making process was under way, armed tribesmen from northwestern Pakistan swarmed into Kashmir in October 1947, forcing the king's hand in calling on India for help and eventually acceding to India. Although Pakistan vociferously denies this, most scholars agree and evidence indicates that the tribesmen were in fact backed by the Pakistani government. A full-scale war ensued, and claims and counterclaims were exchanged by the two sides. On December 31, 1948, a United Nations-sponsored truce was declared, concluding the first of the three wars and numerous border crises over Kashmir. A plebiscite advocated by the United Nations was never implemented, and India rejected holding such a plebiscite. A formal UN-sponsored cease-fire concluded in 1949 divided Kashmir. India would control two-thirds (the state of Jammu and Kashmir), and one-third would be controlled by Pakistan—Azad (Free) Kashmir—and given relatively greater autonomy than its Indian-held counterpart.

In 1965 India and Pakistan again went to war over an uprising in disputed Kashmir. Several years later, in 1971, the two countries fought a war over the creation of Bangladesh from former East Pakistan, with India prevailing. The war broke out when East Pakistanis, ethnic Bengalis with a separate culture and language, sought separation from the rest of Pakistan after years of government oppression. When government crackdowns on the East Pakistanis resulted in thousands of refugees streaming into India from its northeastern borders, the Indian government felt compelled to become involved in the crisis.

Another war was fought in the summer of 1999 in the northern part of Kashmir near the town of Kargil. Of all the confrontations between India and Pakistan, arguably this last war in Kargil had the potential for the greatest damage, because both countries were by this time nuclear states. Neither country seriously considered using its nuclear weapons, however. The continuing issue of Kashmir is examined more closely in the final section of this chapter.

The Cold War Years: Nehru and Gandhi

The rapidly developing Cold War provided an opportunity for Nehru to put his mark on evolving Indian foreign policy. He became one of the founders, along with Egypt's Gamal Abdel Nasser and Yugoslavia's Josip Broz Tito, of the non-aligned movement (NAM). This movement was an attempt by many former colonies to counter the bipolar world and superpower rivalry that had emerged by the 1950s. In reality, though, many NAM member countries such as India and Cuba became very closely aligned with the Soviet bloc. Although lofty in their ideals of disapproving of and not immediately partaking in the costly and dangerous emerging Cold War, many NAM member countries successfully played the Soviets off against the United States and the West in an attempt to gain aid and trade benefits for themselves. This strategy was realist politics in the guise of noninvolvement.

The influence of Mahatma Gandhi, India's most beloved independence figure, inevitably carried over into the early days of India's foreign policy articulation, with nonviolence and peaceful settlement of disputes appearing large in the rhetoric of India's foreign relations. However, this early idealism gradually gave way to pragmatism, particularly in light of India's early and continual antagonism with neighboring Pakistan and later China. Nehru perhaps came as close to embodying Plato's ideal of the "philosopher-king" (the ruler who has such perfect wisdom and morality that the future of the country is best left in his hands) as any contemporary world leader. Yet he was constrained by the realist realization that simply setting an example was not enough. For one thing, India could not expect other countries to follow suit. Moreover, others might interpret any signs of pacifism as weakness. In the end, India's first responsibility was to shore up its defense and protect its national integrity from attacks by others. It could do this by becoming more militarily powerful itself.

Indeed, shortly after Indira Gandhi (no relation to Mohandas) ascended to the position of prime minister in 1966, she oversaw the modernization of the army, which helped India to win the third war against Pakistan in 1971, a war that led to the creation of an independent Bangladesh out of what used to be East Pakistan. Gandhi shared little of Nehru's idealism and philosophical bent and clearly believed that states needed to increase their power in order to increase their security. In fact, she was ruthless in attempting to subordinate neighboring countries like Nepal and Bhutan through the unspoken threat of Indian military action if they disagreed with India's economic and security proposals. Her realist leanings were further apparent in the way she conducted domestic policy, moving quickly after she was elected prime minister to consolidate great power in the position of prime minister and to eliminate from her government those who opposed her policies. It was because of her inability and unwillingness to compromise with Congress leaders who disagreed with her vision that the Congress Party split into the Congress I (for Indira) Party and the Congress O (for organization) Party in 1969.

Gandhi's thinking remained zero-sum for much of her life in politics. For example, in 1975 she chose to move against opposition members and declare a national emergency in India rather than face the prospect of being jailed for breaking election laws during her 1971 campaign. Instead of resigning when she was convicted of the offense (a conviction later overruled by the Supreme Court), she labeled the conviction an opposition ploy and called a national emergency on June 26.[4] More broadly, Gandhi is widely blamed for having caused the ultimate waning of the powerful Congress Party. The local organization of the party suffered through her attempts to consolidate all power at the national level and in her person.

External Factors

The regional and international setting as it applies to India reveals more discontinuity than continuity, more disarray than consensus. With the post–Cold War shift away from a bipolar distribution of power and the Russians no longer able to provide the kind of heavy economic and military support that the Soviet Union once did, India has had to deal with the United States whether it likes it or not. For many Indians, the United States continues to represent the Western imperialism that India has always decried; however, while the rhetoric might sound familiar, real changes are becoming evident in the relationship.

The United States has been India's biggest trading partner for some time now, and U.S. foreign direct investment into the country continues to increase significantly. To the extent that India needs this investment desperately (not least for the development of infrastructure in the communications, technology and power sectors), it understands that investing countries may insist on linking continued economic investment with concessions from India in the nuclear and other spheres. In this sense, increasing interdependence offers both an opportunity for and a potential constraint on Indian foreign policy. Indeed, India has already had to agree with the international nonproliferation regime that it will not transfer nuclear technology and materials to states that seek to build weapons, and in fact has not done so thus far. This concession can be traced back to increased Western pressure on India for restraint in this arena.

In terms of the economy, a power project by the U.S. company Enron represents the largest foreign investment (approximately $2 billion) ever made in India and nicely illustrates the economic constraints India faces. The project got off to a smooth start when the national government granted swifter than normal approval in 1992. However, the Maharashtra state government (where the plant would be located) cancelled the project on grounds that it was exploitative of India (the state changed over in 1995 from a Congress Party-led government to a coalition government that included the nationalist Bharatiya Janata Party, or BJP). Enron, which had already spent $300 million in infrastructural costs, then sued the state government in an international court for reimbursement. When it became clear that the state government might have to repay Enron and that the adverse publicity might jeopardize future foreign investment, the state hurriedly renegotiated and reinstated the deal. As it becomes clearer that India needs increased levels of foreign investment pumped into its economy and that it is in fact more integrated with the world economy today than at any previous time in its independent history, such patently nationalistic responses by some Indian politicians to Western companies and countries are routinely giving way to more measured responses at both the state and central levels. Globalization, as Chapter 1 indicates, certainly does bring new pressures in its wake.

India also may have to make concessions in the human rights arena. Whereas up to this point India's standard response to Western accusations of human rights violations in both Kashmir and elsewhere in the country has been defensiveness and a reiteration of its sovereignty, its increasing economic interdependence with investing countries is almost certain to bring greater scrutiny by the West of its record of police brutality of minorities, both in India and in Kashmir. Since the demise of the former Soviet Union and India's opening of its economy in the early 1990s, it appears that India needs the West more than ever. This new integration with the world economy will continue to serve as a moderating factor on India's foreign policy.

On a more symbolic level, President Bill Clinton made a historic visit to India in March 2000 that created much good feeling and the sense on India's part that the United States was finally recognizing India as an important global actor. It further served to illustrate that the United States has to now deal with a nuclear India whether it likes it or not, much as India has to deal with the world's remaining superpower, whether it likes it or not. India's prime minister, A. B. Vajpayee, reciprocated with a successful visit to the United States in the fall of 2000. Thus the Indo-U.S. relationship appears to be heading toward a new prag-matism that seems to be shedding, albeit in small steps, the shrill ideological rhetoric of the past.

With China, there has been a cautious overall improvement in the relation-ship despite the unresolved border dispute and despite China's occupation of Tibet. Indian prime minister Rajiv Gandhi (the son of Indira Gandhi) agreed in 1988 to set aside border differences to work on the overall amelioration of the relationship, and China made clearly conciliatory statements about India and Kashmir in 1991. This improvement, however, was threatened in the wake of the 1998 Indian nuclear tests. A war of words ensued, with the Indian prime minis-ter openly claiming that one of the reasons for the tests was protection against China's nuclear weapons and their proliferation to Pakistan, and China criticiz-ing India for seeking to be a hegemon in Asia. India found the Chinese reaction somewhat hypocritical in light of its diffusion of nuclear weapons and technolo-gy to Pakistan. Moreover, it found China's reaction contradictory, because China had previously stated that India had the right to keep its nuclear option open. India also found the Chinese position to be somewhat ungrateful in light of India's tacit support of China during the world community's denunciation of the Tiananmen massacre and its continual unwillingness to criticize Chinese policy in Tibet. In the last year, however, academics and businesspersons have contin-ued to exchange visits between the two countries, and the Indians and the Chi-nese have held formal diplomatic meetings at gatherings such as the ASEAN Regional Forum (ARF) in Manila in the fall of 1998.[5] It is possible that the "new world order" pragmatism that is infusing the Indo-U.S. relationship also might be permeating the relationship between India and China and that rapproche-ment might be back on track despite the nuclear test flap. The Tibet issue is con-sidered again toward the end of the chapter.

East Asia has never generated much official interest for India, although many Indians travel to Singapore, Hong Kong, and Thailand and have relatives and friends there. India has always turned farther ashore, to the Soviets, rather than closer home, to East Asia, for its security and economic ties. India's lack of inter-est in East Asia also may stem from its preoccupation with itself as regional power in Asia that has little time for smaller and (according to this view) less-important Asian countries and whose politicians, as Barbara Crossette has argued, believe firmly in India's cultural superiority in the region.[6]

Although India's relations with East Asia have always been puzzlingly limit-ed and continue to be weak, its relations with its immediate neighbors—Bangladesh, Nepal, Bhutan, and Sri Lanka—appear to have gone from close and harmonious during the Nehru era to strained. India is increasingly taking on the role of regional heavyweight. The independent kingdom of Sikkim was taken over by India during the 1970s, and that event may continue to serve as a reminder to Bhutan of the consequences of crossing its powerful neighbor, even as it maintains outwardly cordial and close ties with New Delhi. Ninety-five percent of Bhutan's trade is with India, the Indian military is conspicuously present in Thimpu, Bhutan's capital, and Indian experts frequently travel to Bhutan for consultations with the Thimpu government. In the 1950s, Indian troops may have served as a deterrent to China, which had declared Bhutan part of its territory, along with Tibet.

In 1989–1990 India imposed economic sanctions on Nepal, citing certain violations in trading and work permit rules. Many observers believe that the fact that Nepal was increasingly awarding building contracts to Chinese firms had upset India. The sanctions, effectively blocking Nepal's access to the Indian port of Calcutta, Nepal's closest entry to the sea, generated in Nepal some bitterness toward India and domestic instability that eventually led to the recent constitutional upheavals in that country. India also has been involved in the Tamil struggle for self-determination in Sri Lanka, perhaps, as some have argued, by arming the Tamil militants there. India has claimed that its role in the region stems from the existence of millions of ethnic Tamils in the southern Indian state of Tamil Nadu.

What all this points to, then, is a state of affairs in which India's friendly neighbors of the past are today suspicious and sometimes hostile. India has moved from early idealism to more single-minded realism; beginning with Indira Gandhi, India began to interpret the regional setting in terms of security equaling power. Thus it flexed its economic and military muscle for its neighbors where once friendship and persuasion had prevailed. On a broader scale, both Nehru and Indira Gandhi appeared to have become convinced of the prevalence of realpolitik in relations among states of the world. Until the unraveling of the Soviet Union, India clung to its relationship with the Soviets to balance Pakistan's alliance with the United States. And, although India often blasted the Cold War as dangerous and wasteful and supported smaller former colonies in their struggles, it clearly was not preoccupied with these smaller states (witness its lack of close relations with other Asian countries).[7] Rather, India concerned itself with its secured place in the sphere of Soviet influence, because reality dictated that India be firmly attached to one of the poles in the bipolar world.

Internal Factors

From the end of the Nehru era in 1964 until the early 1970s, well into Indira Gandhi's reign, little domestic political opposition was present in India. Mohandas Gandhi's and Nehru's Congress Party, which had achieved a high profile and eventual success in the independence movement, was clearly the single largest political party in India and had the greatest domestic support. The Congress Party continued to win elections on the national level with significant majorities until 1997, when, for the first time, it was voted out of power in a national election. One reason for its defeat was Prime Minister Indira Gandhi's increasingly visible dictatorial tendencies and her call for a national emergency in the years between 1975 and 1977. The civil liberties guaranteed to the Indian people through the constitution were suspended for an extended period for the first and only time. In the 1977 elections, she bore the consequences for her actions by being voted out of office.

Until the 1970s and arguably into the early 1980s, India's foreign policy appeared to have the support of a domestic consensus. Even later, when opposition parties became more numerous and more vocal, and indeed for the first time in 1977 formed the government, a consensus generally prevailed. The consensus appears to have formed around three main goals of Indian foreign policy: (1) to preserve national security and integrity; (2) to maintain self-reliance so that India, even though it had signed the treaty of Friendship and Cooperation with the Soviets in 1971, could essentially protect itself and be economically self-reliant; and (3) to attain recognition for India as a major player and important power in world politics.[8]

In the early days, because of the prevalence of the Cold War, many of the decisions surrounding these goals were relatively easy. India knew who its friends were, to whom to turn to purchase weapons and technology (the Soviet Union), and what to do and say in which arena in order to claim a higher profile for itself—for example, within the friendly boundaries of the nonaligned movement or the Group of 77, the group of developing countries and former colonies in the United Nations that often spoke with one voice on trade and aid issues. Since the end of the Cold War, even though some consensus around the three goals may continue to exist, the decisions surrounding them have become increasingly difficult and the divisions among the political parties as to just how to attain these goals have become wider. For example, the parties continue to debate openly how much closer India should move toward the United States, and some in the opposition have expressed concern that escalating hostilities with Pakistan might actually stem more from the anti-Muslim rhetoric of the Bharatiya Janata Party and its allies than from Pakistan's provocations. Another subject of heated debate is how to attain economic self-reliance. The old quasi-socialist ideas that drove India's mixed economy until the early 1990s are increasingly giving way to new market-driven options.

The end of the Cold War also coincided with a sea of change in the Indian domestic political scene. Whereas the Congress Party once dominated Indian politics and other political parties were small and fragmented, the Indian political stage today is a decidedly multiparty one, and the Congress Party has lost its dominance—many will argue, forever. Coalition governments appear to have become the order of the day. The Bharatiya Janata Party (Indian People's Party) and its coalition partners have formed the government in India since the mid-1990s. The BJP is a nationalist, fundamentalist (Hindu) party that has at different times railed against the Muslims and other minorities in India as being "un-Indian," spoken out against the secular nature of modern India, and advocated a

Hindu India in its place. Formed out of smaller nationalist and fundamentalist fringe parties, the BJP rose from obscurity in the 1980s to poll the largest number of votes in the 1999 election. It has not yet managed to secure a sole majority in parliament, but it could well do so in future elections, even though the party appears to be fracturing along moderate-extremist lines (the current prime minister, Atal Behari Vajpayee, is a well-respected and influential moderate). During the BJP's rule, India has detonated a nuclear bomb and presided over greatly deteriorated relations with Pakistan, including the war in the Kargil region of Kashmir that was concluded in 1999.

In parliament, there is currently no consensus among political parties on whom India's friends now are, how India can best attain self-reliance, or how it should persuade the world community to recognize it as a major player. Although the United States is still often on the receiving end of hostility from many of the political parties, including the BJP, others realize how badly U.S. foreign direct investment is needed to push the Indian economy ahead. The collapse of the former Soviet Union has left Indians unable to play the West off against the Soviets. Now, realistically, India can turn only to the West for investment, because other Asian investment in India has not historically been very high.[9]

The BJP's influence on Indian foreign policy appears to be one of radicalization: the detonation of the bomb led Pakistan to quickly do the same and led world opinion (at least initially) to view India as a potentially loose cannon. New Delhi and Islamabad, Pakistan's capital, exchange harsh words routinely, and the BJP and its other, more radical political allies such as the Rashtriya Swayam Sevak Sangh and Shiv Sena have seen the ramifications of this strain in India's relations with Pakistan and vice versa. For all its tough talk about the bomb being needed to protect itself (from Pakistan and China, primarily, a position that most politicians and many Indians genuinely subscribe to), today India appears more vulnerable from different quarters than ever.[10]

This discussion of the influence of domestic factors on Indian foreign policy underscores another important factor that must figure in any analysis of India's role in world politics, especially until the early 1990s which signaled the end of the Nehru-Gandhi dynasty.[11] Indian politics until this time was controlled to an extraordinary degree by the dominant personalities of its leaders, particularly Jawaharlal Nehru and his daughter Indira Gandhi. There is little doubt but that both of these leaders were involved in actual decision making rather than delegating it to subordinates, and thus their impact on the foreign policy agenda was great. Examples are India's early involvement in the nonaligned movement, the gestures of friendship to China, and the budding friendship with the Soviet Union from the socialist Nehru who while a student in England avidly studied Fabian socialism (a strand of socialism developed by intellectuals in England in the 1880s that advocated working within the system rather than overthrowing it). Gandhi not only continued the Soviet relationship built under her father, but also steadily cooled relations with the United States, which she found dominating and arrogant. Her view of Richard Nixon, who was U.S. president during the

Bangladesh war, was particularly dim. Indeed, possessing enormous personal insecurity, a trait documented by many of her biographers, Gandhi adopted a leadership style that was highly controlling, and she sought maximum power for her own office. She also mistrusted neighbors and saw the world as essentially conflicted.[12]

Gandhi, then, differed quite a bit from her father in how she conducted domestic and foreign policy, but she did share his socialist outlook. By all accounts, Nehru was open, engaging, conciliatory, and a consensus builder, but there was no doubt that he was also the dominant leader during his tenure. It was as if his mandate as the true successor of the beloved Mohandas Gandhi gave him the confidence to seek advice when he needed it, but also the leeway to act decisively and on his own if the situation demanded it. Although Gandhi was recognized by most Indians as a moral giant—and indeed, as his diminutive *Bapu* implies, as a father (in his case, of the nation)—it was also widely accepted that after forging a broad path for India's foreign relations guided by his beliefs in nonviolence and cooperation, Gandhi left the business of governing to Nehru.

Quite unlike her father, Indira Gandhi relied on a closed and limited circle of confidants. Many scholars have commented that it was in fact her legendary lack of trust and her intense desire to dominate that led ultimately to the weakening not just of the infrastructure of the Congress (I) Party but indeed of the institutions of Indian democracy itself. Another difference was Indira Gandhi's total embrace of realism as the guiding star of foreign policy, whereas Nehru had continued to depend on a moral compass in his conduct of foreign policy. Indeed, Nehru candidly stated in speeches that without the recognition of a "moral law" in national and international relations, India would not be successful in achieving peace. For his daughter Indira, morality was what suited her vision for India.

With the advent of coalition politics in India in more recent times, no single leader has been able to imprint his or her personality on Indian foreign policy.[13] However, it could be argued that the collective character of the BJP, ardently nationalistic and chauvinistically Hindu as it is, has gone a long way in firing religious passions among many Indians against Muslims and has introduced the volatile element of religion and sectarianism into India's dealings with its neighbors.

Contemporary Indian Foreign Policy

As we have seen, then, present-day India has strayed quite far from the early underpinnings of its foreign policy. The end of the Cold War made the non-aligned movement irrelevant. Nehru's dream of a united and interdependent Asia gave way to a reality of increased hostilities and tensions not just between India and Pakistan, but also between India and some of its other South Asian neighbors. Mohandas Gandhi's nonviolent ideals appear to be belied by a total of four wars and numerous other conflicts between India and Pakistan and by a fifteen-year insurgency in India's northernmost state, Kashmir, where blood is spilled almost daily.[14] Only in India's suspicion of the West, which once symbolized colonialism, does there appear to be some continuity with the past. The United States, the enemy of India's friend of many decades, the Soviet Union, and the friend of India's enemy, Pakistan, continues to be viewed with mistrust and misgivings that still give way to open hostility in the Indian press and parliament on occasion.[15] Of course, all these developments are complicated by India's newfound status as a nuclear state.

The Path to the Bomb

One of the most prominent issues confronting India in the post–Cold War period was its decision to detonate a nuclear device. As early as 1948 India had an Atomic Energy Commission, and its Department of Atomic Energy was flourishing by 1954.[16] Although the early nuclear program focused on fulfilling domestic energy needs, the conflict between India and China changed perceptions toward the program. The ongoing conflict with Pakistan, a perception that the United States still sided with this enemy-neighbor, and the firm belief of the ruling government and a majority of the Indian people that more weapons and bombs equaled greater security led India to join the ranks of the declared nuclear weapons states in 1998.

The specific motivations behind India's decision to test the bomb at the time it did are still widely debated. India has continued to make the national security argument, pointing a finger at both Pakistan and China. Others have suggested that the decision grew out of India's oft-thwarted desire to be recognized as a major power in the world and domestic pressures — a powerful and increasingly vocal scientific community that advocated testing and a sympathetic ruling government that had included a nuclear India in its campaign platforms.[17] Perhaps nowhere as much as in the nuclear arena did India continue to label the West as imperialist, often referring to the nuclear nonproliferation regime as one of "apartheid," in which Western countries were trying to keep the rest of the (particularly developing) world out of the nuclear club. A kind of "political psychology" approach to understanding the Indian motivation views the decision as the result of decades of grievances by Indian leaders and the populace that their proper place in the world had not been recognized and their belief that "going nuclear" would make them more "equal" with other nuclear powers. In a more realist vein, India was aware of increasing Chinese assistance to Pakistan's nuclear missile program and felt compelled to regain momentum. It is fair to state that all of these explanations are viable and perhaps played a part in explaining India's motivation.

Although the idealist in Nehru believed that there would never be cause to actually build nuclear weapons, the pragmatist in him had already realized early on in the history of the nuclear program that the option must be kept open by continuing research. However, Nehru probably would have been shocked to learn that in 1998 India did actually produce a bomb and test it, and that it now faces Pakistan with theater nuclear weapons. It also is a great irony that the land of nonviolent conflict resolution can now unabashedly proclaim the benefits of the bomb.

The Conflict with No End: Kashmir

Much of the larger Indo-Pakistani relationship has revolved precisely around the question of Kashmir and who controls it. Although Pakistan has claimed that it is in favor of multilateral discussions on the issue, with Western officials and organizations serving as mediators, India has steadfastly rejected any idea of mediation, claiming that the issue can be settled only by the two parties concerned.[18] Other studies have shown, however, that third party involvement (including Britain, the United States, the United Nations, and Russia) in the various Indo-Pakistani crises have often led to settlements rather than escalation and that, conversely, when third parties are not involved crises have escalated into full-fledged wars.[19] The Indian position up until this day, however, remains averse to what it calls "internationalizing" the issue through third party involvement.

In January 1990 a crisis unfolded that many newspaper reports at the time described as potentially the most serious since the war of 1971. Thousands of demonstrators from Azad, or Pakistan-occupied Kashmir, gathered in the Indian-controlled Kashmir valley and vowed to liberate it from Indian rule. Following the demonstrations, a battle of words erupted between the two countries. India blamed Pakistan for playing a direct role in initiating the crisis and declared it would use force if necessary. Pakistan denied the charge, insisting that the problem had been created by India's continued illegal occupation of the valley. By April the crisis had evolved into the threat of war. The Bush administration, recognizing the crisis as grave, sent Deputy National Security Adviser Robert Gates, accompanied by a U.S. delegation, to both countries. Wise counsel and a political settlement were urged on both sides. As a result, the crisis was averted; by June, prime ministers on both sides were exchanging conciliatory messages and issuing accommodating statements. One can only speculate whether war would have occurred had the United States not intervened in a timely fashion. On the other hand, personal gestures of friendship on either side have not always resulted in long-term positive results. Several months before the Kargil war of 1999, Indian prime minister Vajpayee made a historic and much-feted bus trip into Pakistan as a gesture of goodwill between the two peoples. Journalists on both sides seized on the event as a confidence-building measure to be applauded. Nevertheless, war broke out, and indeed there were reports in the Indian press that Vajpayee was personally affronted that his gesture had been repaid by hostility.

Meanwhile, Kashmiris have become increasingly alienated in the five decades of conflict over their land. India, which in the name of protecting its sovereignty and integrity, has come down hard on the insurgency in Kashmir, has lost favor with many Kashmiris. An increasing number of civilians and former Kashmiri militants, even those who may have disavowed violence, are either "disappearing" or turning up dead. The consensus appears to be that Indian troops are targeting civilians and former militants in an effort to spread fear among Kashmiris and pressure the resistance into compliance.[20] Kashmiris, particularly the youth, have become disillusioned with India's handling of the situation and have turned in increasing numbers to more radical and violent solutions — solutions that Pakistan is happy to support through military assistance.[21]

At the same time, it is extremely difficult for any Indian politician of any political party to voice the possibility that any portion of Indian-held Kashmir would ever be negotiable. In fact, Kashmir has become a quagmire for Indian foreign policy, not just in relation to Pakistan but also in relation to the global community as Kashmiris seek increasingly to internationalize their position and demands for self-determination.[22] In addition, Kashmir has become an obsession with the country itself, with polls revealing that the average Indian is solidly in favor of doing whatever it takes and at great cost to keep Kashmir under Indian control. In recent times, this effort has resulted in numerous daily fatalities for both Kashmiris and the Indian troops who are permanently posted in the Kashmir valley. In its dealings with Kashmir, as with its dealings with other insurgencies within its borders when they arose — from Sikkim and Nagaland in the northeast to Punjab in the west — India has firmly followed the realist tenet of the state as primary actor. It has clung tenaciously to this belief through the global changes of integration and disintegration that have made boundaries more fluid in the post–Cold War world. India has viewed concessions to groups seeking increased autonomy as admissions of weakness on the part of the state and has often interpreted such demands as anti-Indian, a threat to the integrity of the state that should be averted at all costs.

The animosity between India and Pakistan also in some measure reflects the animosity between Hindus and Muslims on the subcontinent, people who have been living together for centuries, but whose ethnic and religious differences continue to matter. Unfortunately, the patriotism of Indian Muslims is routinely questioned whenever tensions between Pakistan and India flare up. When extremist Indian politicians within the BJP and its allies criticize Pakistan, many Indians seize on that as an excuse for baiting Indian Muslims. Both relationships — India-Pakistan and Hindu-Muslim — today suffer from misperceptions, nursed grievances, missed opportunities, and cultural/religious misunderstandings and intolerance. Both relationships also demonstrate the intertwining of domestic issues and foreign policy in India quite effectively.

Meanwhile, the rhetoric on both sides has become louder in recent years. One change on the Indian political scene that has fed the greater acridity of the national and subcontinental discourse has been the BJP's attempts to tear down secularism as one of the tenets of independent India's national consensus. Today, some Indians find it easier to assert Hindu chauvinistic ideas, thereby poisoning the political landscape and forcing all sides to be more extreme. Politics in Pakistan also has become more radical in recent years with the reassertion of religious fundamentalism.

India's dubious actions in the Kashmir crisis and its failure to unequivocally condemn the increasingly frequent attacks against minority religious groups in India have raised questions within the international community of human rights abuses and illuminated the thin line trod by countries between what is domestic and what is international.[23] As in the past, India has continued to assert its sovereignty in essentially denying that any external body has a right to question its actions (or, in the case of attacks against minorities, lack of actions) anywhere within its territory. As for Kashmir, India refuses to allow international human rights organizations such as Amnesty International and Human Rights Watch to monitor the Kashmir valley, even though the Kashmir All-Parties Hurriyat (a loose conference of all Kashmiri groups and parties) has asked for their presence. Again, it appears that realism as a theoretical explanation prevails in this case, and liberalism, which would predict that India would naturally cooperate with international organizations in attempting to comply with international human rights norms, fails to serve as an explanation. Looking to the future, it is still possible that as the Indian economy continues to attract increased foreign investment, the government will find itself in the position of being somewhat more accountable to the international community and mindful of the scrutiny of others in the newly globalized world. To date, however, this has not happened convincingly.

The chaos in Kashmir and the uncertain plight of India's religious minorities also bring forcefully to light the moral slide in the country's dealings with others, even its own citizens. It is hard to imagine the recent attacks on Christians, and indeed the ongoing threats that continue to face the country's Muslims, occurring during the time of Mohandas Gandhi and Nehru. It is even hard to imagine Indira Gandhi succumbing to such tactics, although her ruthlessness in employing her policies during the national emergency did lead to unfair targeting of Muslims. Today, however, such attacks have become a part of the fabric of Indian society and politics, making Indian society fundamentally different from what it was even a decade ago.

Tibet

Another contemporary issue that might require greater attention from India in the future is the status of Tibet. After the Chinese invaded Tibet in 1950, the Dalai Lama fled to India (in 1959) and was quickly given refuge. Since that time, Tibetan refugees have set up a small mirror of Tibet in India in the northern town of Dharamshala. India's willingness to allow Tibetans to seek refuge in India is a lasting testament to Nehru's great concern with questions of moral dimension in domestic and foreign policy; it was the right thing to do. On the other hand, his pragmatism made him careful to articulate a foreign policy that would not aggravate China. Thus officially India regards Tibet as an autonomous region of China. In recent times, Indians have been more reluctant to offer a haven for the Tibetans. When the seventeenth Karmapa (the leader of the Kagyu sect of Tibetan Buddhism and considered the third most important Tibetan spiritual leader) fled to India in 2000, reports and letters to the editor in the Indian press suggested that Tibetans might constitute an increasing security risk to India and a hindrance in India's continued relationship with China.

At the present time, it appears that India is willing to let the status quo continue. The idealism that might have guided India's earlier embrace of Tibetan refugees appears to have now given way to an uneasy acceptance of their presence in India and a reluctance to explore the implications of this presence—and, conversely, of China's presence as a northern Indian neighbor—completely. In the absence of a Nehru at the helm of Indian foreign policy, it is unlikely that India will offer much beyond what it already has to the Tibetan people.

Conclusion: And Miles to Go . . .

Many Indians believe that the nuclear tests constituted an inevitable "showdown" with a world that has treated India with indifference and has refused to recognize its emerging strength, human power, and relevance. Thus for many Indians the tests were an excuse to celebrate India despite persistent problems. It quickly became apparent, however, that the world did not join in this celebration and that India's foreign policy would emerge in a greater shambles from this event, at least in the short term. Indeed, the nuclear tests marked a low point in the steady decline of Indian foreign policy's potential since the days of Nehru and Mohandas Gandhi a half-century ago when hopes for the country associated with decolonization were so high. The recognition that India craves from the world hardly seems likely unless a new and viable consensus can be built around what the country stands for, what it seeks from its relations with its neighbors, and what it sees as its place in the world. Such a consensus would bring Indian foreign policy full circle, back to its roots established by Gandhi and Nehru. These roots have been lost to an unwieldy mixture of realist policies (strong state centrism, a reluctance to deal with sub-state groups, a rejection of international nongovernmental organizations in finding human rights solutions, the seeking of security through military means), psychological overtones (the craving for international recognition, the entrenchment of enemy images of Pakistan and their extension to Muslims of the subcontinent, distrust of third party involvement in Kashmir), and a chaotic intertwining of the domestic with the international.

The success of future foreign policy action in India depends on many factors, not least of which is the domestic situation. How the dominant BJP continues to work with coalition partners, whether it becomes a more inclusive party that heeds the nervousness of India's minorities or whether it radicalizes further, whether fundamentalism and antiforeign sentiment will capture the tone of foreign policy rather than pragmatism and rationalism—all these factors will determine the road that India will take. Many elements will be out of its control. In

Pakistan, for example, India faces an enemy that is disintegrating as a state and whose military government might be willing to take more desperate risks to keep public attention averted from the chaos at home. How China will continue to react to India's search for dominance in the region remains unclear (see Chapter 6). How the government of the day handles these issues will be critical. Thus which government it is and what mandate it has received from the people are of the utmost importance. A government like the BJP-led coalition, which has been forced to dissolve and re-form three times in almost as many years, is bound to be a weak one. It probably cannot provide the much-needed continuity in foreign policy and might be tempted to take actions that might shore up the government's short-term popularity but may not be in India's best long-term interest. Some analysts have interpreted the 1998 nuclear tests in this vein.

What will Indians want for themselves in the new millennium? Will they continue to view Kashmir as land they must fight for? Will they continue to divide along religious and sectarian lines, taking the state further and further away from the vision of Mohandas Gandhi and impeding much-needed progress on economic reform and foreign investment? Will they make good on the promise of their huge wealth of talent and brainpower which has already made India a formidable force in the emerging information technology world? What mandate will they give succeeding governments?

Since the nuclear tests were carried out, there are signs that a welcome new sensitivity is creeping into the way in which foreign policy is being handled. For example, the government's handling of the Kargil war in Kashmir was exemplary—nonprovoking, cautious, and pragmatic. The government also appears to understand that if foreign investment in India is to continue, some movement on the human rights front and efforts to negotiate with Pakistan are necessary. Indeed, when the central government has appeared to drag its feet in encouraging investment, individual state governments such as Andhra Pradesh under chief minister N. Chandrababu Naidu have themselves pursued investors and reaped the benefits of high rates of foreign direct investment in their states.

Whether a new foreign policy can be articulated that will enable India to stabilize its position in the subcontinent and move ahead with the much-needed political, social, and economic reforms remains still to be seen. Two scenarios are possible: one in which India attempts to settle its problems at home and across its borders and press ahead with internal growth and prosperity, or one in which India goes against the promise of all that it has to offer in order to push its internal problems and border insurgencies to their costly and destructive conclusion.

Suggestions for Further Reading

Appadorai, Angadipuram *Domestic Roots of India's Foreign Policy, 1947–1972*. New Delhi: Oxford University Press, 1981.
Bertsch, Gary, Seema Gahlaut, and Anupam Srivastava. *Engaging India: U.S. Strategic Relations with the World's Largest Democracy*. New York: Routledge, 1999.

Gould, Harold, and Sumit Ganguly. *The Hope and the Reality. U.S.-Indian Relations from Roosevelt to Reagan.* Boulder: Westview Press, 1992.
Hagerty, Devin. *The Consequence of Nuclear Proliferation: Lessons from South Asia.* Cambridge: MIT Press, 1998.
Thomas, Raju G. C., and Amit Gupta. *India's Nuclear Security.* Boulder: Lynne Rienner, 2000.

Notes

1. Independent India's first prime minister was by all accounts a literary and philosophical giant. To him, Frost's poem "Stopping by the Woods on a Snowy Evening" reflected the unfinished nature of his own service to the country.
2. The Indian National Congress later became independent India's dominant Congress Party until it split in 1969, at the behest of Prime Minister Indira Gandhi.
3. See, for example, Ian Talbot, *Freedom's Cry: The Popular Dimension in the Pakistan Movement and Partition Experience in N-W India* (Oxford: Oxford University Press, 1996); and Khushwant Singh, *Train to Pakistan,* reprint ed. (New York: Grove Press, 1990).
4. Chapter XVIII, Article 352, of the Indian constitution specifies that the head of state may declare a national emergency and suspend the normal workings of a parliamentary democracy if he or she perceives a national crisis or international security threat to India. Most scholars agree that Indira Gandhi's growing insecurities led her to perceive grave threats to her power by 1975. In response, she called for a national emergency. Opposition leaders were jailed in large numbers and constitutionally guaranteed civil liberties were suspended. The media were censored and an atmosphere of repression, the likes of which had never been experienced before or since, settled on the country.
5. Swaran Singh, "Sino-Indian Ties: Need for Bold Initiatives," Institute for Defence Studies and Analyses, online at http://www.idsa-india.org/an-feb9-6.html.
6. Barbara Crossette, *India: Facing the Twenty-First Century* (Bloomington: Indiana University Press, 1993).
7. India, however, spoke up loudly on ideological issues close to its heart; for example, it was an ardent supporter of minority rights and an opponent of apartheid in South Africa before it became fashionable for most of the world to fall in line against the apartheid regime.
8. Robert Hardgrave, *India Under Pressure: Prospects for Stability* (Boulder: Westview Press, 1984).
9. Barbara Crossette in her book *India: Facing the Twenty-First Century* argues that the cool relationship with East Asia could be attributed in part to Indians' belief in their cultural and moral superiority. It is also true, however, that prosperous Asian countries, notably Japan, have looked to other East Asian neighbors as investment receptacles, rather than South Asia.
10. In all fairness, one must also take into account Pakistan's often-provocative acts. Most scholars and the world media agree that the recent Kargil conflict was initiated by Pakistani infiltrators crossing the line of control in Kashmir. Many recent indications from the new Musharraf government in Pakistan offer no silver lining: the military leader appears to be committed to making the Kashmir issue top priority in Indo-Pakistani relations, without apparently considering the nuclear consequences of escalation.
11. Indira Gandhi was Jawaharlal Nehru's daughter. Her son Rajiv Gandhi became prime minister upon her death and was elected to another full term in his own right. This

has led some scholars of India such as Lloyd and Suzanne Rudolph (in their documentary "Life and Death of a Dynasty") to comment on the importance of dynasty in Indian politics.

12. See, for example, Dom Moraes, *Indira Gandhi: Heiress to Destiny* (Boston: Little Brown, 1980); Nayantara Sahgal, *Indira Gandhi: Her Road to Power* (New York: Unger, 1982); and Surjit Mansingh, *India's Search for Power: Indira Gandhi's Foreign Policy, 1966–1982* (New Delhi: Sage, 1984).

13. It could be argued, however, that the current prime minister, Atal Behari Vajpayee, has imprinted his own moderate, consensual leadership style to halt the BJP's more radical agenda. It is clear though that his position as leader of a ruling coalition is far from the dominant, influential ones that Nehru and Indira Gandhi enjoyed.

14. In addition to separatist demands in Kashmir, India has faced, at different times and with differing degrees of violence, demands for increased autonomy and separatism from groups in the northeast, including the Nagas and the Mizos, and from the Sikhs in Punjab and to a lesser extent from the Tamils in southern India.

15. Like much of India's current foreign policy, this is also in flux, and Washington and New Delhi have moved somewhat closer in recent years, setbacks from the nuclear tests notwithstanding.

16. Pratap Mehta, "India: The Politics of Self-Esteem," *Current History* (December 1998).

17. George Perkovich, "Think Again: NonProliferation," *Foreign Policy* (fall 1998).

18. India claims that the time for a plebiscite was in the immediate aftermath of partition and the first war. It claims that Pakistan has now effectively swayed the area with its propaganda and that a plebiscite today would not reveal the true feelings of the people.

19. Tinaz Pavri, "Help or Hindrance? Third Parties in the Indo-Pakistani Conflict," *Negotiation Journal*, vol. 13, no. 4 (1997): 369–388.

20. Robert Marquand, "Targets of Frustration in Kashmir," *Christian Science Monitor*, August 9, 2000.

21. An indictment of India's policy in Kashmir can be found in Sumit Ganguly, *The Crisis in Kashmir: Portents of War, Hopes of Peace* (Cambridge: Cambridge University Press, 1997).

22. The most recent event that brought Kashmir to the attention of the international community was the 1999 Christmas Eve hijacking of an Indian Airlines airplane en route from Kathmandu to New Delhi. The hijackers were Kashmiri separatists seeking the release of Kashmiri "freedom fighters" (India called them militants) from Indian jails.

23. For example, Indian Christians were the target of almost forty-four separate incidents of Hindu fundamentalist violence from January to August 2000, whereas several years ago such incidents against this particular community were practically unheard of. Robert Marquand, "Christians Still Targets in India," *Christian Science Monitor*, July 18, 2000.

CHAPTER 9

Continuity and Change in Israeli Foreign Policy

Laura Drake

Although small in territory and population, Israel is a central player in one of the world's most conflict-ridden regions—the Middle East—and thus a central player in contemporary international relations. The hostile regional context in which Israel finds itself and its dependence on the United States for military and economic assistance have certainly shaped Israeli foreign policy, especially security policy. As Laura Drake argues in this chapter, Israel's strategies for coping with regional foes and international allies have included both an aggressive military posture and a desire to normalize relations with its regional opponents through diplomatic and economic exchanges. In addition to these important external influences on Israeli foreign policy are internal factors. Drake highlights the role of popular opinion, particularly within the military ranks, as well as Israel's self-definition as a "Jewish state." She discusses the influence of these factors on Israeli foreign policy, including its policy in regard to the complex Middle East peace process.

Israel is an interesting country to compare with others in this book because in many ways it falls between categories of states and thus challenges some of the conventional expectations about its foreign policy. For example, the population of Israel is much smaller than that of France (Chapter 3) or South Africa (Chapter 12). Its overall economic size, which is closest to Iran (Chapter 10), does not make it a major player in the international economy. Yet, the average Israeli enjoys a level of wealth close to that of the citizens of Great Britain (Chapter 2). Israel's importance to world politics, however, stems more from the historical circumstances surrounding its statehood and its alliance with the United States than its position in the world's security or economic structure. Israel, like India (Chapter 8), must balance domestic political factors, such as public opinion represented by political parties competing in regular elections, with external security priorities. Also like contemporary India and Germany (Chapter 4), Israel's fragmented political system requires coalition governments, which can influence the making of foreign policy.

Since its inception in 1948, Israel has faced some unique problems in world politics. Israel's situation is different because the legality of the manner by which it brought itself into existence has been in question from the start, not only in the Middle East region but in much of the rest of the world as well. For these reasons, in Israel, foreign policy has been paramount. Foreign policy, not domestic policy, has dominated Israel's electoral process.

Israel's continued existence in a regional environment so hostile to it has been possible due solely to its superior military power and scientific know-how (imported by the immigrants who came from the West) and the unconditional political, military, and economic support it has received from the United States. This chapter covers the important regional and international factors that affect Israel's day-to-day existence; Israel's strategic imperatives toward the Palestinians, given its self-conception as a specifically Jewish state in accordance with its state ideology of Zionism; Israel's foreign policy making imperatives in the context of the different tracks of the Middle East peace process; and Israel's historical quest for normalization—an end to its pariah status—in the region and in the world at large.

Israeli Foreign Policy during the Cold War

The central concern of Israeli foreign policy, the Arab-Israeli conflict, was not a by-product of the Cold War. It began before the tension between the United States and the Soviet Union had solidified in the post–World War II bipolar system, and it continues even now after the Cold War has ended. During the Cold War, although both superpowers tried their best to align the Middle East along Cold War lines, neither was ultimately successful in this effort. The region's animosities revolved around a totally different and overriding factor—the opposition of the Arabs to what they saw as Israel's existence at the expense of the Palestinians' existence—and neither superpower proved capable of altering the already-established fault line in this region to conform with the Cold War alignment. Nonetheless, the Arab-Israeli conflict did not escape the effects of the bipolar world distribution of power. The changes in the international system, as well as in the regional system, affected Israeli foreign policy, but the long-term constants of Israeli foreign policy existed throughout and beyond the Cold War.

The Regional and International Context

Before the emergence of the peace process, the twenty-two Arab states in the

Middle East, with the single exception of Jordan, opposed Israel's existence in the region. They deemed illegitimate the means of its establishment at the expense of the Palestinian people, who previously—during the Turkish and then British colonialism—existed in exactly the same territorial space. Both sides saw the contours of their people's true homeland as encompassing today's Israel, the West Bank, and Gaza. The Arab states and the Palestinians therefore refused to recognize Israel as a legal sovereign state in the region, and refused any and all forms of interaction with it. Simultaneously, they actively sought its destruction by military means. To supplement the war effort, the Arab states and the Palestinians were largely successful in isolating Israel internationally, leading many if not most states in the world to boycott any form of diplomatic or economic relations with it—turning Israel into a virtual pariah state.

Israel's superior military power, supplemented by the unbroken political, military, and economic support of the American superpower, enabled it to survive this long period of regional enmity and international isolation (1948–1991). The United States has supported Israel since its inception, motivated by several factors: the postwar national sense of guilt about Washington's inability to prevent the genocidal crimes of Hitler toward the Jewish population of Europe, the unique domestic political factors internal to the United States, and Cold War considerations. The Cold War dictated U.S. support for strong regional powers, such as Israel and Turkey, that were seen as militarily capable of responding to a full-scale Soviet invasion. According to U.S. government documentation of the period, the Arab states, even in their combination, were not seen as possessing any credible military might whatsoever. Although the Western economy was vulnerable to any Soviet invasion of these states because of their vast territory and oil wealth, their potential military contribution was seen as limited solely to opening their territory and providing logistical support to those actually repelling the Soviets. Washington would have preferred to have had alliances with both Israel and the Arab states to better contain the Soviet Union, but when forced to choose, it was compelled to choose Israel. Israel's enemies were not seen as capable of defending either themselves or the Mideast region; Israel and Turkey were seen as capable of defending both. The entire peace effort during the Cold War was therefore about creating a situation in which the United States would no longer be forced to choose between them, and such that it would become possible for Israel and the Arab world to stand on the same side of a war against the Soviet Union. The United States never accomplished these goals, and the U.S. support for Israel continues after the Cold War for the other two reasons, namely, as historical "compensation" for the Holocaust, reinforced by the overwhelming domestic political influence of pro-Israeli partisans in the American political system.

A series of Arab military defeats in the first four Arab-Israeli wars (1947–1949, 1956, 1967, and 1973) led to shifts in the Arab posture and a reluctant tolerance of Israel's presence in that region. The military defeat of the Palestine Liberation Organization (PLO), which was founded in 1964 to restore

Palestine to the Palestinians, in an additional Arab-Israeli war (the Israeli invasion of Lebanon in 1982) led to a similar rethinking among the Palestinians approximately a decade later. Prior to the Soviet collapse and the end of the bipolar world system, this reluctant acceptance had led to only a single formal peace treaty, signed by Egypt, the strongest Arab state, with Israel in 1979. Other Arab states opted instead for an unofficial "no war no peace" stance—something less than a military war, but more than a cold war.

The other sets of bilateral negotiations, or tracks, of the peace process (the Syria-Israel, Palestinians-Israel, Lebanon-Israel, and Jordan-Israel dyads) became possible only after the disappearance of the Soviet Union and its strategic clout from the region in 1990 and 1991, and the defeat of Iraq—the strongest Arab power after Egypt—by the U.S.-led coalition forces at about the same time. Since the Arab sides were now strategically helpless, in effect in the hands of the now-established U.S. hegemony in the region and the world at large, they were compelled to enter the same Middle East peace process—largely on Israel's terms of separate, direct bilateral negotiations between Israel and each Arab state—that they had been refusing for decades.

The comprehensive Middle East peace process thus began with the late-1991 opening of a ceremonial international conference in Madrid and was immediately followed up with negotiations along each of the bilateral tracks. In 1993 it produced an Israel-PLO "declaration of principles," known also as the Oslo agreement, which promised peace and recognition between the PLO and Israel as well as limited "self-rule" (civil autonomy) by Palestinians in Gaza and the West Bank. With this Palestinian cover thus secured, Jordan—which had been cooperating with Israel secretly for decades—was able to sign a full and final peace treaty with Israel in 1994.[1] Negotiations for peace treaties followed between Israel and Syria, Israel and Lebanon, and Israel and the PLO.

Long-Term Constants of Israeli Foreign Policy

The most important constant elements of Israeli foreign policy are those that derive from Israel's self-concept. Dedicated to protecting a secure existence according to Israel's own definition of that existence, they will not change unless Israel's self-definition first undergoes change.

Internal Constitution. The first and most important of these constants is the paramount national objective, which is the preservation of an overwhelming and sovereign Jewish majority within any borders Israel can feasibly reach while remaining inside the area of Eretz Israel ("Land of Israel," synonymous with the entire land of Palestine inhabited by Palestinians until late 1947/early 1948, including "Israel proper," or 1948 Israel, plus the territories of the West Bank and Gaza Strip occupied in 1967). Hence, demography is a central feature of Israel's self-defined existence, and protecting it is therefore a top priority. This imposes two constraints on Israeli foreign policy.

First, Israel must not occupy more territory within Eretz Israel/Palestine than it can demographically handle. The occupation of the West Bank and Gaza Strip in 1967 hence presented a unique problem for Israel. The problem was stemmed temporarily by keeping the Palestinian population there under martial law without citizenship rights instead of officially annexing the territory to Israel, while simultaneously making these areas available for settlement by Jewish citizens of Israel. Partly for these demographic reasons, the left-of-center Labor Party disagreed with the unrestrained settlement of Israelis in the heart of Palestinian population density in the West Bank and Gaza Strip that occurred under the right-of-center Likud Party during its years in power (1977–1992). Labor argued that Israel proper, with its population of only five million Jews and one million Palestinian citizens of Israel, could not demographically afford to integrate the non-Jewish two-and-a-half million Palestinians who would come with the West Bank and Gaza Strip territories should Israel try to integrate them. The problem emerged paramount when direct military rule came under Palestinian fire and eventually gave way to the second Intifadah ("popular uprising," akin to an earthquake) of 1987–1989.

There have been a total of three Palestinian Intifadahs. The first Intifadah, a failed war of Palestinian independence from colonial Britain, took place during the years 1936–1939. It was directed against the Zionist militias and Jewish settlements that were in the process of constructing Israel on top of Palestine, and against the British colonial troops who were seen as enabling that effort. The third Intifadah, known as the Al-Aqsa Intifadah, or "Jerusalem Rebellion," began in September 2000 as a war of independence in the West Bank and Gaza based on the Lebanon model of resistance to Israel.

The second Intifadah of the 1980s was not an independence war but was intended to graduate eventually to that level. Centered on resisting the Israeli occupation of Gaza and the West Bank both militarily and through acts of civil disobedience (for example, refusing to pay taxes to the occupation), it did succeed in temporarily eliminating the problem of collaboration with Israel by vulnerable Palestinian individuals. It also gave the Palestinians a sense of optimism about the future because it altered the situation on the ground, requiring a solution. Israeli troops and secret police lost much in the way of physical control of West Bank and Gaza Strip cities, where they could no longer roam at will, especially at night. The end results of this Intifadah were the Oslo agreements of 1993 and 1995.

To deal with the demographic dilemma, the Labor Party in 1992 developed a doctrine known as "separation," a means to separate the Palestinian population from Israel's. To do so, Israel "separated" out the indigestible clusters of territory (large cities and individual village clusters) within the West Bank and Gaza Strip in which the Palestinian population is especially dense. These clusters were given Palestinian "autonomy" or administrative "self-rule." Israel kept the areas surrounding them—the wide open spaces and the territories' international borders with Jordan and Egypt—under direct Israeli rule. The policy, which has been implemented by both parties in Israel unilaterally since late 1992, was embodied in the late Yitzhak Rabin's slogan during his successful 1992 campaign for prime minister: "I have three principles: No to two million Palestinian citizens, no to a Palestinian state, no to a withdrawal to '67" (from the West Bank and Gaza Strip, including East Jerusalem).[2] The Labor Party doctrine of separation accounts for the geographical "leopard-spots" (radically discontiguous and surrounded) character of the "self-rule" jurisdiction of the Palestinian Authority (the Palestinian autonomy government in certain areas of the West Bank and Gaza) under the 1995 interim agreement also known as Oslo II.

A second consequence of Israel's internal demographic constitution in Israel's foreign policy is that Israel must fend off the efforts, whether violent or peaceful, of the Palestinians who share the same space-time as Israeli Jews, to assert their own claim to the land. The relationship between the Palestinian Arabs and the Israeli Jews is unique in world politics, coming into conflict as they did by claiming the same piece of territory as their exclusive national homeland at precisely the same time in world history. Physics dictates that two particles cannot exist simultaneously in the same space at the same time, and hence, the conflict between Israel and Palestine is not over borders but, rather, existence. The central issue of this conflict is which of these two peoples gets to exist as a nation with freedom and independence in this land, with the inherent understanding that national existence is indivisible, whether horizontally (dividing the territory in half, which is not under discussion by anyone) or vertically (two nations sharing one state). Each side understands fully that the completeness of its own national existence can only be at the direct expense of the completeness of the other side's national existence.

The mathematics of it is incontrovertible: the Palestinian-Israeli track of the peace process, if successful, would leave Israel without approximately one-fifth and the Palestinians without approximately four-fifths of the space they jointly consider to be their country. Demographically, it would leave all of Israel's population inside their country. Fully two-thirds of the Palestinian people, however, will have to live outside any part of their country, since the West Bank and Gaza Strip by themselves, as one-fifth of geographical Palestine, cannot physically accommodate the entire Palestinian people—who inhabited the whole of Palestine until late 1947/early 1948. The Israel-Palestine conflict, as demonstrated by these fractions, is a pure example of what is known in international relations as a "zero-sum conflict," one that just happens to pit the strongest power in the region (the Israelis) against the very weakest (the Palestinians). Yet Palestinian core demands in the peace process, unlike those of any Arab state, strike at the very center of Israel's self-concept, threatening either its demographic or territorial existence or both. Thus they are more fearsome to Israel than the demands of Arab states like Syria that Israel withdraw its military forces and settlers from Arab territories like the Golan and southern Lebanon that Israel never claimed for itself in the first place.

Israel's Core Strategic Objectives. The second large-scale constant of Israeli foreign policy over time has been the strategic objective of obtaining Arab state and international political acceptance of Israel's "legitimacy of existence" within its chosen (still fluid but solidifying) borders, and if possible, support or at least acquiescence in Israel's political-military methods. Over the long term this requires that Israel realize a series of practical achievements.

The first of these is the conclusion of bilateral peace treaties between Israel and each Arab state, regardless of what happens with the Palestinians. This requires treaties that contain both recognition and normalization clauses, not merely an end to the state of war. Recognition means that Arab states must agree and behave as though Israel has a legal and ethical "right to exist" as a specifically Jewish state on that piece of land, despite the parallel claim of their Arab Palestinian brethren to the very same. Normalization means the end of the total Arab boycott of physical and communicative interaction with Israel and its citizens (diplomatic, geographic, political, economic, scientific, cultural, and so forth) and the replacement of this blanket boycott with cooperation in all these areas.[3] This Israeli strategy is designed to create an irreversible network of interconnectedness between each Arab state and Israel, which the Arab world interprets as the creation of one-way dependencies on an Israeli hub. Derided by its Arab opponents under the label of *sharq awsatiyyah* (Middle Easternism), many Arabs fear this concept. They believe it to be a plan for the deliberate establishment of Israeli regional hegemony (and further Arab decline) through the creation of Arab dependence on the economy and infrastructure of Israel. Israel, in contrast, hopes that the creation of such networks of interaction and infrastructure would eventually fulfill the long-term Israeli foreign policy objective of eradicating Arab popular enmity toward Israel (or, at least, separating it from any policy implications) by building an economic cost-benefit structure into Israel's future peaceful relations with Arab states.[4]

Arab hostility toward Israel derives from the Arab concept of Israel in its initial condition as an alien collective from the West that came suddenly, one day, to the East, invaded Arab Palestine, expelled 90 percent of its indigenous (Palestinian) population by force of arms and turned them into refugees, then replaced that population with incoming waves of Jewish settler-immigrants from western and eastern Europe, the United States, and elsewhere. Initially, Arab states responded to these events of 1947–1948, known to Palestinians as the *nakbah* (catastrophe, or disaster), by trying to reverse them in war (1948–1949) before they became entrenched, and then after the war had been lost, by refusing to have anything to do with Israel either directly or indirectly.[5] This meant boycotting it completely in every conceivable area of cross-national interaction, with one single exception — the future military battlefield. That condition has lasted for more than fifty years.

A change in the Arab core perception of it as the enemy almost by definition is, Israel believes, the only way to ensure its long-term security; regional acceptance is seen as the only way to guarantee its permanence. This involves the building of irreversible economic, political, strategic, and cultural links with Arab states to the extent that the idea of liquidating Israel eventually becomes

Oslo II Map Outlining Areas A, B, and C

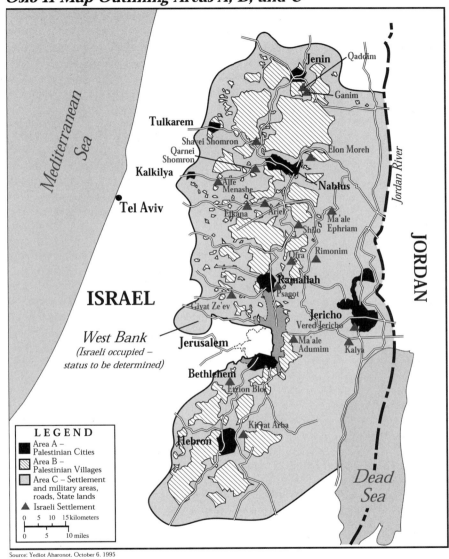

LEGEND

- ■ Area A – Palestinian Cities
- ▨ Area B – Palestinian Villages
- ▨ Area C – Settlement and military areas, roads, State lands
- ▲ Israeli Settlement

0 5 10 15 kilometers

0 5 10 miles

Source: Yediot Aharonot. October 6. 1995

Source: Foundation for Middle East Peace. Reprinted with permission.

unthinkable in the Arab political mindset. Otherwise, the day may come when the Arabs are able to catch up to Israel militarily, invent an asymmetric or unconventional battle strategy, unify their efforts, or obtain the backing of a future great power. The rationale is that the Arabs can lose many wars, due to their vast population and landmass, whereas the Israelis, with their small population and landmass, cannot afford to lose even a single war, much as Washington or New York could not afford to receive even a single incoming nuclear-tipped missile.

The peace treaties that Israel has been seeking from Arab states since its inception would indeed compel Arab states to recognize Israel as a permanent and integral part of the Middle East region, or at least to behave that way in their official conduct of international relations. Eventually, though, Israeli foreign policy makers seek an outcome whereby the idea of an Arab country seeking to liquidate Israel would be just as unthinkable as twenty-first-century Germany seeking to liquidate France. With this goal of greater interconnectedness between itself and the Arab states, Israel's foreign policy is in a sense premised on liberalism's notion that interdependence fosters cooperation and hence, for Israel, greater security.

Israel's strategy of obtaining regional acceptance has involved many building blocks, all aimed at establishing links with other states in the region. Diplomatic representation of Israel and each Arab state in each other's capital cities is considered the minimalist definition of normalization. Only five of the Arab states, including the PLO (a full state member of the Arab League, which comprises all twenty-two Arab member countries and is the region's official interstate grouping), have recognized Israel or established diplomatic relations with it in the context of peace agreements (Egypt, Jordan, Mauritania, and Morocco are the others). Four more (Oman, Qatar, Tunisia, and Yemen) were on the way to doing so, but that process is on hold. Syria will have to reluctantly accept diplomatic exchange if it wishes to get back the Golan, but it is likely that Syria would be even more minimalist than Egypt has been.

Economic cooperation is also an important part of Israel's strategy for normalization. Only with Jordan, however, has Israel established positive economic linkages, including Israeli capital investment in Jordan, the creation of Israeli-capitalized labor camps, or "industrial parks," inside Jordanian territory employing Jordanian cheap labor, the establishment of joint ventures with Jordanian capitalists, and trade exchanges. Infrastructure linkages and normalization of border relations would aid regionwide economic cooperation. Thus, Israel seeks the interconnection of the electricity grids of Israel and surrounding countries, water-sharing arrangements, and a common regional tourism infrastructure. Israel also seeks an agreement with Arab states to allow direct air travel between their countries and Israel, to allow Israeli civilian aircraft to fly over their airspace, and to open their borders to Israeli citizens. Additionally, normalization of border relations means that Arab countries accept Israeli tourists in their countries and that they allow tourists from their countries to visit Israel. Israeli tourists go to both Jordan and Egypt at will, but Egypt strongly discourages its citizens from visiting Israel. In short, Israel wants to establish itself as the region's commercial transportation hub for both oil and water, as well as for foreign tourists.

Israel, seeking to be a "nation among nations" and to be treated as a "normal" country, would like to put an end to what it considers its "abnormal" exclusion from regional organizations and regionally based committees in international organizations. Shunned by the Arab countries, Israel, for example, participates in the European group in the United Nations. Full participation in the regional organizations, however, will not be feasible unless and until the majority of member countries in the Arab League have established "normal" relations with Israel.

Israel also seeks normalization of its relations outside the region. Normal relations were not possible prior to the end of the Cold War, since developing countries and the Eastern bloc were unified in their support for the Arab side, although to varying degrees. Now that the Cold War is over, Israel is able to create global allies through military cooperation (provision of equipment upgrades, new technologies, and targeted sharing of strategic and tactical intelligence). Israel's most recent achievement in this regard is its military alliance with Turkey, which threatens Syria, and in which Israel has also managed to obtain the use of Turkish airspace stretching close to the borders of Iraq and Iran. Israel has also succeeded in achieving a military relationship with China, through equipment upgrades and sales (which in several cases also involved the unauthorized transfer of U.S. technology). Finally, Israel has built up a nuclear relationship with India, from which India benefits from Israel's nuclear knowledge base and in which both states share a common threat from Islamic Pakistan.

Other of Israel's post–Cold War global "normalization" achievements — many of which were accomplished as a result of the emergence of the United States as the sole superpower and world hegemon — entailed the recent recognition of Israel by a majority of the world's nations and the subsequent establishment of diplomatic relations with them. Previously, Israel was a diplomatic outcast in the international community, akin to South Africa; the Palestine Liberation Organization had embassies in more countries than did Israel. Even the Vatican did not recognize Israel, while simultaneously enjoying friendly diplomatic relations with the PLO. Israel also achieved in the post–Cold War environment, with the help of an intense and far-reaching U.S. diplomatic campaign, a revocation of the UN General Assembly's 1975 UN "Zionism-is-racism" resolution.[6]

Israel's Military Doctrine and Strategy. The third constant of Israel's foreign policy since its inception has been the adoption of an aggressive, offensive military strategy and posture toward those Arab countries that continue to proclaim hostility to Israel's existence, a strategy in which geography is king. This, in turn, led to the emergence of a complex military doctrine that has remained constant throughout Israel's history of more than fifty years.

The first element of this doctrine is the dictum that offense is defense.[7] Israel's diminutive geographical configuration, particularly pronounced before Israel's occupation of the West Bank and Gaza Strip in 1967, led to the emergence of the doctrine alternatively known as "preemptive warfare" or "preventive warfare." Shorthand for the dictum of "attack them before they attack you," it means that Israel must be the first to launch an attack in any environment it perceives to be potentially dangerous. The rationale is that Israel cannot afford to be territorially overrun in the initial hours or days of an Arab first strike before it has had time to put its overwhelmingly stronger military forces into action. Israel with its small population does not have a large standing army; thus it requires a twenty-four- to seventy-two-hour warning interval to bring its full strength to bear in any war. Above all, Israel fears the surprise attack that destroys or severely injures it before it can respond; hence the huge psychological toll of the surprise attack on Israeli forces by Egypt and Syria on the Sinai and Golan fronts in 1973. The practical outcome of the preemptive war doctrine is, unfortunately, the occupation of enemy territories and the subsequent establishment of these territories as Israeli security buffers or security zones. Settling Israeli civilians in these areas serves to increase Israel's "strategic depth"—the geo-strategic asset of deep land-mass in front of cities and vital economic infrastructure—an asset that Israel critically lacks. Thus, the first Israeli imperative of defense—"attack first if possible, but if surprised, carry the war to the enemy's territory as rapidly as possible"—has resulted in the creation of a second layer of occupied territory, prompting a new Arab grievance.

The perceived necessity to attack first translates in practice to attacking the enemy state offensively at the first sign of a potential threat in order to avoid any possibility of surprise, or even initiating a controlled escalation of a heated situation so as to enable the preempting state to launch war at a time of its own choosing. This doctrine accounts for Israel's invasion of the Egyptian Sinai in 1956 (with Britain and France, which had joined together to re-occupy the Suez Canal in Egypt) before the Egyptian military could absorb a newly ordered inventory of advanced Soviet weapons. Specific enemy actions that Israel might consider threatening are delineated in advance as "red-lines"; these are then subtly communicated to enemy states as preordained *casi belli* (tripwires, or grounds for immediate war). Thus, in the 1967 war Israel began the fighting by launching a surprise attack on Egypt's air force, reacting to the threat of Egypt's expulsion of the United Nations buffer force and the forward movement of Egyptian troops in the direction of the Israeli border. Egypt, as it turned out, was reacting to a Soviet intelligence report that Israel was on the verge of invading Syria—a warning that turned out to be unfounded—in the hope of deterring Israel from invading its Syrian ally. In a classic instance of the self-fulfilling prophecy, the very Israeli invasion of Syria that was initially a false alarm then in fact took place as a direct result of Egypt's actions to deter it. The result was Israel's occupation of the Golan, Syria's southwestern sector, the return of which is now Syria's price for peace.

The second element of Israeli military doctrine is the dictum of excessive retaliation. The Old Testament metaphor "an eye for an eye" is here translated as "a thousand eyes for an eye." A major part of Israel's deterrence strategy against any type of Arab attack, be it a guerrilla operation or a full-fledged attack by the military forces of an opposing state, is to respond in a multiple of the force of the original enemy attack. In essence, Israel is calling the bluff of the attacking entity or state by concretely threatening to wreak unacceptable levels of destruction through air power, or even to escalate the situation into an all-out war that the Arabs would surely lose.

Third is Israel's establishment and maintenance of an undeclared, last-resort nuclear option while simultaneously preventing any other state in the region from acquiring an unconventional weapons capability.[8] Israel deems this last-resort option necessary in the event that, one day, it should find itself on the losing side of a conventional war. Hence, Israel refuses to sign the Nuclear Non-Proliferation Treaty (NPT) while buttressing U.S. counter-proliferation efforts against Arab states and Iran. Israel's air attack on Iraq's nuclear facilities at Tuwaitha in 1981 is an instance of both this strategic imperative and the "offense is defense" doctrine in general.

Finally, Israel seeks the preservation of unconditional support from the United States at any cost, to the point of overt interference in America's internal foreign policy making processes concerning Middle East policy matters. Israel deems its omnipresent lobbying and pressure apparatus in Washington necessary to guarantee long-term, stable U.S. military and political support under any and all conceivable circumstances. This means ensuring U.S. provision of military equipment and its technological cooperation with Israel; economic grants in the range of $2 billion to $3 billion per year for the purchase of additional military supplies and for the costs Israel incurs in implementing its peace agreements; and finally, international political support, in the UN Security Council and elsewhere. Without a great-power alliance, Israel as a fairly small state in world politics would not be capable either economically or militarily of realizing this vast array of strategies while still retaining its first world standard of living.

External Factors

As is apparent from the above discussion of Israel's core strategic objectives and military doctrine, Israeli foreign policy is very much conditioned by the regional and international environment within which it resides. The most immediate of the external influences on Israeli foreign policy are the postures of individual Arab states, both those opposed to Israel and those reconciled with it. This has historically been the single most important and consistent determinant because it concerns the situation in Israel's immediate geopolitical environment. Israel formulates strategy based on its own political-military ambitions in relation to the individual Arab states, its perceptions of their respective levels of hostility toward Israel, and its assessments of the likely strategies, tactics, and capabilities of Arab states.

Israeli foreign policy is not merely a response to the balance of power in the region but also to regional religious parameters, or Islamic red lines. Jerusalem, both sides of which Israel claims as its "eternal capital," is holy to Christians, Jews, and Muslims alike. Whereas West Jerusalem is part of Israel proper, East Jerusalem, which contains the holy places of all three religions, fell to Israeli occupation in the 1967 war. Immediately upon occupying East Jerusalem, Israel expanded its municipal boundaries to include other surrounding West Bank areas and annexed these to Israel together with East Jerusalem proper, despite its expectation of UN and international condemnation of the move. The site of the Temple Mount, the holiest site of the Jews, sits beneath the Dome of the Rock/Al-Aqsa mosque complex, Islam's third holiest site, from which Muslims believe their last prophet, Mohammad, ascended to heaven. Some religious extremists have thought of blowing up the Islamic shrine so as to allow the Jews to build the Third Temple, thereby hastening the coming (or second coming) of the Messiah. Israel, however, is very careful about preventing this from ever happening, for fear of setting off a region-wide jihad, or holy war.

Israel's freedom of action is also occasionally constrained by the unwritten limits set by the United States. Israel has a free hand in the region—that is, it can do more or less whatever it wants without encountering U.S. opposition—but it does not have a blank check. Washington's unwritten red lines—they are few and never voiced but Israel understands where they are—are in areas where action by Israel would cause irrevocable harm to America's grand strategic interests in the region (for example, in the Persian Gulf). Israel's dependence on the United States, stemming from its need for an alliance with a great power, acts to limit the extent of Israel's normally aggressive military posture toward enemy states. The best recent example of this constraint in action came in 1991: Israel acceded to Washington's request not to respond militarily to the Iraqi SCUD surface-to-surface missile attacks on Tel Aviv and other Israeli cities during the Persian Gulf War. The result of such response would have been the entry of Israel into that war. Since no Arab country would want to be on the same side of a regional war as Israel, the decision to respond would have had unforeseen repercussions on the cohesion of the wartime alliance against Iraq. Had the constraint not been there, Israel's military deterrence strategy of "excessive retaliation" would have dictated, without question, a disproportionate attack (probably an air attack) on Iraq in response to the SCUD attacks in order to preserve the credibility of its deterrent resolve.

Much less significant for Israeli foreign policy are the limits of the international community, from which Israel is generally exempted by the American superpower. Israel historically has had great antipathy toward the United Nations, perceiving hostility from most of the world community, which had cast Israel as a pariah state. Therefore, Israel does not care much about UN resolutions against it, which are never enforced in any case; Israel's policy has always been to put its security or strategic interests above international public relations concerns. The philosophy is approximately the following: We can deal with the public relations repercussions later, but we must protect our security interests today at any cost. International opinion, then, is limited to using international public relations (the only means available in the face of the U.S. veto in the UN Security Council) to punish Israel for some of its greater excesses. Good examples of such world opinion nightmares for Israel arose from Israel's use of phosphorous chemical bombs against the city of Beirut during its invasion of Lebanon and siege of Beirut in 1982, the "breaking bones" tactic used against the teenagers who participated in the second Intifadah in the occupied West Bank and Gaza Strip (1987–1989), and more recently, Israel's attempt in 1996 to bomb the Lebanese Hezbollah (Party of God) in what turned out instead to be a makeshift, hastily erected UN sanctuary camp in Qana, southern Lebanon, for civilians fleeing the fighting.[9]

Internal Factors

Internal constraints on Israeli foreign policy making include both the ideology and the actors. First and paramount is the state ideology, and the core ambitions or aspirations derived from it, and its political culture. The ideology of Zionism, a political-religious-ethnic doctrine that signifies the gathering of Jews from all parts of the world to inhabit an exclusive Jewish state in Palestine, is the core element of Israel's existence as a state, its fundamental "core value," and thus drives all policy. On top of this defining element stand Israel's basic national security objectives and second-level interests, as well as strategies for achieving them, all of which derive from the broad contour set by the founding ideology. Much like the Islamic Republic of Iran, although without its rigid theocratic dictums, Israel sees itself as a country on a mission. As the core value and foundation of Israel's political culture, Zionism sets the parameters in which decision makers choose policy.

Those who translate the state's basic aspirations into implementable policy objectives are members of Israel's broadly defined national security establishment, the most important foreign policy makers in Israel. They include the prime minister and defense minister (who are often combined in one person), the chief of staff of the Israel Defense Forces and the armed forces in general, as well as the intelligence branches, composed primarily of the Mossad (foreign intelligence service), the Shin Bet (internal intelligence service), and the Aman (military intelligence). The foreign minister is usually a somewhat lesser figure, below these others in the national security establishment pyramid. Further down the ladder is a sprinkling of former heads of intelligence agencies, ex-government ministers, retired generals and colonels, and other known influential persons who act as elite opinion barometers and unofficial advisers to the government. Beneath them are the strategic think tanks (Israel's functional equivalents of American think tanks like the RAND Corporation), such as the Jaffee Institute for Strategic Studies, which are often led and manned by retired or semiretired national security figures. Finally, certain select defense correspondents from the Israeli press, as they reflect elite opinion and analysis, are also included, since national security figures often choose to speak through them unofficially while retaining anonymity. In Israel the president is merely a symbolic figure and occasional national ombudsman, like the queen of England, and does not take part in national security decisions.

Israeli prime ministers and their foreign policy platforms have historically defined the main points of debate. This usually takes place along the major party Likud - Labor divide in the center, with the two main parties flanked by far - right and far - left allies. Since 1993 the debate has centered on Oslo. Labor prime ministers Yitzhak Rabin, Shimon Peres, and Ehud Barak have reluctantly accepted territorially based solutions with the Palestinians and Syria as necessary for peace, whereas the Likud prime ministers Ariel Sharon and Benjamin Netanyahu have opposed them, at least in any substantial form. Netanyahu and Sharon were adamant opponents of the Oslo agreements that Labor concluded with the Palestinians, and they have used their terms in office to undermine them and to minimize their territorial dimensions to the greatest extent possible.

The next most important internal policy influence in Israel is the 120 - seat Knesset (parliament) and the political party coalition dynamics surrounding it. Israel is a parliamentary, multiparty system with two major parties, Labor and Likud (center - left and center - right, respectively), and a large number of intermediate and small parties. If the prime minister does not control 61 of the Knesset's 120 seats, he is generally not considered to have a viable or lasting mandate. The dynamics of this process were unfavorably altered when Israel temporarily changed over to a system of direct election of the prime minister during Netanyahu's term. The change unwittingly gave more power to the small - and mid - sized parties by allowing their Israeli supporters to effectively "split" their votes for prime minister and Knesset, thus increasing their representation in the Knesset and making it harder for the prime minister to assemble coalitions and pass legislation. For that reason, the change has since been rescinded. The small handful of Arab and joint Jewish - Arab parties, which together usually hold just under ten seats in the Knesset, are not counted for political purposes here. The prime minister must have a specifically Jewish mandate to be considered credible; therefore he must have the majority of the seats of the Jewish parties, especially when dealing with matters concerning the Palestinians.

Every Israeli prime minister is aware that a series of majority votes of "no - confidence" in the Knesset, usually led by the main opposition party, or the withdrawal of a swing party from the governing coalition, can tear away a government's mandate or topple the government completely at scarcely a moment's notice. Therefore, the credible threat of doing either of these can act as an internal constraint on the prime minister's conduct of foreign policy. No prime minister wants to govern this way: often, in the event the Knesset majority coalition (and hence the perceived legitimacy of the government's policies) is lost, the prime minister will dissolve the government and call for early elections (as Barak did) in the hope of replacing his weak government with a renewed mandate. Usually this issue arises in moments of crisis, when shared national values held at different levels of priority by different sections of Israeli society are in conflict with each other. It can also happen when the major political parties are split on the correct strategy to deal with a critical situation, or on the proper conclusion to be drawn from the national cost-benefit analysis of a given proposed course of action. This is what happened to Ehud Barak in 2001 with the eruption of the third Palestinian Intifadah, after the failure of a critical phase in the "final status" negotiations. The result of the election that followed resulted in the largest landslide victory in Israel's history for the Likud hawk Gen. Ariel Sharon, who was defense minister during the Israeli invasion of Lebanon in 1982. Sharon had campaigned on an end to Oslo, an end to Israeli "concessions," and the forcible suppression of this Intifadah.

Finally, there is the popular opinion factor, which, according to the realist viewpoint, is last on the totem pole of national security decision making in any country, including Israel. Although Israel is a fully democratic political system with regard to its Jewish citizens, individual citizens unaffiliated with the state have access to neither the classified information nor the foreign intelligence that is required for making national security decisions. Furthermore, as ordinary citizens, they lack access to the inner circles of decision makers themselves. Ordinary people know very little about what is actually being discussed and which options are being debated until after decisions have been made. Allowing the public to provide informed input into this process would require leaking out all the classified inputs to such decisions, thus destroying the secrecy that is vital in areas concerning national security policy. Jewish public opinion can, however, pressure the government on an existing, overt long-term policy in which this public is deemed to have standing (such as a war claiming the lives of too many of its citizens and the strategic benefits of which are not deemed by the public to be worth that loss of life).

It must be noted that most of the Jewish popular sentiment that actually influences Israeli foreign policy decisions originates from within the military, usually with soldiers in the field and their families. Every Jewish Israeli citizen (except those exempted for religious Torah study) serves in the Israeli army. Furthermore, the Israeli state has existed in a perpetual state of war and alert since its inception. Both of these factors have led to the Israeli perception that theirs is a citizen army in a total sense. Pressure from the citizen-soldiers serving in southern Lebanon and their families influenced the Israeli national security establishment, despite the relatively low battle casualties from a purely military point of view (several hundred only), to decide to end Israel's twenty-two-year occupation there. The morale among Israeli soldiers in southern Lebanon had reached an all-time low, as Israeli forces there were being slowly bled to death by the innovative asymmetric guerrilla warfare tactics of Lebanon's paramilitary resistance forces, led by the Hezbollah. The Jewish Israeli public responded by demanding that the government do something to stop the ongoing carnage. The Lebanese resistance, in effect, had turned this conflict into what is known in international relations parlance as a "two-level game": it caused the penetration of what was previously an international conflict into Israel's domestic political domain. Israel's strategic planners tried to counter these tactics and failed repeatedly. At a loss, and faced with mounting internal pressure, Israel recognized UN Security Council Resolution 425 of 1978, which demanded Israel's unconditional withdrawal from the Lebanese territory it had occupied for more than two decades. It then proceeded unilaterally to schedule for itself a withdrawal deadline, regardless of the status of peace talks, and to finally withdraw in May 2000.

The military source of popular influence in Israel stems from the combination of two related factors: Israel's small population and its requirement that all Jewish citizens serve in the army, which is in a perpetual state of active warfare. The most important way in which Jewish Israeli popular sentiment affects Israeli foreign policy directly (the opinions of Israel's Arab citizens are not deemed a factor) is therefore in the country's acute sensitivity to Israeli casualties, both civilian and military. In instances in which Israeli soldiers or citizens seem to be dying continuously in the absence of a clear and worthy military objective, and in which the government seems impotent to improve the situation, Jewish popular sentiment can have a huge effect on the decision-making apparatus, either by direct pressure or by forcing a change in the ruling party.

Battle fatigue in the West Bank and Gaza Strip during the second Intifadah was a significant factor in the reemergence of the Labor Party into power. Immediately upon its election the Labor Party established the "separation" policy to get Israeli soldiers out of Palestinian cities and large villages. By implementing separation, the party also had to institute "closure," a system of military permits and checkpoints that prevents the normal movement of Palestinians from one city, town, or village cluster to another within either the West Bank or the Gaza Strip, respectively (internal closure), as well as in and out of these territories to and from Egypt, Jordan, and Israel proper (external closure). The basic purpose of closure is to confine each Palestinian to his or her individual sector of population density while preventing the normal movement of Palestinians through the Israeli-controlled areas that crisscross the West Bank. Permits to cross the checkpoints are thus granted only under very rare circumstances (for example, to Palestinians who collaborate with Israel's secret police). Soon after separation began to be implemented through closure, it was further solidified by the interim agreement (Oslo II) of 1995. This agreement carved the West Bank up into more than 190 densely populated but geographically discontiguous, or separate, areas, with Israel retaining the lands surrounding each of them. These former areas were then turned over to Palestinian administrative "self-rule." The foundations of general closure were therefore preserved for the time being. Thus, the particular arrangement negotiated as part of an international agreement originated in the "battle fatigue" in Jewish Israeli public opinion. Arab Palestinian citizens of Israel, of course, sympathized with their Palestinian brethren in the occupied territories.

Jewish popular sentiment can also have an impact on Israel's broad policy directions in a more general way. The fifty-fifty split in popular sentiment between the Israeli West Bank "annexation" camp (Likud) and the "separation" camp (Labor) resulted in the razor-thin victory of the Likud candidate, Benjamin Netanyahu, in 1996. When Netanyahu was found to be incapable of continuing the peace process, popular sentiment brought Ehud Barak, the new Labor candidate, to power in 1999 in a landslide victory. However, the failure of the Camp David final status talks sponsored by U.S. president Bill Clinton in July 2000, followed in September by the beginning of the third Intifadah brought on by Palestinians frustrated with the effects of "separation" and "closure" on their daily lives, prompted the Jewish Israeli public opinion pendulum to swing back in the opposite (rightward) direction, resulting in the election of Ariel Sharon shortly thereafter.

Contemporary Israeli Foreign Policy

The most important issue in contemporary Israeli foreign policy is the signing of peace treaties with as many Arab states as possible. Still, it is realized that peace with the more distant Arab states is conditional upon reaching agreements with the front-line states. These include Egypt, Jordan, Lebanon, and Syria as well as the Palestinians. Israel successfully completed peace agreements with Egypt and Jordan in 1979 and 1994, respectively. The extent of appropriate Israeli concessions in the other three bilateral tracks—with Syria, Lebanon, and the Palestinians—has been subject to continuous debate within Israel's foreign policy establishment. The most contentious areas of Labor-Likud debate have centered on the degree of territorial withdrawal, settlements, and East Jerusalem on the Palestinian track, and the depth of the withdrawal, if any, on the Syrian track.

The Palestinian-Israeli Track

The Israeli-PLO declaration of principles, or Oslo agreement, was signed by Israeli prime minister Yitzhak Rabin, PLO chairman Yasser Arafat, and U.S. president Bill Clinton on the south lawn of the White House in 1993. That was the beginning of the process, not the end. Many detailed agreements followed, the most important of which was the interim agreement, also known as Oslo II, in 1995, thus launching the "interim period" agreed to in the declaration of principles. The interim period expired in May 1999, and negotiations then turned to focus on implementation issues concerning Israel's military redeployment from various small parcels of West Bank land left over from the interim agreement. The "final status" talks, which were supposed to resolve all the big issues that were deferred in Oslo, began in 2000 but faced impasse on several of these issues. The most important of these issues has been the borders and nature of the Palestinian state or quasi-state.

The most talked-about aspect of the borders issue has been the question of how much of the West Bank and Gaza Strip would be turned over to the Palestinians, usually expressed in percentages. Until the start of the final status talks, the Palestinians had sole control only of the tiny land areas that house their major cities and large villages: these were collectively designated as "Areas A" under the interim agreement. Smaller villages fell under "Areas B," areas in which the Palestinian Authority has controlled civilian affairs while sharing security control with the Israelis. Following the second Israeli army redeployment (three were agreed to in the follow-ups to the interim agreement but the third was never implemented), Areas A and B comprised about 40 percent of the West Bank and Gaza Strip, with Areas A being far smaller, in the single-digit percentages. The remaining 60 percent of the West Bank and Gaza Strip—including the lands adjacent to their borders with Jordan and Egypt—were designated as "Areas C" (see map earlier in chapter). These areas have been controlled exclusively by Israel, available for Israeli civilian settlement and road construction connecting the settlements to each other and to Israel.

An even more important question, however, has been the two issues that would determine the nature of Palestine's future. First is the control of Palestine's entry and exit points. Shall the Palestinian state have control of its gateways to the outside world—its lands bordering Egypt and Jordan, its airport and its seaport in Gaza—or will the Israeli army remain in control of the entrances and exits? A state that does not have sole, sovereign control of its external gateways is not a state. During the Camp David summit of mid-2000, the Israeli establishment showed no sign that it was likely to release control of Palestine's external borders. Some Israelis believe that Israel should control Palestine's entry points even after the final status, so as to enable it to govern the entry of both people and weapons, and to control Palestine's international border in general so as to prevent the new mini-state from aligning itself with hostile forces on the eastern front, such as Iraq, Iran, and Syria.

Almost as important is the issue of internal territorial contiguity for the future Palestine. In the interim agreement, Israel succeeded in carving up the West Bank and Gaza Strip into dozens of tiny geographical areas or land-islands, all of which fell under the designations of A, B, or C. Shall the future Palestinian state be in pieces, or cantons, or shall it have territorial contiguity (aside from the accepted separation by Israel proper of the West Bank and Gaza Strip from each other)? The first Israeli-proposed final status map displayed a Palestinian state in four cantons, three in the West Bank and one in Gaza, with the West Bank cantons separated from one another by areas designated as Areas C, slated for annexation to Israel proper. Later maps, such as the Camp David map, sharply reduced these discontiguities but retained those around East Jerusalem and the main road connecting the northern and southern West Bank.

The second of the four issues, the future of the Palestine refugee communities from the 1947–1948 Palestine war/Israel war of independence, has been among the most difficult of all the issues because it brings into question Israel's demographic goals. The Palestinians have demanded the implementation of their UN-sanctioned "right of return" for any and all of their 3.6 million refugees (including their children and grandchildren) displaced by the Zionist militia organizations—as the British colonial regime was in the process of departing

Palestine — to make room for the establishment of Israel. Fully two-thirds of the Palestinians had already been displaced before the intervention of the Arab states, during the six-month period between November 1947 and May 1948. The Arab states, of course, could not become involved until the British had fully departed the country. This occurred on May 15, 1948, on which date Israel declared itself into existence, and on which date the Arab states then intervened in an attempt to stop it, thus launching the first interstate Arab-Israeli war (1948–1949).

Most of these exiled Palestinians and their descendants live in refugee camps and major cities in Jordan, Lebanon, and Syria, adjacent to Israel. Were Israel to agree to their return, it would destroy the Jewish majority state and lead to a fifty-fifty population ratio at least. This would be equivalent to the liquidation of Israel as it defines itself, which is as a "Jewish state," not a "Jewish-Palestinian state" or "binational state." As Labor's Yossi Beilin has said, the "most reddish" of Israeli red lines concerns the Palestinian right of return: "If the Palestinians will have the right to return, it will not be a Jewish state. The Zionist dream would be over. . . . This is where I draw the line. Our national state would be in danger."[10]

This issue of the 1947–1948 refugees was considered to be among the most intractable of all issues, because it went all the way back to the initial condition of the conflict — in fact it has defined the conflict. Of all the issues in the final status, the refugee issue is the only issue with this characteristic; all the other issues deal with the second-level problems generated by the 1967 war. Israel's solution is to persuade Arab states to resettle most of those refugees in place or have them transferred to a scattering of other countries for resettlement. Limited numbers would be allowed to take up Palestinian citizenship in the West Bank and Gaza Strip. The Palestinians do not want to go anywhere but back to their hometowns in Palestine, and the Arab states, particularly Lebanon, do not want to host them in their countries forever.

The third issue concerns the city of East Jerusalem, which was occupied by Israel during the 1967 war. The other side, West Jerusalem, is part of Israel proper and recognized as such by the peace signatories as well as the international community. It is no longer contested as a territory (although it is contested as a site for the return of 1947–1948 refugees who were displaced from the Palestinian villages that had existed in the area). The Israelis expanded East Jerusalem into adjacent West Bank territory, and then annexed the enlarged area. This annexation was contested. Israel, with Zionism as part of its political culture, sees Jerusalem, the center of Jewish life in antiquity and the location of its holiest religious sites, as its "eternal capital." Palestinians see East Jerusalem as the political, economic, religious, and cultural center of West Bank life, not to mention that the territorial contiguity of the southern and northern regions of the West Bank depends exclusively on it (the closure cut off the single road in 1992). Because of the religious sites, the viewpoints of Arab and Islamic worlds, as well as that of the Vatican, also come into play. Israel's proposed solution has been to substitute outlying areas located near East Jerusalem, such as Abu Dis, for the Palestinian capital. Under Barak, this was amended to include several discontiguous patches of land within East Jerusalem proper. These proposals, however, would solve neither the territorial contiguity problem nor the problem of Israeli military checkpoints blocking free and normal Palestinian access to the city. The Palestinians, for their part, have proposed both shared municipal jurisdiction and shared sovereignty for Jerusalem, with East Jerusalem as Palestine's capital and West Jerusalem as Israel's capital, with special arrangements for the holy sites.

The last of the four issues has been the future of Israeli settlements. More than 300,000 Jewish settlers currently reside in the occupied West Bank and Gaza Strip territory; the army posts and roads providing contiguity among the settlements are also counted as settlement activity. Israel's solution is to incorporate the major settlement blocs, located mainly in the center of the West Bank, and annex them, together with the roads that connect them to Israel. This action would sever the West Bank at its thin midpoint and break it up into several territorially discontiguous cantons. Israel has been prepared to allow most of the smaller and more remote West Bank settlements to become territorially part of the Palestinian state, which Israel hopes will agree to lease at least some of them back to Israel. Otherwise, the settlers currently residing in those outposts would have to be relocated to Israel proper, or to Israeli-controlled areas in the West Bank.

The Syria-Lebanon-Israel Track

The initially separate Israel-Syria and Israel-Lebanon tracks are now intertwined as a result of Syria's having taken on Lebanon essentially as a strategic protectorate beginning in 1991. Thus, Lebanese foreign policy, especially as it pertains to the peace process, is coordinated, or merged, with that of Syria, which has the final say in any decision. This triangular strategic configuration has thus led to the emergence of a single trilateral peace track, comprised of two main issues.

The first of these is Israel's withdrawal from the Golan. The Golan is Syrian territory, occupied by Israel in the 1967 war and annexed unilaterally by Israel in 1981. The dispute is strictly over the location of the boundary: Syria wants Israel to withdraw to the prewar line of June 4, 1967. Israel prefers the 1923 colonial boundary, which was set to define British and French areas of control. The 1967 border would return to Syria the eastern shore of Lake Tiberias, the area from which Israel has been drawing a significant percentage of its water supply. The area in dispute is a small number of square meters, which if not for the water issue would be quite trivial. Israel also wants to maintain a military listening post manned by Israeli army personnel on top of the Golan, which looks down onto Israeli lands below. This area, however, is also a mere twenty-five miles from Damascus, the Syrian capital—thus rendering it of the utmost strategic significance to Syria.

The second issue concerned Israel's withdrawal from southern Lebanon. It also includes dealing with the issue of the Palestinian refugees in Lebanon, in that Lebanon believes Israel is responsible for them and has refused to sign a peace agreement without some provision for their future. Israel would have preferred to pull its military forces out of Lebanese territory in the context of a peace agreement, with Lebanon agreeing to prevent attacks by hostile guerrilla organizations, be they Lebanese or Palestinian, across the southern border into Israel. However, not wishing to pay for that agreement in Syrian currency (the Golan), and faced with mounting battle casualties, a failed military strategy, and the "battle-fatigue" in Israeli Jewish public opinion discussed earlier, Israel decided to withdraw from the "security zone" it had occupied inside Lebanon and to defend its northern border from within Israel itself. Once Israel made this decision, even before the actual troop withdrawal, it immediately began to revert to its old strategy of "excessive retaliation" (against the Lebanese civilian infrastructure and against Syrian forces in Lebanon) as the standard response to any future attacks from that direction. Israel may have to pay for this decision in Palestinian currency, however. The main pitfall of the unilateral withdrawal from Israel's point of view has been to crown tiny Lebanon as the first and only Arab country ever to expel an Israeli occupation force solely by military means. The withdrawal had the clear potential to turn the Lebanese resistance into an example and a model for the coming generation of Palestinians in the West Bank and Gaza Strip. This is precisely what happened, and the result has been the third Intifadah.

Conclusion: Evolving Trends Affecting Future Israeli Foreign Policy

A generational shift is under way in the key Arab countries and in Iran. (Iran is not an Arab country, but since the Islamic revolution in 1979, Iran joined Iraq and Syria as part of the "eastern front" of adversaries opposed to Israel.) The pattern so far seems to be evolving into the stability of hereditary rule in Arab countries where it already exists (Jordan, Morocco, and the southern Gulf monarchies) and a high probability of its establishment or reestablishment in countries where it currently does not exist (Syria, and possibly Iraq, respectively). Iran is a special case, undergoing a process of large-scale populist postrevolutionary reform spawned by the offspring of the revolutionary generation. The nature of the coming rulers in the Middle East will have to be taken into account by Israeli foreign policy makers, since the personal inclinations of the individual rulers tend to define both the ideology and the foreign policy outlook of these countries.

The issue of economic and political globalization is strongest in Iran, but it will eventually come, probably at a much slower pace, to Arab states. The question of interest here is how it will affect Israel. So far the economic liberalizers, not wanting to be "left behind," are accepting peace and normalization with Israel as an inevitable part of globalization and, in some cases, as a source of economic opportunity. The political opponents of the current forms of authoritarianism, however, are the very same elements of civil society and intelligentsia who are among the most fervently opposed to recognition of Israel and normalization with it. They have nothing against globalization per se, but they see no reason why they cannot have globalization without Israel. To this secular-nationalist intelligentsia one must add the "Islamic democratizers," those political Islamists, with many intellectuals among them, who are on the opposing side of Arab secular-authoritarian rule, and who share the antipathy to Israel with their secular-nationalist counterparts in Arab civil society. Together these two highly educated segments have formed a potent antinormalization movement in many Arab countries, first among them Jordan. In any case, Israel will have to deal with Arab populist antinormalization sentiment, since Arab states can afford to go only so far with Israel and its goals of regional interdependence without destabilizing the credibility of their regimes.

Islamism is still alive as a sociocultural force, but as a force capable of taking over states and thus participating in the high politics of international relations, it has undergone a steep decline in recent years. This trend should be expected to continue.[11] The reasons for the decline are numerous, the main one being that radical revolutionary Islamists realized they could not take over Middle Eastern countries without causing massive loss of life, and without thus turning their own people against them in the process. Recent carnage in Algeria, brought on by the reaction to the Algerian military's overturning of an Islamist victory in a democratic election, has cost tens of thousands of lives, and the brutality of the retributions has carried repercussions in other countries as well.[12] Among the Palestinians, the Hamas and Islamic Jihad movements have seen their strength diminished in the wake of Israeli retributions and assassinations, carried out in cooperation with the United States and the Palestinian Authority. Furthermore, the eruption of the third Intifadah marked the reemergence of the secular-nationalist Fatah-PLO organization as the preeminent force in Palestinian politics. The only place in which militant Islamists are flourishing is in Lebanon, where their Hezbollah movement led the recent victory against the Israeli army in southern Lebanon. Still, the Hezbollah knows it cannot attempt to take over multisectarian Lebanon for fear of setting off another civil war. The downward trend of militant Islamism is unmistakable, and this will take a lot of weight off the shoulders of Israeli strategic planners in future years.

Before the 1999 landslide election of Labor's Ehud Barak, the main fault line running through Israeli society had been a fifty-fifty split between the two major political parties—Labor and Likud—and the trends they represented. The chasm divided those who placed peace as the top priority from those who did not and was reflected in the 51–49 vote for the Likud candidate Benjamin Netanyahu in 1996. With Barak's election, it became apparent that this political chasm and its effects had virtually disappeared. This occurred most probably as a result of Netanyahu's term in office—with the ghosts of Yitzhak Rabin's assassination hovering in the background—and its replacement by a centrist consensus on foreign policy. Barak, who then proceeded to stray too far to the left of that center, faced a wholesale loss of support in addition to his Knesset majority. This led him to resign and call for the special prime ministerial election in 2001, which resulted in the movement of the center to the right and the landslide election of Ariel Sharon.

With the closing of the political ranks around a somewhat mobile Israeli center, the old "secular"-religious divide had now come to the surface as the issue most likely to cause an explosion of internal tensions. Unlike the political divide, this cultural one is not an even split. The religious fundamentalists are vocal and powerful, but they are in the minority. Barak's 1999 electoral victory was widely interpreted as a mandate not only for the peace process but also for the secular, modern Western culture.

This is a difference of opinion about what type of society Israel should be. The religious side holds that Israel, as an expressly Jewish state, must be run according to Jewish law. The "secularists" (in quotations because they too want to live in a Jewish state), in contrast, do not want to be bound by Jewish law. They consider the religious side to be theocratic extremists, on the pattern of Iran. Cultural clashes have arisen over such issues as prohibition of driving and other activity on the Sabbath, enforcement of kosher laws, the closing of movie theaters in Jerusalem, protests over scantily clad females on the beach and on advertising billboards, and so forth. This cultural war is being played out in the form of regionalism: Jerusalem is being captured by the theocrats, and the "secularists" are taking refuge in Tel Aviv.

This divide, although not directly related to foreign policy, must be taken into account by the foreign policy making elite. The religious parties, mainly Shas and the National Religious Party, are an important swing factor that can make or break coalitions. It is not unusual for a prime minister to make concessions to these parties on internal religious matters in exchange for their support on this or that foreign policy issue, in order to keep the government intact. The "secularists" in Israel call this blackmail, but it is what coalition politics are all about. Should the regional conflict become more stable in the future, we can expect these internal cultural-religious differences in Israel to grow sharper.

An emerging movement among some members of the Israeli intelligentsia, particularly in the current history sector, has recently taken to questioning Israel's official and popular version of the means by which Israel brought itself into being. Its initiators, known in Israel as the "new historians," in researching questions such as "Did the Palestinians really leave willingly in 1947 and 1948, or did we expel them?" reached certain conclusions that led some of them to question their commitment to Zionism.[13] Although technically on the fringes, many of the historical questions they have been raising were initially spawned by the second Intifadah and Israel's subsequent interactions with Palestinian history in the peace process, and then brought to the fore by the occurrence of the fiftieth anniversary of Israel's establishment in 1998.

Since then, changes have appeared in certain textbooks in Israeli schools that tend to lend more legitimacy to the accuracy of Palestinian claims about their recent history than ever before. Israeli films have been made in which the Palestinian version is presented alongside the Israeli version, drawing feverish criticism and denunciation from mainline Zionists. Recent studies have also shown a diminishing commitment to Zionism as an ideology among Israeli youth, reflecting not so much opposition to Zionism as indifference. This change is most often attributed to the diminishing Arab military threat, and perhaps most important, to the generational passing of the idealism that accompanied Zionism's founding generation. Although the third Intifadah has placed these "new historical" forces on the defensive, they represent a permanent trend. New knowledge, once gained, can never be taken back; one cannot retreat from knowledge into ignorance. Some people have called this the "maturing" of Israel—the ability to let go of some of its founding myths when presented with factual information that is inconsistent with those myths. These emerging trends may remain in the background as they have been, or, as others have speculated, they could eventually lead to. the emergence down the road of a new "post-Zionist era" in Israel.

Into the future, then, we can expect both external and internal trends to influence Israel's foreign policy. These large-scale trends, as in the past, will continue to be more important than the actual mechanics or bureaucratic elements of policy making. That is because Israel's foreign and national security policy is not only about the nature of Israel's overseas interests, as is the case in most other states, but about the nature of its very existence. It should also be noted, though, that internal developments in Arab states and among the Palestinians could radically alter the configuration of the Arab adversaries Israel is now confronting externally and may very well hold the largest impact in the coming decades.

Suggestions for Further Reading

Beilin, Yossi. *Israel: A Concise Political History.* New York: St. Martin's Press, 1992.
Brecher, Michael. *The Foreign Policy System of Israel: Setting, Images, Process.* New Haven: Yale University Press, 1972.
Evron, Yair. *Israel's Nuclear Dilemma.* Ithaca: Cornell University Press, 1994.
Khouri, Fred. *The Arab-Israeli Dilemma.* Syracuse: Syracuse University Press, 1976.
Liebman, Charles S. "The Myth of Defeat: The Memory of the Yom Kippur War in Israeli Society." *Middle Eastern Studies* 29 (July 1993): 399–418.
Morris, Benny. *The Birth of the Palestinian Refugee Problem, 1947–1949.* New York: Cambridge University Press, 1987.
Netanyahu, Benjamin. *A Place among the Nations: Israel and the World.* New York: Bantam Books, 1993.
Pappe, Ilan. *The Making of the Arab-Israeli Conflict: 1947–1951.* New York: Tauris, 1992.
Peres, Shimon. *The New Middle East.* New York: Holt, 1993.
Roberts, Robert J. *Survival or Hegemony? The Foundations of Israeli Foreign Policy.* Baltimore: Johns Hopkins University Press, 1973.
Sachar, Howard M. *A History of Israel from the Rise of Zionism to Our Time.* 2d ed. New York: Random House, 1996.
Said, Edward W. *The Question of Palestine.* New York: Vintage Books, 1979.

Yaniv, Avner A. *Deterrence without the Bomb: The Politics of Israeli Strategy.* Lexington, Mass: Lexington Books, 1987.

Zak, Moshe. "The Jordan-Israel Peace Treaty: Thirty Years of Clandestine Meetings." *Middle East Quarterly* 2 (March 1995): 53–59.

Zureiq, Qunstantin. *The Meaning of the Disaster.* Translated by R. Bayly Winder. Beirut: Khayat's College Book Cooperative, 1956. Originally published as *Ma'na al-Nakbah* in 1948.

Notes

1. Avi Shlaim, *Collusion across the Jordan: King Abdallah, the Zionist Movement, and the Partition of Palestine* (Oxford: Clarendon Press, 1987); Uri Bar-Joseph, *The Best of Enemies: Israel and Transjordan in the War of 1948* (London: Frank Cass, 1987); Yehuda Lukacs, "Sub-Rosa Peace: The Dynamics of Israeli-Jordanian Functional Cooperation: 1967–1988" (Ph.D. diss., American University, 1989).

2. Yitzhak Rabin, the Labor Party candidate, in a debate with Prime Minister Shamir, June 16, 1992, quoted in the *New York Times,* June 17, 1992.

3. For the most exhaustive strategic discussion of Israel's normalization concept, see Shimon Peres, *The New Middle East* (New York: Holt, 1993).

4. For a more thorough discussion of normalization's practical details, see Meir Merhav, *Economic Cooperation and Middle East Peace* (London: Weidenfeld and Nicolson, 1989), and Gideon Fishelson, ed., *Economic Cooperation in the Middle East* (Boulder: Westview Press, 1989).

5. For the classic Palestinian and Arab concept of the *nakbah* of 1947–1948, see the explication by the Arab Christian intellectual Qunstantin Zureiq, *The Meaning of the Disaster,* trans. R. Bayly Winder (Beirut: Khayat's College Book Cooperative, 1956; originally published as *Ma'na al-Nakbah,* 1948).

6. The Zionism-is-racism resolution, officially adopted in 1975, declared Zionism to be "a form of racism and racial discrimination," United Nations General Assembly Resolution 3375, November 10, 1975.

7. For a good geopolitical and resource-based explanation of why Israel cannot afford to fight defensive wars, see Major General Israel Tal, "The Offensive and the Defensive in Israel's Campaigns," *Jerusalem Quarterly* 51 (summer 1989): 41–47.

8. For an excellent strategic discussion of why Israel does not openly declare its nuclear option, preferring "opacity," see Yair Evron, *Israel's Nuclear Dilemma* (Ithaca: Cornell University Press, 1994).

9. When he was defense minister during the 1980s, the late Israeli prime minister Yitzhak Rabin instituted what he called the "iron fist" policy toward the occupied territories, ordering the policy of "force, might, and beatings," part of which meant the bone-breaking policy, in response to the second Intifadah (quoted from the *New York Times,* June 17, 1992). That policy was halted as a result of unexpected levels of international media coverage, which in turn led to an international public relations nightmare for Israel.

10. Yossi Beilin, quoted in *Washington Post,* August 16, 2000, A32.

11. For a particularly interesting in-depth discussion of this subject, see Max Rodenbeck, "Is Islam Losing Its Thunder?" *Washington Quarterly* 21 (spring 1998): 177–193.

12. The Egyptian Islamic Jihad, after witnessing the popular backlash following its attack on Western tourists in Egypt—in the hope of damaging the government economy—decided to formally give up its armed struggle, leaving the Islamist cause back in the hands of the century-old Muslim Brotherhood movement, which does not seek a

revolutionary takeover of the state apparatus. Political Islamists, although strong in Jordan, are not ready to risk inflicting similar bloodbaths by confronting the state head-on. The demise of the Islamist movement's chances in Turkey after a very brief time in partial power—and the continuing decline of political Islam even in Iran, its modern birthplace—has sapped the motivation of other would-be Islamist movements.

13. Benny Morris, *The Birth of the Palestinian Refugee Problem, 1947–1949* (New York: Cambridge University Press, 1987), and Simha Flapan, *The Birth of Israel* (New York: Pantheon Press, 1987), are considered to be the founding works of the Israeli "new historians." Other well-known works by subsequent "new historians" include Ilan Pappe, *The Making of the Arab-Israeli Conflict: 1947–1951* (New York: Tauris, 1992), and Avi Shlaim, "Conflicting Approaches to Israel's Relations with the Arabs: Ben Gurion and Sharett, 1953–1956," *Middle East Journal* 37 (spring 1983): 180–201.

CHAPTER 10

The Changing Character of Iranian Foreign Policy

Paul D. Hoyt

Since the beginning of the Cold War, Iran has been an important country in world politics, receiving attention from the superpowers and other powerful states in the Middle East. Its oil reserves make others dependent on Iran, but this has not provided it with leverage in international relations. Rather, its oil has attracted outside actors—including the British, the Soviets, and the Americans—each trying to control or seek concessions from Iran. Iran has also been affected by geopolitical competition and rivalry, both in the global conflict between the United States and the Soviet Union (particularly with the U.S.–British-sponsored coup against Prime Minister Mossadeq in 1953) and in the regional conflict in the Middle East (particularly with Iraq's invasion of Iran in 1980). In this chapter, Paul Hoyt shows how Iran has attempted to cope with these external pressures along with its desire to play an influential role in the Persian Gulf. Adopting at various times the roles of "pillar," "prophet," and "rogue," Iran has dramatically changed its foreign policy over the years, depending on the worldviews of its leaders. Today, Iran plays the part of reformer, focusing on establishing positive relations with other states.

The importance of Iranian leaders' beliefs in shaping foreign policy parallels the significance of leaders like De Gaulle in France (Chapter 3), Nehru in India (Chapter 8), and Mao in China (Chapter 6). Like those of China, South Africa (Chapter 12), and, until recently, Nigeria (Chapter 11), Iran's political system is authoritarian and provides its people with few avenues of influence on foreign policy. Yet its leaders often reflect Iranian society's core values of anti-westernism and anticolonialism, similar to other developing countries such as Mexico (Chapter 14). Islam, as a belief system, underlies many of the core values that act as parameters of Iranian foreign policy, similar to the role of Zionism in Israeli foreign policy (Chapter 9). As this chapter argues, Iran is an excellent example of a country operating under the effects of external constraints. At times, Iran has followed the path expected by realist theories and was closely aligned with the United States, much like Germany (Chapter 4) and Japan (Chapter 7). At other times, however, it has attempted to remain neutral, rejecting the overtures of superpowers, much like France and India. Iran's attempts at neutrality, however, contributed to the isolation from which it is now struggling to break free.

The he modern state of Iran emerged from the dissolution of the Qajar dynasty in 1921, when Reza Pahlavi seized power and declared himself the shah, or king, of a new dynasty. On August 26, 1941, in the early days of World War II, Iran was simultaneously invaded by the Soviet Union and Great Britain. These two countries, allied more by circumstance than by choice, were concerned with what they perceived to be the pro-Nazi sympathies of the Iranian government. They wanted to deny the Germans access to Iranian oil supplies and create a secure route for transporting war materiel to the Soviet Union. The shah was forced to abdicate on September 16, 1941, in favor of his son, Muhammad Reza Pahlavi, who was considered more pliable by the occupying forces.[1]

Since the time of these events, Iran has been a central player in the international strategic environment, though the nature of that participation has altered radically over the years. Guided by a consistent strategic desire to play an influential role in the Persian Gulf region, Iran's tactics have shifted in response to the differing worldviews of the individuals leading the state. Iran has acted as a "pillar" in the U.S.-led confrontation with the Soviet Union, then as a "prophet" under the guidance of the Islamic leader, Ayatollah Ruhollah Khomeini. Subsequently, Iran has been characterized as a "rogue" in its support for international terrorism, its quest to acquire weapons of mass destruction, and its antipathy toward the Middle East peace process between Israel and her Arab neighbors. Most recently, since the election of Mohammad Khatami as president in 1997, the election of a pro-reform parliament in February 2000, and Khatami's reelection in June 2001, Iran has been seen as a "reformer." This chapter details the major shifts in Iranian foreign policy and discusses the international and domestic political forces that have played an important role in shaping policy; finally, it considers expectations about the future.

Iranian Foreign Policy during the Cold War

Beginning with World War II, other nations increasingly perceived Iran to be of strategic value, making it a target of competition that lasted throughout the Cold War. This perception led to efforts by Britain and the United States to influence Iran's foreign policy orientation, mostly by maintaining the pro-western shah in power.

Iran — The Pillar

A Battlefield of the Cold War. In January 1942 the shah signed a deal with the British and Soviets whereby Iran would assist in the war effort against Germany, mainly by acting as a supply route for western goods to the Soviet Union, which was facing a determined German onslaught. In exchange, both the Soviets and the British agreed to respect Iran's sovereignty and to remove all foreign troops from Iranian territory within six months of the end of the war. These commitments were reaffirmed at a November 1943 conference in the Iranian capital, Tehran, between U.S. president Franklin D. Roosevelt, British prime minister Winston Churchill, and Soviet leader Josef Stalin.[2]

In 1945 Iran emerged as one of the first battlegrounds of the fledgling Cold War. Despite the wartime agreements, Soviet troops remained beyond the six months agreed to at the Tehran conference. More critically, the Soviet Union supported efforts to create two independent areas in the ethnic Azeri and Kurdish sections of Iran's northern territories, which, not coincidentally, bordered on the Soviet Union.[3] The price of Soviet withdrawal was a pledge by the Iranian government (led by Prime Minister Qavam) to support an oil concession for the Soviet Union in Iran and to negotiate a peaceful settlement of the Azerbaijani and Kurdish independence claims. The Iranians acceded. With that agreement in hand, and under pressure from the United States, Britain, and the United Nations, Soviet forces withdrew in May 1946. With the Soviets physically removed from Iranian territory, the Iranian government felt secure enough to attack the secessionist areas and return them to central government control. The oil concession was then rejected by the Iranian parliament (the Majlis). Both the Americans and the Soviets interpreted these events as evidence of each other's bad faith, thus adding fuel to the developing Cold War.[4]

The Mossadeq Crisis and the Turn to the West. Oil was also central to the next crisis in Iranian politics. Beginning in 1949 there was increased sentiment within Iran to nationalize the country's oil industry as a demonstration of independence from the colonial powers. Negotiations with the British-dominated Anglo-Iranian Oil Company proved fruitless, and the situation deteriorated. Finally, in March 1951, the parliament voted to nationalize the nation's oil industry. In April, under great popular pressure, the shah appointed as prime minister a leading proponent of nationalization, the popular nationalist politician Muhammad Mossadeq. Throughout 1951 and 1952 the situation was deadlocked, with the Anglo-Iranian Oil Company — along with the British government — and the Iranians rejecting each other's proposals.[5]

In January 1953 Dwight D. Eisenhower took office as U.S. president as the Cold War intensified worldwide. The Americans regarded Mossadeq's leadership in Iran to be potentially conducive to a pro-Soviet shift in Iranian policy. Mossadeq's behavior was also disturbing to some senior members of the Iranian military, who perceived a dangerous drift toward the left in Iranian politics. Thus, simultaneous plots were hatched to bring down the popular prime minister. The

Americans agreed to a proposal for a joint American–British operation to support the overthrow of Mossadeq. Code-named Operation Ajax, the plan called for a military coup supported by street demonstrations. Launched on August 13, 1953, the operation stumbled initially (the shah, who had been sidelined politically, even fled the country). Eventually it succeeded when the military and civilian demonstrators took to the street. When Mossadeq was removed from office, the shah returned to the throne more powerful than before. [6]

The shah's now elevated political position in the Iranian system made him essentially the only political power in the country. He entered a close relationship with the United States that made Iran a major element in American Cold War policy in the Middle East. Iran became a listening post for American intelligence monitoring the Soviet Union. It also became a major recipient of American military aid in part to facilitate its serving as a bulwark against Soviet advances in the Middle East. This tight relationship was further enhanced by Iran's central role in what was termed the "twin pillars strategy" of the United States during the 1970s. Under this plan the United States increased its support to both Iran and Saudi Arabia (the "twin pillars") as regional guardians of American interests in the Middle East. Iran remained a linchpin in American Cold War policy until the shah fell in the revolution of 1978–1979.[7]

Iran — The Prophet

The roots of the Iranian Revolution go back at least to 1963, when the shah introduced a program of economic and social reforms collectively known as the White Revolution. These included land reform, profit sharing for industrial workers in private enterprises, and female suffrage. Supported by some elements of Iranian society, the White Revolution was rejected by others, including many in the religious establishment who, in particular, opposed land reforms and the extension of voting to women. Opposition leaders also saw the reforms as an unwanted extension of government influence. One of them was the Ayatollah Sayyid Ruhollah Musavi Khomeini, a religious leader in the city of Qom. The Ayatollah was imprisoned for his vocal opposition and later was exiled for condemning a bill granting diplomatic immunity to American military personnel in Iran.[8]

Despite the heightened revenues flowing into Iran from the oil price increases of 1973–1974 (arising from the October 1973 war between Israel and several Arab states and engineered in large part by the shah), the overall socioeconomic political picture grew bleak. Corruption, inflation, and economic mismanagement led to deteriorating conditions for large numbers of Iranians in the lower and middle classes, including the politically powerful merchant class, or *bazaaris*. Socially, the large and visible foreign presence in Iran was considered disgraceful by conservative religious leaders, who rejected western cultural attitudes and practices. In addition, foreigners were anathema to Iranian nationalists, who saw their influence as a form of colonialism. These internal forces increased in visibility and power when the shah began to open up the political system in response to pressure from the United States, during President Jimmy Carter's administration, to improve its human rights record.[9]

This coalition of disparate forces used the limited political opening to demand major reforms from the shah. The tone of these protests changed in 1978, when occasionally violent mass demonstrations took to the streets, demanding that the shah be removed and calling for the return of the exiled Ayatollah Khomeini, who had remained an active political voice even in exile. The situation deteriorated throughout the year, with the shah alternating between concessions and coercion. Neither strategy was effective, and domestic pressure mounted for the shah to leave. Facing the inevitable, the shah left Iran in January 1979, never to return. The royalist government collapsed. Two weeks later, Khomeini arrived in Tehran to an enthusiastic reception by millions of Iranians.[10]

However, the broad coalition of forces that had united in their opposition to the shah was unable to remain cohesive after his departure. Throughout 1979 and 1980 the various political forces in the country struggled for dominance in the emerging political system. Despite these challenges, including armed insurrection by some groups, the faction centered on Khomeini emerged victorious.[11]

"Neither East nor West." As is common with successful revolutions, Khomeini's new government sought to repudiate the previous government's domestic and foreign policies. The close relationship with the United States that had been a centerpiece of Iranian policy and of the Cold War was rejected. The United States was referred to in Iranian pronouncements as "the Great Satan."[12] The United States, in turn, rejected any collaboration with the new Islamic Republic, especially after the U.S. embassy in Tehran was overrun in November 1979 by Islamic students, who held fifty-two embassy staff hostage for 444 days.[13]

Intriguingly, Iran also rejected close ties to the Soviet Union, which it dubbed "the Lesser Satan." The 1979 Soviet occupation of Afghanistan, a Muslim country bordering Iran, was partly responsible for this attitude. In addition, the new Iranian leaders believed that both the capitalism of the United States and the socialism of the Soviet Union were corrupt ideologies. According to Khomeini, such ideologies, with their emphasis on materialism, were to be rejected and replaced by reliance on Islam. Khomeini labeled this dual rejection of both superpowers a policy of "neither east nor west."[14]

Iran–Iraq War. Nonaligned by choice and isolated by consequence, Iran was a solitary country when Iraq invaded on September 20, 1980. Led by Saddam Hussein, Iraq had ambitions of altering the political landscape so that it would emerge as the dominant power in the Persian Gulf region. Saddam was also seeking to end Iran's stated policy of exporting its revolution by calling for un-Islamic governments "to be replaced." Iraq's Sunni Muslim leadership feared that this idea would resonate with Iraq's Shiite Muslim majority.[15]

Iraqi expectations of exploiting the turbulent situation in Iran in order to achieve a quick victory faded as the conflict settled into a lengthy and destructive war of attrition on each side. Condemnatory of both the east and the west, as well as the Arab states aligned with Iraq, Iran became more and more an outcast from the international system, while Iraq benefited from the support of most Arab states and, to a lesser degree, western powers. The war ended in 1988 with no significant territorial adjustments. Both countries had suffered tremendous economic and societal devastation—there were 600,000 Iranian and 400,000 Iraqi dead. At this point Iran's isolation was virtually absolute.[16]

Few countries' journeys through the turmoil of the Cold War were as tortuous and complex as Iran's. From its initial status as a battlefield of the Cold War, Iran then moved into a close orbit with western powers before ending the Cold War's final decade in isolation from it. The next section will examine the external factors that have influenced Iranian foreign policy.

External Factors

Iran's foreign policy for the four decades beginning in 1940 was mostly determined by external factors. Iran's involvement in the two major geopolitical events of the mid-twentieth century—World War II and the Cold War—was dictated by foreign powers' engagements in broader strategic struggles. As predicted by realist theories, the great powers of the period—the United States, the Soviet Union, and to a lesser degree Great Britain—imposed their will on less powerful states. Efforts by the Iranians to assert their independence in foreign policy decision making during World War II and during the Mossadeq period were countered by the great powers pursuing their own agendas. Indeed, Iranian independence was such a threat to the United States and Great Britain that they sponsored the coup against Mossadeq.[17]

Iran was also critical to foreign powers because of its oil. Having access to oil production and gaining concessions were important to both the British and the Soviets in the 1940s and the 1950s, and the nationalization policies of Mossadeq were a direct threat to British and American economic interests. Here, we see the constraining effects of interdependence in the international environment, although in a way usually not accounted for by liberalism. Liberalism expects economic connections between countries to facilitate cooperation. Furthermore, as noted in Chapter 1, states that are most dependent on others are assumed to be the most constrained. In Iran, however, the opposite of both of these expectations can be seen. The great powers' dependence on Iran brought conflict, in the form of a military troop presence, military threat, and a sponsored coup, rather than cooperation. And even though it was Iran that controlled the resource—oil—it was Iran that was most constrained in its foreign policy.

The role of global factors in Iranian foreign policy waned in the late 1970s and throughout the 1980s and 1990s as internal factors related to the new Islamic Republic took precedence. After the revolution, Iran developed an ideology based in part on the rejection of ties with the United States, which was rightly seen as the patron of the shah.[18] The loss by the United States of a valuable ally so superbly located on the border with the Soviet Union runs counter to realist expectations that would anticipate vigorous American efforts to keep Iran in the western orbit. Iran's break with the United States was not followed by an immediate turn toward the Soviet Union. So, in essence, Iran opted out of the Cold War in 1979. This action too was contrary to realist expectations that the great powers would dictate smaller powers' international behavior.

Iran paid a price for opting out of the Cold War. In particular, its isolation from the world economy and the economic and military embargo imposed by the U.S. in response to the hostage crisis had devastating consequences on Iran's domestic economy. Iran's choice to remain nonaligned in the 1980s had also been costly; it meant that Iran had no real allies in its long war with Iraq. The goal of Iran's contemporary foreign policy of emerging from isolation and reestablishing positive relations with other countries is in some ways a recognition by Iranian leaders of the benefits of interdependence — and hence of the importance of external factors.

Although the role of global factors in Iranian foreign policy has varied over the years, the importance of regional factors in Iranian foreign policy has remained a constant; in particular, is Iran's interest in dominating the Persian Gulf region. Regardless of who its leaders were, Iran's regional policy can be seen as one of balancing against the power and interests of other large states in the region, such as Iraq and Israel, and against the coalition of smaller Gulf states. Iran's current opposition to Middle East peace negotiations and its efforts to establish better relations with many Arab states testify to the continuing significance of regional factors in Iranian foreign policy.

Internal Factors

During the 1980s two imperatives guided Iranian foreign policy. The first was the worldview and policy direction of the Ayatollah Khomeini. Adopting the concept and title of the *velayet-e faqih* (supreme jurist), this charismatic leader had virtually unchallengeable authority in the Iranian policy making process.[19] His views were determinative throughout his tenure. Central to those views was the need to confront corrupt regimes in the Middle East, especially when a Shiite population was being oppressed, and the need for Iran to maintain distance from the United States, the Soviet Union, and other governments he considered morally bankrupt.[20] As mentioned in the introductory chapter, individual leaders can be central to a country's decision making and push that policy in directions unexpected by theories of international behavior. The Ayatollah's influence is an excellent example.

The second imperative was the need to persevere in the war with Iraq. The conduct of the war was a constant in Iran's foreign policy throughout the decade. But even here the impact of Khomeini's policy direction is clear. After repulsing the Iraqi attacks of 1980–1981 at tremendous cost, Iran was able to recapture all the territory initially occupied by Iraq. At this point, the Iraqi leaders in Baghdad signaled their willingness to end the conflict. However, a return to the prewar status quo was unacceptable to Khomeini, who insisted that Iran now go on the offensive and move the fight into Iraq. The war continued for another five years before it finally ended with both sides exhausted and essentially in their original territorial positions. It can be argued that Khomeini—as an individual—made a decision to continue the war because his personal views regarding Saddam Hussein, ethnic Arabs, and Sunni Muslims overrode more military-based strategic calculations of Iran's ability to defeat Iraq.

The depth of Khomeini's personal animosity toward Iraq in this conflict was also reflected in his reaction to efforts to end the war in 1988 after staggering losses by both sides. Although finally convinced that Iran's better interests were served by accepting a cessation of hostilities, Khomeini remarked at the time that making peace with Saddam Hussein's Iraq was "like drinking poison."[21]

Both the shah and Khomeini had to deal with certain core values held by Iranians by honoring them or trying to suppress them. These values included anti-imperialism and anti-westernism. The nationalization of the oil industry in 1951, for example, was in part driven by the desire to demonstrate Iranian independence from colonial powers. Both American capitalism and Soviet communism were rejected as corrupt and foreign. There was a strong connection, of course, between anti-western attitudes and Islam. The 1979 revolution brought about both domination by the religious establishment and an isolationist foreign policy, and as pointed out earlier, the idea of exporting the revolution was also connected to Islam.

With the death of Khomeini in 1989, the Iranian political system has become a more fragmented and contentious entity, and the consensus on old core values has eroded. Lacking Khomeini's charismatic appeal, the new *velayet-e faqih,* Ayatollah Ali Khamenei, has been unable to dominate the Iranian political system. From 1989 to 1997 the main political actors in Iran were Khamenei and the president of the Islamic Republic, Hojatolislam Ali Rafsanjani. The differences between the two were generally slight, with Rafsanjani focused on rebuilding the economy, while leaving much of the social and foreign policy to Khamenei and his supporters. Since the late 1990s other political and social institutions—especially the newly elected parliament, the president, students, and the media—have become platforms for advancing alternative policy directions. In brief, the demise of dominant leaders like the shah and Khomeini has facilitated the rise to power of other actors, some of whom question anti-westernism and the role that Islam plays in foreign policy. All of them need to be considered important players in the power structure of Iran.[22]

Contemporary Iranian Foreign Policy

The end of the Cold War was of little direct consequence to Iran. After the revolution Iran had derived virtually no benefits or incurred any costs from the competition between the superpowers. However, Iran had suffered tremendously from the combined effects of the war with Iraq, the economic embargo by the

United States, and the widely held distrust of Iran by most states in the Middle East. The most pressing need driving Iranian foreign policy in the 1990s was to reestablish positive relations at both the regional and international levels.

Many forces converged in this period to push for a new line in Iranian policy. First, the utter devastation wrought by the Iran–Iraq war required a massive and immediate rebuilding of Iran's infrastructure and economy. This required foreign capital and technology and a reduced emphasis on regional confrontations. Second, the leadership after Khomeini's death was more attuned to rejuvenation than to revolution. Finally, the belligerency of Iraq, as evidenced by the invasion of Kuwait in August 1990, removed Iran as the number one perceived threat in the region. This made some Gulf Arab states more open to Iranian overtures. Although some relationships remained poor throughout the 1990s (Israel and the United States are the primary examples), Iran's overall record throughout the decade was one of slowly mending fences at both the regional and international levels.[23]

Regionally Iran has enjoyed some success in improving its position with the other countries of the Middle East. Most of the Gulf states, except Iraq, have been open to Iranian overtures over the past decade.[24] Relations with Syria, which was the sole Arab country to support Iran during the Iran–Iraq war, have remained close. The improvement in relations with Saudi Arabia, the largest of the Gulf monarchies, was a critical factor in Iran's efforts to gain greater acceptance and influence within the Middle East. Relations with Turkey remain proper, since both countries have a mutual interest in maintaining stability in the Kurdish region along their common border.[25]

The situation with Iraq continues to be tense because each side distrusts the other and actively supports opposition groups targeting the other's regime. However, neither side appears to have any interest in renewing the fighting of the 1980s. The other regional issue in which Iran plays an active role is that between Israel and Lebanon and Israel and the Palestinians. Unwilling to accept Israel's presence in what it sees as Muslim lands, Iran has been a vocal critic of the Middle East negotiations, which it believes ultimately will legitimize Israel's presence. Iran has been an active supporter of groups such as the Lebanese Hizballah (a militant Shiite group in southern Lebanon) and the Palestinian Hamas, both of which have resisted the presence of Israel in their countries.

After the Israeli withdrawal from its self-declared security zone in southern Lebanon in May 2000, the Iranian leadership faced a choice of what its future policy in Lebanon would be. With Iran as a long-time supporter of the Hizballah movement, the question is open as to what Iranian policy (as well as Hizballah policy) will be in the future.

At the international level, Iran has had mixed success in moving away from the isolation of the 1980s. Iran has developed positive relations with most of the central Asian states that emerged from the dissolution of the Soviet Union in the early 1990s (Kazakhstan, Kyrgyzstan, Uzbekistan, Turkmenistan, and Tajikistan). Combining religious appeals with economic opportunity, Iran has sought to develop ties with these states, especially as part of an effort to serve as a transit route for the developing petroleum and natural gas deposits of the Caspian Sea basin. Improved relations with these states would have the dual benefit of providing Iran with lucrative contracts for shipping oil from the Caspian Sea basin across Iran to port facilities in the Persian Gulf and for extending Iran's political network. Iran has also developed important trading ties with China and Russia.[26]

Another area of improvement has been with the states of the European Union. Iranian-European relations suffered for decades over such issues as the killing of Iranian dissidents living in Europe, allegedly by Iranian intelligence agents, and the Salman Rushdie affair. The latter incident occurred when Rushdie, a Muslim writer living in Britain, was judged by Ayatollah Khomeini to have written a book blasphemous toward Islam. Khomeini authorized a bounty for anyone who would kill Rushdie. In recent years, the relationship with European Union states has changed: Rushdie is no longer a target and Europeans are more aware of commercial opportunities in Iran.

Relations with the United States have shown only minimal improvement over the past two decades. Iranian-U.S. ties, which were broken following the Iranian Revolution, have generally remained bitter. The U.S. policy presence in the Middle East is an unwelcome intrusion that Iran sees as a hindrance to its sovereignty. An embargo on Iranian exports (especially oil), the imposition of economic and diplomatic sanctions, efforts to deny Iran access to certain technologies and weapon systems, the freezing of $12 billion in Iranian assets in the United States, and overt calls by U.S. policy makers for a dramatic political change are all interpreted in Iran as provocative acts designed to subvert Iranian interests and sovereignty. The United States argues that Iran seeks to acquire weapons of mass destruction, acts as a sponsor of international terrorism, and actively works to undermine the peace process between Israel and its neighbors. Such alleged actions have led to Iran's being labeled as a "rogue state" in American foreign policy rhetoric (along with such other states as Iraq, North Korea, Cuba, and Libya).

Iran—The Rogue

The "rogue state" depiction has had serious repercussions in Iran. Bilaterally, such actions as Iran's appearance on the U.S. State Department's list of state sponsors of terrorism serves to maintain sanctions against Iran that seriously affect its ability to rebuild from the Iran–Iraq war, develop its all-important oil industry, and improve its overall standard of living. On a broader scale, even though no other states have placed such extensive sanctions against Iran, many honor at least some aspects of U.S. sanctions. This again has implications for Iran's ability to break out of its twenty-year isolation. The United States has sought to extend the effects of its sanctions through such policies as the Iran–Libya Sanctions Act of 1996. This act seeks to limit foreign investment in

Iran's energy sector by denying companies access to the American market if they invest more than $1 million in Iran's oil industry. The U.S. Congress has also passed the Iran Non-Proliferation Act of 2000, which can be used to place sanctions on any states that aid Iran's efforts to acquire weapons of mass destruction.

As the 1990s came to a close there were some indications on both sides of a willingness to consider a thaw. Hopes for improved relations between Iran and the United States were given a boost in 1998, when Iran's newly elected president, Muhammad Khatami, gave a speech carried on CNN in which he called for a slow warming of ties between the "great civilizations" of Iran and the United States. This initiative was well received in the United States, but further movement has been slow. After Khatami spoke about the desire for closer relations between the two civilizations (but not the two governments), there were interactions such as sporting events and academic exchanges. U.S. policy makers were pleased by the results of Iran's parliamentary elections in 2000, which brought to power a large majority associated with President Khatami's reform efforts. In an act as important symbolically as it was economically, the United States lifted the embargo on Iranian pistachios, carpets, and caviar—the biggest export items from Iran after oil and natural gas. But the future relationship between these two states remains unclear.[27]

Iran—The Reformer

The government of Iran has been under further pressure for reform since the election of Khatami as president in 1997. A former minister of culture forced out of office in 1992 for permitting too much free speech in newspapers, Khatami won a shocking landslide victory in 1997 for the reformist wing over the candidate endorsed by conservatives centered on Ayatollah Khamenei. Although heavily supported by women, young voters, and those generally frustrated by the social and economic dislocations of the past twenty years, Khatami remains weak within the institutional centers of power. In the Iranian political system, the president is not constitutionally the most powerful figure. The president is generally weaker than the supreme jurist—the life-time position held previously by Khomeini and currently by Khamenei. Further, all decisions of the president and the parliament must be accepted by the Council of Guardians, which rules on whether any new laws are contrary to Islam. Political battles among these power centers have been constant for the past four years.[28]

In foreign policy Khatami has made strong efforts to ingratiate Iran with broader regional and international forces. He has made numerous visits throughout the region, moving Iran closer to such countries as Saudi Arabia, Kuwait, and Bahrain. These countries had rejected Iran for most of the previous fifteen years, fearing its revolutionary and antimonarchical fervor and its hegemonic ambitions in the Gulf. More broadly, as mentioned earlier, Khatami made overtures to the United States. His visit to Italy in 1999 was the first visit by an Iranian leader to a western country since the revolution. He shepherded through improved relations with the states of the European Union. These overtures reflect shifts in the balance of power in Iran's ruling elite.[29]

Further foreign policy moves by Khatami are likely since the balance of power shifted again after the 2000 parliamentary elections in Iran. Previous iterations of the legislature were dominated by conservatives and thus served as a powerful brake on the president's reformist agenda. The elections gave candidates affiliated with Khatami's reformist line a dramatic victory, capturing well over two-thirds of the seats. Although the Council of Guardians and the Council of Experts remain dominated by conservatives, public opinion heavily favors a new direction for Iranian policy, as indicated by Khatami's landslide reelection in 2001.[30]

Overall, Iran has made great strides in moving away from its years of isolation. Currently, it faces no serious security challenges from other Middle Eastern states and in fact is seen as a key player in the region. For example, Iran hosted the 1997 summit of the Organization of the Islamic Conference — a multilateral organization designed to coordinate policy among fifty-six governments. Internationally, Iran's relations with many key players in Europe and Asia have improved, though problems with the United States continue.

Future Challenges

As with all governments in an interdependent world, Iran's foreign policy in the future will be influenced by the actions of others. Acquiring foreign investment capital, for example, will be in part a function of the willingness of foreign companies to invest in Iran. Such actions can be affected by Iranian policy but in the end will remain the decision of outsiders. Similarly, the U.S. decision to lift sanctions is subject to American considerations of national interest and domestic politics. Here, too, Iran can influence the American position, but it cannot determine it. This basic fact makes policy making, not to mention policy success, a difficult task.

With a number of critical issues unresolved, the future direction of Iranian foreign policy is uncertain. Any Iranian government, no matter its ideological orientation, will face several challenges:

- *Population growth.* Iran's population is large (more than 65 million in 2000), rapidly growing (approximately 4 percent population increase per year), and young (more than 50 percent of the population is currently under twenty). The ability of any Iranian government to meet the basic needs of this growing population will be a critical factor in the legitimacy of that government.
- *Infrastructure building and economic growth.* Iran still suffers from the dual effects of the Iran–Iraq war and U.S. sanctions. Overcoming these obstacles to economic development, in part by providing jobs for the growing population, will be critical.
- *Foreign direct investment.* Economic progress in Iran will likely best be facili-

tated through the acquisition of foreign investment, especially in some of the large sectors such as energy and telecommunications. Access to foreign capital and technology will be key to any take-off of the Iranian economy.

- *Islam and globalization.* As evidenced by the parliamentary and presidential elections in Iran in 2000 and 2001, there is a large sentiment for seeking both economic growth and social reform. Different views abound as to the possibility of integrating Shiite Islamic views with more western values. A common debate in Iran revolves around the possibility of importing goods, technology, and ideas from the western world without diluting, if not despoiling, the country's Islamic character.
- *Regional issues.* Gaining access to the potentially very lucrative oil and gas industry of the Caspian Sea basin (most likely as a transit route), determining its stance toward the Arab-Israeli peace process, and dealing with Iraq (with or without Saddam Hussein) and the Gulf, all will continue to be a part of Iran's foreign policy agenda.
- *Iran's global relationships.* Iran's security and economic future will remain tied at least in part to the broader international setting. Continued access to western capital and technology, access to Russian and Chinese military assets, and removal of the U.S. sanctions will all help Iran meet its needs.
- *Iranian independence in an interdependent world.* A strong element in Iran's post-shah worldview is the belief that foreign powers, especially the United States, are unwilling to accept Iranian sovereignty. For example, Washington interprets Iran's efforts to bolster its military power as efforts to establish Iranian hegemony in the oil-rich Gulf region. The continuation of such differences will undoubtedly slow, if not paralyze, Iran's achievement of its goals, as there likely would be repercussions in terms of access to capital and technology.

The resolution of these issues is mainly dependent on two forces. The first is the continuing transformation of the Iranian political system. At present, reformers appear to be in the ascendancy, given the results of recent presidential and parliamentary elections, but other powerful political institutions are still controlled by conservatives. The second is the ability of the reformers and conservatives to deliver on the economic and social concerns of the population.

Conclusion

When we examine the conduct of Iranian policy over the past sixty years, two basic patterns emerge. The first is Iran's continuing interest in dominating the immediate region, the Persian Gulf. Arms acquisition, conventional and unconventional, both under the shah and the Islamic Republic, demonstrates that interest. Whether for defensive purposes, as the Iranians claim—to counter the Iraqi threat or to balance against the American presence in the region—or for more aggressive reasons, as the Americans assert—to intimidate the small Gulf states or to threaten Israel—is difficult to determine. But this basic pattern in

Iranian policy seems to be ongoing, despite radical changes in Iran's internal organization and foreign relations.

The other pattern is that the mechanisms that Iran uses to pursue its goal of regional dominance seem to vary according to the worldview of the country's dominant figure. The shah was an ardent anticommunist who moved Iran closer to the west, resulting in a strong relationship with the United States, poor relations with the Soviet Union and China, and a close relationship with Israel, which the shah saw as a counterbalance to Iraq. Relied on as one of the two "pillars" of American containment strategy in the Middle East, the shah enjoyed tremendous power and influence in the Gulf region.

With the ascendancy of Ayatollah Khomeini, a reversal in Iranian tactics occurred, although the same basic goal remained. Khomeini's views about the United States and the Soviet Union—the "Great Satan" and the "Lesser Satan"—led him to seek the removal of all foreign influence in the region. Calls to export the Iranian Revolution and overthrow Arab monarchies considered too supportive of the American position in the Middle East (that is, Saudi Arabia) were designed to remove America's ability to influence events in the region. Part of the logic of Iraq's attack on Iran (and subsequently Gulf states' support of Iraq during the war) was to thwart what was seen as the Iranian drive toward regional hegemony.

In recent years, Iranian pursuit of regional dominance has continued but with different approaches. In the current situation of divided leadership, the conservative wing, led by those such as Khamenei, has continued the basic policy direction set by Khomeini. These leaders see the pursuit of weapons of mass destruction, support for groups such as Hizballah and Hamas, confrontation with Israel, and refusal to consider improving relations with the United States as ways of minimizing foreign intervention in the Gulf. The reformers, led by Khatami, also worry about foreign domination but see some benefit from broader interactions. This tactic seeks to lessen the western role in the Gulf, especially in terms of military presence, by pursuing a more accommodating line with the Gulf region and even with the west. The idea is to lessen the perceived threat emanating from Iran so that there will be less need to confront that country.

The ultimate rationale underlying Iranian foreign policy will be debated for years to come. Some will see an aggressive Iran striving for hegemony in the Gulf region, while others will view Iran as more defensive, trying to play a legitimate role in the Gulf free from foreign intervention. The evidence can be interpreted both ways. It also will depend on the outcome of political battles currently being fought in Tehran, Washington, Riyadh, and elsewhere. What will be constant is Iran's effort to play a leading role in the Gulf. Whether it does so as a pillar, a prophet, a rogue, a reformer, or even some yet-to-emerge style will, in large part, reflect the worldviews of the leading political figures in the Islamic Republic.

Suggestions for Further Reading

Arjomand, Said Amir. *The Turban for the Crown: The Islamic Revolution in Iran.* New York: Oxford University Press, 1988.

Bill, James A. *The Eagle and the Lion: The Tragedy of American-Iranian Relations.* New Haven: Yale University Press, 1988.

Bulliet, Richard. "Twenty Years of Islamic Politics." *Middle East Journal* 53 (1999): 189–200.

Chubin, Shahram. "Iran's Strategic Predicament." *Middle East Journal* 54 (2000): 10–24.

Cottam, Richard. *Iran and the United States: A Cold War Case Study.* Pittsburgh: University of Pittsburgh Press, 1998.

Ehteshami, Anoushiravan. *After Khomeini: The Iranian Second Republic.* London: Routledge, 1995.

Gasiorowski, Mark J. *U.S. Foreign Policy and the Shah: Building a Client State in Iran.* Ithaca: Cornell University Press, 1991.

Hooglund, Eric. "Khatami's Iran." *Current History* 98 (1999): 59–64.

Kazemi, Farhad. "The Iranian Enigma." *Current History* 96 (1997): 40–43.

Keddie, Nikki. *Iran and the Muslim World: Resistance and Revolution.* New York: New York University Press, 1995.

Keddie, Nikki, and Mark Gasiorowski, eds. *Neither East nor West: Iran, the Soviet Union, and the United States.* New Haven: Yale University Press, 1990.

Mackey, Sandra. *The Iranians.* New York: Plume, 1996.

Masoud, Tarek. "Misreading Iran." *Current History* 97 (1998): 38–43.

Rajaee, Farhang. "A Thermidor of Islamic Yuppies? Conflict and Compromise in Iran's Politics." *Middle East Journal* 53 (1999): 217–231.

Roy, Olivier. "The Crisis of Religious Legitimacy in Iran." *Middle East Journal* 53 (1999): 201–216.

Schirazi, Asghar. *The Constitution of Iran: Politics and the State in the Islamic Republic.* London: I. B. Tauris, 1997.

Sick, Gary. *All Fall Down: America's Tragic Encounter with Iran.* New York: Random House, 1985.

Notes

1. See James A. Bill, *The Eagle and the Lion: The Tragedy of American-Iranian Relations* (New Haven: Yale University Press), 1988; Richard Cottam, *Iran and the United States: A Cold War Case Study* (Pittsburgh: University of Pittsburgh Press), 1988; Mark J. Gasiorowski, *U.S. Foreign Policy and the Shah: Building a Client State in Iran* (New York: Cornell University Press), 1991; and Gary Sick, *All Fall Down: America's Tragic Encounter with Iran* (New York: Random House), 1985.

2. Ibid.

3. The Azeri, who inhabit the region covered by northwest Iran and what is now Azerbaijan, are an ethnic group distinct from the Persian majority in Iran. They speak Azeri and are Shi'a Muslim. The Kurds inhabit a region incorporating parts of Iran, Syria, Turkey, and Iraq. They are a distinct ethnic group and follow the Sunni branch of Islam.

4. See Bill, *The Eagle and the Lion;* Cottam, *Iran and the United States;* and Gasiorowski, *U.S. Foreign Policy and the Shah;* Sick, *All Fall Down.*

5. Ibid.

6. See Bill, *The Eagle and the Lion;* Cottam, *Iran and the United States;* and Gasiorowski, *U.S. Foreign Policy and the Shah.*

7. Ibid.
8. See Bill, *The Eagle and the Lion;* Cottam, *Iran and the United States;* Gasiorowski, *U.S. Foreign Policy and the Shah;* Sick, *All Fall Down;* and Said Amir Arjomand, *The Turban for the Crown: The Islamic Revolution in Iran* (New York: Oxford University Press), 1988.
9. Ibid.
10. Ibid.
11. Ibid.
12. Nikki Keddie and Mark Gasiorowski, eds., *Neither East nor West: Iran, the Soviet Union, and the United States* (New Haven: Yale University Press), 1990.
13. See Bill, *The Eagle and the Lion;* Gasiorowski, *U.S. Foreign Policy and the Shah;* Arjomand, *The Turban for the Crown;* and Sick, *All Fall Down.*
14. Keddie and Gasiorowski, *Neither East nor West;* Arjomand, *The Turban for the Crown;* Richard Bulliet, "Twenty Years of Islamic Politics," *Middle East Journal* 53 (1999):189–200.
15. Keddie and Gasiorowski, *Neither East nor West;* Nikki Keddie, *Iran and the Muslim World: Resistance and Revolution* (New York: New York University Press), 1995.
16. Keddie, *Iran and the Muslim World;* Shahram Chubin, "Iran's Strategic Predicament," *Middle East Journal* 54 (2000): 10–24.
17. See Bill, *The Eagle and the Lion;* Cottam, *Iran and the United States;* Gasiorowski, *U.S. Foreign Policy and the Shah;* and Sick, *All Fall Down.*
18. Keddie and Gasiorowski, *Neither East nor West;* Arjomand, *The Turban for the Crown;* Bulliet, "Twenty Years of Islamic Politics."
19. Asghar Schirazi, *The Constitution of Iran: Politics and the State in the Islamic Republic* (London: I. B. Tauris), 1997.
20. Keddie and Gasiorowski, *Neither East nor West.*
21. Ibid.
22. Bulliet, "Twenty Years of Islamic Politics;" Anoushiravan Ehteshami, *After Khomeini: The Iranian Second Republic* (London: Routledge), 1995; Eric Hooglund, "Khatami's Iran," *Current History* 98 (1999): 59–64; Olivier Roy, "The Crisis of Religious Legitimacy in Iran," *Middle East Journal* 53 (1999): 201–216; and Schirazi, *The Constitution of Iran.*
23. Bulliet, "Twenty Years of Islamic Politics;" Chubin, "Iran's Strategic Predicament."
24. One exception is the United Arab Emirates, a small country in the Persian Gulf. The United Arab Emirates and Iran are locked in a disagreement over who should control three islands in the Gulf.
25. Chubin, "Iran's Strategic Predicament;" Hooglund, "Khatami's Iran."
26. Ibid.
27. Hooglund, "Khatami's Iran;" Farhang Rajaee, "A Thermidor of Islamic Yuppies? Conflict and Compromise in Iran's Politics," *Middle East Journal* 53 (1999): 217–231.
28. Bulliet, "Twenty Years of Islamic Politics;" Ehteshami, *After Khomeini;* Hooglund, "Khatami's Iran;" Rajaee, "A Thermidor of Islamic Yuppies?" and Schirazi, *The Constitution of Iran.*
29. Chubin, "Iran's Strategic Predicament;" Hooglund, "Khatami's Iran."
30. Hooglund, "Khatami's Iran;" Rajaee, "A Thermidor of Islamic Yuppies?"; and Roy, "The Crisis of Religious Legitimacy in Iran."

CHAPTER 11

Leadership and Ambition in Nigerian Foreign Policy

Olufemi A. Babarinde and Stephen Wright

Strengthened by its oil revenues, Nigeria has sought to play an active role in both Africa and the world. Regionally, Nigeria has served as an important player through its leadership in the Economic Community of West African States (ECOWAS), its vocal criticism of South Africa's apartheid policy, and its support of independence movements in Angola and Zimbabwe. In the world arena, Nigeria, Africa's most populous state, has been an active participant in international organizations and has persistently sought a seat on the United Nations Security Council. The country's importance drew a visit from President Jimmy Carter in 1978, the first official visit by a U.S. president to an African country, and from President Bill Clinton in 2000. However, Nigeria's legacy of corruption and military regimes has led to many economic problems such as difficulty securing foreign investment. These problems, compounded by Nigeria's internal difficulties, including ethnic and religious clashes, have led some observers to predict the ultimate demise of Nigeria.

Nigeria shares several similarities with other developing countries included in this book. As one might expect, external factors are a central influence on the foreign policy of Nigeria. In particular, Babarinde and Wright illustrate how democratization pressures and globalization are playing a key role in shaping the country's foreign policy. For globalization, Nigeria can be compared with other countries that are not democratic, such as China (Chapter 6) and Iran (Chapter 10), or are in a transition to democracy, such as Russia (Chapter 5). The direct influence of the United States and European powers also is important. Yet Nigeria is not completely at the mercy of forces and actors in the international system. Like other developing countries, such as India (Chapter 8), Brazil (Chapter 13), and Mexico (Chapter 14), Nigeria has at times played an activist, nonaligned role in global politics that frequently conflicted with U.S. and European interests. The importance of leadership in the creation of foreign policy also mirrors the other developing countries in this book.

Since achieving independence from Britain in October 1960, Nigeria has attempted to pursue a foreign policy of leadership within and on behalf of the African continent, but with varying levels of ambition, enthusiasm, and success. This ebb and flow of foreign policy have been influenced by a combination of factors, both domestic and external, but, as Chapter 1 revealed, it is very difficult to separate the overlapping influences. It is clear, however, that much of Nigerian foreign policy has been affected by the country's resource base of petroleum (oil), a "domestic" factor, and yet the value of that resource to Nigeria hinges on its price in international markets and Nigeria's position within the global political economy.[1] Since the early 1970s, petroleum sales have accounted for approximately 95 percent of the country's export earnings, and efforts to diversify the economic base have yet to succeed.

For all but ten years between 1960 and 1999, Nigeria was ruled by military governments, some of whom performed better than others in the foreign policy arena.[2] Thus the continuity and change characterizing Nigeria's foreign policy are influenced just as much by the different dynamics of internal leadership (adept/inept, military/civilian) as by the changing global environment within which the country operates. All Nigerian governments have been tainted by corruption, some on a grander scale than others. But at least such national shortcomings have been softened by large petroleum revenues, which have buoyed optimism and maintained Nigeria's credentials as the "leader" or "champion" of the African continent.

Nigeria both reflects and contrasts with the predominant foreign policy profile of West Africa and of the continent as a whole. Africa has been a marginalized continent for centuries; Africans were brutally victimized and enslaved by Europeans during colonization and had their countries' borders drawn arbitrarily by the imperial powers in the late nineteenth century. Nigeria in its modern geographical form took shape only in 1914 as British colonizers sought to amalgamate disparate territories and peoples into a governable unit, with little or no respect paid to historical patterns of development. Today, Nigeria strives to maintain political stability and territorial integrity in increasingly unfavorable circumstances. Notably, economic marginalization offers the daunting prospect of exclusion from the mainstream international economy through the uneven and unequal pressures of globalization and e-commerce.[3]

To many observers, African states appear destined to remain commodity producers and bit players in the global economy, despite major efforts by numerous international agencies, including the International Monetary Fund (IMF) and the World Bank, to change their status. Debts, structural adjustment, and low levels of development by any index cast a shadow across the continent in contrast to the high-tech boom and euphoria found across most of the North.[4] Democratization has certainly been witnessed in Africa, but democratic successes within the continent are relatively few, often tenuous, and prone to reversal. Indeed, many consider these democratic experiments to be desperate efforts by autocrats to hold on to power and to placate extraneous interests such as the World Bank and the United States, rather than grassroots, populist movements. The implosion of states in the 1990s, such as Liberia, Rwanda, Sierra Leone, and Somalia, provides examples of extreme cases of misfortune, but many other countries also are in periods of difficult social unrest, including Nigeria. Overall, few African states possess the internal cohesion or economic resources to be "active" players or "medium" powers in world politics, and most maintain a limited role even in subregional politics.

Nigeria reflects many of these African dilemmas, but it also offers a contrast in critical ways. Its population of some 120 million accounts for roughly 15–20 percent of the continent's population. Besides being one of the world's largest producers of petroleum (normally in the top seven), it has substantial reserves of natural gas, virtually untapped until recently. As such, its economic profile is one of the continent's strongest, especially in contrast with that of many of its neighbors in West Africa.

Despite decades of military rule, Nigeria has a robust yet embryonic civil society in which, for the most part, domestic and foreign policies can be debated freely and openly. Although there have been many areas of disagreement within domestic policy, the objectives and aspirations of Nigeria's leadership in the foreign policy arena have attracted a consensus. Two republics under civilian governments (1960–1966 under Prime Minister Alhaji Abubakar Tafawa Balewa and 1979–1983 led by President Alhaji Shehu Shagari) were not particularly successful in carrying out domestic or foreign policy initiatives, and their overthrow by the military was greeted widely with relief.[5] It is still too early to draw conclusions about the civilian government of President Olusegun Obasanjo, which came into office in May 1999; it has had severe problems in stabilizing tensions within the domestic arena. Nigeria's military governments, which have not been automatically disparaged, have all attempted to play active roles in foreign policy. The governments led by Yakubu Gowon (1966–1975), Murtala Muhammed (1975–1976), and Olusegun Obasanjo (1976–1979) worked to promote Nigerian leadership in Africa and a viable nonaligned strategy for the country in world affairs. The increasingly predatory rule of later military heads of state—Muhammadu Buhari (1984–1985), Ibrahim Babangida (1985–1993), Sani Abacha (1993–1998), and Abdulsalam Abubakar (1998–1999)—certainly diminished respect for the military as an institution, especially because Babangida and Abacha pursued more openly corrupt and personalist foreign policies.[6] Before turning to the domestic decision-making environment and the role of civilian and military elites, this chapter will examine the overall characteristics of Nigeria's foreign policy within its African context and its specific elements during the Cold War.

Nigerian Foreign Policy during the Cold War

Nigeria is one of the most analyzed countries in Africa. Although it is difficult to summarize accurately the overall continuity and change in the country's foreign policy since independence in 1960, political economy approaches do indicate continuity in underdevelopment and exploitation.[7] Moreover, it is possible to isolate five main themes of foreign policy that were pursued fairly consistently throughout the Cold War period, and to some extent are still being pursued. All of these themes reflect a realist perspective—that is, Nigeria's leadership emphasized the state and its ability to pursue a rational and coherent foreign policy.

Foreign Policy Themes

The first theme is an emphasis on the West Africa region and the desire to exert a form of subregional political and economic hegemony. This desire manifested itself in massive aid flows across the region, Nigeria's leadership in the formation of the Economic Community of West African States (ECOWAS) in 1975, and its intense diplomatic activity within the region.[8] Moreover, in the 1990s and early 2000s Nigeria was a significant (and controversial) military presence in the ECOWAS Monitoring Group (ECOMOG) in Liberia and Sierra Leone.[9]

The second critical theme characterizing Nigeria's foreign policy has been its vocal, and often financial, support for liberation movements within the continent. This support was most noticeable in Nigeria's strident backing of anti-apartheid movements and the neighboring front-line states (FLS) which opposed the white minority-ruled South Africa, as well as its open intervention in the Angolan and Zimbabwean decolonization/peace processes in the 1970s. Nigerian leaders perceived their country to be a "distant" member of the FLS in the struggle against South Africa.

The third theme of Nigeria's foreign policy has been its consistent friendship and alliance with Western countries, most notably in the economic arena.[10] Despite its protestations of nonalignment or positive neutrality, Nigeria's core economic relationships, especially in the crucial petroleum and gas sectors, have been with Western multinational corporations. After the mid-1980s, this relationship widened because of Nigeria's chronic economic problems and debt and its reliance on the International Monetary Fund and World Bank for structural adjustment support and debt rescheduling. Despite its initial stiff resistance, the Nigerian economy has been forced to open up increasingly to foreign investors and ownership, because much of the nationalization and indigenous ownership legislation of the 1970s and 1980s was repealed during the 1990s. Even so, a joint delegation from the IMF and World Bank found in February 2001 that Nigeria needed to do much more to stabilize privatization and to encourage foreign direct investment.

The democracy, transparency, and accountable government that could perhaps have improved domestic and foreign economic policy choices have been largely absent from Nigeria since it declared independence. The latest transition to civilian rule took fourteen tortuous years (1985–1999), and the "civilian" government that took office in May 1999, led by retired general and former military head of state Olusegun Obasanjo, has very uncertain prospects of survival. Brought in during flawed elections that international observers could not legitimize, the government is currently attempting to improve economic conditions and control the regional and ethnic violence that, in the past, has provided a golden opportunity for military intervention. In January 2001, in a desperate act, Obasanjo fired his cabinet of ministers, but that step produced little improvement in the condition of the country. Nigeria is a classic example of what Larry Diamond has called a "hollow democracy."[11] Oil revenues have been squandered repeatedly on bad projects or diverted corruptly into personal overseas accounts (Sani Abacha is said to have created an illicit personal fortune overseas of $4.3 billion), and little economic diversification has occurred to provide a stronger basis for a more viable foreign policy.

The fourth theme of foreign policy complements the third in that successive governments have maintained fairly cool relations with the socialist bloc in contrast to their widely publicized policy of "neutrality" and "nonalignment." Certainly, Nigeria has engaged in some trade and military sales with these countries, notably the Soviet Union and Soviet bloc countries during Nigeria's civil war in the late 1960s, but these links pale in significance when compared with trade with the Western countries.

The fifth and final theme of Nigeria's foreign policy during the Cold War period was its strong endorsement of and enthusiasm for the work of international organizations. Nigeria was most active in the United Nations (UN) and used this and other organizations to boost its own foreign policy positions and aspirations, including its ongoing quest for a permanent seat on the UN Security Council. The country's status was certainly aided by the presence of Nigerian troops in UN peacekeeping operations, including those in Congo, Burma, Lebanon, Rwanda, Yugoslavia, and Somalia.

Important Issues during the Cold War

When Nigeria achieved independence in October 1960, the government was strongly influenced by the attitudes of its conservative Islamic leadership. In the debates of the early 1960s leading to the establishment of the Organization of African Unity (OAU) in 1963, Nigeria was firmly in the camp of the foreign policy "moderates" who favored a loose, intergovernmental association of states. The more radical idea of a federation of states was promoted by Kwame Nkrumah (Ghana), Modibo Keita (Mali), and Sékou Touré (Guinea), who were outspoken critics of Western imperialism and neocolonialism and who appeared to have close links to the Soviet and Chinese blocs. Such tensions in West Africa made

Nigeria appear to be more conservative in the foreign policy arena than perhaps it really was. In economic policies, various governments promoted at both federal and regional levels close cooperation with Western companies, particularly British, and British military personnel maintained an active partnership with their Nigerian counterparts. Notwithstanding these realities of its foreign policy actions, the Nigerian government remained a strong vocal supporter of the policy of nonalignment, arguing for a more balanced perspective of Cold War rivalries. However, there were almost no linkages with the Soviet Union until the mid-1960s.

Within the space of eighteen months in 1966–1967, domestic and foreign policy orientations were challenged. Two military coups in 1966, both heavily influenced by interethnic hostility, ushered in the first of many military governments, which ruled the country for all but four years from 1966 to 1999. The assassination of key leaders of the federal government and two regional premiers in January 1966 exacerbated serious regional ethnic tensions, which had been brewing for more than a decade between the "ruling" Hausa-Fulani of northern Nigeria and the Yoruba and Igbo groups of the south, as well as with many of the smaller ethnic groups. These tensions quickly deteriorated into a three-year civil war during 1967–1970, in which the eastern (Biafran) region, predominantly Igbo, sought secession from the federation. The caution with which Western governments approached the civil war (based on concerns for access to the oil-rich eastern region and public opinion support for the Biafrans) forced the federal government to seek new alliances with the Soviet Union. This changed the character of the country's nonalignment strategy and allowed successive leaders to be more openly critical of the West in their foreign policy pronouncements. Although Nigeria's pro-Western leanings were revived during the 1970s under Gowon's leadership, there was more willingness to be more strident in nonalignment strategies, fueled by the confidence of booming oil revenues.

Nigeria's foreign policy assertiveness coincided with a corresponding sense of vulnerability in the West with the collapse of the Bretton Woods free trade system in 1971 and the OPEC (Organization of Petroleum Exporting Countries) oil crisis in 1973. Perhaps pushing an open door, Nigerian policy makers became more aggressive in the Cold War environment in promoting foreign policy agendas against the wishes of the U.S. and European governments. With the widespread support of virtually all Nigerians, the period 1975–1980 marked the heyday of Nigeria's influence in African and global politics. Its leadership was most marked in interventions related to Angolan independence in 1975, when Nigeria came down forcefully in support of the communist faction over the opposition of the United States, and with Zimbabwean independence in 1980, when the government nationalized British Petroleum's operations inside Nigeria in order to influence the views of the British government over Zimbabwe. In addition, Nigerian governments were active in various peacekeeping and mediation efforts in Chad, in the Western Sahara, and in conflicts between Tanzania and Uganda and between Ethiopia and Somalia.

The push for increasing sanctions against apartheid South Africa also was a key platform of foreign policy and a core element of the country's nonaligned Cold War posture. Nigerian governments opposed the diplomatic policies of the West toward South Africa which called for "quiet diplomacy" and "constructive engagement"; they favored a much more aggressive stance. Much talk was heard in the late 1970s about Nigeria acquiring a nuclear arsenal to match its prestige and status in the continent and abroad and to challenge South Africa militarily in its own backyard. Nigeria led the African boycott of the 1976 Olympic Games to isolate South Africa and was one of the only states to boycott the 1978 Commonwealth Games. Such an activist and successful foreign policy pushed Nigeria into the ranks of the respected "middle-level" powers, a place that its leaders hoped to maintain indefinitely.

In West Africa, Nigeria saw an opportunity to check French political and economic hegemony (all Nigeria's neighbors are former French colonies) by working to create the Economic Community of West African States in 1975. The creation of this trading group of sixteen (now fifteen) West African states was brought about by Nigeria's diplomatic skills and financial largesse. Indeed, Nigerian "oil diplomacy" in the early 1970s won over reluctant francophone countries, which continued to maintain close links to France. The establishment of ECOWAS provided Nigeria with a renewed international presence after the debacle of its civil war, a regional market over which to exert influence, and a visible success in pushing African states toward nonalignment. Nigeria continues to provide leadership for ECOWAS, but the gains for Nigeria have not been as strong as were predicted in the 1970s.

During the early 1970s, Nigeria led negotiations on behalf of the African, Caribbean, and Pacific (ACP) states with the European Union (EU) on the issues of North-South trade and broader development. Nigeria's first attempt to broker an accord with the EU was in 1966, but the so-called Lagos Initiative was stillborn because of complications arising from the civil war. The next attempt by Nigeria to establish formal ties with the EU began in 1973 as part of British accession to the EU. At first, Nigeria intended to negotiate a bilateral relationship with the EU, but those negotiations were soon changed to multilateral ones on behalf of the former British colonies in Africa. Given Nigeria's diplomatic clout, these talks were then broadened further to include all African states as well as Caribbean and Pacific states, and they culminated in agreements contained in the Lomé Convention of 1975.[12] Nigeria's leaders had calculated that Nigeria's leadership of the ACP would provide the country with a sphere of influence from which to launch and pursue its own foreign policy agenda. And, to a degree, they were right. Eventually, financial largesse across the continent, the country's large population, its peacekeeping roles around the world, and the grudging respect shown by Western leaders won Nigeria the title of "giant of Africa." This status was sealed by Jimmy Carter's official state visit to Nigeria in 1978, the first to Africa by a sitting U.S. president.

After the early 1980s, however, the deterioration of Nigeria's petroleum fortunes combined with other factors to lead to an apparent decrease in leverage in foreign policy matters. Some scholars have asserted that Nigeria's influence in the late 1970s was somewhat illusory or exaggerated in any case, particularly because the country's "oil weapon" could not be used without causing immense damage to the Nigerian economy itself. In the early 1980s, Chief Obafemi Awolowo, a prominent Yoruba political leader, even cautioned against the use of Nigeria's oil, a commodity that was (and remains) vital to the country's economy, to conduct its foreign policy against apartheid South Africa. The ineptitude and corrupt depravity of the Shagari administration (1979–1983) led senior Nigerian foreign policy analyst Ibrahim Gambari to conclude that in the 1980s "Nigeria appeared to be a demographic and economic giant on the continent, but a political and diplomatic dwarf in African affairs."[13] The country's rapid economic collapse led to the introduction of structural adjustment programs in 1986.[14] Nigeria then found it very difficult to pursue an "activist" foreign policy, in part because the country possessed few economic resources with which to threaten the West or to shower on neighboring African states. The International Monetary Fund and World Bank pressured the Babangida administration to alter domestic and foreign economic policies in line with the tenets of neoliberalism. Nigerian governments continued to try to play a limited activist role within Africa, partly assisted by the rapid collapse of many other national economies, but the end of the Cold War in 1989 contributed to a different playing field for foreign policy within Africa, marked by new Western perspectives about the continent, as well as by the emergence of South Africa as a "legitimate" player in African affairs to rival Nigeria.

External Factors

The approach to the study of African foreign policy has changed since the pioneer studies of the 1960s and 1970s. This evolution has been influenced not only by advances in foreign policy analysis (see Chapter 1) and their application to the continent, but also by the changes in the political and economic environment within which African states pursue their foreign policy today. In the 1960s and 1970s, the approach to the study of foreign policy was what is now considered "traditional"[15]—that is, based on a realist perception of the state as a rational actor. Scholarship emphasized a range of factors, including the impact and legacy of colonialism on the emerging states and the importance of mineral and agricultural resources for economic development. Decision making within states was considered primarily elitist in nature, in which the "big man" (such as Gowon or Obasanjo), either individually or with a very small group of advisers, made policy to promote the country's national interest. The notable foreign policies of African states, like those of Nigeria, included strong support for coordination of policy within international governmental organizations, especially the United Nations; the promotion of nonalignment within the Cold War; and the maintenance of security and protection of national borders and newly won sovereignty. At the continental level, hostility to apartheid South Africa was a common denominator of the foreign policy of almost all states.

Although some of these factors are still salient today, several developments in the 1990s altered the way that foreign policy is conceived and perceived in Africa in general and Nigeria in particular. These factors, many of which were discussed in Chapter 1, include the end of the Cold War in 1989, the reexamination of the realist perspective on foreign policy, the sweep of the twin giants of liberalization and globalization, and the difficulty African states confronted in trying to agree on common economic and political agendas, whether regionally or continentally. Consequently, the questions posed (and answered) in this chapter about African, and Nigerian, foreign policy since the end of the Cold War have been reconstituted to take account of such changing dynamics.[16] Such questions reflect concerns with globalization and interdependency and focus on the declining capacities of the state, whether economic, political, or military, and the increasing role of the International Monetary Fund and World Bank in defining economic policies. The responses to these challenges have varied from one African country to another, but the preference for regional and even continental solutions appears to be growing. Nigeria continues to pin hopes on the success of ECOWAS for building regional strength and prosperity.

The mounting pressures for democratization coming from both within and outside the continent have become an important foreign policy issue. During the 1990s, numerous Nigerian dissident groups were operating in exile in the West, providing new foreign policy challenges for the military regimes. The European Union and the United States placed great weight on the democratization of Nigeria and the end to military governments and imposed sanctions (along with the Commonwealth) on the country in the mid-1990s when this did not occur. However, the importance of Nigeria's oil to Western corporations, led by Shell, limited the impact of those sanctions. The oil companies placed pressures on the British, French, and American governments not to impose tough sanctions, and notably oil exports were not affected.

The dire need for debt rescheduling and foreign investment also allowed Western governments, nongovernmental organizations (NGOs), and agencies such as the World Bank and International Monetary Fund to leverage an agenda of democratization and good governance in addition to liberal economic reforms. Such interdependency requires Nigerian domestic politics to take account of these external parameters. But will this most recent expansion, or "third wave," of democratization take root in Africa, or are reversals likely? The answer to this question is certainly a great concern within Nigeria itself. Most observers believe the Obasanjo government will be hard-pressed to survive the combination of political, economic, religious, and ethnic pressures currently challenging the country's stability, possibly throwing the country into another round of military government, or worse. Yet beyond that worry are the very different conceptions about what "Nigerian democracy" should actually look like. Should it be based on Western models of liberal democracy, and how can grassroots participation be promoted?

The reluctance of global powers to be physically present on the continent since 1990, at least in a security sense, has left peacekeeping more in the hands of African peacekeepers than at any time since the independence era. How then can such new foreign policy challenges be addressed? Linked to this, the realist concept of sovereignty is a difficult one to grasp today in an era of porous borders, globalization, and overlapping domestic and foreign agendas. Efforts such as the integration of EU member states deliberately challenge traditional conceptions, as do extensive plans for regional unity in other parts of the world. In Africa in general, and increasingly in the relatively strong state of Nigeria, the concept of sovereignty has something of a hollow ring, though the trappings and symbols of office (palaces, airlines, fleets of bullet-proof cars) certainly remain evident. Nigerian governments have tended to be unrepresentative of the "Nigerian nation," even when legitimized by an election. Borders are increasingly difficult to police, as people move back and forth across them somewhat at will. In other countries, the artificiality of the border and of sovereignty is accentuated by the many ethnic groups that are divided by state boundaries and therefore are wracked with political unrest. How can anyone talk of sovereignty in Sierra Leone or Somalia, where the collapse of government has left sovereign power in the hands of the "warlords" with the most guns on the street?[17] Today, the pressures on "sovereign" states in Africa are increasing, making the study of foreign policy all that much more complex.

Internal Factors

Of the many domestic factors discussed in Chapter 1 that influence foreign policy, students of African foreign policy have long emphasized the role of a small elite or a single leader as the key variable in decision making, and often with good reason. More recently, they have placed increasing emphasis on the role of interest groups and bureaucratic politics in foreign policy making, although there remains a dearth of scholarship on Africa to test these ideas rigorously.

Leaders and Foreign Policy

In the Nigerian context, the formal or constitutional structures of decision making are not particularly helpful in understanding the processes at work. The First Republic (1960–1966) was a parliamentary system in which the prime minister had great latitude to pursue foreign policy within the fairly limited constraints laid down by the federal legislature. During the Second Republic (1979–1983), and currently under the Obasanjo government, a U.S.-style president is monitored and held accountable by the Nigerian Senate, but again the legislative body has little real power over decisions. Throughout the various military regimes, some form of military ruling council acted as the official decision-making chamber, but these groups probably provided only nominal controls at best over the head of state.

Individual heads of state have undoubtedly controlled foreign policy debates and outcomes at crucial times, but the true picture is more complex than that. During the First Republic, the country's conservative policies were strongly influenced by Tafawa Balewa, the country's prime minister, and Alhaji Ahmadu Bello, the northern regional premier. Both were conservative Muslims who favored the status quo in terms of close economic relations with the West, especially Britain. But their interpretation of Nigeria's national interest was not automatically supported by non-Muslims within the country. Partly as a result, both leaders were assassinated in January 1966 in Nigeria's first military coup. A radical shift in Nigerian foreign policy in 1975–1976 can be easily attributed to the ousting of the more conservative Yakubu Gowon (a Christian from the Middle Belt) by the more dynamic and radical Murtala Muhammed (a northern Muslim) and his federal commissioner for external affairs, Brig. Gen. Joseph Garba. Likewise, few scholars doubt that foreign policy in the 1990s was very closely controlled by heads of state Ibrahim Babangida and Sani Abacha. However, their policies increasingly pursued personal financial interests and objectives at the expense of the interests of the country as a whole, thereby undermining realist perspectives on "rationality."

But even "great men" cannot always control policy, and in Nigeria many other actors are involved in the development and implementation of the country's foreign policy. During the Second Republic, for example, President Alhaji Shehu Shagari, another conservative Muslim northerner who had served as a federal commissioner for trade under Gowon, left much of foreign policy making to others. Chapter 1 raised questions about who exactly makes decisions, and in whose interests, but it is difficult to be certain of the answers. Many agencies and other actors within the domestic establishment are involved. For example, the foreign policy bureaucracy, notably the External Affairs Ministry, plays some role in shaping goals and implementing foreign policy objectives. Such a role has often been accentuated under military governments, though even then the military had the final say. The former external affairs minister and later Nigerian ambassador to the United Nations Ibrahim Gambari has noted that when he served in government there was normally considerable policy formulation and discussion within the ministry and with government officials, but that critical decisions were usually made solely by the military government itself.[18] Indeed, a case could be made that this ministry has not really been a key player in the formulation of foreign policy.

Interest Groups and Lobbies

In addition to the External Affairs Ministry, numerous quasi-official think tanks and agencies, normally staffed by policy specialists and academics, formulate ideas and policy alternatives in the foreign policy arena. These agencies include the Nigerian Institute for International Affairs (NIIA), the Nigerian Institute for Policy and Strategic Studies (NIPSS), and the Nigerian Institute for Social and Economic Research (NISER).[19] In fact, Bolaji Akinyemi, the first director of the NIIA, who served in the 1970s and 1980s, became the minister for external affairs in the mid-1980s, and Joseph Garba assumed the leadership of the NIPSS in the late-1990s.

The opinion of other elites, whether political, military, or business, also shapes some of the broader parameters within which policy is conceived. These groups can operate in the public eye. Academics, the media, trade unions, and NGOs (such as human rights movements and pro-democracy groups) are very active in political and economic commentaries and may occasionally shift opinions and policies. One example of this is the government's abrogation of the Anglo-Nigerian defense pact in 1962 (although the essential elements of the defense agreement were kept by the Tafawa Balewa government). University students in the south, trade union activists, and others who favored nonalignment influenced the government's decision. Another example is the government's 1986 decision to reject an IMF loan. That decision was strongly influenced by the Nigerian Labour Congress (NLC) and the Academic Staff Union of Universities (ASUU). However, the powers of persuasion of these groups should not be inflated, particularly under praetorian governments. Trade unions such as the National Union of Petroleum and Natural Gas Workers (NUPENG) learned this costly lesson.[20] In recent years, pro-democracy groups such as the Campaign for Democracy (CD) and the National Democratic Coalition (NADECO) have clearly been important actors in attempting to pressure government decisions, but their role has been perhaps more significant in pressuring Western governments than in altering the policy of Nigeria's recent military autocrats. Likewise, NGOs based in Western countries, such as Amnesty International and Human Rights Watch, have been significant actors in attempting to influence outcomes in Nigerian foreign policy.

Elites acting behind the scenes are probably more influential in shaping policy than one might think. Retired military generals, for example, have a very significant influence through their valuable resources and connections. It is estimated that Nigeria can boast the most retired millionaire generals at the age of forty of any country in the world—but few obtained such stature through legitimate means. As for business leaders, the fluid rules of the Nigerian economy allow some to gain incredible wealth, and policies that promote access to opportunities—for example, fixed exchange rates, access to foreign exchange, government contracts—give them the motives and capacity to influence policy and to oppose the further opening of Nigeria's economy to liberalization. These elites are generally opposed to genuine moves toward democratization, because such actions would threaten their control over the state. One famous elite group is known as the Kaduna mafia.[21] This undefined group of northern business leaders is alleged to have provided immense influence over policy decisions during the past two decades or more.

Nigeria's political economy, with its distinct nature, exercises a significant influence over foreign policy, whether intended or not. During the First Republic, each region was allowed to pursue its own foreign policy, so there was a multiplicity of (often competing) foreign policy positions. Religion and ethnicity continue to be stark features of the political landscape, and at times certainly are factors in the orientation of foreign policy, such as in relations with Israel and the Arab states. Nigeria is a complicated mosaic of several hundred distinct ethnic groups, and much of domestic politics, including political parties and interest groups, revolves around their interrelationship. An integral part of this problem has been the struggle between the largest ethnic groups—the Hausa, Yoruba, and Igbo—for political supremacy. Ethnic politics also has been complicated by the role of numerous minority groups, who often have felt excluded from the Nigerian state. Deliberate state engineering has tried to maintain a "federal character" within government and external policy, but recently these ethnic tensions have been exacerbated by structural adjustment, economic hardship, and political chicanery.[22]

The linkages among ethnicity, regionalism, and foreign policy are exemplified by the civil war of 1967–1970, which was deliberately internationalized by Biafran separatists to push their cause. The superpowers and European countries found themselves drawn into the conflict in indirect ways.[23] The thorny questions of diplomatic relations with Israel, representation in Lagos by the Palestine Liberation Organization, and membership in the Organization of the Islamic Council (OIC) all probe Christian-Muslim tensions and tendencies within the body politic.

Such factors also feed into the patrimonial disposition of Nigeria, whereby state resources are considered prizes to be distributed to regional and ethnic groups, and foreign economic policies are pursued to produce illicit spoils for those groups.[24] For example, the value of the national currency, the naira, is heavily contested by internal elites who benefit from its higher exchange rate, and politics can influence this rate as much as external economic conditions can. Similarly, the continuing division and subdivision of the country into smaller and less-viable units—from three regions in 1960 to thirty-six states in 2000—has less to do with internal democracy than with the struggle by elites to gain access to federal funds and "spoils." Elite wealth tends not to be produced, but rather extracted from the state.[25] And, as Alex Gboyega points out, the instability of political life accentuates the speed by which a particular elite must extract, leading to "fast-feeding frenzies" in which "civilian and military rulers and candidate rulers alike regard their incumbency as a turn at the trough, necessarily limited, assuredly enriching."[26]

The federal pie is made up almost entirely of petroleum revenues. Agriculture had accounted for the lion's share of export revenue in the 1960s, but it was displaced by petroleum in the 1970s. In 1980, petroleum earnings peaked at about $25 billion, but by the end of that decade they had dropped to a low of $4.2 billion and generally remained at that level throughout the 1990s. In Nigeria, petroleum is essentially the key influence on foreign policy.[27] The heyday of petroleum revenues coincides with Nigeria's most activist of foreign policy postures. The blatant misappropriation of petroleum revenues over the past three decades has left the country in a much weaker foreign policy position than it should be in and has certainly contributed to the country's external debt of $33 billion in 2001. As Gambari states, "The management of the petroleum resources has been so inept and often corrupt that the country's oil 'boom' has almost become its economic and social 'doom.'"[28] Against this dire backdrop, we now turn to Nigeria's contemporary foreign policy.

Contemporary Nigerian Foreign Policy

The 1990s was an era of difficulty and missed foreign policy opportunities for Nigeria, and changed circumstances gave rise to a modified form of interdependency within the global arena that was detrimental to the country. Part of this change was linked to an economic downturn in the price of oil that reduced the economic potential of the country. [29] The relative absence of foreign investment flows into the Nigerian economy other than in the oil and gas sectors also limited potential growth. The failure to create any high-tech industry left the country sidelined and marginalized in the globalization and e-commerce booms of the early twenty-first century, and there was little sign that ECOWAS could provide the regional economic boost or a strong regional trade market that many predicted at its inauguration in 1975. On a brighter note, however, the upward surge of oil prices in 2000 and 2001 promised some respite to the Nigerian economy, if utilized properly.

At home, the economic difficulties coincided with the political misfortune in having intransigent and venal military governments in office. The Babangida (1985–1993) and Abacha (1993–1998) military regimes promised much initially in terms of openness and democratization, but led the country down an opposite path, stifling human rights and prospects for transparent government with panache. Both leaders, who were masters of political intrigue and chicanery, had already participated in multiple military coups over the years. They divided, mesmerized, and intimidated their opponents, brought the country to a standstill, and offered "transition without end."[30] As for foreign policy, they pursued it not in the best interests of the country but more for their own personal financial gain. Manipulation of civilian party politics and cancellation of the transitions to civilian government planned for 1990, 1992, 1993, 1994, and 1998 left the country in political limbo, drained finances and energy, and tainted the country's foreign policy. After all, democratization was the watchword elsewhere. The imprisonment of Moshood Abiola, a prominent Muslim Yoruba businessman who by all accounts had won the presidential election of June 12, 1993, which was quickly annulled by Babangida, divided the country and caused simmering ethnic resentment to boil up, especially in the southwest from where Abiola hailed. These tensions were heightened when Abiola died in detention. In response, Western governments increased economic sanctions and withheld foreign investment and debt rescheduling. The big push for economic liberalization, announced as a key platform of the 1995 budget, was not implemented and thus did not produce results. In June 1998, the country was essentially rescued by the inopportune death of Abacha, who appeared to be headed toward succeeding himself in August as the elected civilian president; he was the sole nominated candidate of all five hand-picked political parties. His military successor, Gen. Abdulsalam Abubakar, another Muslim northerner, quickly announced a timetable for the return to civilian rule and handed over power to the elected Obasanjo in May 1999.

Relations within Africa

Within the African continent, Nigeria has had few dramatic foreign policy successes of which to be proud. Nigeria's championing of South African liberation was useful in the 1970s and 1980s, but since the death of apartheid and the downfall of the Soviet Union, there has been little role for Nigeria to play. Indeed, the rise of a postapartheid South Africa raised a particular kind of challenge to Nigerian foreign policy. In terms of political leadership, the charismatic qualities of South African president Nelson Mandela cast a shadow over the questionable personality of Sani Abacha, who called Mandela a "fake." South Africa posed a natural challenge to the ongoing quest for continental leadership that Nigeria pursued, most notably in the form of a permanent seat on the UN Security Council, and Nigerians generally supported their governments in standing up against South Africa. In economic terms, South Africa offered much better opportunities for Western investors than did Nigeria, and so that country received far more attention than did Nigeria. As a result, relations between the two countries deteriorated rapidly, and by the end of 1995 Nelson Mandela was calling for Nigeria's expulsion from the Commonwealth and full-blown oil sanctions against the country.[31] Since the death of Abacha, there has been some fence mending, most notably at the presidential level, but relations remain uneasy.

In West Africa, the centerpiece of foreign policy, Nigeria maintained some semblance of leadership and hegemony in the 1990s, in part because the capacity of most of its neighbors was diminished. Nigeria's expulsion of more than a million "illegal" West African aliens in the early 1980s did little to support the spirit of the ECOWAS treaty, and despite various agreements on freedom of movement and currency transactions, the performance of ECOWAS has been modest. Illegal trade has far outstripped legal trade, a development that has helped government ministers personally rather than government coffers collectively. In many instances, the lingering interests and actions of France have thwarted Nigerian ambition in the region. The CFA franc, the currency linked to the French franc and used by the fourteen African nations joined in a monetary union, remains important in West Africa because it is thought to be a more stable (and useful) currency than the Nigerian naira, which has been dramatically devalued over the past decade.

The end of the Cold War, combined with the debacle of U.S. intervention in Somalia in 1992–1993, led to a marked disinterest in superpower engagement in the continent. The breakdown of law and order in Liberia and Sierra Leone in the early 1990s spurred the creation of the regional peacekeeping force, ECO-MOG, to which Nigeria contributed the largest contingent. The creation of ECOMOG was a bold departure in African peacekeeping, and although its creation was in violation of both the OAU and ECOWAS charters, the force gained support across Africa, in the West, and within the UN.[32] Besides, the undertaking was consistent with European and U.S. calls from the early 1990s for African peacekeeping forces to police Africa. Although successive governments had provided significant financial support across the region, the mobilization of ECO-MOG was the first time Nigeria had overtly exerted military force outside of its own borders. The irony of the situation was not lost on observers in the 1990s: the Nigerian military was using force outside its borders to restore normalcy, peace, and democracy, but was using force inside its borders to prevent democracy. ECOMOG's failure to achieve its objectives, combined with the costs to Nigeria in money and men, led to increasing opposition in Nigeria to the peacekeeping adventure. Nigerian military officers within ECOMOG, who were linked closely to the government at home, were accused of running illicit drug and diamond smuggling rackets, allegations that undermined Nigeria's role in the region. Moreover, Babangida had a close personal friendship with President Samuel Doe in Liberia, along with significant personal business interests in that country. And Abacha was perceived as having a significant personal financial stake in Sierra Leone, which was cited as a reason for Nigeria's intervention there. But the argument also could be made that Nigeria's national interests were fostered by a military presence and some semblance of peace and unity within West Africa. After 2000, when British peacekeepers became more heavily involved in the region because of the lack of success of the ECOMOG force, it was uncertain what role Nigeria would continue to play.

Relations with the West

Relations with the West have been somewhat agonizing for all parties. Western countries, spearheaded by the United States, Britain, and France, have used their own foreign policies to push for greater accountability, openness, and democracy in Nigeria over the past decade, but they have been constrained by the importance of Nigerian oil to their multinational corporations and economies. Even when relations with Nigeria were at the lowest point, Western governments could not bring themselves to countenance major economic sanctions against Nigeria, and so their condemnations appeared hollow and ineffectual. From the perspectives of the Babangida and Abacha administrations, the support of the West was needed to maintain the flow of foreign investment and debt relief so desperately needed. And so these dictators were forced to play along and implement some of the reforms requested by the West, the International Monetary Fund, and the World Bank. Both leaders also played Western powers off each other by offering favors and trade incentives from time to time. Babangida often leaned toward Germany, whereas Abacha favored France (at one time recommending that French become an official language of Nigeria and injecting the French hybrid political system into his proposed new constitution). Both were attempting to keep options open and neutralize the influence of Britain, the Commonwealth, and the United States.

Relations with the United States went from bad to worse during the 1990s, as Nigeria's political intransigence, economic incapacity, and crime and corruption hardened the view of Washington. Nigeria's pariah status also was heavily influenced by internal pressure groups within the United States, led by TransAfrica, which joined with Nigerian democratic groups in exile in order to maintain very vocal opposition to the military dictators. By the mid-1990s, the United States and Nigeria had little or no high-level contact, and as late as 1998 President Clinton studiously avoided the "giant" of Africa on his tour of the continent.

After Abacha's death and the return to civilian rule, these relations were dramatically reversed. High-level contacts were resumed, and even President Clinton made a high-profile visit to Nigeria in August 2000. Obasanjo's close personal links with Jimmy Carter forged two decades earlier helped to consolidate ties with the Clinton administration, which was keen to help promote the nascent Nigerian democracy. Efforts to promote foreign investment were intensified, and Obasanjo was courted not only in the United States, but also throughout Europe as he shuttled incessantly from capital to capital. However, as noted in Chapter 1, it is important to distinguish between rhetorical or formal policy and pronouncements, on the one hand, and the reality of implemented foreign policy, on the other. Unfortunately, the chronic political and economic problems that Nigeria faced could not be so easily swept aside by pronouncements or official visits. Despite the change of leadership, the fabric of elite and ethnic rivalries—and corruption—appeared unchanged, and there was little evidence that renewed friendship with the West would bring any immediate reversal of fortunes to a collapsing Nigerian political economy.

"New" Foreign Policy Issues

Much has been written in the international relations literature about the changing nature of world politics, and Chapter 1 described its overall impact on foreign policy. The nature of foreign policy has changed as well to include "new" policy issues and challenges. Many of those facing Nigerian policy makers are transnational or transsovereign in character and so challenge traditional notions of realism.[33] The Nigerian state is not the only actor involved in foreign policy actions. Democratization and globalization clearly influence the economic and political environments in which Nigeria operates, and the global marketplace is becoming an increasingly difficult one in which to compete. How exactly can Nigeria and other developing countries kick-start diversification into high-tech industries when they have so little experience with such production? How can new channels of production be engineered when the country has been "locked" into primary production for centuries? How can Nigerian companies become important foreign economic actors? Globalization is challenging traditional patterns of both foreign and economic policy, and so far Nigeria has been unable to meet this challenge.

The foreign policies of other countries on issues such as drugs, health, and the environment have had a major impact on Nigeria. Many of those fighting the war against drugs view Nigeria as one of the leading transshipment centers for the global trafficking of narcotics. Moreover, government efforts to combat this trade have been questionable, and observers have alleged that many in government have had a hand in this trade. The United States in particular has placed significant pressure on Nigeria to tackle the problem, but efforts to stop this trade have had relatively little success. Such activities, combined with other widely publicized criminal activities within the country, have served to deter foreign investors from entering the Nigerian market.

On the health front, Nigeria's collapsing health networks and the rise of AIDS cases have become foreign policy issues, locking government horns with those of Western pharmaceutical companies and leading NGOs to become more involved in providing health care and assistance within the country.

As for the environment, Nigeria has been in the global spotlight because of the significant political and environmental problems in the main oil-producing delta region of southeastern Nigeria, particularly in areas populated by the Ogoni. The Ogoni, who are among the poorest people in Nigeria and who have horrific economic, health, and literacy problems, live in a land degraded by environmental pollution. Yet the oil wells in Ogoni land provide tremendous wealth for the Nigerian state and its controlling elite. When in the early 1990s an environmental rights movement, the Movement for the Survival of the Ogoni People (MOSOP), challenged federal government policies and the flow of money into the hands of the elite, it met with brutal force.[34] MOSOP also pursued its own foreign policy in spreading its message of resistance around the world. The execution of Ogoni dissidents, the "Ogoni Nine," including the well-respected writer Ken Saro-Wiwa, in November 1995 following a sham military trial proved to be a foreign policy disaster for the Abacha government. It was eventually overcome, however, because Western governments refused to countenance oil sanctions. Nevertheless, environmental groups continue to lobby against multinationals active in that region, notably Shell, and so continue to pose problems to the vitality of the petroleum sector. Despite the Obasanjo government's promises to bring change, the brutal suppression of dissidents appears to be continuing, with little change of policy.

Conclusion: Foreign Policy Projected

Crystal balls have long failed international relations scholars of whatever theoretical bent. Moreover, Chapter 1 reveals that these scholars often put forward overlapping and contradictory theories in trying to provide a clear understanding of the nature of foreign policy. Readers may wish to keep these cautions in mind as they consider the various issues presented in this section that suggest possible areas of foreign policy success and concern in Nigeria.

The first issue is the viability of the Nigerian state, and that of many of its neighbors. The collapse and disintegration of African countries have long been predicted, but with the exception of the creation of Eritrea out of Ethiopia and the collapse of the Somali state in the early 1990s, there has been no substantial redrawing of the African map since the creation of the Organization of African Unity in 1963. Its members, acting in enlightened self-interest, decided to maintain the territorial status quo. Within Nigeria, the success of the federal forces in the 1967–1970 civil war halted the immediate prospects of dismemberment of the country, but in recent years there have been increasing calls for confederalism and even for secession by various dissatisfied ethnic communities. The country is not even close to resolving long-standing ethnic and religious issues, as demonstrated by the chronic instability and religious strife in 2000–2001 over the introduction of Islamic or *Shari'a* law in various northern states. Questions about whether Nigeria as a state has outlived its usefulness and could join the growing list of "collapsed states" abound.[35] The widespread support for the perpetuation of the Nigerian state may help to keep the various ethno-religious entities glued together, but disintegration is a real possibility that would naturally alter all the foreign policy scenarios.[36]

A second issue is foreign policy and economic relations within West Africa. Nigeria's hegemonic status within the region is not likely to be challenged, but it is difficult to identify any actor that will provide the momentum for further regional integration. Although trade within the region increased significantly just after the inauguration of ECOWAS, legal intraregional trade remained at roughly 10 percent of the aggregate trade of member countries in the 1990s. Moreover, cooperation in the region appears difficult, infrastructure is shriveling, and democratization seems to be stumbling, even though there have been some policy breakthroughs in the form of creating a transregional highway, eliminating visas for ECOWAS nationals, and introducing the regional travelers check. The current crises in Liberia, Sierra Leone, and Guinea do not augur well for the region. In short, ECOWAS has progressed very little in more than twenty-five years of existence, and chronic political and economic circumstances currently do not provide an ideal platform for growth in the near future. And yet the Abuja Declaration of 1991 calls on states to build on regional cooperation to create an African Economic Community by 2025. Such a step is definitely needed, but the pathways and policies to reach that goal are unclear. Nigeria's foreign policy leadership also is somewhat questionable at this stage.

A third issue is Nigeria's economic development. Nigeria is as heavily dependent on oil revenues today as it was twenty years ago. Its reserves of oil and natural gas guarantee Nigeria a healthy income in the coming years, and therefore some basis for foreign economic policy, but Nigeria needs to undergo an economic transition and diversify into high-tech and nonpetroleum products. The gap between the "high-tech haves" and "high-tech have-nots" is widening, and the prospect of global economic apartheid (North versus South) is becoming increasingly apparent. The correlation between the lack of technological development and the efficacy and respectability of Nigeria's foreign policy has been evident for some time, but this is likely to increase in coming years. Nigeria has the resources, both human and material, to attempt the leap into the twenty-first century economy, but that leap will require several changes, not least of which is the transition to a permanently stable, accountable, transparent political environment that will attract the foreign investment needed to spur economic development.

And so the final issue is one on which all others hinge: Can Nigeria reverse its forty-year nightmare of inept and often corrupt government and usher in stable, accountable, civilian government on which society can build? Or will the "third wave" be reversed and the pendulum swing back again in Nigeria to military rule, as many Nigerians and pundits fear? There is no guarantee that a civilian government will perform better in the foreign policy arena than past military governments, but a strong civil society should provide the necessary ingredients to create a stable political economy. Perhaps Nigeria's foreign policy could then become more activist and confident. Without such change, Nigeria could over the next decade become relegated to the role of a peripheral West African player with little or no credible foreign policy options outside of its political space. Successive governments have frittered away opportunities over the past forty years, and there is no clear indication of how that familiar path will be changed.

Clearly, then, the international community will have an important role to play in shaping Nigeria's domestic and foreign policy agendas over the next decade, "because, in the context of uncivicness, praetorianism, and deepening national economic crisis and dependence, it is now the only potential agency of restraint on Nigeria's institutional horizon."[37] External pressure is essential to helping create stable, civilian government in Nigeria,[38] and foreign policy is inextricably linked to the outcome of the domestic struggle. If Nigeria does become a failed state, the implications for the rest of the continent are immense. Even if political stability is miraculously achieved, the economic challenges facing Nigeria look almost insuperable. On that road Nigeria would not be without company, because such extreme marginalization appears to be the path along which most African states are unfortunately headed.

Suggestions for Further Reading

Diamond, Larry, Anthony Kirk-Greene, and Oyeleye Oyediran, eds. *Transition without End: Nigerian Politics and Civil Society under Babangida.* Boulder: Lynne Rienner, 1997.

Falola, Toyin. *The History of Nigeria.* Westport, Conn.: Greenwood Press, 1999.

Gambari, Ibrahim A. *Theory and Reality in Foreign Policy Making: Nigeria after the Second Republic.* Atlantic Highlands, N.J.: Humanities Press International, 1989.

Ihonvbere, Julius O., and Timothy M. Shaw. *Illusions of Power. Nigeria in Transition.* Trenton: Africa World Press, 1998.

King, Mae C. *Basic Currents of Nigerian Foreign Policy.* Washington, D.C.: Howard University Press, 1996.

Lewis, Peter M., Pearl T. Robinson, and Barnett R. Rubin. *Stabilizing Nigeria: Sanctions, Incentives and Support for Civil Society.* New York: Council on Foreign Relations, 1998.

Osaghae, Eghosa E. *Crippled Giant: Nigeria since Independence.* Bloomington: Indiana University Press, 1998.

Notes

1. For surveys of Nigerian foreign policy, see Mae C. King, *Basic Currents of Nigerian Foreign Policy* (Washington D.C.: Howard University Press, 1996); A. B. Akinyemi, S. O. Agbi, and A. O. Otunbanjo, eds., *Nigeria since Independence: The First 25 Years,* vol. 10, *International Relations* (Ibadan: Heinemann, 1989); Olajide Aluko, *Essays in Nigerian Foreign Policy* (London: Allen and Unwin, 1981); and Timothy M. Shaw and Olajide Aluko, eds., *Nigerian Foreign Policy: Alternative Perceptions and Projections* (London: Macmillan, 1983). For useful chapters on Nigerian foreign policy, see Julius Emeka Okolo and Stephen Wright, "Nigeria," in *The Political Economy of Foreign Policy in ECOWAS,* ed. Timothy M. Shaw and Julius Emeka Okolo (London: Macmillan, 1994), 125–146; and Stephen Wright and Julius Emeka Okolo, "Nigeria: Aspirations of Regional Power," in *African Foreign Policies,* ed. Stephen Wright (Boulder: Westview Press, 1999), 118–132.

2. For general surveys of Nigeria, see Toyin Falola, *The History of Nigeria* (Westport, Conn.: Greenwood Press, 1999); Eghosa E. Osaghae, *Crippled Giant: Nigeria since Independence* (Bloomington: Indiana University Press, 1998); Stephen Wright, *Nigeria: Struggle for Stability and Status* (Boulder: Westview Press, 1998); and Tom Forrest, *Politics and Economic Development in Nigeria* (Boulder: Westview Press, 1995).

3. James H. Mittelman, ed., *Globalization: Critical Reflections* (Boulder: Westview Press, 1996); Claude Ake, "The New World Order: A View from Africa," in *Whose World Order? Uneven Globalization and the End of the Cold War,* ed. Hans-Henrik Holm and Georg Sorenson (Boulder: Westview Press, 1995), 1–17.

4. For surveys of the African predicament and the continent's role in world politics, see Sola Akinrade and Amadu Sesay, eds., *Africa in the Post–Cold War International System* (London: Pinter, 1998); John W. Harbeson and Donald Rothchild, eds., *Africa in World Politics: Post–Cold War Challenges* (Boulder: Westview Press, 1995); Christopher Clapham, *Africa and the International System: The Politics of State Survival* (Cambridge: Cambridge University Press, 1996); Peter J. Schraeder, *African Politics and Society: A Mosaic in Transformation* (Boston: Bedford/St. Martin's, 2000); and Ralph I. Onwuka and Timothy M. Shaw, eds., *Africa in World Politics: Into the 1990s* (New York: St. Martin's Press, 1989). Also see Stephen Wright, "The Foreign Policy of Africa," in *Foreign Policy in World Politics,* 8th ed., ed. Roy C. Macridis (Englewood Cliffs, N.J.: Prentice Hall, 1992), 330–356.

5. Larry Diamond, *Class, Ethnicity and Democracy in Nigeria: The Failure of the First Republic* (Syracuse: Syracuse University Press, 1988); and Toyin Falola and Julius O. Ihonvbere, *The Rise and Fall of Nigeria's Second Republic* (London: Zed, 1985).

6. Wole Soyinka, *The Open Sore of a Continent: A Personal Narrative of the Nigerian Crisis* (New York: Oxford University Press, 1996); Jimi Peters, *The Nigerian Military and the State* (London: Tauris Academic Studies, 1997); and Peter Lewis, "From Prebendalism to Predation: The Political Economy of Decline in Nigeria," *Journal of Modern African Studies*, vol. 34, no. 1 (1996): 79–103.

7. Julius O. Ihonvbere and Timothy M. Shaw, *Illusions of Power: Nigeria in Transition* (Trenton: Africa World Press, 1998); William Graf, *The Nigerian State: Political Economy, State Class and Political System in the Post-Colonial Era* (London: James Currey, 1988); Julius O. Ihonvbere and Timothy M. Shaw, *Towards a Political Economy of Nigeria: Petroleum and Politics at the (Semi-) Periphery* (Aldershot: Avebury, 1988); Claude Ake, ed., *Political Economy of Nigeria* (Harlow: Longman, 1985); and I. William Zartman, ed., *The Political Economy of Nigeria* (New York: Praeger, 1983).

8. Julius Emeka Okolo and Stephen Wright, eds., *West African Regional Cooperation and Development* (Boulder: Westview Press, 1990).

9. See Olufemi Babarinde, "Regionalism and African Foreign Policies," in *African Foreign Policies,* ed. Stephen Wright (Boulder: Westview Press, 1999), 215–236.

10. R. A. Akindele and Bassey E. Ate, eds., *Nigeria's Economic Relations with the Major Developed Market-Economy Countries, 1960–1985* (Lagos: Nelson and NIIA, 1988); and Toyin Falola and Julius O. Ihonvbere, *Nigeria and the International Capitalist System* (Boulder: Lynne Rienner, 1988).

11. Larry Diamond, *Developing Democracy: Toward Consolidation* (Baltimore: Johns Hopkins University Press, 1999).

12. Olufemi A. Babarinde, *The Lomé Conventions and Development* (Aldershot: Avebury/Ashgate, 1994).

13. Ibrahim A. Gambari, *Theory and Reality in Foreign Policy Making: Nigeria after the Second Republic* (Atlantic Highlands, N.J.: Humanities Press International, 1989), 13.

14. Thomas J. Biersteker, ed., *Dealing with Debt: International Financial Negotiations and Adjustment Bargaining* (Boulder: Westview Press, 1993).

15. Vernon McKay, *African Diplomacy: Studies in the Determinants of Foreign Policy* (New York: Praeger, 1966); Olajide Aluko, ed., *The Foreign Policies of African States* (London: Hodder and Stoughton, 1977); and Ali A. Mazrui, *Africa's International Relations: The Diplomacy of Dependency and Change* (London: Heinemann, 1977).

16. Stephen Wright, "The Changing Context of African Foreign Policies," in *African Foreign Policies,* ed. Stephen Wright (Boulder: Westview Press, 1999), 1–22.

17. William Reno, *Warlord Politics and African States* (Boulder: Lynne Rienner, 1998).

18. Gambari, *Theory and Reality in Foreign Policy Making.*

19. Gabriel O. Olusanya and R. A. Akindele, eds., *The Structure and Processes of Foreign Policy Making and Implementation in Nigeria, 1960–1990* (Lagos: NIIA/Vantage, 1990).

20. Under the Abacha government, union leaders were summarily dismissed and arrested. Their successors were handpicked by Abacha and imposed on the unions.

21. B. J. Takaya and S. G. Tyoden, *The Kaduna Mafia* (Jos, Nigeria: Jos University Press, 1987).

22. Okwudiba Nnoli, *Ethnicity and Development in Nigeria* (Aldershot: Avebury, 1995).

23. John J. Stremlau, *The International Politics of the Nigerian Civil War, 1967–1970* (Princeton: Princeton University Press, 1977); and Suzanne Cronje, *The World and Nigeria: The Diplomatic History of the Biafran War, 1967–1970* (London: Sidgwick and Jackson, 1972).

24. Richard Joseph, *Democracy and Prebendal Politics in Nigeria* (Cambridge: Cambridge University Press, 1987).

25. See Pade Badru, *Imperialism and Ethnic Politics in Nigeria, 1960–1996* (Trenton: Africa World Press, 1998); and Julius O. Ihonvbere, *Nigeria: The Politics of Adjustment and Democracy* (New Brunswick: Transaction, 1994).

26. Alex Gboyega, "Nigeria: Conflict Unresolved," in *Governance as Conflict Management: Politics and Violence in West Africa*, ed. I. William Zartman (Washington, D.C.: Brookings Institution, 1997), 150.

27. Peter O. Olayiwola, *Petroleum and Structural Change in a Developing Country: The Case of Nigeria* (New York: Praeger, 1987).

28. Gambari, *Theory and Reality in Foreign Policy Making*, 5.

29. There was a mini-boom during the Gulf War, but much of the extra revenue was squandered in ECOMOG peacekeeping and private bank accounts.

30. Larry Diamond, Anthony Kirk-Greene, and Oyeleye Oyediran, eds., *Transition without End: Nigerian Politics and Civil Society under Babangida* (Boulder: Lynne Rienner, 1997). Also see *Nigeria's Third Republic: The Problems and Prospects of Political Transition to Civil Rule*, ed. Bamidele A. Ojo (Commack, N.Y.: Nova Science, 1998); and Julius O. Ihonvbere, "Are Things Falling Apart? The Military and the Crisis of Democratisation in Nigeria," *Journal of Modern African Studies*, vol. 34, no. 2 (1996).

31. Paul-Henri Bischoff and Roger Southall, "The Early Foreign Policy of the Democratic South Africa," in *African Foreign Policies*, ed. Stephen Wright (Boulder: Westview Press, 1999), 154–181.

32. Karl P. Magyar and Earl Conteh-Morgan, eds., *Peacekeeping in Africa: ECOMOG in Liberia* (London: Macmillan, 1998); and Gunnar M. Sorbo and Peter Vale, eds., *Out of Conflict: From War to Peace in Africa* (Uppsala: Nordiska Afrikainstitutet, 1997).

33. Maryann K. Cusimano, *Beyond Sovereignty: Issues for a Global Agenda* (Boston: Bedford/St. Martin's, 2000); and Anders Hjort af Ornas and M. A. Mohammed Salih, eds., *Ecology and Politics: Environmental Stress and Security in Africa* (Uppsala: Scandinavian Institute of African Studies, 1989).

34. Abdul Rasheed Na'Allah, ed., *Ogoni's Agonies: Ken Saro-Wiwa and the Crisis in Nigeria* (Trenton: Africa World Press, 1998); and Ken Saro-Wiwa, *Genocide in Nigeria: The Ogoni Tragedy* (Port Harcourt: Saros, 1992).

35. Jeffrey Herbst, "Is Nigeria a Viable State?" *Washington Quarterly*, vol. 19, no. 2 (1996).

36. See, for example, Rotimi Suberu, "Integration and Disintegration in the Nigerian Federation," in *Regionalisation in Africa: Integration and Disintegration*, ed. Daniel C. Bach (Oxford: James Currey, 1999), 91–101.

37. Larry Diamond, "Postscript and Postmortem," in *Transition without End: Nigerian Politics and Civil Society under Babangida*, ed. Larry Diamond, Anthony Kirk-Greene, and Oyeleye Oyediran (Boulder: Lynne Rienner, 1997), 479. This quotation refers to the Babangida and Abacha administrations but remains salient in the current era.

38. Peter M. Lewis, Pearl T. Robinson, and Barnett R. Rubin, *Stabilizing Nigeria: Sanctions, Incentives and Support for Civil Society* (New York: Council on Foreign Relations, 1998).

CHAPTER 12

South African Foreign Policy:

A New Regime in a New World Order

Kenneth W. Grundy

During the Cold War, South Africa's foreign policy was dominated by the issue of apartheid (racial segregation). Because that policy became increasingly controversial as the world became more conscious of human rights, South Africa's leaders were forced to continually defend their country's domestic policies. Then, in the early 1990s, South Africa experienced a dramatic change in its political system. The new regime, led by President Nelson Mandela, set out to transform South Africa, which included making significant changes in both its domestic and foreign policy. In this chapter, Kenneth W. Grundy describes how postapartheid South Africa has incorporated new actors in the foreign policy process, has tried harder to play a positive role in the region, and has attempted to infuse its foreign policy with a moral element. Grundy goes on to explain that even though South Africa is no longer criticized for its apartheid policies, the external critics have not disappeared. Now South Africa has come under pressure for its relations with Cuba, Libya, and Iran, and it is being urged to play a greater leadership role in Africa.

South Africa can be compared with other countries on several dimensions. For example, the major change in the South African political system and the subsequent effects on its foreign policy can be compared with similar changes in Russia (Chapter 5). South Africa also can be compared with countries like Nigeria (Chapter 11) and Brazil (Chapter 13), because each seeks an active role in a region generally made up of weak countries. Yet despite this position of relative power, South Africa continues to suffer from underdevelopment like China (Chapter 6), India (Chapter 8), and Iran (Chapter 10), and thus some of the central goals and substance of South African foreign policy are similar to those characterizing the foreign policies of these countries. Finally, the South Africa foreign policy process, in particular its degree of centralization, is comparable to that of several countries, including France (Chapter 3) and Mexico (Chapter 14).

South Africa emerged from World War II as a member in good standing of the victorious Western alliance. Its prime minister, Jan Christian Smuts, was one of the founders of the United Nations in 1945. But its white minority was determined to maintain a social system that segregated and exploited its nonwhite majority. The electoral victory of the National Party (NP) in 1948 systematized this injustice. The new government entrenched a racist system widely known by the Afrikaanse term *apartheid*. South Africa had become, in the words of its foreign minister, "the polecat [skunk] of the world."

As more and more states gained independence and membership in the UN and other international bodies, South Africa found itself increasingly isolated.[1] Members of the minority regime insisted on their right to organize South African society as they pleased, even though apartheid violated the evolving universal tenets of social acceptability. For most of the postwar era, the world community moved toward a more open and uniform set of human rights norms, while South Africa headed in the opposite direction. In a hostile world—and in a region where South Africa's very name was anathema—survival was everything. For South Africa, an outcast state, foreign policy became an indispensable vehicle for defending apartheid.

This chapter begins by describing the foreign policy dilemmas of the apartheid regime from 1948 until its demise in 1989. It will look at the external factors affecting South Africa's foreign policy, as well as some internal factors such as the centralized foreign policy process, and the composition of the foreign policy constituency as perceived by the National Party government. After a four-year transition, a majority-based government was established in 1994 that sought to represent, for the first time, the aspirations of the disadvantaged masses. How did this "New" South Africa, as it was called, change the pattern of policy making and the direction of policy itself? Several themes stand out, including South Africa's leadership in southern Africa and the democratization of foreign policy making.

This chapter then examines a few specific issues, such as the postapartheid efforts of Pretoria, South Africa's administrative capital, to encourage trade and development, its negotiations with the European Union, its commitment to human rights (which includes its efforts to change the policies of the military government in Nigeria), its resistance to efforts by the United States to shape Pretoria's relations with "problematic states," and the contentious question of the recognition of China. Finally, this chapter tries to make sense of this revolutionary foreign policy thrust in a world itself undergoing radical shifts in the basis of state power.

South African Foreign Policy during the Cold War

The Cold War presented the racist government with an opportunity to use the global power struggle between communism and anticommunism as a means of weakening the domestic opponents of apartheid. By identifying its chief opposition—the African National Congress (ANC) as well as liberal whites and leftist revolutionaries—in Cold War terms and by seeking itself to be included in the anticommunist confraternity, Pretoria worked to isolate antiapartheid activists, to rationalize its antirevolutionary stance in broader, global terms, and thus to neutralize opposition from the Western world. In doing so, Pretoria tried to characterize apartheid not as a human rights issue, but as one of Cold War import by merely arguing that any effort to destabilize southern Africa or to undermine Western "civilization" there would contribute to the communist tide. South Africa's rhetoric about what its defense establishment labeled "total onslaught" tried to establish that South Africa was the prime target of a concerted communist offensive. Through the post–Cold War years, Pretoria shifted the rationalization for minority rule from a purely race-based argument predicated in terms of alleged racial superiority to one based ostensibly on "group" rights. Each separate ethnic group became eligible to have a self-governed, "independent" homeland. Never, however, was it proposed that the land and resources of the country be distributed equitably.

To accept that South Africa's foreign policy was Cold War-driven was to endorse, in a fashion, Pretoria's strategic leitmotif. Few believed that by opposing apartheid the West was furthering the communist cause. Insofar as the Western governments swallowed the Cold War distortions coming out of Pretoria, South Africa's foreign policy enabled the regime to survive beyond its numbered days.

A "Dual" Policy: Avoid Regional Isolation and Maintain Ties with the West

In the years leading up to F. W. de Klerk's 1989 assumption of the presidency from P. W. Botha and the February 11, 1990, release from prison of ANC icon Nelson Mandela, South Africa's foreign policy was two-pronged.[2] It consisted of a firm and even proactive defense of apartheid within South Africa and in the surrounding region, coupled with an economic and diplomatic determination to be accepted as a member of the loose Western anticommunist coalition. Thus South Africa resisted the nonaligned countries' efforts to ostracize it in international organizations and in various trading constellations and occasionally offered concessions to selected neighboring governments and opponents of apartheid in order to co-opt them into collaboration. Insofar as it succeeded—and overall it did not—this two-pronged approach demonstrated to the West that South Africa was flexible and open to change. Through it all, however, one goal stood out clearly: maintain the white advantage.

Pretoria's domestic policies and politics always had foreign policy ramifications. Whether it was changing the laws on trade unions, detaining political opponents, silencing a newspaper, maneuvering around a racially charged funeral, altering the guidelines for secondary education, or maintaining segregated sports, everything resonated abroad. Simply put, the world community began to challenge the traditional legal defense of domestic policy, which maintained that a sovereign state can do as it pleases with its citizens within its territorial jurisdiction. Pretoria needed to find a more convincing rationalization for its increasingly unpopular domestic arrangements.

In pursuing its objectives, Pretoria thought it imperative that the leaders of the antiapartheid movement be denied an endorsement of legitimacy by the international community. But, given the ANC's broad-based support internally, especially in the high-profile black middle class and in the religious community, such a denial proved impossible. For example, Chief Albert Luthuli, the ANC's president, and Anglican bishop Desmond Tutu, an active advocate of nonviolent resistance to apartheid, were awarded Nobel Peace Prizes in 1961 and 1984, respectively. Although members of the outlawed South African Communist Party (SACP) were highly placed and influential in the African National Congress, inside South Africa and in exile, the ANC could not be regarded as either a pawn of Moscow or largely a tool of the Communist Party. Instead, the two movements, the SACP and the ANC, more accurately perceived themselves as allies in a common struggle.[3] From the 1960s to the 1980s they came together in the ANC, the only viable organization fighting apartheid. When in the 1980s the insurrection took flight under the internal United Democratic Front (UDF), the ANC found a powerful and agile collaborator inside the country. The UDF was an umbrella confederation of hundreds of antiapartheid groups, representing a wide spectrum of progressive thought.

Efforts to discredit this popular coalition proved convincing only for those already obsessed by the fear of a communist takeover. Thus a few members of the conservative governments of Ronald Reagan, Margaret Thatcher, and Helmut Kohl and of parties to their right sought to denigrate the ANC, but in the end even they were not prepared to buy Pretoria's line. As the Soviet Union began to lose its capacity (and stomach) to vie for influence in Africa, Pretoria was left alone in a critical world, swimming against the current of universal values, including majority rule, tolerance, decolonization, racial equality, and human rights. Mounting black resistance thus found a sympathetic ear throughout the world.

In addition to undermining the ANC, operating largely from exile, the regime also sought to isolate and weaken other governments in the region that opposed South Africa's racial order. Originally, Pretoria's aim was to surround itself with friendly or at least weak or compliant neighbors that would accept and thus legitimize the white regime. Until the 1960s the rest of the region was controlled by the colonial powers. But then Great Britain withdrew from Malawi and Zambia in 1964 and from the so-called High Commission Territories (Botswana,

Lesotho, and Swaziland) in 1966 and 1968. Through the 1960s and 1970s South Africa sought to shore up a security bloc of white powers (the settler government in Rhodesia and the faltering Portuguese colonial regimes in Mozambique and Angola), but in the mid-1970s the Portuguese occupation collapsed. Once Rhodesia's experiment with its Unilateral Declaration of Independence failed in 1980, South Africa found itself surrounded by black states, most of which were critical and some openly hostile to Pretoria. Only Namibia remained, administered by South Africa and defended by its defense force. But even there, South Africa's rule was none too secure. Pressure from an indigenous liberation movement (the South West African People's Organization), the United Nations, and external powers was mounting.

The Ultimate Fallback: Armed Forces

Beginning in the late 1970s South Africa used military power to dominate the region. This strategy included efforts to weaken opposition movements based in nearby territories and preemptive strikes to destabilize and embarrass governments in the region. Meanwhile, the global powers and their proxies had been drawn into southern Africa. In each conflict, the United States and the Soviet Union identified allies and enemies and sought to use them for their Cold War purposes. Likewise, various actors in the region sought to exploit their Cold War links for their own local ends. But for the peoples of southern Africa, the Cold War was always a secondary consideration, important only insofar as it could enable them to fulfill their immediate aspirations of racial equality, self-government, economic development, and majority rule. Indeed, the great struggle between the ideological forces of communism and capitalism had chiefly utilitarian consequences in southern Africa. And even though South Africa's effort to destabilize neighboring regimes succeeded, it proved a flawed policy, for it failed to stem the resistance to apartheid.

While the Cold War lingered on, South Africa's rulers fought efforts to exclude the country from international organizations. The pressure on South Africa at the UN intensified. On issues such as the treatment of South Africa's Indian population, apartheid, and South Africa's mandate/trusteeship over Namibia (South West Africa), Pretoria found itself repeatedly criticized, censured, ostracized, and penalized. Other international bodies, many in the UN family of organizations, also took steps to expel or silence South Africa.

To opponents of apartheid—a varied lot that ranged from pacifist and Christian church groups to freedom fighters prepared to sabotage and disrupt minority society—the evil posed by this racial order was so odious that they were prepared to insist that any association with the evil apartheid state was an outrage. Nevertheless, South Africa remained integrated within the Western economic system in trade, investment, and technology flows.[4] The dominant Western industrial powers would have preferred to continue economic relations as usual and at the same time express their displeasure with South Africa's racist order. It was, after all, the wicked political system that should be condemned. Some argued that the economic links were an altogether different matter, a lever by which the West could force South Africa to change. To the more liberal critics of apartheid, the selective application of antiapartheid policies made sense. Weaken the supporters of apartheid, they urged, but do not abandon the opponents of apartheid within South Africa's borders. "Constructive engagement," some called it, and it is a familiar counterargument to sanctions.

Militant opponents of apartheid, the ANC, and its allies in the developing world, the socialist bloc, as well as some nongovernmental organizations in the West challenged and attacked all relations with Pretoria and the South African power structure. Sporting, cultural, and religious ties were suspended. Antiapartheid groups pressured corporations to withdraw from South Africa, to stop trading with South Africa, and, where that failed, to adopt codes of conduct that empowered the black workforce. To diehard militants, South Africa was a pariah that deserved total rejection. Moreover, even though Pretoria failed in the long run to limit sanctions sufficiently to provide more than symbolic contact with its chosen partners, the most fanatical antiapartheid activists regarded the West as appeasers at best and allies of apartheid at worst.

In the end, South Africa's regional policy was a policy of desperation, propelled by and dependent on its security establishment. The country simply lacked the resources and cohesion to shape the larger power relationships. Reliance on securocrats virtually sealed South Africa's fate. Behaving as if "total onslaught" were a reality contributed to the isolation that South Africa feared the most. The business community, the Department of Foreign Affairs, scientists, and the intellectual and artistic communities found it increasingly difficult to maintain relationships abroad. Regional military operations seemed calculated to sabotage the diplomatic process.

Meanwhile, a kind of ebb and flow characterized regional relations. Unable to force its neighbors to expel its enemies and to deal openly and cooperatively with South Africa, Pretoria reverted to military steps. Eventually, a targeted government would knuckle under to the pressure and reluctantly call for accommodation with Pretoria. But the interests of the vulnerable black governments and those of Pretoria were fundamentally incompatible. Soon the *modus vivendi* collapsed, leading to more economic warfare and possibly more military strikes. The net impact was further isolation of South Africa and a strengthening of opponents' resolve to bring down the minority regime. Eventually, South Africa's policy makers recognized the futility and costliness of their efforts. The regime was ready to adapt, but as little as possible. South Africa had entered an era of tense and yet profound transition. Foreign policy needed a new set of bearings. This chapter will examine this new foreign policy after considering the external and domestic influences on South Africa's foreign policy.

External Factors

Because foreign policy can best be understood as an extension of a country's domestic politics, it is important to place South Africa's foreign policy in such a context. Who makes foreign policy, and how do those people assume policy-making positions? It is also vital to know how they perceive the national interest. This was especially true during the apartheid years when Pretoria's insularity reflected the embattled sense of being alone in a hostile world and besieged within the country by an African majority. The "new" South Africa, with essentially new constituencies, has different values and different prospects. But the elements of continuity cannot be ignored either. Thus this section begins by outlining how South Africa progressed from defending apartheid to projecting democracy.

During the post–World War II era, foreign policy making was dominated by the state. According to Deon Geldenhuys, it was an "oligarchic-bureaucratic" system.[5] Decision making was concentrated in the hands of a small group of senior government ministers. Not only was the majority black population excluded, but so were the white electorate, pressure groups, and even the legislature and the ruling National Party. Foreign policy was divorced from social discourse. As for its substance, Pretoria's foreign policy posture basically identified with the core values of its pinched white constituency; it explicitly rejected the values of the majority.

That authoritarian/bureaucratic oligarchy was narrow indeed. The prime minister and the ministers of foreign affairs and defense and their most senior advisers had a voice in the process, but even as the circle was widened, the views expressed tended to be fairly uniform. In the 1970s and 1980s the Department of Information and the intelligence community were included, briefly. Independent of government, the business community had a role, but by no means officially. In fact, the oligarchy widened as the National Party felt compelled to include more actors in the process in order to garner support domestically. Overall, however, foreign policy was a focused, top-down enterprise, fashioned to defend apartheid and the "South African way" in a hostile world.

A New Domestic Scene and a New Thrust in Foreign Policy

After several years of difficult, prolonged, sometimes secret negotiations, a new political dispensation was agreed on and legitimized in the national election of April 1994.[6] The compromise transitional constitution (adopted in 1993 and finalized in 1996) featured the Government of National Unity (GNU). The GNU was designed to smooth the transition to majority rule and to provide the minority parties with a sense of participation and security. It featured in turn a multiparty cabinet of twenty-seven ministers and twelve deputy ministers, appointed for five years. The first cabinet comprised twenty-six members of the ANC majority, nine members of the National Party (plus F. W. de Klerk as executive deputy president), and four members of the Inkatha Freedom Party (IFP).

The IFP is a Zulu-based party strong in KwaZulu-Natal province. The composition of the GNU roughly reflected the partisan distribution of seats in Parliament. The National Party withdrew from government in May 1996.

The seven "principles" of foreign policy developed by the ANC before the 1994 election called for promoting human rights, democracy, justice and international law, peace, the interests of the continent of Africa, and regional and international economic cooperation, thereby leading to the consolidation of a democratic South Africa. The GNU was determined to exploit the "moral space" that Mandela's ascension to power provided. Moreover, South Africa saw itself as a leader, a catalyst for the rest of Africa, because of its unique position at the "confluence" between North and South. South Africa already has an economy that produces industrial and primary products, and it possesses a sophisticated infrastructure. Yet it is located in Africa, and its population is culturally diverse and lives in disparate modes, traditional and twenty-first century. These characteristics, it would seem, were crafted to rationalize a vigorous role for South Africa in the South and particularly in its backyard. Indeed, its first foreign policy efforts demonstrated that intention. South Africa quickly joined the Organization of African Unity in May 1994 and the Southern African Development Community (SADC, formerly the Southern African Development Coordination Conference) in August 1994.

In important respects, the new thrust in foreign policy was a backlash against the old regime's preoccupation with realist foreign policy models that assumed that world politics is primarily a struggle among self-interested states for power in an anarchic world. The apartheid state had implicitly rejected interdependence. In fact, realism had fit apartheid well because of its state-centric perspective that enabled it to refuse to conform to external values and to change its domestic social system.

In the end, it was Pretoria's stubborn unwillingness to appreciate the profound impact of the globalizing world economy on the South African economy and on apartheid that brought the de Klerk government to power and the establishment to its senses. The last white government and the first majority government shared a sensitivity to the emerging world political economy. It was either that or risk a debilitating economic collapse. This shift to an acceptance of globalization and a desire to apply its tenets on South Africa's terms enabled the new regime to proceed with enthusiasm. In doing so, the ANC, determined to totally reject apartheid, tossed overboard any foreign policy perspectives associated with the old regime.

Regional Integration

Today it is expected that Pretoria will serve as the conscience and engine of the region. Forces in the region and beyond assume that South Africa will follow up its own political "miracle" by fostering mini-miracles elsewhere. South Africa's gross national product of $133 billion accounts for some 80 percent of the region's GDP. Moreover, the country's economy is more balanced than that of any other African country, and its population of nearly 45 million is racially diverse—77.2 percent black, 10.5 percent white, 8.8 percent colored (mixed race), 2.5 percent Asian, and 0.9 percent unspecified[7]—and relatively well educated. On the business front, South Africa attracts job seekers and its businesses invest in the region and beyond.

Yet some observers wonder how long South Africa can sustain these advantages.[8] And how can it lead without appearing to bully its weaker neighbors? The new government wants to be active but to cooperate with others as equals. There is already resentment, however, that the new South Africa may be throwing its weight around. As a country surrounded by poverty, famine, war, and instability, it is no wonder South Africa is regarded as a regional heavyweight. Thus the redefinition of South Africa's policy is not its emphasis on the region, for neutralizing southern Africa was central to the defense of apartheid. The redefinition is in the changed temperament of relations within the region—cooperative instead of hostile, multilateral as well as bilateral.

Despite South Africa's desire to cooperate, interests often clash, especially on matters of trade, transportation, infrastructure, immigration, investment, and economic policies regarding local businesses. Domestic political pressures dictate that foreign policy not be made in a vacuum, no matter how much officials in the government's Union Buildings want cordial relations with their counterparts beyond the borders.

These varying interests are reflected in what Robert Davies, an ANC member of Parliament, calls the "variable geometry" that exists in international relations in the region.[9] He argues that there are basically three approaches to regional integration in southern Africa.[10] The first involves trade or market integration. The Preferential Trade Area (PTA, also known as the Common Market for Eastern and Southern Africa, COMESA), which South Africa has chosen not to join, is the current regional example. Because the PTA seeks to promote trade links by breaking down tariff barriers, it clashes with the Southern Africa Customs Union (SACU), which allows duty-free movement of goods only among the member states of South Africa, Botswana, Lesotho, Swaziland, and Namibia. SACU is a holdover from the apartheid years, but Pretoria clings to it; South Africa and its SACU partners still have elements of protectionism in place that they seem reluctant to abandon. Before deciding whether to join the PTA, Pretoria sought to negotiate its relationship with the European Union, an outcome that will have a profound effect on the SACU and Southern African Development Community states. The PTA considers itself the first step toward a free trade area, a customs union, a common market, and eventually an economic and then political union. SADC also seeks to establish a regional free trade policy.

The second approach to regional integration is to seek functional integration. Called the SADC approach, it focuses on project cooperation. Within SADC, regional cooperation is propelled topically, as individual member states are assigned responsibility for coordinating efforts in specific areas such as infrastructure, food, energy, manpower development, mining, tourism, and health. South Africa belongs to SADC chiefly because SADC's ad hoc and selective approach to economic change can be used more easily by South Africa for activities it supports.

The third approach is one of more ambitious development integration, in which cooperating governments seek to balance benefits and obligations. Those who advocate this approach fear that market-driven trade liberalization will inevitably lead to unhealthy concentrations of growth and development in some countries and stagnation in others. Because of its already strong economic base, South Africa is likely to reap all the advantages of this scenario, and the weaker countries will suffer the disappointments.

The ANC claims that it wants to be more involved in regional affairs. It acknowledges that democracy in South Africa depends on regional growth and development, but it also admits that existing relations in the region are uneven and that regional growth and stability are central to South Africa's commonweal. Its leaders agree that South Africa cannot succeed as an island of prosperity in a sea of poverty. But they add that it is not yet an island of prosperity.

Overall, despite the rhetoric southern Africa has made little progress toward integration. Davies asserts that SADC and COMESA represent "weak commitments by weak states to weak organizations."[11] Statism and regionalism do not easily go together. Most leaders, many of whom pretend to champion greater regional integration, still follow the minimalist approach, because to open their domestic politics to regional forces might threaten their tenure. In a fifteen-page update on the first three years of the "new" foreign policy, the ANC devoted less than a single page to regional affairs. And most of that focused on regional "problems" posed by illegal immigration, drug trafficking, and organized crime.[12] Pretoria seems to have no comprehensive strategy for regional cooperation and integration, and, even if it did, without extensive financial investments it would not make a great deal of difference. Its more vulnerable neighbors are as likely to conjure up fears of the giant within the region as those of the giants beyond.

South Africa is most intimately linked to the SACU states (Botswana, Lesotho, Swaziland, and Namibia). Originally negotiated in 1969, the Southern Africa Customs Union created a tariff regime that collects and distributes customs and excise revenues and applies a formula by which such monies are distributed among member states. Despite disagreements and periodic renegotiations, the less-developed member countries stay involved and seek a larger voice in SACU's decisions.

Within the Southern African Development Community, which is a second and larger circle of linkages, negotiations have been concluded to create new trading relationships among its fourteen member states, and special arrangements have been drafted to protect the least-developed SADC members. When established in 1980, SADC's predecessor, the Southern African Development Coordination Conference, had provided the structure for regional development. Its members had originally been motivated by a desire to reduce their trade and infrastructure ties with apartheid South Africa. But their efforts had been less than inspiring; there were simply too many pressing demands, not the least of which were Pretoria's efforts to destabilize these polities. Now that Pretoria is a member in good standing of SADC (since August 1994), SADC's goals include integrating South Africa's economy into the regional flow and using South Africa's economic weight to jump-start the region's development.

Such intentions are a reaffirmation of a historical pattern that goes back to the nineteenth century. South Africa has always treated the region and beyond as its hinterland.[13] During the colonial era, infrastructure development patterns confirmed South Africa as the hub of the region. In a way, the new South Africa is merely taking up where the country left off in the pre-apartheid era—that is, it is seeking to normalize historical relations that reflect the geographic realities of economic interdependence. This aspect of contemporary South African foreign policy reflects the geopolitical drives of earlier governments in Pretoria. In fact, there is a continuity here that realists can appreciate—no matter what the values or ideologies of the regime in power, the external givens force it, for reasons of state, to behave in a statist way.

The commitment to region also may be a response to regionalization elsewhere around the world. Whether it is the highly institutionalized framework of a European Union or the looser structure of a North American Free Trade Agreement (NAFTA) or an Association of Southeast Asian Nations (ASEAN), the impulse to form a regional bloc is unmistakable. Reinforcing that drive is the fear that Africa may be marginalized, the sense that Africa will be left out of a rapidly globalizing world, and the equally pressing fear that even if Africa were to clamber aboard the economic express, the nature of globalization would work to the disadvantage of weak southern states. Regional development still depends heavily on trends in the world economy. In this sense, South Africa may see regional economic integration as a defensive strategy to protect itself from and take advantage of gravitational forces elsewhere.

The fact is that Africa has long been on the margins of the world's economy, in a peripheral position in the world's division of labor. This situation has become even more apparent today as other states on the periphery have managed to become mini-engines of growth. African states are tied into the global economy, but largely as supplicants, seeking debt relief, economic assistance, investment, trade preferences, and so forth. Though a state may possess the trappings of statehood and may be formally independent, it soon learns that it must seek to balance the demands of its polity and people with the realities of a world of states of varying degrees of power and assertiveness. As pointed out in Chapter 1, the distribution of power and a state's position in the international system can affect a state's foreign policy. The systemic variable thus dovetails with realist thinking about foreign policy, but a realism that has a broader basis for state power and one that accounts for the swirling exigencies of globalization. No matter what policies South Africa pursues, in the West it is regarded as African and thus situated in a violent, brutal, corrupt, despotic continent. South Africa is wary of being tarred with the brush of the continent. Yet when the current South African president, Thabo Mbeki, recently traveled to Europe and America, he found himself having to answer for Zimbabwe's land seizures and the chaos in Central and West Africa. It would be as if Washington were forced to apologize for the corruption in Mexico.

As fearful as Africa's leaders are of outside forces, they also are not entirely at ease with the economic forces closer to home. Some see South Africa as a threat. A larger regional market (110 million versus 45 million) may mean economies of scale, but it does not automatically translate into purchasing power and prosperity for all. Given the extreme poverty and civil dislocation throughout the region, the form of regional economic institutions is important. A market-driven model might lead to growth, but it also might amplify the inequities. Without state intervention, corporate decisions about capital, labor, and growth tend to cluster in already established nodes of growth. South Africa, therefore, has an advantage in attracting investment over its neighbors, many of which are in danger of becoming nothing but suppliers of raw materials (water, hydroelectric power, agricultural products) and labor, which could strangle South Africa's already oversupplied labor market and overtaxed social services.

Zimbabwe, the second most important economy in the region, has reason to fear that South Africa will draw away the factors of growth and leave the rest of the region in its tracks. This fear is compounded by South Africa's protectionist tariff regime, vestiges of a powerful business community that shielded particular industries. In textiles, clothing, automobiles, and chemicals, for example, industrial giants prevailed on government to buffer them from European and Asian competition. Many are still powerful domestic interests close to decision makers.

Internal Factors

In one important respect, South Africa presents a picture of apprentice actors engaged in the foreign policy-making process. The installation of a majority government in 1994, with its attachments to different constituency groups, totally changed the composition of government and Parliament. But in other respects, various internal nongovernmental actors continue to try to influence foreign policy as they had before.

This section first examines the changing roles of the governmental actors in South Africa—specifically, the legislature and the executive branch—and then describes the nongovernmental actors, including the business community, think tanks, and organized pressure groups.

Parliament

Within Parliament, profound elements of change and intriguing elements of continuity are at play. To begin with, the actors are new. Seventy-five percent of the members of Parliament during Mandela's tenure and 82 percent of the current Parliament come from parties that represent voters who were without standing in the previous order. The African National Congress, which alone holds 266 seats in the current 400-seat Parliament, was a banned, unlawful party when the National Party ruled. Conversely, only 17.7 percent of the current seats are held by minority white parties. Although it is problematic whether Parliament has a vigorous and unified voice in foreign policy making, the fact is that the governments that these overwhelming majorities support constitute a revolutionary sea change in the locus of power in Pretoria.

Before 1994 Parliament was conspicuously passive about foreign affairs. Decision making was concentrated in the hands of the cabinet and top bureaucrats in the Department of Foreign Affairs. If it did voice opinions about foreign issues, Parliament did so in the annual budgetary debates on foreign affairs and defense, in response to the ministers' speeches, or in isolated written or oral questions posed to the ministers. Foreign policy also was a subject in the censure debate at the beginning of each new session of Parliament and in the prime minister's vote debate.[14] The result was a compliant body, supportive of the government of the day. There were no organs of Parliament through which the legislature could contribute creatively to the process of foreign policy making. Moreover, government, maintaining that secrecy about foreign relations was imperative, imposed a culture of secrecy on all matters foreign—a step taken easily when a Parliament was securely in the ruling party's camp. Likewise, when the National Party caucus met there was little more than pronouncements from party leaders and not much discussion.[15] Even in the NP study groups on foreign affairs, defense, and national security, which met monthly when Parliament was in session, communication usually flowed from the top down. Simply put, in the apartheid years Parliament was hardly a preeminent institution through which the public expressed its views on foreign affairs—unless one might suggest that the South Africans seldom had strong views about foreign affairs.

The relationship between Parliament and the executive in the new constitutional framework is still evolving. Nevertheless, it can be argued that current members of the legislature are determined to have a voice and some oversight responsibility. This they seek to do through a system of committees that empowers legislators "to monitor, investigate, enquire and make recommendations relating to any aspect of the legislative programme."[16] Thus the Portfolio Committee on Foreign Affairs is seeking to develop expertise in its subject area, and its chair is longing for a regular structure for inputs from the legislature and some role for its members in decision making.[17] Not only are Parliamentarians on a steep learning curve, but they also are in the process of devising procedures and organs of oversight when little in the past worked. It has not been easy. Members of the executive branch continue to make decisions with little legislative input. Indeed, as one analyst has concluded: "We still do not know who makes foreign policy decisions in this country. What we do know is that it is not Parliament."[18]

The Executive Branch

From the perspective of the executive, structurally little has changed.[19] The responsibility for policy making and implementation emphasis still rests with the president, deputy president, ministers of foreign affairs, defense, finance, trade and industry, and the deputy ministers, departmental directors general, and personnel from a few "overseas" missions. Many but not all the individuals once in government jobs have been replaced (although in the Department of Foreign Affairs even these changes have been gradual), but continuity in many respects has been maintained.[20] Eventually, however, serious discontinuities will be manifested as the democratic ideal gains currency among members of Parliament and interest groups begin to reflect a broader spectrum of the populace.

In its passage from global rejection to enthusiastic acceptance, South Africa needs time to reshape its organs of foreign policy. To be sure, organizationally African regional and multilateral relations have been upgraded. But Europe and North America still play central roles in the activities of the Department of Foreign Affairs. Although the budget for the 2000–2001 financial year allocates R187.2 million for bilateral relations in Africa and R202 million for Asia and the Middle East, R492.7 million have been earmarked for the Americas and Europe.[21]

In the late 1980s the department began to recruit personnel from outside the white community. During the transition period, awkward efforts were made to absorb at least five "foreign services" into the South African foreign service — those of the black homelands of Transkei, Bophuthatswana, Venda, and Ciskei (all of which were terminated in 1994) and the ANC's "diplomatic corps" in exile. Today, South Africa maintains ninety-one diplomatic missions — twenty-five in Africa, twenty-one in Asia and the Middle East, twenty-six in Europe, fifteen in the Americas, and four multilateral embassies.[22] But at the very top (at the level of director general, deputy directors general, and chief directors), the Department of Foreign Affairs inherited either whites from the previous regime or blacks formerly associated with the South Africa-trained but woefully inexperienced foreign services of the ex-homelands. At first, few former ANC officials were co-opted for the chief director level. Those who head missions abroad, however, have been drawn from ANC loyalists. In 2000, the government announced a transformation plan for changing the race and gender profiles of various management levels and missions. To aid the transformation process, the Foreign Service Institute is attempting to train new recruits and to retrain experienced diplomats. Because the number of South African missions abroad has almost doubled, this opening up of the foreign service could occur without too much displacement of existing officers. The foreign affairs budget, however, has not kept pace with these developments, leading to criticism of the allocation of funds, especially the fact that missions in North America and Europe continue to receive disproportionate funding. The newer priorities tend to receive funds after additional resources are made available.

Criticism of the pace of change continues. For one thing, the first "new" foreign minister, Alfred Nzo, was less than dynamic. As a result, the department he headed did not provide the sort of leadership many had hoped for. Others complain that there has been a "lack of foreign policy"—that is, a lack of carefully crafted goals and strategies to guide workers in the field. The culture of democracy with its preoccupation with consultation and "mandates" is not an easy environment in which to make foreign policy. In the first few years of the GNU, what passed for foreign policy was a general era of good feeling for South Africa abroad. President Mandela and Deputy President Mbeki traveled widely to raise investment capital and show the flag. Foreign policy was ad hoc, reactive, and the foreign minister and his department kept a low profile. Secrecy, nonresponsiveness to public opinion, and insensitivity were no longer acceptable behaviors. Yet the Department of Foreign Affairs seemed reticent to encourage a more open and dynamic foreign policy or to coordinate its activities with defense, with other departments secondarily associated with foreign affairs, and with nongovernmental and other foreign policy actors. South Africa's foreign policy tended to be identified with President Mandela and his global ramblings and pronouncements rather than with a structured scheme emanating from the ministry or the department.

Nongovernmental Actors

As pointed out in Chapter 1, economic interest groups can be an important source of foreign policy. South Africa is no exception. Outside of government, a variety of associate actors seek a role in specific foreign policy questions. Central are the major corporations, keen to structure the investment atmosphere, relations with the industrial West and its collaborative economic institutions, trade policies, and the overall framework for growth and development. Given the continued concentration of wealth in South Africa, it would be unfathomable if these voices were stilled. They think of themselves as good corporate citizens and believe that, because South Africa's economy would flounder without their cooperation, they are entitled to open doors and sympathetic ears. Thus numerous trade organizations, the South African Chamber of Business, the Afrikaans Handelinstituut, the Chambers of Commerce and Industry, exporters' organizations, banks, economic development organizations, and individual corporations are actively involved in trying to influence thinking in Pretoria's Union Buildings. In addition, independent think tanks, often financed by the corporate community, have relatively close relations with decision makers in government. The South African Institute of International Affairs, various university departments and research centers, the South African Foundation, and the Institute for Defence Policy are among the many voices that chime in at policy-making time. Because the government would like to approach policy making in inclusive, interactive ways, the openness of the process contributes to its fuzzy reputation.

But it is a marked improvement over the patterns of decision making in the minority government years.

Contemporary South African Foreign Policy

In May 1994 South Africa launched a new era of foreign policy, one in which it was no longer necessary to rationalize and justify the internal political order to the outside world. From the start, South Africa became in some respects the poster child for democratic government in Africa. President Nelson Mandela and his Government of National Unity were held up as models for other regimes in Africa to emulate. Many governments in the West and in Africa called on South Africa to play an active leadership role in African affairs, especially in conflict resolution, economic development, race relations, and cultural tolerance.

Understandably, South Africa still has a full and costly domestic agenda. The twin problems of excessive crime and widespread unemployment mean that scarce resources need to be dedicated to generating economic growth and redistribution (many social services are not available to the masses). Such nettlesome problems are tied in with the issue of reconciliation. How does the government hope to reassure the economically powerful white population and yet be true to its promises of upgrading the lives of South Africa's most disadvantaged citizens? And as the GNU focuses on economic growth, despite of and because of its rhetorical commitment to its African brothers, the foreign policy agenda gravitates toward those countries that are in a position to invest in, trade with, and make economic assistance available to South Africa. To many, foreign policy seems tilted toward the industrial West to the detriment of the region and the African continent.[23] This bias does not sit well with those on the left of the ANC, the SACP, and the trade unions. Militants see such policies as little more than a continuation of the proclivities of the National Party government that they fought to eliminate.[24] However transformed the new South Africa may be, it does not begin with a clean slate. The past constrains what the new state can do.[25]

To grapple with the long-standing, pent-up, largely economic and social demands of the overwhelming majority of its citizenry, the government must concentrate principally on domestic affairs. As government officials see it, their first order of business is to strengthen the economy in order to draw in the previously disadvantaged sectors of the populace and thereby enable them to participate fully in the South African transformation. Without a vibrant economy, the regime cannot create employment or generate the revenue needed to pay for the expanded social services demanded by the majority. By creating new jobs and bringing new revenue into government coffers, the regime aims to stabilize the polity as a participatory democracy. Although the government would not admit it publicly, to retain popular support it must be committed to "South Africa first" —that is, to delivering the material goods and services formerly allocated on racial grounds. In this sense, foreign policy is a product of amorphous domestic pressures. and the ultimate payoff of foreign policy is expected to be at home.

This section, rather than survey all South African foreign policy issues, highlights a few and seeks to understand how they were decided and what basic motives prevailed. It examines South Africa's policies toward relations with the European Union and the Nigerian military regime, the development of bilateral relations with two so-called "problematic" actors, and the dilemma over which China to recognize.

Trade and Investment

Early on, Deputy Foreign Minister Aziz Pahad put it succinctly, "Our European policy is essentially an outward projection of South Africa's domestic imperatives—economic and social."[26] South Africa's priorities are increasingly seen as "investment, investment, investment; trade, trade, trade," to quote South Africa's ambassador to Germany.[27] With entities worldwide trying to gain customers and investment, South Africa must scramble to compete. So, in 2000, President Mbeki established the International Investor Council to elicit the views of distinguished international business leaders on how to meet the challenges of development and globalization.

With this perspective, Pretoria seeks to strengthen its ties with the West and with those Asian-Pacific states in a position to facilitate South Africa's economic transformation. Although it wishes eventually to assume its leadership role among countries of the South, South Africa knows that the costs in time, energy, and treasure to be such a leader would slow down its own economic growth, development, and domestic stability. At this point, South Africa does not want to gauge every trading partner, every potential investor against some absolute standard of human rights and democracy. In other words, South Africa cannot afford to be choosy in the world of finance and trade. Besides, open efforts to befriend all comers reflect a domestic regime committed to reconciliation and one determined to rev up the economy so that domestic interests can find reasons to support foreign policy. The business community certainly identifies with this orientation. But local populist forces—the unions, the churches, students, and those on the left of the ANC—need to be convinced that there will be spillover to benefit the disadvantaged populace.

In fact, South Africa's recent history leaned toward an active government role in the economy. Apartheid was defended by mercantilist trade policies, rigid foreign exchange controls, and substantial state-owned and -managed sectors of the economy, including steel, armaments, petroleum, electricity, post and telecommunications, and transportation. Similarly, the ANC, with its strong Marxist tradition, had been inclined toward nationalization of certain industries and heavy government regulation of private businesses. Trade liberalization is the opposite of mercantilism. The extent to which leaders of the new South Africa have rapidly embraced free trade and a policy structure attractive to investment from abroad has surprised long-term observers.

As part of that shift, the Mandela government entered into negotiations with the European Union in 1996 to arrive at a free trade arrangement between the two parties. Europe is South Africa's biggest trading partner; imports from the Continent make up more than 47 percent of total imports, and exports to Europe make up nearly one-third of total exports. Negotiations between South Africa and the EU should not be seen in isolation. External factors, such as World Trade Organization liberalization, EU expansion and reform of its agricultural policy, and the free trade agenda of various southern African organizations, especially SACU, complicated the talks. What South Africa does toward Europe clearly will have an impact on its regional role.

The Trade, Development, and Cooperation Agreement (TDCA), which came into force on January 1, 2000, between the fifteen member states of the EU and South Africa, is a detailed, complicated, two-hundred-page agreement covering ten thousand individual products, time scales for phasing in changes (over a twelve-year period), and linkages across sectors. Essentially, a free trade regime has been achieved. It provides that 86 percent of EU exports to South Africa shall be exonerated from customs duties for twelve years and that 95 percent of South African exports to the EU shall be duty-free for ten years.[28] The concessions offered by South Africa indicate Pretoria's determination to conclude such an agreement in order to normalize relations with the industrial world. Could a better deal have been reached? Perhaps. But South Africa's negotiating team was inexperienced, government departments were divided, and business involvement in the process was spotty. Yet some sort of deal was necessary in view of the government's approach to economic development and political economic change.

Human Rights and the Moral Imperatives

South Africa's leadership is torn by the imperatives of morality, state building, and economic management. That, coupled with the reality that moral decisions are seldom simple and clear, poses problems for Pretoria.

The Nigerian Military Government. In several early challenges, South Africa's policy produced a less-than-satisfactory result. For example, when President Nelson Mandela sought to damp down the Nigeria crisis in November 1995, he emerged with his reputation sullied.[29] The Nigerian military had seized power in 1993 and nullified the June 1993 presidential elections, detained the winner, and interred dozens of journalists and critics. It also had sentenced prominent figures to prison and arrested and put to death nine ethnic Ogoni activists, including the writer Ken Saro-Wiwa. In doing so, the military was prepared to defy the Commonwealth of Nations and the world community. At first by quiet diplomacy, Mandela, Deputy President Mbeki, and Bishop Tutu tried to persuade the Nigerian government to be less despotic and not to execute the high-profile

Saro-Wiwa. Meanwhile, South Africa was being buffeted by conflicting moral demands: to defend human rights, to provide leadership in African diplomacy, to stand by states that stood by the ANC in the antiapartheid struggle, and to be critical of major multinational corporations (for example, Shell Oil, against which the Ogoni Nine had been protesting). Mandela preferred to go slow toward Nigeria in the face of the divisions in the ANC and other criticism. Indeed, the man of principle at first seemed reluctant to back up his principles with threats. Instead he chose verbal persuasion.

But South Africa's intercession failed. In a pique of personal hurt, Mandela, who had taken the lead on the policy of "constructive engagement," then reversed his policy on Nigeria and pushed for sanctions against the regime he now labeled "an illegitimate, barbaric, arrogant military dictatorship." South Africa cosponsored (with the United States) a resolution in the UN General Assembly condemning the hanging of the Ogoni Nine and Nigeria's persistent violations of human rights. Pretoria also supported Nigeria's suspension from the Commonwealth for two years and sought to lobby other African states in support of sanctions. But Mandela was not successful. By April 1996 most of Nigeria's critics, including South Africa, had retreated to nearly normal relations with that crisis-ridden country. South Africa's first major experience with a putatively moralistic foreign policy had ended in frustration and embarrassment.

U.S. Reactions to Pretoria's Relations with "Problematic" States. Despite South Africa's commitment to growing economic ties with the West, it is not prepared to relinquish parts of its independence just to please states with significant economic clout. This stand was made clear when South Africa sought to expand its relations with states hostile to the United States and Great Britain. The new majority government is determined to reach beyond the established actors with which the previous government dealt—that is, to those states that supported the ANC during the struggle for majority rule and, among them, Cuba, Libya, and Iran.

As a sovereign state, South Africa is free to maintain relations with any state. Officially, however, South Africa seeks bilateral relations that are developed within the framework of UN resolutions and other international initiatives. Maintaining relations is not necessarily equated with approving a state's domestic or foreign policies. In adhering to these principles, President Mandela and those on the left of the ANC were determined to open relations with governments that had supported the ANC's struggle. But as straightforward as this may seem, it is not so simple in practice.

Certain elements in the United States are inclined to view any relations with Cuba as a threat to U.S. interests. Members of Congress in particular have pressured Pretoria to shun relations with Cuba. Contact is, in their eyes, a violation of the U.S. embargo on Cuba, in place since 1962. Elements opposed to Cuban leader Fidel Castro regard South Africa's involvement with Cuba chiefly in symbolic terms, a direct affront to their position. Pretoria, however, does not see it as affront to Washington; after all, trade between Cuba and South Africa is minimal, and closer ties are a symbolic change in policy from the previous government, as well as a gesture of solidarity with the South.

Cuba–South Africa relations came to the fore in early 1996 when President Mandela announced that President Fidel Castro had been invited to South Africa. In the 1970s and 1980s Cuba had assisted Angola and the ANC in fighting the apartheid military forces through its some fifty thousand troops in Angola. Because of these close supportive ties, Cuba was invited to open an embassy in Pretoria in May 1994, and it concluded several agreements with South Africa.[30] Despite a harsh letter in July 1995 from four influential members of the House of Representatives to the South African ambassador to Washington, the issue seems to have blown over. Bilateral relations between South Africa and Cuba and between South Africa and the United States are friendly, and no particular tensions exist over the issue in South African politics. Washington tried to push, South Africa would not budge, and relations eventually were smoothed.

Clearly, then, South Africa is determined to be its own boss and to resist any pressure from richer or more powerful states. It is the sort of behavior that characterized postcolonial states three decades ago. Sometimes it leads to foolish or forced policies, but they are at least South Africa's policies. As the apartheid era passes into history, debts to governments that supported the ANC will fade as those governments fade. Insofar as such policies are more than symbolic and they are driven by the country's interests, other countries seem content to accept South Africa as it pursues such policies, with a minimum of criticism. The United States, for example, is not about to jeopardize its good relations with Pretoria over such "side" issues. And when Washington gets too pushy, South Africa asserts its independence. On one occasion, President Mandela admonished the United States to stop interfering in regional conflicts and to stop regarding itself as the gendarme of the world. South Africa prefers diplomacy to pressure, and local solutions to global ones. For its determination to be independent, the government has earned praise domestically, even from elements that do not usually agree with it. In this regard, such relatively unimportant policy stances are parlayed into powerful nationalistic messages, and the ANC gains popularity among those — the young, the economically destitute, and the militant — who often criticize government. The ANC wants to distance itself from its predecessors, especially because it is often accused of devoting the lion's share of its energies to cultivating ties with the industrial West.

The Two Chinas. Moral ambiguity marked the issue of which China to recognize.[31] The "two Chinas dilemma" was the first substantive foreign policy issue to face democratic South Africa that was not posed in response to breaking issues elsewhere — that is, the decision was made, presumably rationally, without the need to rush. As such, on view were the full play of interests and the political pressures and reasoning that preceded South Africa's decision to switch recognition from the Republic of China (Taiwan) to the People's Republic of China (PRC). Coming into play were the practical economic advantages attending both Chinese claimants, as well as historical, political, and ideological factors. The debate over recognition was heated and revolved around the impact of four factors in shaping policy: human rights, trade and investment, obligations to traditional allies, and the relative importance of financial support for political parties.

Before the 1994 elections both Chinas had dabbled in South African affairs. During the apartheid years, Taiwan and Pretoria had developed close ties as two so-called pariah states. Trade relations were extensive, and Taiwanese businesses invested heavily in South African industry, especially in the nominally independent sham states called *bantustans* or homelands that Pretoria had created out of rural wastelands and that the rest of the world refused to recognize. Diplomatic, military, and cultural links were encouraged. Meanwhile, important trade relations between South Africa and the PRC also were put in place, often secretly through the medium of Hong Kong. In addition, secret contracts tied South Africa's state-run armaments industry to Beijing. As for relations with South Africa's liberation movements, at first the PRC felt alienated from the ANC. The Soviet Union supported the SACP, which was allied with the ANC. Thus as a reflection of Sino-Soviet competition, China chose to support the Pan-Africanist Congress (PAC), a weak and corrupt organization. But the PAC faltered, and by the mid-1980s nominal ANC-SACP-PRC ties of solidarity were established.

With Mandela's release from prison and the legalization of the antiapartheid movements, observers widely expected that a postapartheid government would switch recognition from Taiwan to the PRC. On a 1993 trip to Taiwan, Mandela even hinted as much, but it was not to be so easy. The debate lasted two years in the press, in the foreign policy-making establishment, in the business and academic communities, and among formerly muted or powerless interest groups.

In a nutshell, those who favored continued recognition of Taiwan stressed China's human rights record and Taiwan's movement toward democracy. After all, South Africa had only recently launched the democratization process itself, and, given Mandela's moral stature, South Africa should seize the high ground. Less prominent in the argument for recognition of Taiwan was the fact that sources in the Taiwanese ruling party had reportedly anted up $5 million to support the ANC's 1994 election campaign.

Those who favored switching recognition to the PRC took the realist position. China has over a billion people, a quarter of the earth's population, and is a tempting market. It is a powerful and growing military and economic force, and it is a permanent member of the UN Security Council as well as a leader of the bloc of less-developed countries. South Africa's desire to reform the United Nations and gain a seat itself on the Security Council means that assistance from the PRC is imperative. Moreover, the PRC supported the liberation struggle while Taiwan initially stood by apartheid Pretoria.

For the ANC government, this decision was not an easy one. It had come to power with its own mandate to incorporate human rights into foreign policy, and Taiwan looked better at this than the PRC. And the decision had to be made during the transformation process when paralysis, not definitude, stalked the halls of government.

Meanwhile, for the first time interest groups participated publicly in the foreign policy process. Those who identified with the ANC were unsure of their roles. Should they continue to support the party or move into a more critical mode? Many of these organizations began to debate their own identities. Some chose to function as components of a civil society and to focus their efforts on the narrow concerns of their group. Others were divided—the business community and labor, for example. Both Taiwan and the PRC sought to influence members of Parliament, the media, and the academic and research communities. Even within the executive branch, divisions arose. The Department of Trade and Industry, responsible for trade promotion, threatened to outflank the Department of Foreign Affairs, which was divided.

From May 1994 to the announcement in November 1996 that the government planned to switch recognition to the PRC was a disputatious time. Statements showed the indecision. Even the foreign minister at one point said he saw no reason to switch recognition. Midway through the debate the South African government tested the possibility of "dual recognition." The pro-Taiwan faction urged Mandela to pursue concurrent diplomatic representation of both the PRC and Taiwan. Taipei was supportive, but Beijing would have none of it. In the end, Mandela overruled the wavering establishment. The PRC was pressing for a decision; Hong Kong was about to be returned to China. Business pressures were coalescing in favor of the PRC. If South Africa was going to assume its presumed leadership position in Africa, it would have to resolve this question in keeping with the overwhelming majority of African and world states.

When it came, the decision to recognize the PRC was made without the knowledge of either the foreign minister or the foreign policy bureaucracy. On November 26, 1996, Mandela announced that retaining diplomatic relations with Taiwan was inconsistent with South Africa's activist role in international organizations. South Africa would recognize China as of December 1997. Thus the realist position prevailed. And the decision making took place at the very top, the president's office.

In all of these decisions was the hand of Nelson Mandela. It speaks to his loyalty to those who stood by his people, to his effort to demonstrate that South Africa is a different sort of country, and to his willingness to pay for and risk the reproaches of the Great Powers in order to make a statement of principle. That such posturing had little to do with the overall needs and thrusts of South African foreign policy, that in these instances symbolism seemed to be a substitute for substance, troubled him little. In these controversial decisions, he and South Africa had it both ways—a low-cost, low-risk gesture toward solidarity in a practical context.

Conclusion

To outsiders, South Africa sometimes appears to base its foreign policy on the moral values that were articulated during the struggle for majority rule. To progressives and revolutionaries alike, apartheid South Africa was propped up by a world system based on realpolitik. On coming to power, the ANC spoke of serving as a revolutionary force, not only domestically but also in terms of regional and world affairs. Yet at the same time it was practical enough to realize that foreign policy must be predicated on the national interest, itself a product of the internal political contest. To base policy on the ideals of the revolution, it is first necessary to strengthen South Africa regionally and to seek to transform South Africa into an economically strong and politically stable state.

The result is that the new South Africa lacks a clear conception of itself and, as a result, displays something of a dual personality. While mouthing both its intention to lead the African Renaissance (yet struggling to avoid accusations that it is throwing its weight around on the continent) and its willingness to be the standard-bearer for the South and for the nonaligned movement, South Africa also recognizes the need to strengthen its links with the states central to its economic recovery.

A foreign policy that evinces a split personality is not unusual. In the past, other innovative and revolutionary regimes behaved in similar ways. On gaining statehood, the United States sought to reshape the world system in favor of republicanism. Likewise, the Soviet Union held out for a revolutionary classless approach to foreign policy and diplomacy. In time, though, reality set in, and each found that it was a territorial state forced to operate in a world of territorial states. South Africa's foreign policy displays many of the characteristics of newly independent or revolutionary states. It seems to be searching for a role for itself even as it displays the convictions of a state on a mission. But it is being forced to learn the limits of statecraft and to appreciate that no matter how focused it may be, the day-to-day demands of its citizens and its particular constituencies obligate it to behave in the interests of those who matter, the political heavyweights in the South African polity. Moreover, revolutionary enthusiasm has a way of dissipating over time, especially when it seems to go unrewarded. Those with power eventually find a way of asserting themselves. If this is so, and if South Africa is not able to take off economically, it may be in for an extended period of civil unrest. With the pandemic of HIV-AIDS threatening the subcontinent, South Africa's economic future looks less promising.

In the foreign policy arena, there is a wide gap between foreign policy rhetoric and reality, and reality is beginning to win out. Economic realities in particular leave Pretoria with fewer foreign policy options. Calls to promote human rights, to lead the region without being heavy-handed, and to force the West to share its largesse with Africa grow less convincing, even as they are more frequent. As a model for the African Renaissance, as the continent's conscience, South Africa at first was able to demand attention. But time may tarnish that model, for South Africa's haves of all races seek security, not revolution, and their preoccupation with domestic affairs has led them to try to manipulate foreign policy for their immediate gain.

Since the downfall of apartheid, South Africa has benefited from great leadership. Nelson Mandela's strength was in domestic politics, less so in the realm of foreign affairs, except as a symbol of integrity and virtue. He may have stepped down, but his legacy lives on. The current president, Thabo Mbeki, served his apprenticeship under Mandela and learned his lessons well. Moreover, Mandela himself continues to field requests from South Africa and other African states to engage in diplomacy, mediate disputes, and lead by example. In some ways, he is being asked to use his prestige to shame his colleagues into righteous behavior. But charisma is a rare commodity. Other leaders operate in more pedestrian ways; more dependent on political support and pressure, they are less free to fly on their own. Not that Mandela was divorced from political realities — he never was. But his own stature did more to shape those realities than will his successors'.

The new South Africa lives with ambiguity. Its foreign policy making is characterized by thematic ambiguity. It wants to stress human rights and democracy and the African Renaissance, but it finds itself drawn to address the immediate demands of the economy, trade, investment, assistance, growth, and jobs. These demands lead in turn to an ambiguity about its geographical focus. Does it emphasize its leadership role in Africa? Or does it tend to its immediate surroundings, the southern African region? Even in that context, there is a danger of being too assertive, too nationalistic, as issues of trade, immigration, health, crime, and so forth loom larger each year. Meanwhile, South Africa's leaders appreciate the fact that without massive capital injections from beyond Africa, South Africa's future is suspect. The West, therefore, must be attended to. South Africa has a sophisticated and diverse economy, capable of considerable productivity and sensitive to disruption. It is a quasi-Western state situated in Africa and populated largely by Africans. It is, then, both industrialized and traditional in its character and makeup. The pressures on government reflect this diversity. Who decides foreign policy is pretty well set; the executive branch at the highest levels is paramount. Parliament and the foreign policy bureaucracy so far only have a marginal influence. Input from the corporate community is strong, as are the pressures from various nongovernmental groups representing the mass of South Africans. Policy will be worked out in the play of politics. This period is, for South Africa, one of experimentation, a shakedown cruise in which the captains thus far have displayed considerable skill and courage. The long-term prospects, however, are daunting.

Suggestions for Further Reading

Barber, James, and John Barratt. *South Africa's Foreign Policy: The Search for Status and Security, 1945–1988*. Cambridge: Cambridge University Press, 1990.

Carlsnaes, Walter, and Marie Muller, eds. *Change and South African External Relations*. Johannesburg: International Thomson Publishing, 1997.

Grundy, Kenneth W. *South Africa: Domestic Crisis and Global Challenge*. Boulder: Westview Press, 1991.

Mills, Greg, ed. *From Pariah to Participant: South Africa's Evolving Foreign Relations, 1990–1994.* Johannesburg: South African Institute of International Affairs, 1994.

Mills, Greg. *The Wired Model: South Africa, Foreign Policy and Globalization.* Cape Town: Tafelberg, 2000.

South African Journal of International Affairs, South African Institute of International Affairs, Johannesburg.

South African Yearbook of International Affairs, an annual survey and edited collection by the South African Institute of International Affairs, Johannesburg.

Swatuk, Larry A., and David R. Black, eds. *Bridging the Rift: The New South Africa in Africa.* Boulder: Westview Press, 1997.

Toase, Francis H., and Edmund J. Yorke, eds. *The New South Africa: Prospects for Domestic and International Security.* New York: St. Martin's Press, 1998.

Notes

1. A detailed narrative can be found in James Barber and John Barratt, *South Africa's Foreign Policy: The Search for Status and Security, 1945–1988* (Cambridge: Cambridge University Press, 1990). For my analysis and interpretation, see: Kenneth W. Grundy, *South Africa: Domestic Crisis and Global Challenge* (Boulder: Westview Press, 1991).

2. P. W. Botha served as prime minister from 1978 to 1983 and state president from 1984 to 1989, when he suffered a stroke. In February 1989, he resigned as leader of the National Party, and in August he was replaced as president by F. W. de Klerk, who then was elected for a five-year term in September. In a dramatic speech to Parliament on February 2, 1990, de Klerk announced the unbanning (legalization) of the ANC, the South African Communist Party, and the Pan-Africanist Congress; the lifting of restrictions on thirty-three antiapartheid organizations; and the release of political prisoners. One week later, Nelson Mandela was unconditionally released from prison after twenty-seven years of incarceration. He soon was named deputy president of the ANC, making him effectively its leader. Its president, Oliver Tambo, had been partially disabled by a stroke in 1989.

3. See Stephen Ellis and Tsepo Sechaba, *Comrades against Apartheid: The ANC and the South African Communist Party in Exile* (Bloomington: Indiana University Press, 1992).

4. See Kenneth W. Grundy, "Intermediary Power and Global Dependency: The Case of South Africa," *International Studies Quarterly* 20 (December 1976): 553–580.

5. Deon Geldenhuys, *The Diplomacy of Isolation: South Africa's Foreign Policy Making* (Johannesburg: Macmillan, 1984), 247–249.

6. For a historical review of the struggle for majority rule, an overview of this process, and an analysis of the contemporary political scene, see Kenneth W. Grundy, "South Africa: Transition to Majority Rule, Transformation to Stable Democracy," in *The Uncertain Promise of Southern Africa,* ed. York Bradshaw and Stephen N. Ndegwa (Bloomington: Indiana University Press, 2000), 27–66. Foreign policy is covered in *From Pariah to Participant: South Africa's Evolving Foreign Relations, 1990–1994,* ed. Greg Mills (Johannesburg: South African Institute of International Affairs, 1994).

7. Data supplied by the Central Statistical Office, 1999. Also see *European Yearbook, 2000* (London: Europa Publications, 2000), 3306.

8. Patrick J. McGowan, "The 'New' South Africa: Ascent or Descent?" *South African Journal of International Affairs,* vol. 1, no. 1 (1993): 35–61.

9. Robert Davies, "Promoting Regional Integration in Southern Africa: An Analysis of Prospects and Problems from a South African Perspective," in *Bridging the Rift: The*

New South Africa in Africa, ed. Larry A. Swatuk and David R. Black (Boulder: West-view Press, 1997), 116.

10. Ibid., 111–112.
11. Quoted in Swatuk and Black, *Bridging the Rift,* 231.
12. "Developing a Strategic Perspective on South African Foreign Policy: ANC Discussion Document Released in July 1997 Prior to Their Annual Conference at Year End," *South African Journal of International Affairs* 5 (summer 1997): 170–184; see especially p. 180.
13. Kenneth W. Grundy, *Confrontation and Accommodation in Southern Africa: The Limits of Independence* (Berkeley: University of California Press, 1972), chap. 7.
14. In a parliamentary system based on the British model, the leader of the opposition introduces a motion of censure as the first order of business in each legislative year. If the motion carries, which seldom happens, the prime minister is expected to call a new election and then resign. The debate on censure usually ranges widely over broad policy issues, including foreign affairs. Likewise, a prime minister's "vote" refers to the budget for his or her office. Though relatively small, the issue is seen as a chance to debate the government's policy directions.
15. Geldenhuys, *Diplomacy of Isolation,* chap. 3.
16. "Rule 52," *Revised Standing Rules for the National Assembly and for Joint Business and Proceedings of the National Assembly and the Senate,* February 1995.
17. Raymond Suttner, "Parliament and Foreign Policy," in *South African Yearbook of International Affairs, 1996* (Johannesburg: South African Institute of International Affairs, 1996), 142.
18. Jo-Ansie van Wyk, "Parliament and Foreign Affairs: Continuity or Change?" *South African Yearbook of International Affairs, 1997* (Johannesburg: South African Institute of International Affairs, 1998), 197.
19. Even though the ministries are periodically reorganized. See Marie Muller, "The Institutional Dimension: The Department of Foreign Affairs and Overseas Missions," in *Change and South African External Relations,* ed. Walter Carlsnaes and Marie Muller (Johannesburg: International Thomson Publishing, 1997), 51–72.
20. As part of the compromise agreements leading to the 1994 election, the new regime is obligated to retain the personnel from the past until they retire.
21. African National Congress Newswire (ANC Daily News Briefing), "Foreign Ministry Gets R1,32bn Budget," February 24, 2000, online at http://www.anc.org.za/anc/newsbrief/.
22. Ibid.
23. Representative critiques can be found in Swatuk and Black, *Bridging the Rift.*
24. See Peter Vale, "Continuity Rather than Change: South Africa's 'New' Foreign Policy," *Indicator South Africa* 12 (winter 1995): 79–84.
25. Jack Spence, "The New South African Foreign Policy: Moral Incentives and Political Constraints," in *The New South Africa: Prospects for Domestic and International Security,* ed. Francis H. Toase and Edmund J. Yorke (New York: St. Martin's Press, 1998).
26. Quoted by Spence, "New South African Foreign Policy."
27. As quoted in the *Weekly Mail and Guardian,* August 4, 1995, 23. Also see Fred Ahwireng-Obeng and Patrick McGowan, "The EU-SA Free Trade Arrangements," *South African Journal of International Affairs* 6 (winter 1999): 101–112.
28. "The SA-EU TDCA: A Business Perspective," *SAIIA Intelligence Update,* March 2000.
29. See Larry Swatuk, "South African Foreign Policy toward Nigeria: No Room/Will/Time/Desire for Adventure" (Paper presented at the annual meeting of the International Studies Association, Toronto, March 18–22, 1997).

30. Adam Gordon, "Cuba and South Africa: Prospects for Partnership," *South African Journal of International Affairs* 3 (winter 1996): 149–172.
31. For background and analysis, see Chris Alden, "Solving South Africa's Chinese Puzzle: Democratic Foreign Policy Making and the 'Two China' Question," *South African Journal of International Affairs* 5 (winter 1998): 80–95.

CHAPTER 13

Brazil:

The Emergence of a Regional Power

Scott D. Tollefson

As South America's largest country, in terms of population, geography, and economy, Brazil has been an important regional actor. Brazil has been a central factor in keeping peace in the region, forming Mercosul—the world's third largest trading agreement—and, more recently, supporting democracy in the region. During much of the Cold War, Brazil maintained a relatively independent foreign policy toward the United States on issues such as oil, Cuba, and communist China. With the Cold War over and the foreign affairs–oriented Cardoso in power as president, Brazil's foreign policy has become increasingly diversified. For instance, Brazil has expanded its trading partners to include Asia and Portuguese-speaking African countries. Brazil has also become a global player on environmental issues because of the Brazilian rainforest. The country's continuing desire to be a permanent member of the Security Council is but one example of its goal to become an increasingly important global actor.

Brazil's foreign policy has been closely associated with its leaders. The president of Brazil, as in most other developing countries, has a great amount of influence on foreign policy, even after Brazil turned to democracy. Brazil's transition to democracy can be compared to the recent changes in the political systems of South Africa (Chapter 12) and Russia (Chapter 5). Dramatic changes in Brazilian foreign policy, however, were not forthcoming, partly because of the gradual nature of the political transitions and the overriding influence of the Ministry of Foreign Relations across the democratic and authoritarian systems. Brazil can also be compared to Mexico (Chapter 14) due to its geographic location in the Western Hemisphere. Unlike Mexico, however, Brazil has not been overly concerned with infringement on its sovereignty. Like Mexico and many of the other developing countries in this volume such as Nigeria (Chapter 11) and China (Chapter 6), Brazil's contemporary foreign policy focuses on economics and liberal trading policies. Similar to South Africa, Brazil has taken the lead in regional integration efforts, although Brazil's motive for this is partly to counter U.S. influence in South America.

Brazil, the largest country geographically in Latin America, with 48 percent of the South American landmass, also has the largest population in Latin America, with 173 million people. Geographically, it is the fifth-largest state in the world; only Russia, China, Canada, and the United States are larger. Brazil's economy is the largest in Latin America and the ninth largest in the world. Its continental size, its abundant resources, its demographic and economic prominence in Latin America, and the fact that it shares boundaries with every country in South America except Chile and Ecuador all play a role in shaping Brazil's foreign policy. With the rapid growth in its population and economy in the latter half of the twentieth century, Brazil began to take a more active role on the world stage, a development that has begun to gain attention.[1]

Brazil was a colony of Portugal from the time the Portuguese discovered it in 1500 to its independence in 1822. Developments during the colonial period affected Brazil's foreign policy as an independent nation. The most important development was the geographic expansion of Brazil. The Treaty of Tordesillas between Portugal and Spain in 1494 gave Portugal control over the "bulge" of Brazil—only a fraction of what is currently Brazil. During the seventeenth and eighteenth centuries, Portuguese adventurers known as *bandeirantes* (the term comes from *bandeira*, the Portuguese word for flag) expanded westward, in search of riches. In so doing, they dramatically increased Portugal's territorial claims. Those claims were recognized in the Treaty of Madrid of 1750, which rejected the Tordesillas accord in favor of the principle of *uti possidetis*, or ownership by occupation.[2]

It is significant that the territorial disputes between Spain and Portugal were settled in relatively peaceful fashion. With the exception of Argentina during its war with Brazil in the late 1820s over the Banda Oriental (now known as Uruguay), Spanish American countries have recognized Brazil's territorial claims. This has led to Brazil's image as a peaceful state in its relations with its neighbors. The Portuguese-Spanish rivalry has continued to manifest itself, especially in Brazilian-Argentine relations, but that rivalry never led to war between Brazil and Argentina after Uruguay was established as a buffer state.

After Brazil's independence, major relations were with its mother country, Portugal. In time, England, the world's leading commercial power in the nineteenth century, became the dominant foreign power in Brazil. England provided Brazil with over half of its imports in the 1800s. After the turn of the century, the United States, which had become a global imperial power in the aftermath of the Spanish-American War in 1898, became Brazil's major external partner.

In large measure, it was Brazil's rivalry with Argentina, which had become more independent in its relations with the United States, that drove Brazil to turn to the United States. This presaged a common theme of the twentieth century: the jockeying between Brazil and Argentina to have the upper hand in relations with the United States.

The most important person in the definition of Brazil's foreign policy after independence was José Maria da Silva Paranhos, the baron of Rio Branco, who was Brazil's foreign minister from 1902 to 1912. The bold leadership of the baron of Rio Branco was an important factor in establishing the three main tenets of Brazil's foreign policy: (1) the resolution of conflict through diplomatic means; (2) an ongoing rivalry with Argentina for influence in South America; and (3) a special relationship with the United States. These tenets guided Brazil's foreign policy through much of the twentieth century. Brazil did not experience war with any of its neighbors after the War of the Triple Alliance (also known as the Paraguayan War; 1865–1870). The rivalry with Argentina remained strong until the 1980s, at which point it gave way to efforts at economic integration between the two countries. Although Brazil's special relationship with the United States lasted for about half a century, it was tested by the very independent foreign policy that Brazil adopted in the 1950s and accentuated in the 1960s and especially the 1970s.

Brazilian Foreign Policy during the Cold War

During the Cold War, Brazil was often viewed as a "contingent power" in the international system, meaning that Brazil's power derived from manipulating the "great power" rivalries.[3] According to the "contingent power" view, Brazil was viewed as important only to the extent that it was relevant to the East-West calculus of power.[4] Although Brazil's foreign policy was shaped to a large extent by the U.S. relationship with the Soviet Union (especially until the late 1950s), viewing Brazil as nothing more than a contingent power is a mistake because it ignores Brazil's own foreign policy interests and the internal dynamics that shaped Brazil's foreign policy.[5]

The initial phase of the Cold War virtually coincided with Brazil's 1946 Republic (1946–1964), a period in which Brazil's presidents were elected democratically. On the domestic front, Brazil experienced rapid industrialization, urbanization, and modernization, all of which placed major strains on Brazil's embryonic democracy.[6] In foreign policy, Brazil grew much closer to the United States from 1946 to 1951, under President Eurico Dutra, a former general. Brazil played a positive role in the formation of the United Nations and the Organization of American States. In 1952 Brazil was "rewarded" for its support of the Allies during World War II, when it signed a major military assistance agreement with the United States, the first of its kind in the Americas.

Brazil, however, became increasingly frustrated with the lack of U.S. interest in Latin America. U.S. attention was focused on the rebuilding of war-torn

Europe and Japan. As a result, Brazil refused to support U.S. involvement in Korea in the early 1950s. Getúlio Vargas, Brazil's independent-minded leader from 1930 to 1945, re-emerged as a democratically elected president from 1951 to 1954, and again, balanced Brazil's ties with the United States with a heavy dose of nationalism, which included the nationalization of Brazil's petroleum resources.

Brazil's president Juscelino Kubitschek (1955–1960) unveiled an independent foreign policy, which influenced an entire generation of Brazilian diplomats. The Cuban Revolution of 1959 strengthened that independent stance. In that watershed event, Fidel Castro defeated Fulgencio Batista, a dictator who had close ties to the United States. The success of the Cuban Revolution emboldened the new generation of Brazilian diplomats in their efforts to distance Brazil from U.S. influence. President Kubitschek's successor, Jânio Quadros (1961), became even more independent in his foreign policy. In a *Foreign Affairs* article, Quadros wrote that Brazil was "a new force on the world stage." In a defiant tone, he added, "Not being members of any bloc, not even the neutralist bloc, we preserve our absolute freedom to make our own decisions in specific cases and in the light of peaceful suggestions at one with our nature and history."[7] Quadros's successor, President João Goulart (1961–1964) continued with an independent foreign policy. Goulart was sympathetic to the Cuban Revolution and failed to support the United States on numerous multilateral initiatives against Cuba. Furthermore, Goulart opened trade missions with communist countries, such as China.

A military regime took power in Brazil with a coup on March 31, 1964, and remained in power for twenty-one years. Five army generals took turns as "presidents." The first was Humberto de Alencar Castelo Branco, who ruled from 1964 to 1967. He represented a moderate wing of the military that was pro–United States. One of his first actions as president was to break diplomatic relations with Cuba. In April 1965 his government played a major role in the U.S.-led intervention in the Dominican Republic. As a result, the United States reciprocated with record-level foreign aid. From 1964 to 1967, only India, Pakistan, and South Vietnam received more official aid from the United States.[8]

The governments of Eurico Dutra (1945–1951) and Castelo Branco were anomalous. They represented a pro–U.S. position that increasingly gave way to an independent posture on the part of Brazil. Castelo Branco's successor, Artur da Costa e Silva (1967–1969), represented the hard-liners within the military, who eschewed close ties with the United States and adopted a much more nationalistic tone. For instance, Brazil refused to adhere to the 1967 Treaty for the Prohibition of Nuclear Weapons in Latin America (Tlatelolco treaty), which sought to create a nuclear-free zone in Latin America. All the major countries in South America signed and ratified the treaty, with the exception of Argentina, which signed the treaty but did not ratify it until 1994. Chile and Brazil signed and ratified the treaty, but with the reservation that the treaty would not enter into force until all other eligible states (meaning Argentina) had signed it. In 1994 Argentina, Chile, and Brazil finally brought the Tlatelolco treaty "into force." Brazil also refused to sign the 1968 Nuclear Non-Proliferation Treaty, which sought to limit the spread of nuclear weapons, despite the fact that 187 countries became signatories to the treaty.

Under Costa e Silva, Brazil began to implement neomercantilist, protectionist trade policies in an attempt to boost exports and limit imports. From the time he came to power in 1967, Brazil and the United States have engaged in numerous trade disputes. Emílio Médici (1969–1974) continued in the nationalist mode, and, for example, unilaterally claimed a 200-mile territorial sea for Brazil, which departed from the U.S.-led effort to maintain a 12-mile zone. The more expansive definition of a territorial sea was significant for Brazil because of its long coastline on the Atlantic Ocean and the potential resources along that coastline. Médici also sought to develop the Amazon through the creation of a Transamazon highway. This national integration scheme was viewed ominously by Brazil's Spanish-American neighbors in the region, who feared that Brazil's growing prominence along its borders would threaten their regional interests. Under Médici, Brazil also began to take a much more assertive role in Africa. For example, Brazil supported the pro-independence movement in Angola, against the interests of Portugal and the United States and in favor of the Soviet Union.

Médici's successor, Ernesto Geisel (1974–1979), presided over the most nationalistic foreign policy of the military leaders. Geisel signed a major accord of nuclear cooperation with West Germany, in a direct challenge to the United States, which strongly opposed the accord. Brazil broke with the United States and supported the Soviet-aligned government in Angola after its independence. Brazil also began to develop a major armaments industry in an attempt to break Brazil's dependence upon the United States for military hardware. Geisel's foreign minister, Azerdo da Silveira, sought to "multilateralize" Brazil's foreign relations by pursuing ties with all regions of the world, turning increasingly to Latin America. In 1978 Brazil signed a treaty with seven countries in the Amazon region. This was Brazil's way of asserting leadership in South America. Brazil's behavior under Geisel and Azerdo da Silveira can be described as moving away from, but not against, the United States. Brazil's final military president, João Figueiredo (1979–1985), worked to preserve many of the gains of the Geisel administration, especially in the area of regional economic integration. Figueiredo was especially interested in improving relations with Argentina, providing the early foundation for the Common Market of the South (Mercosul in Portuguese; Mercosur in Spanish).

The restoration of democracy in Brazil in 1985 coincided with a major recession in Brazil. From 1985 to 1991 Brazil's foreign relations were focused primarily on trade and financial issues. President José Sarney (1985–1990) maintained proper relations with Washington, D.C., but did not make major changes in the foreign policy that had been established under military rule. Therefore, the change in regime resulted in very little immediate change in Brazil's foreign relations. In part this was a reflection of the conservative pace and nature of Brazil's transition to democracy, which was negotiated behind closed doors between the military and leaders of the opposition. Sarney was not even identified with the opposition; he had been a leader of the pro-military party within the Congress.

In summary, during the Cold War Brazil became increasingly independent in its foreign policy. Brazil sought to increase its autonomy vis-à-vis the United States. This was a natural step in Brazil's economic growth and search for export markets. It also reflected Brazil's frustration with its "junior" status in its relationship with the United States.

External Factors

The history of Brazilian foreign policy reveals a country that has struggled with its relationship to the great powers in the world—first in its colonial relationship with Portugal and more recently in its relationship with the dominant power in the hemisphere, the United States.[9] Brazil has vacillated in how close it has tied its foreign policy to U.S. interests. In the early years following World War II, Brazil signed a military agreement with the United States, and in the middle 1960s the first military governments in Brazil were supportive of U.S. policy in Latin America, particularly U.S. Cuban policy. For most of the rest of Brazil's history in the twentieth century, however, Brazil has chartered a fairly independent, although not directly confrontational, approach toward the United States. Various theoretical approaches have been used to explain Brazil's foreign policy, and many of them point to the external factors that constrain or provide opportunities for Brazil and Brazil's relationship with the United States.

Realism: Brazil as a Geopolitical Power

At first blush, realism does not seem to explain Brazilian foreign policy particularly well. According to realism, Brazil would be expected to be significantly constrained in its choices, because it is not one of the major powers in the world. Although this does seem to capture some of Brazil's foreign policies, it fails to account for the fairly independent policies, particularly in the 1950s, when Brazil refused to support U.S. involvement in Korea and when it nationalized its petroleum resources; in the 1970s, when Brazil embraced independent nuclear policies and unilaterally abrogated a military agreement with the United States; and in the 1980s, when it increased its military ties with pariah states such as Iraq and Libya. Yet Brazil's geopolitical strengths—the source of its independent foreign policies—are the types of factors that classical realist theory points to as important components in state capabilities and in their relationships with other states.

Geopolitics concerns the relationship between power and geography. For generations, Brazil's size and abundant geographical natural resources have led many to characterize Brazil as having great geopolitical power. The roots of geopolitical thinking go back at least a century to European and American theorists. Within Latin America, Brazil became the bastion of geopolitical thought, although Argentina and Chile also had a rich tradition in geopolitics.[10] In Brazil,

Gen. Golbery do Couto e Silva became one of the world's leading exponents of geopolitical thinking, and unquestionably the most important in the Americas in the latter half of the twentieth century.[11]

Geopolitical theorists point to Brazil's vast territory, population, and economic potential. According to this view, it is because of these power capabilities that Brazil has relatively more freedom in the international system to exercise its influence and follow an independent foreign policy. Furthermore, although the geographical borders that Brazil shares with many other South American countries might produce the opportunity for regional conflict, Brazil is described as "geopolitically satisfied," meaning that it does not have any claims on territory that are not recognized by the international community. In contrast, Argentina, Bolivia, and Ecuador are "geopolitically frustrated" because they have lingering territorial claims. The lack of territorial disputes has given Brazil the opportunity to adopt a relatively peaceful foreign policy within the region.

Geopolitical thought was challenged with the rise of interdependence. The OPEC oil price hike in 1973 exposed Brazil's Achilles' heel—its dependence on imported petroleum. The second oil price hike, of 1979, further eroded the notion of Brazil's geopolitical status. With the end of the military regime, and with the move toward regional integration, geopolitical thinking has lost much of its clout in explaining Brazil's foreign policy. The geopolitical focus on conflict has given way to theories that emphasize economic capability and economic relationships in an interdependent world.

Neo-Marxism: Brazil as a Dependent Power

In the late 1960s and early 1970s, dependency theory emerged as one of the most important interpretations of international relations.[12] Although many U.S., European, and even African social scientists embraced this approach, it was Brazilian sociologists such as Theotonio dos Santos and Fernando Henrique Cardoso (later elected president of Brazil in 1995) who received some of the greatest attention. Dos Santos's definition of dependency is still the most cited: "By dependency we mean a situation in which the economy of certain countries is conditioned by the development and expansion of another economy to which the former is subjected."[13]

Cardoso and Enzo Faletto (from Chile) argued against rigid notions of dependency, and pointed instead to "situations of dependency." In their classic study, *Dependency and Development in Latin America,* they wrote: "We conceive the relationship between external and internal forces as forming a complex whole whose structural links are not based on mere external forms of exploitation and coercion, but are rooted in coincidences of interests between local dominant classes and international ones, and on the other side, are challenged by local dominated groups and classes."[14]

The major contribution of Cardoso and Faletto was to link external forces with internal forces. As the introductory chapter to this book suggests, it is not always easy to determine whether a particular factor affecting foreign policy behavior is external or internal. Although Cardoso and Faletto focus initially on external factors (in this case, a capitalist system of domination), they note that internal factors, such as who rules, are shaped by externalities.

In a parallel and related development, Immanuel Wallerstein's notion of world systems posited that the emergence, from 1450 to 1640, of a single capitalist world economy, created a world division of labor, between the "core" industrial economies and the "peripheral" nonindustrial countries.[15] The world systems approach also led scholars to link external with internal factors.[16] One approach, for example, posited the interaction of three major actors in Brazil: multinational corporations, the national bourgeoisie, and the state.[17] Although most of these and related studies were written by sociologists, their theory had important implications for the study of politics, international relations, and Brazil's foreign policy.

Like realism, dependency theory expects lesser powers — the countries in the "periphery" of the world economy — to have little room for independent foreign policy initiatives. This is because they are highly dependent on other states for trade and investment and only produce goods such as raw materials that do not earn much profit. It is also because the links between internal and external actors posited by dependency theory and world systems theory operate to benefit the capitalist classes at the expense of the masses. Thus, in Brazil, the multinational corporations, the ruling class, and the government would all benefit from a Brazilian foreign policy that did not challenge the economic interests of the largest capitalist power, the United States.

This expectation, like realism, does not account for the fairly independent foreign policies that Brazil pursued, particularly the protectionist trade policies and the nationalization of oil resources. Perhaps this is because Brazil does not fit the mold of a peripheral country, even though it was Brazilian scholars who significantly developed dependency theory. Although certainly dependent on other countries for goods, Brazil, more than many in the "developing" world, enjoys a relative abundance of resources. Furthermore, any dependence that Brazil has on the world economic system has not necessarily harmed it. On the contrary, Brazil is the ninth largest economy in the world and has experienced many periods of great economic growth.[18]

By the late 1980s and early 1990s, dependency theory was no longer very influential as an explanation of foreign policies in Latin America. In many ways dependency theory is a victim of globalization and the adoption across much of the globe of neoliberal economic policies that stress the advantages of interdependence. That Cardoso was a leading dependency theorist and later, as the president of Brazil, became a champion of neoliberalism is one of the great ironies of Brazilian politics. Despite its demise, dependency theory captures an external-internal dynamic that can still be used in the analysis of a country's foreign policy.

Liberalism and Interdependence: Brazil as a Regional Power

In the post–Cold War era, the most important external factor shaping Brazil's foreign policy has been globalization. Brazil has responded to globalization by adopting a neoliberal economic policy—reducing tariffs, privatizing many state-owned enterprises, and exercising fiscal restraint. As a result, the scope of the state has been reduced and Brazil has experienced a period of macroeconomic stability, sustained growth, and relatively low inflation. Also, foreign direct investment (FDI) in Brazil's economy has increased dramatically, making Brazil the fourth highest investment destination in the world, after the United States, the United Kingdom, and the People's Republic of China. In 1999 FDI inflows reached a new record in Brazil, $31 billion; in 2000 FDI inflows nearly matched that level, at $30.6 billion.[19]

Brazil's major response to globalization has been to pursue a vigorous regional policy. A watershed event in Brazil's foreign relations occurred on March 26, 1991, when Mercosul was created to allow for the free circulation of goods, services, and factors of production among the member countries of Argentina, Brazil, Paraguay, and Uruguay. Later, Bolivia and Chile joined Mercosul as associate members. In terms of trade, Mercosul has succeeded spectacularly. The third largest trading pact in the world, it is by far the most significant trade bloc in Latin America. The share of trade between Brazil, Argentina, Paraguay, and Uruguay increased by 400 percent from 1990 to 1998.[20] Intraregional trade in the total exports of Mercosul countries increased from 8 percent to 21 percent between 1991 and 1996.[21] This led two observers to conclude that "Mercosul stands out as the first Latin American integration project to achieve a reasonable degree of success."[22]

The most important relationship within Mercosul has been that between Brazil and Argentina, the two largest members of Mercosul in terms of territory, population, and gross domestic product (GDP). In 1995 Brazil accounted for 70 percent of the GDP of Mercosul.[23] Because of Brazil's large economy, the interdependent relationship with Argentina has been asymmetrical.[24] Despite the asymmetries in the relationship, Brazil and Argentina have begun to cooperate in many arenas and have gone so far as to create a "strategic alliance" with the Rio Declaration of 1997, in which both countries agreed to a broad agenda of military cooperation.[25] The more cooperative relationship between Brazil and Argentina is consistent with liberalism's expectation of the effects of greater interdependence between countries. As economic ties grow and multiple channels connect economies and societies together, states no longer see conflict as in their interests.

Mercosul is much more than an economic venture. It has led to greater integration between the member nations in the financial, political, social, military, and even cultural arenas. Because of this broad integration, Mercosul blurs the boundaries between foreign and domestic policy. For example, in order to strengthen the trade regime (foreign policy), both Argentina and Brazil have coordinated macroeconomic policies (domestic policy).

An even more stunning example of the blurred relationship between foreign and domestic policy concerns the political system requirements in the treaty. The Mercosul agreement states that democracy is a precondition for membership in the trade pact. On several occasions Paraguay, which has faced a turbulent process of democratization since the end of the Alfredo Stroessner regime in 1989, has been threatened by a coup. On at least one occasion, Brazil and Argentina have used the "democracy clause" to support prodemocracy elements within Paraguay.

Brazil's participation in Mercosul raises important issues related to sovereignty. Although Brazil has conceded some sovereignty in its relations with Mercosul, it is far less than the level of concessions made by members of the European Union (EU). In essence, the supranational elements of Mercosul are not nearly as developed as those in the EU. This is because Mercosul, in name a common market, is in fact a customs union — a lower level of integration. In contrast, the EU is a monetary union, which is a higher level of integration than a common market. It is unlikely that Mercosul will ever approach the level of integration seen in the EU.

Internal Factors

The number of actors involved in the formulation of Brazil's foreign policy has expanded in the post–Cold War era.[26] Generally, state actors have the greatest influence, but nonstate actors are increasing their influence in the foreign policy making process.[27]

State Actors

Brazil is a modern nation with a fairly modern bureaucracy. On foreign policy issues, Brazil's executive branch generally takes the initiative. The major players within the executive branch are the president, the various ministries, and the military. At the regional level, governors wield considerable power, but most foreign policy is established in the capital, Brasília.

At the helm of the executive branch is the president. Very few limitations are placed on presidential power in foreign policy, although treaties require congressional approval. Presidents can choose, however, whether they want to be active in foreign policy, such as Cardoso, or more passive, such as Itamar Franco. Leadership matters, but the president has a major say in how much that leadership matters.

President Cardoso has played the most vigorous foreign policy role since President Vargas. In part this reflects Cardoso's preference for international affairs over domestic ones. It also reflects his considerable expertise in the international arena and his command of various languages. Another irony of the Cardoso presidency is that many of his ties to the international community were established in exile, after the military regime forced him to leave Brazil because of his leftist views and opposition to the government.

An example of Cardoso's leadership role in the formulation of foreign policy was his sudden invitation to all South American heads of state to Brasília in September 2000. The summit was unprecedented and served to underscore his leadership among Latin American heads of state. It also further asserted Brazil's growing role as regional leader.

Brazil's Ministry of Foreign Relations (often called Itamaraty, the name of its original office building in Rio de Janeiro) has been the most important Brazilian institution involved with foreign policy. It has a rich tradition, and its diplomats are widely considered the best in Latin America. The diplomats are recruited from a large pool of applicants, and approximately one in one hundred applicants is admitted to the ministry. Once selected, the young diplomats receive a vigorous education. The Ministry of Foreign Relations has given Brazil's foreign policy a remarkable consistency across many decades and various types of political systems. Numerous presidents have exercised considerable leadership in international affairs, but Itamaraty has been able to shape policy as it sees fit. Itamaraty maintains its bureaucratic control in part by placing a diplomat in every ministry. Most ministries have an external section, in which the diplomat plays a prominent role.

One of the questions that has emerged, given President Cardoso's bold leadership on foreign issues, is whether Brazil will be able to maintain such a prominent role once Cardoso is no longer president. It seems likely that Itamaraty will provide bureaucratic continuity to what has seemingly been a personal initiative. It is also probable that unless another strong leader comes along, Brazil's influence in foreign issues will diminish slightly, although the main tenets of Cardoso's policy are likely to be perpetuated.

With the adoption of the neoliberal model for economic policy, the ministries involved with economic and financial matters have increased their scope and influence. The Central Bank plays a prominent role, establishing monetary policy. Not as independent as the Federal Reserve is in the United States, the bank retains a fair amount of autonomy. The Ministry of Finance also plays an important role in shaping Brazil's economic policy. On many commercial and financial issues, the director of the Central Bank and the minister of Finance wield greater power on the international scene than the minister of Foreign Relations. Other ministries, such as the Ministry of Science and Technology, play a role on issues within their arena. For example, the ministry has been involved in negotiations with other countries to purchase surveillance technology for the Amazon region. Generally, however, ministries acquiesce to the leadership of Itamaraty.

Brazil's military has played a remarkably modest role in the formulation of foreign policy. Even when the military was in power, from 1964 to 1985, it allowed the civilians within Itamaraty to take the lead in formulating foreign policy. Military presidents, such as Geisel, could provide for major shifts in policy, such as in Brazil's nuclear contracts with West Germany. Still, much of that policy was filtered through the bureaucracy (in this case, Itamaraty). Under President Figueiredo, the military was eager to expand the export of arms to other countries. While Figueiredo may have provided the broad outlines of that policy, it was a young diplomat by the name of Paulo Tarso Flecha de Lima who articulated that policy and coordinated it with industry and the military. As a result, there were virtually no incidents in which civilians within Itamaraty were at complete odds with the military government. This ability to adapt to domestic regime change has kept Itamaraty in the driver's seat of foreign policy.

Since 1985 the military's prerogatives have declined in almost all areas. The military voices its opinion on issues related to security: military exchanges, drug trafficking in border areas, nuclear accords, and so forth. But even in these areas, they accept the leadership of Itamaraty. Consistent with theories on interdependence, the growing complexity in Brazil's relations with its neighbors has lowered the relative importance of security issues. As a result, the military has played a diminishing role in the formulation of foreign policy and has not contested that role.

One issue that blurs the distinction between foreign and domestic policy is the Amazon. Some elements within the military have taken a fairly strident view, accusing international actors, both state (especially the United States) and nonstate (especially environmental groups), of having designs on the Amazon. The army in particular has sought to develop portions of the Amazon, creating a series of outposts along its Amazon borders, in a program dubbed Calha Norte. The military is also concerned about drug trafficking in the Amazon area and the perceived militarization of the Colombian conflict by the United States. Finally, the military is concerned about large areas of land that the Brazilian government has ceded to indigenous groups. These various "Amazon" issues overlap and involve many state and nonstate actors, both within and outside of Brazil. The military may have opinions, but the final policies are generally filtered through Itamaraty and the president.

Brazil's Congress is playing a growing role in foreign policy but seems unwilling to expand its influence dramatically. In large measure, this is because elections are rarely won or lost on issues related to foreign policy. Legislators, therefore, focus their energy on domestic issues, which are of greater interest to the electorate.

Nonstate Actors

The neoliberal economic model adopted by Brazil has led to an expansion of nonstate actors in the formulation of Brazil's foreign relations. They include quasi-state actors, such as political parties, and a range of nonstate actors.

Brazil's political parties do not place a great emphasis on foreign policy. The major exception is the Workers' Party (Partido dos Trabalhadores, or PT), whose platform is very nationalistic. The PT is wary of U.S. influence in Brazil and opposes the neoliberal model adopted by the Cardoso government. The Brazilian Social Democratic Party (Partido da Social Democracia Brasileiro, or PSDB) has major ties to other Social Democratic parties in Latin America and Europe, but those ties do little to shape Brazil's foreign policy orientation.

Brazil's electorate, as Chapter 1 suggests is the case for many countries, has little control over the final policy formulated in the foreign arena, but it can shape the broad parameters of that policy. For example, the Brazilian electorate has denied the PT the presidency on every occasion since the transition to democracy, which suggests that the voters do not accept the more nationalistic platform of the PT. That could change, but probably not before the PT moves toward the center. In many ways, the PSDB under Cardoso has appropriated much of that center in the political spectrum, and the electorate seems reasonably satisfied with the resulting policies.

The private sector has some impact on the shaping of Brazil's foreign policy, but the great number of competing interests in that sector makes it difficult to generalize. For example, Brazil's business, commercial, and industrial elites place some pressure on the foreign policy decision-making system, but their influence tends to be sectoral and focused on specific legislation. Industrialists have a powerful federation (the Federação das Indústrias do Estado de São Paulo, or FIESP), but industries differ among themselves when they are dealing with issues such as trade protection. Some industries are more competitive than others within Mercosul. The equation may change in relation to Brazil's membership within the proposed Free Trade Area of the Americas (FTAA). That is, an industry that may be competitive in relation to Uruguay (Mercosul) may not be able to compete with the United States (FTAA).

Actors involved with specialized issues such as the environment have also become more influential. They often have ties to international networks and organizations. As a result, the formulation of foreign policy has become more fragmented. Nonetheless, the Ministry of Foreign Relations retains considerable leverage in foreign policy formulation.

Although the academic community is not a strong political actor, its focus on international relations can provide some of the information and analysis necessary to elevate the level of discussion on foreign policy. A new generation of Brazilian scholars, working almost exclusively on Brazil's foreign relations, has emerged. The universities most prominently involved in this kind of research are the University of Brasília, the Catholic University in Rio de Janeiro (especially its Instituto de Relações Internacionais, or IRI), and the University of São Paulo.

Brazil's press provides excellent analysis of foreign relations. The newspapers that are most prominent in this coverage are *Gazeta Mercantil, O Estado de São Paulo, Folha de São Paulo, Jornal do Brasil,* and *Correio Brasiliense.* Magazines such as *Veja, Isto É,* and *Época* provide regular reports of international affairs. Major television companies accompany presidents on their international trips and provide adequate coverage. The role of Brazil's press is to inform the public and to call attention to contradictions or inconsistencies in Brazil's foreign policy. Such a role leads to a more transparent foreign policy and provides for greater accountability of policy makers. For example, a press report in 1987 that Brazil was involved in military technology exchanges with Israel at the same time that

Brazil was selling weapons to Iraq and Libya was met with considerable consternation at Itamaraty, which was forced to explain its position. Later reports that Brazil had dug a deep shaft with the potential for underground testing of a nuclear device led President Fernando Collor de Mello to openly challenge Brazil's nuclear policies.

The Internet has revolutionized the ability of citizens and scholars to follow Brazil's foreign relations. In the 1980s several universities, academic centers, and newspapers in Brazil maintained files of articles on Brazil's foreign relations. In the 1990s most of these institutions moved to an electronic mode. Access to information, however, does not necessarily equate with greater influence on foreign policy matters.

Contemporary Brazilian Foreign Policy

Brazil's current foreign policy demonstrates the continued importance of leaders and their initiatives. Since the end of the Cold War in 1991, Brazil has had three democratically elected presidents: Collor de Mello (1990–1992), Franco (1992–1994), and Cardoso (1995–present). President Collor de Mello sought to impose a neoliberal economic model on Brazil and to improve ties with the United States, but he was impeached on corruption charges. Franco was a "caretaker" president, who finished out Collor de Mello's term and made few changes to Brazil's foreign policy. Under these three leaders, Brazil's foreign policy has matured in the areas of security, economic, regional, global, and environmental policies.

As mentioned earlier, President Cardoso's previous experience as foreign minister and finance minister has made him one of Brazil's most important presidents in the realm of foreign relations. During his years of exile Cardoso lived in Chile, the United States, and France and speaks Spanish, English, and French fluently. A common criticism of Cardoso is that he is too interested in foreign relations, a charge that has rarely been leveled at Brazilian presidents.

Cardoso has sought to bring maturity to Brazil's foreign policy, without giving up any of Brazil's autonomy. For example, one of the major goals of Brazilian foreign policy is to gain for the country a permanent seat on the Security Council of the United Nations. Whereas in the past Brazil had been strident about such membership, under Cardoso, Brazil has been vigorous but quieter in this pursuit. Under Cardoso, Brazil has also played a leading role in defusing the tensions between Peru and Ecuador over border issues. Brazil is one of four guarantors of the Peru-Ecuador accord of 1942 (Rio Protocol), which brought an end to the 1941 war between Peru and Ecuador. The two countries skirmished again in 1995. Cardoso presided over the ceremony when the presidents of Peru and Ecuador flew to Brasília to sign a new peace accord on October 26, 1998. Cardoso has also played a major role in strengthening democratic forces in Paraguay. On several occasions democracy has been challenged in Paraguay, and in each case Cardoso has stepped in to support democracy in that country, with a "carrot and stick" strategy. In effect, Cardoso has threatened to remove Paraguay from Mercosul in the event of a military coup d'état. Those efforts have been coordinated with Argentina, which is also interested in political developments in Paraguay.

Under Cardoso, and in the aftermath of the Cold War, Brazil's foreign policy has focused on the following themes: economics; multilateralism; regionalism and integration; security, defense, military, and nuclear relations; and the environment.[28] That diversification reflects the rise of interdependence in international relations noted by liberalism, and it is a challenge to realism's proposition that security is the only or dominant concern of states. Liberalism recognizes many of the domestic factors that shape international behavior and is broader in its themes. Consistent with liberalism, the diversification in themes in Brazil's international relations continues to this day.

Since the end of the Cold War, Brazil has sought to expand its ties with other countries and regions. No longer are the ideological constraints of the Cold War in place to limit Brazil's involvement across the globe. Brazil continues to have close ties to the United States and Western Europe but has increased its visibility in Africa and in Asia. Brazil has played a particularly vigorous role (especially in the commercial arena) in former Portuguese colonies, such as Angola and Mozambique, where the Portuguese language plays to Brazil's comparative advantage.

Brazil has also begun to play a more mature role in the areas of security, defense, the military, and nuclear relations as well. During the Cold War, Brazil was willing to maintain a major military presence along the Argentine border, engage in the export of arms to Iraq, and develop a nuclear program with virtually no oversight by international agencies. As noted earlier, under Cardoso, however, Brazil drafted a defense plan in 1997 that explicitly states that Argentina is no longer a threat to Brazil's national security interests. As a result, Brazil moved many of the troops from its southernmost army command to other commands across the country. Brazil's relations with Argentina, once tense, are better today than they ever have been. Brazil also no longer exports arms to pariah states such as Iraq. Finally, Brazil's nuclear programs are now under full-scope international safeguards, and Brazil's cooperation with Argentina on nuclear issues has become a model for other countries.

Brazil's environment has also received growing attention from abroad and from within Brazil. The "internationalization" of the Amazon has irked many Brazilian officials (especially military officers), who view such international meddling in the Amazon as a threat to Brazil's sovereignty. Under Cardoso, Brazil has purchased and developed the technology necessary to better monitor the Amazon. Domestically, a growing coalition of citizens interested in environmental issues represent a new force in Brazilian politics.

Since the mid-1980s, when the debt crisis became particularly acute, Brazil's foreign policy attention has shifted to the economic realm. Today, tensions between Brazil and the United States in regard to commerce are more prominent than ever.[29] As a result, economic issues are near the top of Brazil's foreign policy agenda and are being handled through proper bilateral and multilateral channels. The emphasis on regionalism and economics in contemporary Brazilian foreign policy is most clearly seen in Mercosul and Brazil's response to U.S. economic policy in Latin America.

Brazil has used Mercosul as a tool to assert its regional leadership and to counter U.S. influence in the hemisphere. For example, the United States proposed, in December 1994, the creation of a Free Trade Area of the Americas by the year 2005. Brazil has sought to stall the FTAA, in large measure because the FTAA is viewed as a U.S.-initiated proposal that would expand the North American Free Trade Agreement (NAFTA) to the detriment of Mercosul and Brazil. Brazil would prefer to consolidate and expand Mercosul, making it the model for a broader regional trade area.

Brazil's attempt to stymie the FTAA reflects its strategy of "pacing and hedging," a term used by Thomaz Guedes da Costa. According to Guedes da Costa, "Brazil prefers to move gradually and with caution in expanding regional cooperation in order to gain time to establish a general sense of unity and direction for the country and its neighbors in the international arena. At the same time, Brazil must hedge its strategy against possible negative effects in the future."[30]

According to Guedes da Costa, Brazil has opted for a regional strategy for its entry into global policy.[31] This is, perhaps, what would be expected of a "middle power" with aspirations for great power status. Brazil is in no position to challenge the United States in much of the world, but it *is* in a position to assert itself within South America. Brazil has sought, for example, to improve cooperation between Mercosul and the European Union although a full alliance between the two trading blocs seems unlikely.[32]

Brazil will likely continue to seek a regional strategic option as a response to globalization. Brazil will play the regional "card" when necessary—in cooperation with the EU, and against the FTAA. It will pursue a bilateral course on certain issues, such as maintaining close ties with Lusophone (Portuguese-speaking) Africa. And it will use a multilateral path on some issues, such as its desire to become a permanent member of the United Nations Security Council. This varied approach provides Brazil with a considerable range of options as its foreign policy responds to external factors.

Conclusion

In the post–Cold War era, Brazil has emerged as a regional power, willing to assert itself on the international stage. It has exercised a growing leadership role in Latin America while seeking to avoid the negative image of a regional hegemon. Brazil's leadership role will bring about occasional clashes with the sole superpower in the international system, the United States, which seeks to maintain its influence in Latin America.

Perhaps no foreign policy goal is as important to Brazil as regional integration. The forming of Mercosul by Brazil after the Cold War has led to a higher level of cooperation among the member countries. Such cooperation has important implications for commerce, democracy, and security within the region.[33]

The major clashes between the United States and Brazil will be in South America. As the leader of Mercosul, Brazil has sought to forestall the U.S.-led FTAA. Brazil would prefer to expand Mercosul, thereby increasing its influence in Latin America. Brazil will also continue to clash with the United States over the U.S. war on drugs in the Andean region, especially in Colombia. In addition, because of concerns with sovereignty, Brazil will seek to limit any U.S. influence in the Amazon region. Compared with Mexico, however, Brazil suffers from very little "sovereignty anxiety."

Cautiously, but firmly, Brazil will seek to expand its influence internationally. It will continue to seek a permanent seat on the Security Council of the United Nations, and it will attempt to increase its influence in the former Portuguese colonies in Africa. And to further its interests, it will continue to work in multilateral organizations.

International relations theory suffers from a Eurocentric bias. Middle powers like Brazil are poorly understood, especially at the internal level. These obstacles notwithstanding, as Brazil continues to assert itself internationally, interest in understanding Brazil's foreign policy will almost certainly grow.

Suggestions for Further Reading

Becker, Bertha K., and Claudio A. G. Egler. In *Brazil: A New Regional Power in the World Economy*. Cambridge: Cambridge University Press, 1992.

Desch, Michael C. *When the Third World Matters: Latin America and United States Grand Strategy*. Baltimore: Johns Hopkins University Press, 1993.

Hurrell, Andrew. "Brazil as a Regional Power: A Study in Ambivalence." In *Regional Great Powers in International Politics*. Ed. Iver B. Neumann. New York: St. Martin's Press, 1992.

Purcell, Susan Kaufman, and Riordan Roett, eds. *Brazil under Cardoso*. Boulder: Lynne Rienner, 1997.

Roett, Riordan. *Mercosur: Regional Integration, World Markets*. Boulder: Lynne Rienner, 1999.

Schneider, Ronald M. *Brazil: Foreign Policy of a Future World Power*. Boulder: Westview Press, 1976.

Selcher, Wayne, ed. *Brazil in the International System: The Rise of a Middle Power*. Boulder: Westview Press, 1981.

Notes

1. For example, see Larry Rohter, "Brazil Begins to Take Role on the World Stage," *New York Times*, August 30, 2000.
2. For an excellent discussion of Brazil's westward expansion, see E. Bradford Burns, *A History of Brazil*, 3d ed. (New York: Columbia University Press, 1993).
3. See Stanley E. Hilton, *Brazil and the Soviet Challenge, 1917–1947* (Austin: Universi-

ty of Texas Press, 1991); Hilton, *Brazil and the Great Powers, 1930–1939: The Politics of Trade Rivalry* (Austin: University of Texas Press, 1975). See also Hilton, "The United States, Brazil and the Cold War, 1945–1960: End of the Special Relationship," *Journal of American History* 68 (December 1981): 599–624. In much of this literature Brazil is viewed in relation to great power rivalries. This fits in the tradition of "contingent power"—that is, a derivative power, which comes from manipulating the great power rivalries—see David Vital, *The Survival of Small States* (Oxford: Oxford University Press, 1971). See also Frank D. McCann, *The Brazilian-American Alliance, 1937–1945* (Princeton: Princeton University Press, 1973).

4. For a realist's view of Latin America, see Michael C. Desch, *When the Third World Matters: Latin America and United States Grand Strategy* (Baltimore: Johns Hopkins University Press, 1993).

5. J. Gregory Oswald and Anthony J. Strovers, *The Soviet Union and Latin America* (New York: Praeger, 1968).

6. See Gerald K. Haines, *The Americanization of Brazil: A Study of U.S. Cold War Diplomacy in the Third World, 1945–1954* (Wilmington, Del.: Scholarly Resources Books, 1989).

7. Quoted in Riordan Roett, *Brazil: Politics in a Patrimonial Society*, 4th ed. (Westport, Conn.: Praeger, 1992), 186.

8. Albert Fishlow, "Some Reflections on Post-1964 Brazilian Economic Policy," in *Authoritarian Brazil: Origins, Policies, and Future*, ed. Alfred Stepan (New Haven: Yale University Press, 1973), 84.

9. Some of this theory section is taken from Scott D. Tollefson, "International Relations," in *Guide to the Study of Brazil in the United States*, ed. Paulo Roberto de Almeida (forthcoming).

10. See Golbery do Couto e Silva, *A Geopolítica do Brasil*, 2d ed. (Rio de Janeiro: José Olympio, 1967); also Carlos de Meira Mattos, *A Geopolítica e as Projeções de Poder* (Rio de Janeiro: José Olympio, 1977).

11. Golbery do Couto e Silva, *Conjuntura Política Nacional: O Poder Executivo e Geopolítica do Brasil* (Rio de Janeiro: Livraria José Olympio Editora, 1981).

12. See Peter Evans, *Dependent Development: The Alliance of Multinational, State, and Local Capital in Brazil*, 2d ed. (Princeton: Princeton University Press, 1981). Evans is influenced by some of the leading Brazilian dependency theorists, such as Fernando Henrique Cardoso and Enzo Faletto; see their *Dependency and Development in Latin America* (Beverly Hills: University of California Press, 1979).

13. Theotonio dos Santos, "The Structure of Dependence," *American Economic Review* 60 (May 1970).

14. Cardoso and Faletto, *Dependency and Development in Latin America*, xvi.

15. Immanuel Wallerstein, *The Modern World-System: Capitalist Agriculture and the Origins of the European World-Economy in the Sixteenth Century* (New York: Academic Press, 1974).

16. Richard Graham, ed., *Brazil and the World System* (Austin: University of Texas Press, 1991).

17. Evans, *Dependent Development*.

18. Todd S. Purdum, "California, Rising, Passes France on Its Climb," *New York Times*, June 15, 2001; based on data from Los Angeles County Economic Development Corporation.

19. Brazilian Embassy, Washington, D.C., *Brazil Economic Briefing*, No. 01/2001, based on information from Brazil's Ministry of Finance; available at http://www.brasilemb.org/beb/default.htm.

20. Rubens Barbosa (Brazilian ambassador to the United States), "The United States and Brazil: Strategic Partners or Regional Competitors?" in *Thinking Brazil* (newsletter of Brazil at the Wilson Center Project), No. 2, August 2000, 5.

21. Lia Valls Pereira, "Toward the Common Market of the South: Mercosur's Origins, Evolution, and Challenges," in *Mercosur: Regional Integration, World Markets*, ed. Riordan Roett (Boulder: Lynne Rienner, 1999), 7.

22. Ricardo Markwald and João Bosco Machado, "Establishing an Industrial Policy for Mercosur," in Roett, *Mercosur: Regional Integration, World Markets*, 63.

23. Pedro da Motta Veiga, "Brazil in Mercosur: Reciprocal Influence," in Roett, *Mercosur: Regional Integration, World Markets*, 25.

24. Asymmetries are also found in other relationships within Mercosul. For a discussion of the implications of asymmetrical interdependence, see Robert O. Keohane and Joseph S. Nye Jr., *Power and Interdependence*, 3d ed. (New York: Longman, 2001), esp. 9–19.

25. Roett, *Mercosur: Regional Integration, World Markets*, 3.

26. See Riordan Roett, *Brazil in the Sixties* (Nashville: Vanderbilt University Press, 1972); Roett, *Brazil in the Seventies* (Washington, D.C.: American Enterprise Institute, 1972); Roett, *Brazil: Politics in a Patrimonial Society* (New York: Praeger, 1999); Roett, "The Foreign Policy of Latin America," in *Foreign Policy in World Politics*, ed. Roy C. Macridis, 8th ed. (Englewood Cliffs, N.J.: Prentice Hall, 1992; originally published in 1958); Roett, "Brazilian Foreign Policy: Options in the 1980s," in *Authoritarian Capitalism: Brazil's Contemporary Economic and Political Development*, ed. Thomas C. Bruneau and Philippe Faucher (Boulder: Westview Press, 1981); Roett and Scott D. Tollefson, "Brazil's Status as an Intermediate Power," *Third World Affairs* 1986: 101–112; Susan Kaufman Purcell and Riordan Roett, eds., *Brazil under Cardoso* (Boulder: Lynne Rienner, 1997). See also Wayne Selcher, *Brazil in the International System: The Rise of a Middle Power* (Nashville: Vanderbilt University Press, 1972), and Selcher, *Brazil's Multilateral Relations: Between First and Third Worlds* (Boulder: Westview Press, 1981).

27. See, for example, Wayne Selcher, "Brazil's Foreign Policy: More Actors and Expanding Agendas," in *The Dynamics of Latin American Foreign Policies: Challenges for the 1980s*, Westview Special Studies on Latin America and the Caribbean, ed. Jennie K. Lincoln and Elizabeth G. Ferris (Boulder: Westview Press, 1984).

28. See, for example, Michael A. Morris's focus on maritime concerns in *International Politics and the Sea: The Case of Brazil* (Boulder: Westview Press, 1979).

29. For an analysis of such disputes, see Ellene A. Felder and Andrew Hurrell, *U.S.-Brazilian Informatics Dispute* (Washington, D.C.: Johns Hopkins Foreign Policy Institute, School of Advanced International Studies, 1988).

30. Thomaz Guedes da Costa, "Strategies for Global Insertion: Brazil and Its Regional Partners," in *Latin America in the New International System*, ed. Joseph S. Tulchin and Ralph H. Espach (Boulder: Lynne Rienner, 2001), 91.

31. Ibid.

32. See Wolf Grabendorff, "Mercosur and the European Union: From Cooperation to Alliance?" in Roett, *Mercosur: Regional Integration, World Markets*, 95–109.

33. Roett, *Mercosur: Regional Integration, World Markets;* David Pion-Berlin, "Will Soldiers Follow? Economic Integration and Regional Security in the Southern Cone," *Journal of Interamerican Studies and World Affairs* 42 (spring 2000): 43–69.

CHAPTER 14

Mexico:

Balancing Sovereignty and Interdependence

Michael T. Snarr

With one of the largest populations in the region, Mexico stands as a relative giant among Latin American countries. Its political culture reflects Mexico's revolutionary history and its perseverance through the many external challenges to its national sovereignty and territorial integrity. Michael Snarr argues that this characteristic of Mexico's political culture has resulted in an orientation toward international affairs that emphasizes the country's autonomy. Indeed, despite bordering on the only remaining superpower, Mexico exhibits a remarkable degree of independence in its foreign policy choices. Yet in the wake of adoption of the North American Free Trade Agreement, it is experiencing tremendous pressure to adopt neoliberal international trading practices and to open its economy to foreign investment. These conflicting tendencies toward autonomy and interdependence have resulted in important changes both domestically and in the realm of foreign policy.

Mexico recently experienced a significant change in its domestic political landscape when the long-ruling Institutional Revolutionary Party (PRI) lost the 2000 presidential election to an opposition candidate. This transition can be compared with the fall of the Liberal Democratic Party in Japan (Chapter 7). Moreover, Mexico's move toward democracy, although different in nature, can be contrasted with transitions toward democracy in countries such as Russia (Chapter 5) and South Africa (Chapter 12). The Mexican struggle for political autonomy while striving to develop economically is similar in many ways to struggles under way in other former colonies such as India (Chapter 8), Nigeria (Chapter 11), and Brazil (Chapter 13). Yet Mexico's proximity to the United States brings some potential for economic integration not unlike that experienced by countries of the European Union, such as Great Britain (Chapter 2), France (Chapter 3), and Germany (Chapter 4). Like China (Chapter 6) with its Tiananmen Square uprising, Mexico has had to deal in recent years with opposition to the regime by the Zapatistas, peasant soldiers in the southern state of Chiapas. This rebellion has attracted international attention and altered the country's foreign policy.

Mexico has the tenth largest economy in the world and is the fourth largest exporter of petroleum, but it is often overlooked in discussions about world politics. Even within the United States, Mexico is largely ignored by the media, and U.S. citizens generally know little about it (except perhaps its vacation areas such as Cancun and the immigrants it produces for the U.S. labor market). This lack of knowledge persists even though the United States and Mexico share a two thousand-mile-long border and Mexico is the second most important trading partner of the United States (just behind Canada).

This chapter seeks to redress this knowledge gap by offering an overview of Mexican foreign policy. It begins by briefly examining the historical context of Mexico's external relations. Next, it explores the major influences, both internal and external, on Mexican foreign policy, and then examines how that foreign policy is dealing with current issues, including the North American Free Trade Agreement (NAFTA), the U.S. "bailout" of Mexico, drug trafficking, and the conflict in Chiapas. The concluding section takes a closer look at the prospects for Mexican foreign policy in the near future.

Mexico's foreign policy is better understood in the context of the country's history. One very important historical dimension is the repeated violations of Mexican sovereignty by other countries. Mexico came under the rule of Spain in 1521 when Spanish explorer Hernando Cortés conquered the indigenous Aztecs in what is now Mexico City. Although Mexico achieved independence from Spain in 1821, it soon faced another enemy, this time from the north.

In 1836 Texans declared their independence from Mexico and gained recognition from several countries as an independent nation. By 1846 war had broken out between Mexico and the United States, which had annexed Texas the year before. The war, referred to in the United States as the Mexican-American War, is known in Mexico as the War of the North American Invasion. By 1848, when the war ended, Mexico had suffered many military defeats, including the U.S. occupation of Mexico City. The Treaty of Guadalupe Hidalgo, which brought the war to a close, recognized the U.S. annexation of Texas, and Mexico also had to relinquish its claim to California and part of New Mexico. Indeed, Mexico lost half its territory to the United States.

During the nineteenth century, Mexico's troubles from external enemies were not limited to the United States. In 1838 the French blockaded and bombarded the eastern port city of Veracruz in an attempt to collect unpaid Mexican debts. Even more serious was Napoleon III's decision to conquer Mexico and impose French control through a puppet, Austrian archduke Ferdinand Maximilian. In

1861 England, France, and Spain had joined forces to occupy Veracruz as part of an effort to force Mexico's payment of unpaid debts. But when England and Spain learned of Napoleon's intention to install Maximilian as ruler, they withdrew their troops. In June 1863 the French captured Mexico City and appointed Maximilian the emperor of Mexico. He served as monarch until 1867, when Napoleon, bowing to Mexican resistance, U.S. pressure, and criticism from home, withdrew his troops. Maximilian was soon executed by Mexican forces.

In 1876 a new era in U.S.-Mexican relations dawned. The new president, Porfirio Díaz, embraced closer relations with the United States and Europe by opening Mexico to foreign investment. Not all Mexicans, however, were pleased with this phase of Mexican politics known as the Porfiriato (Porfiriato Díaz remained in power from 1876 to 1910, with the exception of only four years) nor with the consequences of foreign investments. These investments only intensified the concentration of wealth in the hands of a few and the control of foreign companies over the Mexican economy. Such factors, combined with others, such as Díaz's refusal to abide by democratic principles, led to the Mexican Revolution, a decade-long civil war that began in 1910.

Mexican sovereignty was violated yet again during the Mexican Revolution. In 1914 President Woodrow Wilson, unhappy about the way Mexican president Victoriano Huerta had obtained office (by arranging the assassination of his predecessor), refused to recognize the Mexican president. In fact, the United States sent military aid to northern Mexico, seeking to overthrow Huerta. Eventually, the U.S. military occupied Veracruz, and U.S. aid to Huerta's opponents, combined with the occupation and blockade of Veracruz, played a key role in the demise of the Huerta regime.

In each of the historical instances just described, Mexico's borders were penetrated by a foreign country, explicitly violating Mexican sovereignty. As a result, for most of the twentieth century Mexican foreign policy sought to guard the country's sovereignty and steadfastly support the principle of nonintervention. For example, Article 27 of the new constitution adopted during the Mexican Revolution proclaimed that all mineral deposits within Mexican borders were to be controlled by Mexico and, if necessary, expropriated by the Mexican government. Mexico thus claimed ultimate control over foreign mining and oil companies. Article 51 of the new constitution stated that, in nearly all cases, Mexicans must possess a majority (51 percent) share of any companies operating inside Mexico. Articles 27 and 51 can be viewed as a reaction to the Díaz era, because they specifically sought to avoid the degree of foreign control over the economy that occurred during the Porfiriato. Taken together, these two articles can be seen as part of a larger theme called "Mexicanization," which is defined by Camp as "a revolutionary principle stressing the importance of Mexicans and Mexico, enhancing their influence and prestige."[1] In other words, Mexico was for Mexicans first, foreign interests second.

Mexico asserted its sovereignty in 1938, when Mexican president Lázaro Cárdenas seized the resources of the seventeen foreign oil companies operating in Mexico. This expropriation or nationalization of the oil companies was prompted by their poor treatment of Mexican workers and refusal to obey a Mexican court decision that called for improved treatment of the workers. This event served as a precursor to Mexico's foreign policy stance during the Cold War years, which is discussed in the next section.

Mexican Foreign Policy during the Cold War

During the Cold War years, Mexico continued to confront the United States on occasion over the issue of sovereignty and the principle of nonintervention in Mexican affairs. In 1954, for example, the United States pressured Latin American countries to condemn Jacobo Arbenz, a left-wing Guatemalan president who threatened U.S. interests with his land reform program. Mexico and Argentina were the only two countries that rejected such a resolution by the Organization of the American States (OAS), a regional organization made up of the United States and Latin American countries and designed to coordinate members' policies. A decade later, Mexico and three other Latin American countries refused to support the U.S. intervention in the Dominican Republic, designed to prevent a communist regime from taking power.[2] Then, during the 1980s, Mexico clashed with the United States over U.S. policy in Central America. Similarly, Mexico has been the staunchest Latin American critic of the U.S. embargo and various attempts to isolate Cuban president Fidel Castro. In particular, Mexico refused to follow the other Latin American countries in breaking off relations with Castro, despite pressure from the United States and the OAS.

Mexican foreign policy during much of the Cold War period reflected to some extent the leader in power. For example, Mexican president López Mateos (1958–1964) was relatively active internationally, and he traveled abroad often during his tenure. He eschewed close relations with both the United States, by taking a noninterventionist position in Cuba, and the Soviet Union, by criticizing the Soviets' role in the Cuban missile crisis. His successor, Díaz Ordaz (1964–1970), focused more on domestic politics. Unfortunately for Díaz Ordaz, the defining event of his presidency was the 1968 Tlaltelolco massacre just prior to the Olympic Games in Mexico City, when Mexican police opened fire on antigovernment student protestors, killing hundreds of civilians. In the wake of this tragic event, President Luis Echeverría (1970–1976) assumed an internationally active foreign policy, especially in issues related to the developing countries. He traveled extensively throughout the world and promoted the economic interests of developing nations through the United Nations General Assembly. These policies and others, such as his support of leftist leaders like Fidel Castro in Cuba and Salvador Allende in Chile, alienated him from the United States. Luis Echeverría was succeeded by López Portillo (1976–1982), whose foreign policy was less radical than that of his predecessors. During his presidency, international economic realities (the oil crisis) and the discovery of large additional oil reserves in Mexico held great promise for Mexico's future; the country seemed poised to become a significant world actor. Unfortunately, López Portillo mismanaged the economy and ended up accepting an economic restructuring package from the International Monetary Fund (IMF).[3] Despite the different styles and ideologies of these presidencies, Mexican foreign policy was characterized by moderate cooperation with the United States, a careful eye toward Mexican sovereignty, and a principled stand on the issue of nonintervention. A break from the past came with López Portillo's successor, Miguel de la Madrid.

A dramatic shift in both domestic and foreign policy occurred in 1982, when Miguel de la Madrid (1982–1988) was elected president. He broke with past policies of strong state involvement in the economy and moved Mexico toward neoliberal economic policies. Among other things, neoliberalism includes privatization of state-owned industries, free trade, and fewer restrictions on foreign investment. The emphasis on free trade led Mexico in 1986 to join the General Agreement on Tariffs and Trade (GATT), an international organization designed to promote free trade among its members. In short, under neoliberalism the role of government in the economy is significantly reduced. These economic policies marked a significant break from the past several decades when Mexico's foreign trade policy included significant government regulations.

De la Madrid's successor, Carlos Salinas, was even more strongly committed to neoliberal policies. Salinas favored economic liberalization, especially privatization, and integrating Mexico into the world economy. In 1993 Salinas signed the North American Free Trade Agreement which drew the Mexican economy uncharacteristically close to those of Canada and particularly the United States. Some groups within Mexico, especially many indigenous ones, opposed NAFTA, and thus it was no coincidence that on January 1, 1994, the same day that NAFTA went into effect, a rebellion broke out in the southern Mexican state of Chiapas (this conflict is discussed in greater detail later in this chapter).

In 1994 Ernesto Zedillo, a third neoliberal, was elected president of Mexico. Zedillo essentially continued the economic policies of his two predecessors. Because Zedillo, like de la Madrid, inherited an economic crisis when he assumed the presidency, Mexico had to institute another round of economic reforms, including an IMF structural adjustment plan. In addition, Mexico borrowed billions of dollars from the United States, an arrangement that, like its participation in GATT and NAFTA, further eroded Mexican sovereignty. This give and take between interdependence and sovereignty is arguably the central theme of Mexican foreign policy.

On December 1, 2000, Vicente Fox became the first non-PRI president in seventy-one years. Fox will likely bring many changes to Mexico's foreign policy. His early performance and likely foreign policy direction are discussed in the conclusion of this chapter.

External Factors

Mexico Prior to 1982

Mexico's emphasis on sovereignty and adherence to the principle of nonintervention that led it to chart a foreign policy that often conflicted with the policies of the United States are noteworthy. As Chapter 1 pointed out, in a bipolar system a middle power is pressured to become a compliant partner of one of the major powers and ultimately relinquish autonomy in its foreign policy for the sake of security. Although Mexico was much more closely allied with Washington than Moscow during the Cold War, Mexico could not be considered compliant.

A good example of Mexico's defiance of the United States was the situation in Central America in the 1980s. The region was rife with conflict between groups friendly to the United States and those allied with the Soviet Union. Despite U.S. president Ronald Reagan's aggressive anticommunist stance toward the region, Mexico stood firm in defiance of Washington. In fact, Mexico, along with Colombia, Panama, and Venezuela, formed the "Contadora Group," which sought to bring peace to the region and offer an alternative to Washington's military solution. In this sense, the realist assumption (see Chapter 1) that Mexico would ally itself closely to the United States did not hold.

Thus Mexico's foreign policy behavior up to 1982 (and since 1982 to an extent) contradicts the expectations of scholars who have written about the foreign policy of the "dependent" state. For example, the compliance approach, which is rooted in realism, argues that the foreign policy of developing or "dependent" countries will coincide with the foreign policy of the "core" country (in Mexico's case, the United States)—that is, weaker states do not have the power to defy the interests of the more powerful states.[4] Another approach within the dependent state foreign policy literature is the "consensus" approach. This approach agrees that the foreign policy of weaker states will generally coincide with the wishes of the dominant, or core, state, but because of shared values rather than coercion.[5] In other words, the elites in the dependent and core states share similar views, and therefore the dependent state's foreign policy will coincide with the interests of the core state. Mexico's independent foreign policy record does not mean that the United States or other external constraints do not exert some influence on its decisions, but that these influences have not been as strong as one would expect.

Interdependence theories also are not very useful in explaining Mexico's foreign policy during much of the Cold War. Mexico maintained a relatively high degree of sovereignty during the first three decades of the Cold War, and its economic policy focused on diversifying the country's economy so it would not become dependent on outside economic forces. In carrying out this so-called import substitution industrialization, Mexico sought to produce a variety of industrial products so it would not have to buy them from the United States and Europe and therefore be dependent on them (not to mention pay for these expensive imports). It was not until the early 1980s that Mexico began to adopt the idea, discussed in Chapter 1, that countries could best create wealth by specializing and integrating themselves into the world market.

Mexico since 1982

Two international and regional circumstances—democratization and economic interdependence—have led to important changes in Mexico's foreign policy process and substance, respectively. Democratization has introduced new voices into the policy-making process, and economic interdependence has resulted in a dynamic tension between Mexico's historical desire to guard its sovereignty and its desire to become integrated into the global economy.

The international trend toward political liberalization, including greater democratization, has taken root in much of Latin America, including Mexico. For example, Mexico has historically opposed the role of foreign observers in its elections as an affront on its sovereignty. However, in both the 1994 and 2000 presidential elections Mexico gave in to foreign and domestic pressure by allowing domestic and foreign observers. Another sign of democratization is the recent break in the domination of the Chamber of Deputies, Senate, and the presidency by the Institutional Revolutionary Party, which had controlled these institutions since 1929. These changes will likely have an important impact on the foreign policy process and the foreign policy behavior of Mexico. Additional domestic changes stemming from democratization are discussed in the concluding section of this chapter.

As noted earlier, because Mexico's most recent presidents, including Fox, have supported economic interdependence, today's economy is much more outward looking. Moreover, the global and regional shift toward greater interdependence can be credited with influencing Mexico's move toward a neoliberal economic policy. International organizations such as the World Trade Organization (WTO), IMF, and World Bank, as well as the major international economic powers (especially the United States), have pushed developing countries to adopt neoliberal policies.

One issue credited with coaxing de la Madrid and Mexico down this new economic path was the debt crisis of 1982. Despite the discovery of additional reserves of oil the decade before, oil prices had dropped significantly, hindering Mexico's ability to pay off its foreign debts. After nearly defaulting on its debts, Mexico moved to restore confidence in its economy by adopting IMF structural adjustment policies. Since this crisis, Mexico has continued to move toward more free market-oriented policies.

Internal Factors

Because external factors such as Mexico's relationship with the United States are limited in their ability to explain Mexico's foreign policy, we now turn to internal influences. Historically, the president of Mexico has been the dominant decision maker in the country's domestic and foreign policy. Strong, centralized power dates back to the time of the Aztecs in the thirteenth century and has been a consistent feature of Mexican politics throughout the modern period. This presidential dominance is often referred to as "presidentialism." In the face of a dominant executive, Mexico's bicameral legislature, which consists of a Chamber of Deputies and a Senate, is relatively weak. Historically, presidential bills have only rarely not passed the legislature. This reality mirrors the situation in other developing countries.

The president's supremacy over domestic and foreign policy has been strengthened by two additional factors. First, because the Institutional Revolutionary Party controlled the legislature and the presidency for several decades, the legislature rarely played an independent role in foreign policy decisions. Second, the structure of the PRI was corporatist—that is, societal groups did not compete against one another, but were incorporated into the party structure. Essentially, this meant that labor, peasants, and "popular sectors" (much of the middle class) were inside the ruling coalition rather than outside as they are in most competitive democratic systems. This arrangement offered obvious benefits, such as permanent access to the government. On the negative side, the ability of these groups to act independently was limited. Presidential power was thus further strengthened because of its control over these groups.

The news media in Mexico, many of which are owned or influenced by the government, have historically been supportive of the government. Until recently, television news was dominated by the government and thus gave much greater coverage to the PRI. The Mexican government also has controlled the newspapers. Although Mexico today has many independent newspapers, for many years its government used its monopoly on newsprint to control critical voices. In addition, because many newspapers receive a significant portion of their money from government advertisements, newspapers are constrained in the degree to which they can criticize the government. Negative coverage of the government or the PRI risked a loss of income from government advertising. Mexico's recent move toward democratization, however, has begun to change many of these practices.

As for other important influences on foreign policy in addition to that of the president, Mexico's historical experiences are cited widely. In attempting to explain Mexico's foreign policy behavior, many scholars have concentrated on the importance of the Mexican Revolution at the beginning of the twentieth century.[6] The revolution is revered in contemporary Mexican culture, from its prominent place in history books, to monuments placed throughout the country, to the rhetoric of politicians. Engle aptly draws the connection between the revolution and Mexico's concern for its sovereignty: "Mexican foreign policy, it may be simply stated, is an extension into international affairs of principles and practices developed and tested in the Mexican Revolution."[7]

Some scholars argue that the emphasis on the revolution has led Mexico to adhere to several related principles. According to Brandenburg, the four "cornerstones" of Mexican foreign policy are "national sovereignty, juridical equality, national self-determination, [and] nonintervention in the domestic affairs of another nation."[8] Similarly, McShane enumerates six principles of Mexican foreign policy: "(1) the self-determination of all nations; (2) the principle of nonintervention; (3) nationalism and the right to independence; (4) collective security, disarmament, and the pacific settlement of disputes; (5) the juridical equality of all nations; and (6) respect for and strict adherence to the principles of international law."[9] Mexico has followed these principles on several important foreign policy decisions, despite U.S. wishes to the contrary.

These principles of Mexican foreign policy fall under the heading of political culture. As Chapter 1 points out, the political culture of some countries is considered an important influence on their foreign policy despite problems in measuring it. Van Klaveran emphasizes the importance of political culture to Latin American foreign policy: "Although history and culture are extremely broad categories that do not readily lend themselves to operationalization, it is obvious that they have a strong influence on foreign policy. Right or wrong, historical interpretations and myths permeate the perceptions of foreign policy-makers and enjoy tremendous popularity with the general public."[10] Because Mexico, of all the Latin American countries (with the exception of Cuba), has most consistently resisted U.S. pressure,[11] the influence of political culture on foreign policy is a very compelling explanation of Mexico's foreign policy during much of the Cold War.

Contemporary Mexican Foreign Policy

The current foreign policy issues facing Mexico are not unique to that country. For example, drug trafficking, free trade, and foreign debt are issues facing the rest of Latin America. Like other countries in the region, Mexico has followed the regional (and global) pattern of increased economic interdependence. The first two foreign policy issues examined in this section—the North American Free Trade Agreement and the U.S. bailout of Mexico—are economic-oriented. This examination of these issues will elaborate on the central actors, their positions, and the politics of the issues in order to illustrate some of the concepts mentioned in the preceding theoretical discussion. The third and fourth issues are the national security issues of drug trafficking and the uprising in Chiapas.

NAFTA

Nowhere is the increasing interdependence more obvious than in Mexico's economic policy. Mexico has joined the rest of Latin America (except Cuba) and most of the countries of the world in adopting neoliberal economic policies. During much of the twentieth century, Mexico's economic policies were inward looking—that is, Mexicans were required to own 51 percent of foreign companies doing business in Mexico, and imports were subject to high tariffs and bureau-cratic interference. One of the most visible signs of Mexico's shift toward an out-ward-looking economy occurred when it joined the North American Free Trade Agreement with the United States and Canada. Unlike the complex ties charac-terizing the European Union, integration among these three countries has focused solely on trade and investment. Among the NAFTA countries, obstacles to trade have been dramatically reduced. In fact, by the year 2009 all tariffs on Canadian, Mexican, and U.S. goods are scheduled to be eliminated. Restrictions on foreign investment also will be reduced. Since the early 1990s Mexico has signed free trade agreements with Bolivia, Chile, Colombia, Venezuela, and five of the six Central American countries. More recently, Mexico has discussed trade agreements with Argentina, Brazil, Paraguay, and Uruguay (the so-called Mer-cosur countries), which are part of a free trade bloc. These multiple treaties could even lead to a hemisphere-wide free trade agreement, which, since a 1994 sum-mit of leaders from the region, has been referred to as the Free Trade Area of the Americas.

By joining NAFTA, Mexico shifted toward interdependence with its neigh-bors to the north. But what were the primary forces responsible for Mexico's decision to take such a step? External factors were certainly one force. The move-ment toward free trade has been a global and regional phenomenon affecting all countries, and the U.S. desire to sign a trade agreement with Mexico magnified the external pressure already on Mexico to move in that direction. The influence of external factors, however, must not be overestimated. For example, during the 1980s Mexico rejected a U.S. proposal for a free trade agreement between the two countries.[12] In fact, President Salinas initially courted Europe and Asia in his bid to integrate the Mexican economy into the global economy. It was not until this effort failed that he turned to the United States.

This situation suggests that internal factors also played a role in the Mexican decision to sign NAFTA. One key internal factor was Salinas's strong support for free market policies. Presidents de la Madrid, Salinas, and Zedillo each held degrees from U.S. Ivy League schools predisposed toward the neoliberal eco-nomic model: "The political education of Carlos Salinas . . . was grounded in a new vocabulary and buttressed with concepts so shocking that politicians even a decade earlier would have considered them sheer madness."[13] From the outset of Salinas's administration, it was clear that the development strategy he preferred was significantly more free market-oriented than those of his predecessors (with the exception of de la Madrid). Thus Salinas's preferences were an important fac-tor in the decision to join NAFTA.

The importance of Salinas's role in the decision to join NAFTA was but-tressed by the relative lack of domestic constraints on his power. The PRI dom-inated the Mexican Senate at the time NAFTA was signed, and because the PRI-dominated legislature rarely opposed the president (who was of the same party for seventy-one years), passage of NAFTA was relatively easy. Mexico's opposition parties also were generally supportive. The National Action Party

(PAN) was free market-oriented, and, although the Democratic Revolutionary Party (PRD) sought to make changes to the treaty, it was supportive of the agreement in general.[14] The final vote in the Senate, 56–2, reflected the lack of opposition to the treaty.

Other domestic actors were either supportive of NAFTA or remained quiet. For example, although many Mexican workers may have opposed NAFTA, the corporatist relationship between the unions and the PRI seriously constrained their ability to oppose the agreement.[15] But what about public opinion? Many Mexicans did oppose NAFTA and held protests, but they in general supported the agreement. The Mexican populace was very conscious of Mexican sovereignty, but most did appreciate the economic opportunity that the United States provided. In a 1989 poll examining Mexican perceptions of what they liked about the United States, "economic opportunities" was at the top of the list, far ahead of "its wealth," "democracy," and "equality for all." Although public opinion alone was not enough to shift Mexico's economic policy, it may have made passage of NAFTA more palatable.[16] Alternatively, one could argue that because the media were dominated by the government (and thus supportive of NAFTA), very little information was made available about the effects of NAFTA on the Mexican people.[17] There also was evidence that the public did not understand the treaty. For example, one poll found that "45.8 percent of those interviewed believed NAFTA would make it easier for Mexicans to get jobs in the United States."[18]

If the neoliberal policy direction, and more specifically the decision to join NAFTA, is for Mexico such a dramatic shift away from its principled foreign policy position stressing protection of its sovereignty, should the political culture explanation of Mexican foreign policy be discarded? There is no doubt that closer economic relations with the United States has led Mexico to greater economic interdependence between the United States and Mexico. Since signing NAFTA, U.S.-Mexico trade has grown steadily. As a result, some experts on Mexican foreign policy charge that Mexico's economic policy has seriously reduced the country's sovereignty.[19] This move toward greater interdependence supports liberalism's notion (see Chapter 1) that the fortunes of countries have become more intertwined in recent years. Thus Mexican sovereignty has been compromised to an extent, but the consequences of interdependence and loss of sovereignty should not be overstated. Interdependence does not necessarily go hand in hand with an asymmetrical, or one-sided, loss of control over sovereignty. Rather, interdependence signifies a mutual loss of sovereignty, because countries are "dependent" on each other. As Carlos Fuentes, the Mexican novelist and political analyst, argues, this dependence extends to both parties: "The vast asymmetry of power between the United States and Mexico is less and less significant with each passing day. If in the past, Mexico got pneumonia when the U.S. caught a cold, today we get the flu together."[20] Or as another well-known political analyst (Mexico's new foreign minister), Jorge Castañeda, has said: "Mexico affects the United States in ways and intensities that are qualitatively distinct from those of years gone by."[21] Therefore, it can be reasonably argued that Mexico's move toward greater interdependence has not resulted in a relatively weaker position in the international system vis-à-vis the United States.

Indeed, interdependence has not prevented Mexico from maintaining its strong commitment to nonintervention and self-determination. For example, from 1948 to 1997 Mexico had consistently low levels of agreement with the United States on UN General Assembly votes when compared with the rest of Latin America. Given its more independent foreign policy, it was not surprising that Mexico took this position from 1948 to 1982, but it was surprising that, after its shift in foreign policy, Mexico's position did not soften during the 1982–1997 period. Some might argue that UN votes are relatively unimportant to the United States, but it is critical to note that Mexico maintains this stance even on UN votes that have been identified as "important" by the U.S. State Department.[22] This behavior over the last two decades suggests that, at least in the United Nations, Mexico has maintained its strong support for self-determination even as it becomes more economically interdependent.

Finally, one cannot expect Mexican policy to remain static in a rapidly changing world—even Cuba has moved toward a more open economy. Thus in absolute terms Mexico has shifted toward interdependence, but in relative terms—that is, compared with other Latin American countries—Mexico is still protective of its sovereignty and principles such as self-determination. It appears, therefore, that it is too early to discount the political culture explanation of Mexican foreign policy.

In summary, it can be argued that a combination of external factors and internal factors led to Mexico's decision to sign NAFTA. Externally, global shifts toward greater economic integration and U.S. pressure to sign NAFTA were important. An important internal factor was the development strategy preferred by Mexican presidents.

The U.S. "Bailout"

Closer trade and investment links between Mexico and the United States have also led to greater interdependence in other economic areas. A recent example was the so-called U.S. "bailout" of Mexico. Soon after taking office in 1994, President Zedillo, bowing to economic pressures, including an overvalued Mexican peso, devalued the peso. This devaluation led to, among other things, a loss of confidence in the Mexican economy and the departure of investors, who sold off their pesos and pulled capital out of Mexico. Eventually, Mexico fell into a deep recession. To reestablish confidence in the peso, President Bill Clinton moved to rescue the Mexican economy with a multibillion-dollar loan package. But because Congress opposed the package, Clinton instead pulled funds from the Treasury Department's Stabilization Fund, which did not require congressional approval. The Clinton administration also solicited funds from the IMF. The final package included over $50 billion in support for the Mexican economy. In an unprecedented move, Mexico used its oil reserves as collateral for the loan.

Such a gesture would have been unimaginable prior to the de la Madrid and Salinas administrations. Ever since President Lázaro Cárdenas expropriated Mexico's oil industry in 1938, Mexicans have zealously guarded their sovereignty over oil. The discovery of additional reserves during the 1970s even emboldened Mexico to assume an aggressive leadership role in the world community that sometimes clashed with U.S. interests. In short, oil has been considered sacrosanct, which makes Zedillo's action perhaps the starkest example of the erosion of Mexican sovereignty. It is interesting to note, however, that this loss of sovereignty did not necessarily result in a one-sided dependence on the United States. As Purcell points out, the "economic crisis in Mexico would have involved the United States even if NAFTA had not existed. NAFTA, however, had raised the U.S. stake in the Mexican economy considerably. In fact, it had made Mexico as much a domestic policy issue for the United States as the United States had traditionally been for Mexico."[23] Thus Mexico's loss of sovereignty was not unilateral. The United States also has become dependent on Mexico to the point that U.S. politics is tied closer than ever to Mexican politics.

Drug Trafficking

For years, Mexico has been a conduit for drugs entering the United States from South America, but only recently has this issue become so contentious, especially within U.S. domestic politics. This confrontation, in its most recent form, pits the U.S. Congress and its "certification" program against countries like Mexico and Colombia. Through the certification process, begun in 1986, Congress determines whether a country like Mexico is cooperating with the United States in its fight against drugs. Countries that fail the test are "decertified" and subject to immediate sanctions. Mexico has not been decertified, probably because of U.S. concerns about the economic disruption that might result in the United States and fear of the sharp political acrimony that might erupt between the two countries, similar to the finger pointing on both sides of the border produced by the annual certification debates in Congress.

In recent years, the certification process has become very political and very public. Congressional opponents to the certification of Mexico have been very vocal in their criticism of Mexican efforts to stem the flow of drugs into the United States. For example, Democratic senator Dianne Feinstein of California has pointed to the pervasive corruption in Mexican society in which drug cartels essentially buy the loyalty of the local police forces, the military, and even members of the executive branch. For its part, Mexico has worked hard to convey the image of a country cooperating with the United States. Yet many Mexicans chafe at the U.S. pressure on drugs, and public support in Mexico for a war on drugs is relatively low (after all, drugs are a significant source of revenue for Mexico). If anything, Mexico's cooperation with the United States stems more from domestic concern about the power of the drug cartels, which may be responsible for violence throughout Mexico, including the high-profile murder of a presidential candidate and a Catholic cardinal. In the end, then, Mexico does not hide its strong opposition to the certification process and often frames the issue as a consumption problem. In a 1997 interview, Jesus Silva-Herzog, the Mexican ambassador to the United States, said, "There is no question that there is a problem . . . but why [is] there . . . no mention whatsoever about consumption, about the demand problem? Once the drug gets into the U.S. border what happens? Is the Los Angeles Police, or the San Francisco Police able to stop the drugging in their areas . . . ?"[24] Similarly, just prior to his inauguration in 2000, President Vicente Fox criticized the United States for not taking more responsibility for its drug problem: "The United States year after year blames us. Why? Who lets the drugs into the United States? Who is doing gigantic business in the United States, then sends down millions of dollars that corrupt Mexican police officers and government officials?"[25]

In view of the importance of the drug issue to the United States and the difficulty the United States faces in trying to control its own border, it can be argued that while the United States can put some pressure on Mexico, the United States is also *dependent* on Mexico. This dependence allows Mexico, to a great extent, to move at its own pace in the fight against drugs. On this issue, then, Mexico has moved toward greater *interdependence* in its foreign relations with the United States.

Chiapas

Chiapas, the southernmost Mexican state, is one of the poorest regions of Mexico, but it is rich in many natural resources. In Chiapas, which has a relatively high concentration of indigenous people, land ownership is very unevenly distributed, literacy rates are low, and infant mortality is high. Given these factors, it was no coincidence on January 1, 1994, the day that NAFTA went into effect, a small group of poorly armed rebels called the Zapatista National Liberation Army (EZLN), or Zapatistas, staged a revolt and successfully captured several towns in Chiapas. The uprising by the mostly indigenous peasants sought to expose the poverty and corruption in the region. It also highlighted frustration with the increased economic competition that NAFTA would bring to Chiapas. Considering their small numbers, the Zapatistas were quite successful. Their leader, Subcommandante Marcos, is an eloquent speaker, who has effectively utilized the media and the Internet. In a very short period of time, Chiapas had captured world attention.

For Mexico, Chiapas presented a foreign policy dilemma on at least two fronts. First, an armed rebellion could scare away foreign investors. Second, Mexico had to deal with foreign criticism of alleged human rights abuses. As foreign governments watched the Chiapas ordeal unfold, they were often critical. International nongovernmental organizations (NGOs) such as Americas Watch, a well-known human rights group that monitors and reports on human rights violations, also closely observed the conflict and, aided by the Internet, became key players in the Chiapas situation. Others along the sidelines were various groups with religious links and that focus on human rights and development such as Witness for Peace and the Christian Peacemaker Teams. To Mexican officials, these criticisms by foreign governments and NGOs (and especially their presence in the region) represented an affront to the country's sovereignty. In line with Mexico's emphasis on nonintervention and self-determination, Mexican officials reacted to their critics, both foreign governments and private citizens, by strongly condemning the foreign meddling. Then, in the wake of a massacre in the town of Acteal of forty-five civilians (including children) by a paramilitary group, Mexican officials blasted foreign intervention, declaring they would not stand for outside interference in the domestic affairs of Mexico. Their reactions to individuals who had come to Mexico to observe, and in some cases participate in, pro-Zapatista activities, were even more severe. Dozens of men and women were expelled, including U.S. citizens and European priests.

To anyone unaware of the historical context of Mexico, the government's reaction in this situation might seem severe. One would expect the Mexican government's response to the rebels and foreign actors to be moderated by the country's position in the international spotlight. More important, it had just joined into an economic trade agreement with two countries that prided themselves on respect for human rights. But this case serves as an example of how Mexico, despite its increasing incorporation into the global economy, still clings to its strong sense of nationalism and the principles of nonintervention.

Conclusion

The next two decades in Mexico promise to be very similar to the last two. The prominent issues today such as drug trafficking and economic development will not be resolved anytime soon. Issues not discussed in this chapter, such as transborder pollution and illegal immigration, also are likely to persist. Internal tension is not likely to abate either. Given the unusually large gap between the rich and poor in Mexico, domestic groups such as the EZLN and the Popular Revolution Army (ERP), a radical Marxist group operating in the state of Guerrero, will continue to operate in Mexico. As a result, international human rights organizations, the United States, and other countries are likely to continue to press Mexico on the human rights front, but that pressure will probably be met with Mexican resistance, and, if the past is any guide, Mexico will continue to vigorously protect its sovereignty.

Yet as the United States and Mexico become more interdependent, Mexico's outlook toward the United States, in particular its suspicions based on its past relations with its neighbor to the north, may soften. Cultural interaction may contribute to a reduction in tensions. One has only to visit Mexico and see the pervasive influence of McDonald's, Burger King, MTV, as well as Barney, Winnie-the-Pooh, and Santa Claus piñatas to conclude that Mexico will have a difficult time maintaining its culture and sense of history. The increasingly open Mexican economy, spurred on by NAFTA, will act as a catalyst for these cultural ties. The result may well be a reduction in Mexico's historic nationalism vis-à-vis the United States.[26]

The converse is also possible—heightened nationalist feelings on both sides of the border. A recent example illustrates the kinds of conflicts that can arise under NAFTA. Although the NAFTA agreement allows Mexican truckers to travel on U.S. highways, the U.S. government has limited that right because of its concerns about the safety of Mexican trucks. Some U.S. sectors also worry that drug smuggling will become more prevalent if Mexican truckers are given this freedom. Mexican officials have been outraged by this perceived violation of NAFTA, and some blamed it on President Clinton's pandering to the Teamsters Union, which feels threatened by Mexican truckers willing to work for lower wages. Confrontations like this will surely emerge frequently and may have the effect of heightening nationalist feelings on both sides of the border.

Without a doubt, the most dramatic event to occur in recent years in Mexico was the election on July 2, 2000, of Vicente Fox to the presidency. His election, under the banner of the National Action Party (PAN), is evidence of the increasing democratization under way in Mexico. The degree of change Fox will bring to Mexico's foreign policy is uncertain. He campaigned on a platform of increased free trade, including support for NAFTA and more links with the European Union. He also pledged to fight drug trafficking in cooperation with the United States, and, unlike previous Mexican administrations, to cooperate in the extradition of Mexican drug traffickers to the United States. There also were signals that the Fox administration would reduce restrictions on foreign observers in Chiapas.

On the surface, many of these policies sound very similar to those of Fox's three neoliberal predecessors, and if these policies are fully carried out, they could lead to a deepening of interdependence and a relaxation of Mexico's historical emphasis on sovereignty. Given that the PAN is considered to be ideologically closer to the United States than the PRI, these policy positions should not be surprising. Such a move would cast doubt on the importance on political culture's influence on Mexican foreign policy. Yet Fox has taken some positions that signify continuity with Mexico's historical concern with sovereignty. He has publicly rejected neoliberalism's extreme reliance on the market. In the area of drugs, despite Fox's pledge for further cooperation on drug trafficking, he also has called for the end of the certification process. In direct dealings with the United States since taking office, the bulk of his actions appear to be directed toward creating a *strengthened* position toward the United States. In fact, it was recently reported that Mexico, under Fox, has begun to establish a new, more assertive relationship with the United States: "Fox has brought new confidence to a nation that historically has been defensive and inward-looking. Armed with that assurance, Fox has vowed to forge a more equal relationship with the United States on such sensitive subjects as illegal immigration, drug smuggling and regional diplomacy."[27]

In a recent meeting between Mexico's foreign minister, Jorge Castañeda,[28] and U.S. secretary of state Colin Powell, Castañeda expressed Mexico's intentions to reinforce its relations with Cuba despite U.S. opposition to Castro. At the same time, in the U.S. Congress moves are under way to eliminate the certification process.[29]

But will Fox be able to implement his policy preferences? The Mexican legislature, no longer under the thumb of a sole political party, will likely play a larger role in policy making. Indeed, as democracy continues to expand, it is reasonable to assume that the opposition parties in the Mexican legislature will begin to demand a greater role in foreign policy. Analysts also point out that Fox's party, the PAN, is not unified. Fox is part of a more moderate wing that clashes on some issues with conservative PANistas.

These changes point to an exciting time of transformation in Mexican foreign policy. One thing seems likely though: even with these impending changes, Mexico's history will play a role in its foreign policy in the years to come. As Carlos Fuentes notes, "The greatness of Mexico is that its past is always alive, . . . Memory saves it, filters, chooses, but it does not kill."[30]

Suggestions for Further Reading

Camp, Roderic Ai. *Politics in Mexico: The Decline of Authoritarianism.* New York: Oxford University Press, 1999.

Castañeda, Jorge. *The Mexican Shock: Its Meaning for the U.S.* New York: New Press, 1995.

Fuentes, Carlos. *A New Time for Mexico.* Los Angeles: University of California Press, 1997.

Handelman, Howard. *Mexican Politics: The Dynamics of Change.* New York: St. Martin's Press, 1997.

Meyer, Michael C., William L. Sherman, and Susan M. Deeds. *The Course of Mexican History.* 6th ed. New York: Oxford University Press, 1999.

Purcell, Susan Kaufman, and Luis Rubio, eds. *Mexico under Zedillo.* Boulder: Lynne Rienner, 1998.

Riding, Alan. *Distant Neighbors: A Portrait of the Mexicans.* New York: Vintage Books, 1984.

Smith, Clint E. *Inevitable Partnerships: Understanding Mexico-U.S. Relations.* Boulder: Lynne Rienner, 2000.

Notes

1. Roderic Ai Camp, *Politics in Mexico: The Decline of Authoritarianism* (New York: Oxford University Press, 1999), 40.
2. Alan Riding, *Distant Neighbors: A Portrait of the Mexicans* (New York: Vintage Books, 1984), 342.
3. The International Monetary Fund is an international organization designed in part to assist countries facing balance-of-payment deficits. Countries that receive financial assistance from the IMF must adopt its structural adjustment policies. In Mexico, these policies entailed, among other things, a decrease in public spending, which

included a reduction in subsidies for domestic companies, and a subsequent reduction in real wages.

4. Eugene R. Wittkopf, "Foreign Aid and United Nations Votes: A Comparative Study," *American Political Science Review* 65 (1973): 868–888; Neil R. Richardson, *Foreign Policy and Economic Dependence* (Austin: University of Texas Press, 1978); and Neil R. Richardson and Charles W. Kegley, "Trade Dependence and Foreign Policy Compliance: A Longitudinal Analysis," *International Studies Quarterly* 24 (1980): 191–222.

5. Bruce Moon, "The Foreign Policy of the Dependent State," *International Studies Quarterly* 27 (1983): 315–340; and Bruce Moon, "Consensus or Compliance? Foreign Policy Change and External Dependence," *International Organization* 39 (1985): 297–329. More recently, several studies have highlighted the ability of dependent states to exercise latitude in their foreign policy. See William J. Biddle and John D. Stephens, "Dependent Development and Foreign Policy: The Case of Jamaica," *International Studies Quarterly* 33 (1989): 411–434; Jeanne A. Hey and Lynn M. Kuzma, "Anti-U.S. Foreign Policy of Dependent States: Mexican and Costa Rican Participation in Central American Peace Plans," *Comparative Political Studies* 26 (1993): 30–62; Jeanne A. K. Hey, "Compliance, Consensus and Counterdependence: Foreign Policy in Ecuador," *International Interactions* 19 (1994): 241–261; and Michael T. Snarr, "Latin American Foreign Policy towards the United States from 1948–1978: Exploring the Salience of Development Strategies," (Ph.D. diss., Ohio State University, 1995).

6. James F. Engle, "The Revolution and Mexican Foreign Policy," *Journal of Inter-American Studies* 16 (1969): 518–532; Olga Pellicer de Brody, "Mexico in the 1970s and Its Relations with the United States," in *Latin America and the United States: The Changing Political Realities*, ed. Julio Cotler and Richard R. Fagen (Stanford: Stanford University Press, 1974); Wolf Grabendorff, "Mexico's Foreign Policy: Indeed a Foreign Policy?" *Journal of Inter-American Studies and World Affairs* 2 (1978): 85–92; John F. McShane, "Emerging Regional Power: Mexico's Role in the Caribbean Basin," in *Latin American Foreign Policy: Global and Regional Dimensions*, ed. Elizabeth G. Ferris and Jennie K. Lincoln (Boulder: Westview Press, 1981); Guy Poitras, "Mexico's Foreign Policy in an Age of Interdependence," in *Latin American Foreign Policy: Global and Regional Dimensions*, ed. Elizabeth G. Ferris and Jennie K. Lincoln (Boulder: Westview Press, 1981); and Guadalupe González, "The Foundations of Mexico's Foreign Policy: Old Attitudes and New Realities," in *Foreign Policy in U.S.-Mexican Relations*, ed. Rosario Green and Peter H. Smith (San Diego: Center for U.S.-Mexican Studies, 1989).

7. Engle, "Revolution and Mexican Foreign Policy," 532.

8. Frank Brandenburg, *The Making of Modern Mexico* (Englewood Cliffs, N.J.: Prentice-Hall, 1964), 320.

9. McShane, "Emerging Regional Power," 192. Also see Rosario Green and Peter H. Smith, "Foreign Policy in U.S.-Mexican Relations: Introduction," in *Foreign Policy in U.S.-Mexican Relations*, ed. Rosario Green and Peter H. Smith (San Diego: Center for U.S.-Mexican Studies, 1989).

10. Alberto Van Klaveran, "Understanding Latin American Foreign Policies," in *Latin American Nations in World Politics*, ed. Heraldo Muñoz and Joseph S. Tulchin (Boulder: Westview Press, 1996), 47. Also see Daniel C. Levy, "Mexico: Sustained Civilian Rule without Democracy," in *Democracy in Developing Countries: Latin America*, vol. 4, ed. Larry Diamond, Juan J. Linz, and Seymour Martin Lipset (Boulder: Lynne Rienner, 1989), 481; and Jon Hurwitz, Mark Peffley, and Mitchell A. Seligson, "Foreign Policy Belief Systems in Comparative Perspective: The United States and Costa Rica," *International Studies Quarterly* 37 (1993): 245–270.

11. The emphasis in this chapter on Mexico's resistance to the United States does not mean that the two countries are always at odds. In fact, the two often agree on issues and cooperate frequently.

12. Jorge Casteñeda, *The Mexican Shock: Its Meaning for the U.S.* (New York: New Press, 1995).

13. Michael C. Meyer, William L. Sherman, and Susan M. Deeds, *The Course of Mexican History*, 6th ed. (New York: Oxford University Press, 1999), 670.

14. Howard Handelman, *Mexican Politics: The Dynamics of Change* (New York: St. Martin's Press, 1997), 152.

15. Ibid., 155.

16. Camp, *Politics in Mexico*, 212.

17. Judith Adler Hellman, "Mexican Perception of Free Trade: Support and Opposition to NAFTA," in *The Political Economy of North American Free Trade*, ed. Ricardo Grinspun and Maxwell A. Cameron (New York: St. Martin's Press, 1993), 195.

18. Casteñeda, *Mexican Shock*, 55.

19. See Julie A. Erfani, *The Paradox of the Mexican State, Rereading Sovereignty from Independence to NAFTA* (Boulder: Lynne Rienner, 1995), 178–179; and Guadalupe González and Jorge Chabat, "Mexico's Hemispheric Options in the Post–Cold War Era," in *Foreign Policy and Regionalism in the Americas*, ed. Gordon Mace and Jean-Philippe Thérien (Boulder: Lynne Rienner, 1996).

20. Carlos Fuentes, *A New Time for Mexico* (Los Angeles: University of California Press, 1997), 160.

21. Castañeda, *Mexican Shock*, 13.

22. For nearly a decade during the 1980s and 1990s the State Department was required to identify the votes it considered "important." See U.S. Department of State, *Report to Congress on Voting Practices in the United Nations* (Washington, D.C.: U.S. Department of State, 1985–1991). Also see Michael T. Snarr and Christina Ralbovsky, "Regime Change and Mexican Foreign Policy since WWII" (Paper presented at a meeting of the International Studies Association, Washington, D.C., February 1999).

23. Susan Kaufman Purcell, "The New U.S.-Mexico Relationship," in *Mexico under Zedillo*, ed. Susan Kaufman Purcell and Luis Rubio (Boulder: Lynne Rienner, 1998), 110.

24. Online NewsHour, "Mexico and Drugs," February 27, 1997, online at www.pbs.org/newshour.

25. Interview online at http://www.cnn.com/2000/WORLD/americas/11/26/mexico.fox.ap/.

26. Camp, *Politics in Mexico*, 215–216.

27. Mary Jordan and Kevin Sullivan, "Mexico Steps into Spotlight," *Washington Post Foreign Service*, January 31, 2001, A14.

28. Fox's selection of Castañeda is significant because Castañeda is not ideologically affiliated with the PAN. He has been critical of neoliberal economic policies in general and of NAFTA in particular.

29. Jane Perlez, "Mexico Warns of Colombia Drug War Spillover," *New York Times*, January 31, 2001.

30. Fuentes, *A New Time for Mexico*, 216.

CHAPTER 15

Domestic and International Influences on Foreign Policy:

A Comparative Perspective

Ryan K. Beasley and Michael T. Snarr

States in contemporary world politics face many challenges. Various conditions and interests both from outside and from within the state influence foreign policy. Differences in states and their international circumstances conspire to paint a diverse picture of the ways in which they conduct themselves in international affairs. Thus far in this book, however, we have examined individual countries separately. It is now time to draw some conclusions based on the countries we have examined and the theories we have outlined. Our conclusions, of course, will be limited by the countries we selected to study and by the theories of foreign policy we have chosen to highlight.

The selection of a wide variety of countries affords us many opportunities to investigate similarities and differences in foreign policies, and in particular, how various forces operate to influence a country's international involvement. Although the thirteen countries we present offer a wide variety of national experiences and international ambitions, they are but a small sample of the diversity of foreign policies evident around the world. China and Japan are no more truly representative of all Asian countries, than Italy, Switzerland, and Norway are reflections of the European countries we have chosen to explore. Certain groups of states, such as very small states Barbados, Liechtenstein, Fiji, and very poor states Chad, Sudan, Ecuador, are not represented at all.

Despite being limited by our relatively small sample, we can still seek out certain common features, certain fundamental similarities within the set of countries we examine. In doing so we will use the "comparative method," which involves selecting things to examine—in this instance, states and their foreign policies—and determining common patterns. You should have already noted that some of the chapters, such as that on Russia, conclude that realism is effective at explaining that country's foreign policy, whereas other chapters, such as the chapter on Mexico, fault realism and favor other theoretical perspectives.

It is important to remember, however, that this is not a competition between and among theories of foreign policy. We offer no preeminent theory that explains the most, offers the "best" insights, or in some other way overpowers the other, "weaker" theories. Indeed, the theories we chose to examine have thus far withstood the test of time fairly well. They each offer a different yet compelling version of why states behave as they do in world politics. Some theories attempt to explain particular decisions, and other theories attempt to explain more general patterns.

To illustrate, imagine trying to explain why a car accident happened. We might choose to focus our attention on the skills of the drivers of the cars. Alternatively, we might pay particular attention to the visibility problems at the accident scene caused by trees and the position of the sun. Finally, we might explain the accident by attending to the increase in traffic in the area due to recent economic growth and expansion of the city. Each factor operates at a somewhat different level of analysis — from the individuals, to the immediate environment, to the overall system. All three types of factors — actors, immediate circumstances, and systemic conditions — contribute to almost all accidents. But in certain circumstances, specific explanations seem to outweigh others. We would certainly be hard-pressed to claim that traffic patterns wholly explained an accident when the drivers were intoxicated. Alternatively, we would be remiss if we pointed only to faulty drivers when the given intersection accounts for most of the car accidents in the city. Many skillful drivers negotiate the intersection without incident, but surely something about the intersection itself promotes accidents. One particular set of factors will lead to conclusions about the causes of accidents different from the others — and hence to different conclusions about how to prevent accidents in the future.

Ultimately, we are not interested only in isolating the various causes and influences behind a particular country's international behavior. We are also interested in informing, evaluating, and revising the theories that we have developed as students of foreign policy. The many perspectives that exist regarding foreign policy are a testament not only to the complexity of foreign policy itself but also to the debates and disagreements that continue to flourish among scholars. We are still faced with many unanswered questions. Having closely examined thirteen different countries, however, we are in a good position to address some of those questions.

Important Questions for Comparative Foreign Policy

Of the many important questions facing foreign policy scholars several stand out. First, how does a state's military power systematically influence its foreign policy? This question drives to the heart of realism and is increasingly important in the post–Cold War world as old powers decline and new powers arise. Second, how does economic interdependence alter a state's foreign policy? Many have argued that increasing economic interdependence and globalism are the most important changes now occurring in the international system. Understanding the role of economic interdependence in foreign policy is one of the most significant issues facing foreign policy scholars today. Third, what is the role of culture and identity in shaping foreign policy? As the Cold War system fades, not only are the distribution of power and wealth being altered, but the very roles states play in the international system are changing, and many states appear to be struggling to find a new identity. Fourth, does public opinion alter or constrain leaders in the realm of foreign policy? In a sense, this question asks whether people matter in determining their country's foreign policy. As countries move toward democratic systems, it is important to know whether such systems will give citizens greater influence in world affairs. Fifth, does foreign policy respond to changes in the nature of the government? Although many regimes have endured for long periods of time, numerous changes have occurred in state governments. Finally, do leaders and their characteristics matter when it comes to shaping foreign policy? In the face of a changing international landscape, leaders find themselves in potentially powerful yet uncertain positions. Whether leaders themselves can influence a state's foreign policy becomes an important question to answer. By comparing several countries facing a variety of circumstances we can begin to provide some answers to these challenging questions.

Is Military Power an Important Influence on Foreign Policy?

As is emphasized in Chapter 1, realism expects that the countries with the strongest militaries will attempt to maintain their powerful position in relation to other countries. Russia and China are powerful states that are particularly concerned with maintaining their military power relative to the United States — arguably the most powerful actor in the current international system. Both countries are relatively independent and autonomous actors with strong military and nuclear capabilities to provide them with considerable security. Thus, they have not sought to entangle themselves in many strategic alliances. "Middle powers," however, often seek to ally themselves with a more powerful state or to play major powers off of one another in order to gain advantage. During the Cold War, many middle powers chose either the United States or the Soviet Union as an alliance partner. Generally, such an alliance leads to a loss in the middle power's sovereignty. By comparing the foreign policies of states with varying levels of military power we can begin to answer the question of whether military power is an important influence on foreign policy.

Alliances and Their Constraints. Germany and Israel provide insight into the question of alliances as a tool for overcoming military shortfalls or excessively conflictual circumstances. Israel's small size, combined with its geostrategic placement in the Middle East and close proximity to several hostile countries, make it an interesting case for examining military power, alliances, and foreign policy. Like Israel, Germany, a relatively powerful country (yet not a superpower), exhibits a high level of reliance on the United States and the North Atlantic Treaty Organization (NATO) alliance for its security. This reliance was especially noticeable during the Cold War. Germany allowed NATO troops as well as U.S. and British nuclear weapons on German soil, and Germany was the only NATO country to have its entire combat forces put under NATO control. In turn, Germany was protected under the "nuclear umbrella" of the United States and Britain. Israel was never compelled to accept foreign troops on its soil, but it clearly has emphasized its military, expending a great deal of its resources, time, and effort dealing with security threats. The fact that Israel has a relatively strong military compared with its neighbors in the Middle East can be explained largely by its having developed a close relationship with the United States. Israel receives billions of dollars in military aid annually from the United States to enhance its security.

In many ways, this is exactly the type of behavior that realism predicts from countries with relatively weak militaries that are facing threats to their national survival. If Israel cannot survive on its own in a self-help world, then it must rely on others and sacrifice some of its autonomy in doing so. Despite several noted exceptions, Germany's geostrategic location in the heart of Europe, combined with a perceived threat from a powerful regional actor (the Soviet Union and its allies), offers a compelling explanation of why Germany sought an alliance with the United States during the Cold War. Such alliance-seeking behavior was not an easy choice for Germany, since its experiences in the two world wars promoted a domestic climate that was not very supportive of such action. That Germany relinquished its sovereignty in exchange for increased security, despite the inhospitable domestic climate for doing so, is rather consistent with the realist perspective.

Avoiding Alliances and Stressing Independence. The experience of France is somewhat similar to that of Germany. France, like Germany, has a relatively powerful military and during the Cold War often sought to strengthen its ties to NATO. Unlike Germany and Israel, however, France does not appear to have relinquished nearly as much autonomy in its foreign policy. Rather, despite its clear status as a middle power, France continued to act as a dominant power. As pointed out by Steven Philip Kramer in Chapter 3, France "did not play the 'good ally' to the United States." Indeed, France appeared less constrained by the Western alliance than did Germany or Great Britain. For example, not long after the Cold War began, France and Great Britain invaded Egypt to halt Egyptian nationalization of the Suez Canal, counter to U.S. wishes. Unlike Great Britain, France would repeat similar acts in the coming decades. French president Charles de Gaulle demanded equal partnership for France in NATO, a proposition that was unpalatable to the United States. Instead of backing down and accepting the U.S. position, France expelled NATO from its headquarters in France and ended its participation in the integrated military command. In addition, France chartered an independent foreign policy course through its relative openness toward the Soviet Union.

Mexico is a relatively weak country that shares a border with the United States. It also does not suffer from the geostrategic problems that France, Germany, or Israel have. Although it has suffered strained relations, including several breaches of its physical borders by the United States, unlike France, Germany, and Israel, Mexico has enjoyed a long period of relative safety from a wide variety of external threats. Bordering the United States, Mexico has not had to fear

Soviet invasion or threats from neighbors who do not recognize its right to exist. Hence an explicit security relationship has not been sought with a stronger power. On the other hand, it could be argued that Mexico enjoyed a de facto security arrangement with the United States. Given its proximity to the United States, and U.S. interests in the area, it is likely that few states would contemplate significant military action against Mexico for fear of U.S. involvement.

Mexican foreign policy, however, parallels France's (and Brazil's) in that it occasionally follows policies that directly conflict with the wishes of the United States. Although there is disagreement over the level of Mexican dependence on the United States during the Cold War (and since), few would dispute that Mexico was more independent in many of its foreign policy positions than realism would anticipate. In Chapter 14 Michael T. Snarr points to Mexico's foreign policy on issues such as U.S. intervention in Central America and Cuba, and its voting patterns in the United Nations. In these cases, Mexico specifically took a policy line in direct contradiction to that pursued by the United States. Given Mexico's size and geostrategic location, its foreign policy often seems to challenge traditional realist predictions.

In sum, military power does tend to be an important influence on states' foreign policies. As discussed in the introductory chapter, realists emphasize the importance of the distribution of power within the international system, especially military power. This would lead one to expect that during the Cold War's bipolar system, states like Germany and Israel would join a major power in an alliance to increase its security, as these states did. Forming such an alliance with a stronger military power is certainly not without costs. As noted by Laura Drake in Chapter 9, Israel "does not have a blank check," and by enhancing its security, Israel has had to sacrifice a degree of autonomy—such as Israel's concession to the United States that it would not retaliate for Iraqi SCUD attacks during the Persian Gulf War. Presumably, from a realist perspective, these costs do not outweigh the benefits, and thus we see rational, self-interested states seeking self-preservation by acquiring power through strategic alliances.[1] This picture does tend, however, to hide some problems that such an extensive focus on external threats and military force faces. Not only does realism occasionally have trouble explaining the independent courses that states such as France and Mexico pursue, but realism's focus on military security in an anarchical world seemingly gives short shrift to the economic side of international relations and foreign policy.

What Is the Role of Economic Interdependence in Foreign Policy?

Increasingly, one can discern a trend toward potentially entangling economic commitments that connect countries in a complex web of trade and finance. From an economic liberal point of view, this makes sense because, as noted in Chapter 1, all states will benefit if they cooperate in a global economic system with each state specializing in what it is relatively better at producing. These commitments, however, come with costs. As Brian Ripley points out in his chapter on Chinese foreign policy, this web "of political and economic interdependence prevents states—even powerful ones—from acting with complete autonomy in world politics." This idea is echoed throughout this volume, as countries increasingly struggle with the tension between national sovereignty and international interdependence.

All the countries we examine are struggling to deal with economic integration and its associated interdependence, but not all of them experience interdependence in the same fashion. You will recall from Chapter 1 that some states are dependent, or what we would call asymmetrically interdependent, and that this serves to further limit their ability to choose their own foreign policies. Several of the countries we examine are significantly affected by their dependent relationship with the industrial countries of the North. We can investigate the effect of such dependency by looking for similarities among such countries and by comparing these countries with those that are considered to be less dependent. In sum, two overarching questions arise with regard to interdependence: why do some countries embrace the costs of interdependence more readily than others, and how do such interdependencies affect the foreign policies of different countries?

Interdependent and Dependent States in Integration. Great Britain, France, and Germany are all members of the European Union (EU). Despite the economic benefits that all three could derive, we see somewhat different approaches to and different degrees of enthusiasm for economic integration. Moreover, economic integration has affected each of these countries somewhat differently. British foreign policy toward the EU has been one of hesitation, preferring to define the country as "*with* but not *of* Europe." France and Germany, in contrast, have emphasized economic integration to a much greater extent. The French initially decided to sacrifice some economic autonomy in the pursuit of security and regional influence, reasoning that having Germany as a strong economic partner with French leadership might well prevent it from becoming a strong military foe. Since that time the European Union has significantly affected French foreign policy making, giving issues a decidedly "European" flavor. Germany, like France, has been decidedly "pro-Europe," but Germany's entrenchment as a central economic power in Europe offers it a decidedly different perspective on European integration from that of France. Instead of seeing integration as a path toward regional influence and competition with U.S. power, Germany initially embraced integration as a way to prove its willingness to be part of the European and global communities and the Western alliance. Even today, German preferences for European integration are partly motivated by a desire to demonstrate a commitment to multilateralism.

In contrast to the countries of Europe, much of the rest of the world had economic interdependence thrust upon them. Colonies were systematically exploited for economic gain, and their economies were often transformed to meet the needs of the colonial power. Upon independence, many of these countries were left with a narrow range of export commodities, an underdeveloped domestic economy, and little prospect of industrialization and further economic development. Often the primary basis of income was foreign trade, which tied their economies to their former colonial power and in some ways made them dependent on it. The new countries were left, in other words, with scant choice but to embrace the international economic system. Some, however, struggled to maintain autonomy and to avoid what they viewed as the immoral, self-serving, and economically destructive exploitations of the wealthy Western countries.

Mexico's import substitution strategy during much of the Cold War reflects its frustration at foreign domination (by the United States) and its long-term commitment to autonomy and noninterference from outside forces in its internal affairs. Indian independence from Britain was partly the product of consumer boycotts of British goods (giving rise to the "home spun" motto, which promoted consumption of domestically made clothing over that imported from Britain). Subsequently, Indian foreign policy charted a "third course," which steered it clear of excessive international entanglements. Mexico, however, finally succumbed to pressures toward further economic integration. Beginning in 1982, Mexican president Miguel de la Madrid began to liberalize the economy, increasingly focusing on export strategies in place of import substitution. Tinaz Pavri observes in Chapter 8 that India continues to struggle with issues of foreign investment and international economic integration, as Indian officials recognize that "increasing interdependence offers both an opportunity for and a potential constraint on Indian foreign policy."

Some countries, like Nigeria and Iran, have found themselves with a particularly valuable export commodity — oil. Iran's foreign policy has long been shaped by the extremely strong interest of foreign powers in preserving access to cheap Iranian oil. Indeed, the West supported the shah of Iran partly in an effort to secure access to oil in the region, and until the revolution in 1979 Iranian foreign policy was largely favorable to its Western patrons. In Nigeria, oil is the primary source of national income, and managing its production and sale abroad occupies a significant amount of attention in the realm of foreign policy. This is true despite a substantial amount of domestic resistance to opening the Nigerian economy to foreign investors and ownership. Both Iran and Nigeria have been compelled to be players in the growing international economy by virtue of their wealth of a high-demand resource. Each country, however, is vying to limit losses of sovereignty associated with increasing economic interdependence.

We might profitably contrast the hesitant approach South Africa has exhibited to regional economic integration with Brazil's formation of and heavy involvement in Mercosur. Both countries are regional powers faced with the task of improving their economic standing, and both have histories plagued by repressive regimes and democratic shortfalls. Thus they occupy somewhat similar positions in the international system. Yet each has chosen a different approach to the issue of economic integration. Brazil emphasizes economics in its foreign policy, paying special attention to regional integration. But this does not imply a wholehearted endorsement of globalization. Indeed, Brazil has jealously guarded its relationship with the countries involved in the Mercosur regional trading bloc and has opposed further efforts by the United States to expand the North American Free Trade Agreement into the Southern Hemisphere. In contrast, Kenneth W. Grundy notes in Chapter 12 that despite favorable rhetoric regarding economic exchange and growth, South Africa "has made little progress toward integration," partly because of pressure from domestic groups who fear that breaking down trade barriers will harm their interests. Moreover, South Africa continues to struggle with its post-apartheid status and increasingly is focusing on its declining internal conditions at the expense of its external economic opportunities.

Causes and Consequences of Interdependent Foreign Policies. Such differences between Brazil and South Africa have a variety of specific causes, such as the availability of regional trading partners, the level of institutional stability, and so forth. But let us consider the question at a more general level. For instance, are decisions by countries to further their economic integration primarily driven by internal factors or external factors, or by some combination of the two? Interdependence is an external factor that may constrain state behavior, but do such interdependencies arise primarily from external forces pulling states into ever greater connection, or do they arise from the internal characteristics of states themselves?

In some cases, external forces alone do not propel the turn toward greater economic integration and the opening of national borders to international commerce. Rather, internal economic and political conditions combine with external pressures and opportunities to do so. Mexico and Brazil embraced liberal reforms in the face of massive foreign debt, and Great Britain increasingly embraced the European Union only with considerable prodding from the administrations of Margaret Thatcher and John Major. In China, internal decisions among politburo members best explain economic reforms and the drive toward increasing integration in the global economy. The currently prevailing reform-minded faction within the Chinese Communist Party is the primary engine behind liberalization and economic changes. Should that configuration change, we might expect rather dramatic shifts in the character of Chinese economic strategies.

Japan's economic development and foreign policy during the Cold War hinged critically on a stable international system and an abundance of trading opportunities. Initially driven by U.S. demands for a stable and economically successful Japan, foreign policy makers embraced an export-led growth strategy that has widely been held as a model for developing countries. Ironically, however, Japan retained a fairly mercantilist, or "state-first," approach to international economic relations, establishing a variety of domestic hurdles aimed at foreign competitors and guarding its balance of trade surpluses both regionally and internationally.

Japan's experience with the Asian financial crisis of 1997 also effectively illustrates not only the constraints that economic interdependence imposes on foreign policy but also the challenges that can arise as a result of that very interdependence. In Chapter 7, Akitoshi Miyashita refers to the financial collapse in

Asia as a "contagion" that affected Japan because the country had located its production and its investments within the region. Ultimately, the crisis prompted Japanese decision makers to propose an "Asian Monetary Fund" and to engage in a variety of economic foreign policy initiatives. Interdependence is clearly a two-way street, both limiting and prompting foreign policy choices.

Global and regional economic integration is certainly of profound importance to states as they attempt to chart a course through international waters. As suggested in Chapter 1, states may sacrifice autonomy in the pursuit of economic gain. Indeed, economic integration of the levels experienced in the European Union can actually alter the decision-making process within states. Still, despite the fact that economic interdependence may be a check on the anarchy of the international system, this alone does not place specific limits on states. Indeed, states differ, for both internal and external reasons, in regard to how much they embrace interdependence, even when it serves their objective interests. Yet all states reside within a global economy that affects their relationships with other states and the interests within their borders. Balancing the changes that arise from globalization is one of the key challenges facing foreign policy decision makers in the twenty-first century.[2]

Has the Post–Cold War Created an Identity Crisis?

Another suggestion introduced in Chapter 1 that can now be explored across several countries deals with "political identity." To the extent that the citizens of a state view themselves and their history and traditions in a particular way, the state may be said to have a particular "identity." A state's identity may be rooted in its political culture, that is, the values, norms, and traditions that are widely shared by its people and are relatively enduring over time. The notion of "identity" is somewhat similar to "public opinion" in that they both involve the attitudes and values of the citizens of the state, but there are some important differences. Public opinion is typically viewed in terms of immediate policy questions ("should we go to war or not?"), whereas identity is a more general orientation toward political affairs ("we must preserve our autonomy"). Leaders may be driven to particular policies in order to accommodate or appease the citizens' views, or public opinion. Political identity does not necessarily require the recognition by political leaders of public sentiment—it is part and parcel of the underlying vision of the state itself.

The end of the Cold War and its effect on the international system transformed the circumstances of many states around the world and the way in which various states viewed their role in world politics. Several of the chapters emphasize cultural proclivities and national identities as influences on foreign policy. Often, identity is closely related to a state's status in world affairs. Kramer argues in Chapter 3 that one of France's primary goals is "to maintain France's status as a great power." In Chapter 2 Brian White indicates that one of Tony Blair's foreign policy priorities was "an attempt to establish a new international role and identity for Britain." Russia, too, is struggling with its own post–Cold War identity crisis and, as Paul D'Anieri argues in Chapter 5, this is affecting its policies toward Ukraine and other post-Soviet states, as well as certain issues in Russian relations with the United States.

Identity and Interests. Two countries in particular stand out as illustrative of the role of national identity in foreign policy. Both Japan and Germany, defeated in the Second World War, are very restrained in their foreign policy initiatives and international involvement. Both chapters dealing with these countries begin with the contrast between the relative importance of the state and the state's relative lack of leadership in global affairs, especially those involving military engagements. Jeffrey S. Lantis talks in Chapter 4 of a "German political culture of restraint," and in Chapter 7 Akitoshi Miyashita points to a very pacific posture adopted by Japan.

Here, however, we have different interpretations of whether this restraint can be attributed to political culture and political identity or to the rational interests of the state. Miyashita argues that Japanese restraint "stems not so much from its unique culture or peculiar political system but rather naturally from certain objective conditions that are unique to Japan." Again, this reflects the underlying question of whether different political cultures, transplanted into similar objective circumstances, would in fact follow decidedly different foreign policy agendas.

Are culture and identity in actuality a simple expression of realist self-interest, or are they something deeper, perhaps even psychological, that guide the thinking and actions of foreign policy makers? Can it be argued that the self-interest of a state can manifest itself in a variety of forms, including expressions of national culture or national identity. Surely, no countries wish to establish an identity as a weak and backward state, and to some extent all the countries examined in this book are striving for greater status and recognition on the world stage. From India's detonation of a nuclear device to China's drive to gain admission into the World Trade Organization (WTO), countries' "national" aspirations consistently involve gaining greater international recognition and more regional importance—what a realist might argue is simply the pursuit of power.

Patterns of Identities. Similarities across countries are quite evident regarding the aspirations of state strength and international standing. Russia's crushing of Chechen separatists parallels India's harsh treatment of many Kashmiris. Emphasizing autonomy and state strength, Pavri indicates in Chapter 8 that "India has viewed concessions to groups seeking increased autonomy as admissions of weakness on the part of the state and has often interpreted such demands as anti-Indian, a threat to the integrity of the state that should be adverted at all costs." Illustrating a resolve to stem a declining international image and prevent internal instability, D'Anieri notes in Chapter 5, "Gaining the approval of the international system for Russia's vision of itself is of crucial importance for Russia, which has lost much of its historic territory, has had to fight to keep Chechnya, and is hobbled by the weakness of the state."

We can also see similarities in the aspirations of countries that have suffered under colonialism (India, Nigeria, South Africa), or that have been subjugated to a peripheral role in international affairs by a dominant actor or actors (Brazil, Iran, Mexico). Each of these countries, in various ways, is seeking to re-establish its previous importance or attain its underlying yet frustrated potential. As Ripley notes in Chapter 6 regarding early Chinese foreign policy, "In some respects, Chinese foreign policy makers were challenged to overcome the 'century of humiliation,' when, prior to the 1949 revolution, the nineteenth-century great powers practiced imperialism. These legacies from the past, perhaps exacerbated by the desire to overcome a perception of 'backwardness,' reinforced a sense of vulnerability, suspicion of outside powers, and strong nationalist sentiment." The power disparities that once served to promote colonial conquest and unabashed imperialism are now being manifested as national aspirations and wounded resolve.

It is tempting, then, to conclude that such similarities across countries reflect the pervasiveness of power politics and rational self-interest, and that "culture" and "identity" are mere window dressing to more central motives. Yet each country also has something undeniably unique in its history and culture that appears to be of real importance in guiding its foreign policy. Perhaps each country aspires to its own particular international character based on its history and identity, even while those aspirations are uniformly power-seeking and self-interested. Mexico's noted desire for autonomy and noninterference may parallel that of China's, but India downplays such a motive relative to its desire to be a regional leader, and South Africa's identity turns more on overcoming its racist past than on preventing outside forces from shaping its destiny. Israel's existence as a state is fundamentally wed to its Zionist ideology, what Laura Drake refers to in Chapter 9 as "a political-religious-ethnic doctrine that signifies the gathering of Jews from all parts of the world to inhabit an exclusive Jewish state in Palestine." This vision for Israel conveys a core value that might be considered self-interested but that surely represents a unique manifestation of that self-interest in the context of Israel's history and regional circumstances.

National identity and culture, then, do provide some explanation of the foreign policy behavior of states. One way to think about national culture and national identity is to consider them to be the repository of state interests. As states face circumstances that emphasize certain interests (national survival, autonomy and independence, and so forth), a culture or identity may arise that internalizes those interests, and thus foreign policy may be constructed to serve the national identity, and thereby the state's interest. A particular culture or identity may well serve the "interests" of the state, but it is the manifestation of that interest in the form of identity and culture that translates the interest into specific foreign policy. This also implies that responding to changes in international conditions may be difficult for states with strong national identities. Clearly, if identity and culture are repositories of state interests, they are not likely to change as abruptly as objective interests. Indeed, this might account for a post–Cold War identity crisis, as states' objective conditions and interests face rapid changes while their Cold War or pre–Cold War identities linger.

Another way to think about national culture and national identity is that they themselves shape what are perceived to be the interests of the state. Thus they serve not as repositories of interests but as sources of interests. Although culture and identity almost certainly arise from a state's circumstances and history, they may well promote a particular vision of what is in the state's interest. This begins to suggest that "objective" interests are not really so objective, as there must be some lens through which circumstances are viewed. This would, in turn, raise serious questions about the practice of attributing objective interests to states, as realists tend to do. In whatever fashion national culture and national identity are viewed, the countries represented in this volume certainly illustrate the importance of such factors on the conduct of foreign policy.[3]

How Is Foreign Policy Affected by Public Opinion?

Chapter 1 suggests a potentially complex relationship between whether or not a country is a democracy and the influence of various societal forces on that country's foreign policy. It is commonly assumed that democracies are constrained by public opinion and a variety of interest groups, whereas nondemocracies are not, but the picture is generally more complex. In the realm of foreign policy, leaders of both democracies and nondemocracies might be unconstrained by the specific attitudes of the public (even when the public has clearly articulated its attitudes on foreign policy) but still be limited by the general prevailing orientation or "mood" of the public. Additionally, to understand the relationship between a society and its foreign policy it is important to know whether or not a democracy is new and in the process of consolidating itself and developing avenues for citizen participation in politics. Thus, it is helpful to compare democracies, nondemocracies, and "transitional" democracies in exploring the role of public opinion on foreign policy. China and Iran are clearly not democracies by most measures. France, Germany, Great Britain, Israel, and Japan, in contrast, are well-established democracies that have endured for a relatively long period of time. South Africa and Russia are recent, limited democracies, each struggling to consolidate and define the role of the public in political affairs. These countries serve as the focal point of our examination of the relationship between democracy, public opinion, and foreign policy.

Nondemocracies and Democracies. Overall, the nondemocracies support the conventional wisdom that public opinion does not drive foreign policy in such political systems. Although recently a variety of political actors in Iran have gained platforms for expressing their views and concerns, Paul D. Hoyt notes in Chapter 10 that for much of that country's modern history powerful individuals who suppressed or minimized the conflicting political impulses of society have dominated its foreign policy. First the shah and then the Ayatollah Ruhollah Khomeini exercised their individual judgments and preferences in foreign policy quite independently of the will of the people. Yet, it should be noted that Iranian foreign policy under Khomeini reflected certain anti-western and anticolonialism "core" values held by the public. China, too, has an elite leadership that, although at times divided, has generally dictated the direction of Chinese foreign policy. Indeed, the crackdown in Tiananmen Square in 1989 effectively illustrates the limitations (and dangers) of Chinese citizen participation in the affairs of state. However, as in Iran, China is dealing with increasing pressures for citizen participation in the political process, and the limited influence of the public on foreign policy in the past may not necessarily be a good predictor of its impact in the future.

France, Germany, Great Britain, and Japan, stand in fairly sharp contrast to both China and Iran in regard to the potential influence that citizens have on foreign policy. Yet, at least historically, foreign policy in these states has been highly centralized, so they have not always lived up to the democratic ideal. In Chapter 3 Kramer says, "Centralized authority in the making of French foreign policy is the result of a long history of a strong, unitary state and a weak civil society in which the influence of regional or local governments, or secondary associations between the state and the individual, has been discouraged." In Chapter 2 White quotes David Vital in arguing that in British foreign policy, "for almost all practical purposes the Executive is unfettered" and a domestic consensus has prevailed on many foreign policy issues, leaving little room for public opinion to make a difference. In Japan the political party elites and the powerful bureaucracy, in alliance with business interests, have long directed foreign policy. Political party elites also play an important role in Germany, as they do in France and Great Britain, yet it is the public that determines who these elites are. Beyond the obvious avenues of electoral participation, as Jeffrey Lantis points out in Chapter 4, the "collective attitudes and perceptions of average citizens may shape the elite discourse by ruling certain initiatives 'in' or 'out' of political bounds." Foreign policy initiatives in democracies, are indeed sensitive to and at times constrained by the collective political attitudes of the citizens.

In Great Britain's foreign policy, particularly on the issue of Europe, bipartisanship and consensus are increasingly lacking. Indeed, in Chapter 2 White argues that British foreign policy is clearly influenced by the domestic environment and that "core values and underlying beliefs of the British people . . . set boundaries for foreign policy makers." In Japan the "strong state" that allowed foreign policy to be more elite driven was based on a national consensus that economic growth was Japan's priority. That consensus, and thus Japan's state, may now be eroding. All of this suggests a pattern in these democracies: although foreign policy is centralized and many decisions are made without the direct input of citizens, central values indirectly affect who is elected and set parameters for policy makers. Furthermore, although historically the public has not been particularly involved and influential in foreign policy, internal and external changes are promoting a shift in the relationship between public opinion and foreign policy. This relationship is starting to resemble the conventional wisdom that assumes policies in democracies are responsive to the will of the people.

In Israel, another long-standing democracy, foreign policy is also in the hands of the national security establishment, as discussed in Chapter 9. Still, the nature

of the political system significantly conditions the role of public opinion in foreign policy. Like Germany, Israel is frequently governed by coalitions of political
parties, but unlike Germany those coalitions are somewhat more tenuous and
involve more parties. The frequency with which elections are held in Israel
prompts some nearly continuous concern regarding the "current mood" of the
public, as dissolution of the cabinet and subsequent elections determine who will
guide subsequent policy. Moreover, the central nature of foreign policy issues in
Israeli public life can amplify the importance of citizen views, because Israeli citizens are likely to be concerned about foreign policy matters. Essentially every
Jewish citizen is mandated to serve in the army and thus there is, as Drake discusses in Chapter 9, a strong connection between society and the military. To the
extent that foreign policy submits soldiers to peril, and this is often the case in
Israel, popular sentiment does have the potential to pressure decision makers.

New Democracies in Transition. During apartheid, notes Grundy in Chapter
12, a small, elite group of decision makers who "explicitly rejected the values of
the majority" dominated foreign policy in South Africa. The 1994 elections,
however, arguably gave citizens more opportunities to influence the course of
South African foreign policy. Clearly, the majority is now represented, and thus
the new democratic regime could represent a stronger connection between the
people and the state. However, the process of defining the relationship between
the popularly elected parliament and the executive branch has not clearly
resolved into potential avenues of influence running from the citizen to the foreign policy apparatus. Instead foreign policy remains a "top-down" enterprise.
Still, as noted in Chapter 12, changes in the making of foreign policy are increasingly likely "as the democratic ideal gains currency among members of Parliament and interest groups begin to reflect a broader spectrum of the populace."
Already evident are a wide variety of interests groups seeking influence over
South Africa's economic policies.

Russia, like South Africa, is in the process of defining the relationship
between its government and its citizens. This process is complicated by the fact
that Russian foreign policy making is informal and uninstitutionalized, thus
obscuring the appropriate avenues for citizen influence. Nevertheless, public
opinion, although not at the heart of the foreign policy process, does play some
role in Russia. Similar in some fashion to its role in Great Britain and Germany,
Russian public opinion offers some guideposts for various foreign policy initiatives and is a concern among politicians, who must have at least some popular
appeal in order to gain or retain office. Russia is like South Africa in that the
institutional structure for the making of foreign policy is somewhat uncertain.
South Africa has clearly retained an executive structure that could accommodate
a wider variety of societal interests and actors than that of Russia, but the process
of doing so is not complete. As in both China and Iran, the history of centralized, hierarchical, and insulated foreign policy making lingers despite impressive
changes in the political landscape.

Clearly, there is no neat and orderly relationship between the type of regime (established democracy, new democracy, or nondemocracy) and the impact of public opinion. Each of the countries examined have some similarities as well as differences. Notably, although Iran is not a democracy in the same way as Great Britain or the United States, it does hold elections and does have a representative body (the Majlis) for the expression of the will of the people. And increasingly the will of the Iranian public is in favor of new foreign policy directions. Moreover, German foreign policy, generally sensitive to the public's opinion, has at times deviated from popular sentiment, as when Konrad Adenauer led Germany toward rearmament in the 1950s despite popular resistance.

It is tempting to conclude that democracies express the will of the public in foreign policy more so than nondemocracies or transitional democracies, but the evidence from the countries we examine is mixed. A simple ordering from "more democratic" to "less democratic" hides important differences. The mechanism of the public's influence seems to reside primarily in the will of political leaders to embrace popular sentiment and allow it to influence foreign policy decisions.[4] But there is no clear formula guiding our expectations as to when this will happen. Certainly having more avenues for communicating public opinion to policy makers, as is typically the case in democratic governments, will highlight the public's attitudes in the minds of the foreign policy leadership, but the consequences of ignoring public sentiment are clearly not lost on elites in the more hierarchical political systems.

How Does Foreign Policy Respond to Change in Regimes?

In order to explore the relationship between domestic factors and foreign policy further, we can examine the degree of continuity of foreign policy in those countries that have experienced relatively recent and dramatic domestic transformations or a change in regime. Because realism and liberalism tend to focus on external factors to explain foreign policy, they would expect a great deal of continuity in foreign policy when international conditions remain the same—even if domestic conditions are changing rapidly. South Africa, Russia, and Iran have each undergone rather dramatic change and exceptional and abrupt transformations of their domestic political landscapes. Mexico has experienced somewhat more moderate, although significant, political changes in the recent past. The election of President Vicente Fox in 2000 marked the end of the long-ruling PRI monopoly of national power. Finally, Great Britain has enjoyed relative stability as a long-standing democracy. Although Great Britain has variously alternated between a Labour Party and a Conservative Party government, these leadership changes have been fairly routine, not challenging the fundamental nature of the political system. To the extent that regime changes affect foreign policy, we might expect to see dramatic changes in foreign policy in Russia, Iran, and South Africa, moderate changes in Mexico, and relative continuity in Great Britain.[5]

Dramatic Regime Change. Russia's domestic transformation was quite sudden and dramatic. The country moved from a communist regime and a centrally planned economy to a multiparty, semipresidential system and forms of free market capitalism over the course of a few years. In Chapter 5 D'Anieri makes the point that despite these shifts the "degree of change in foreign policy has not matched the revolutionary changes in domestic politics." He adds that "[i]n light of this disconnection between drastic change in Russia's domestic life and substantial . . . continuity in foreign policy, it appears that we must look to other, more continuous factors, to explain Russia's foreign policy today." Although we see a complex relationship between domestic and foreign policy, this insight regarding continuity in the face of dramatic domestic transformation effectively illustrates the difference in viewpoint of those focusing on external as opposed to internal factors. The continuity between Russian and Soviet foreign policy suggests that the nature of the regime does not make a significant difference.

The Iranian revolution at the end of the 1970s marked a tremendous transformation of both Iran and the region generally. With the shah deposed after ruling for more than twenty-five years and the emergence of the Ayatollah Khomeini as the new leader of Iran, significant changes in foreign policy emerged. Indeed, in Chapter 10 Hoyt indicates, "[a]s is common with successful revolutions, Khomeini's new government sought to repudiate the previous government's domestic and foreign policies." Although the revolution in Iran was not related to the end of the Cold War, as was the transformation in Russia, the consequences were equally, if not more, profound. The changes in Iranian foreign policy included open hostility toward the United States (the former ally and political supporter of the shah), a significant step away from the Soviet Union, and a long and costly war with Iraq. Thus, in contrast to the situation in Russia, significant internal changes were directly related to altered foreign policy directions.

In South Africa the nature of regime change was also dramatic. As Grundy notes in Chapter 12, foreign policy leading up to the de Klerk regime "consisted of a firm and even proactive defense of apartheid within South Africa and in the surrounding region, coupled with an economic and diplomatic determination to be accepted as a member of the loose Western anticommunist coalition." After the ascension of power of the ANC, foreign policy changed rather dramatically. Indeed, Grundy goes on to say, "the ANC, determined to totally reject apartheid, tossed overboard any foreign policy perspectives associated with the old regime." This resulted in an increased cooperative attitude toward regional actors and increased reliance on multilateralism, although, Grundy notes, an underlying consistency with some pre-apartheid policies remains:

> In a way, the new South Africa is merely taking up where the country left off in the pre-apartheid era—that is, it is seeking to normalize historical relations that reflect the geographic realities of economic interdependence. This aspect of contemporary South African foreign policy reflects the geopolitical drives of earlier governments in Pretoria. In fact, there is a

continuity here that realists can appreciate — no matter what the values or ideologies of the regime in power, the external givens force it, for reasons of state, to behave in a statist way.

The different impact of regime change on Russia on the one hand and Iran and South Africa on the other could be attributed to the nature of the change itself. Although the Russian change was dramatic, sweeping in both new economic practices as well as political institutions, it was one driven by changes initiated by the ruling leaders themselves. Mikhail Gorbachev himself — who to this day remains a committed Communist — began a process of democratization, *glasnost* (openness) and *perestroika* (restructuring), that ultimately (and unintentionally) dislodged the Communist Party from power. The opposition, in an important sense, was within the regime itself. Reformers sought change, not wholesale revolution. The restoration of democracy in Brazil in 1985 also saw this type of change. As Scott D. Tollefson notes in Chapter 13, foreign policy change did not accompany democratization because of "the conservative pace and nature of Brazil's transition to democracy, which was negotiated behind closed doors between the military leaders of the opposition. Sarney [the new president] was not even identified with the opposition; he had been a leader of the pro-military party within the Congress."

In both Iran and South Africa, the opposition had virtually no say in governmental affairs until assuming the reins of power. Indeed, the Ayatollah Khomeini had been imprisoned and exiled by the previous regime, and Nelson Mandela spent twenty-seven years in jail as an opponent of the apartheid regime. Boris Yeltsin, in contrast, was a member of the politburo of the Communist Party, and the current Russian president, Vladimir Putin, worked in the KGB.

Moderate Regime Change and Leadership Change. The recent significant redistribution of political power among domestic actors in Mexico has not immediately translated into a new foreign policy direction. Arguably, the greatest change in Mexican foreign policy began in the early 1980s with the adoption of liberal trading policies under the de la Madrid regime. But perhaps it is too early to place a definitive label on the new leadership in Mexico in regard to its foreign policy orientation. Indeed, the new administration is showing early signs of continuing its concern about sovereignty, and President Fox has confronted the United States about U.S. policies on both immigration and drugs.

Great Britain represents a stalwart of regime stability. Yet, despite this stability and a relatively unchanging rhetoric regarding foreign policy, British foreign policy has undergone notable substantive changes associated with changes in the ruling party. Gauging the exact level of change in foreign policy can be a tricky business, but the resignation of Thatcher, the defeat of her Conservative Party, and the landslide victory of Tony Blair and his New Labour Party clearly heralded new directions in British foreign policy. Yet it is safe to say that here we see more gradual changes than those in South Africa or Iran. In many ways, the changes in British foreign policy are directly related to both the end of the Cold

War as well as the increasing impact of European integration on Britain. In this sense, external factors seem to yield important variations in foreign policy. Still, domestic factors cannot be too heavily discounted in that they continue to play a significant role in shaping foreign policy.

What Is the Role of Leaders in Shaping Foreign Policy?

Given all the preceding forces operating to influence the foreign policies of states, it might seem that little room is left for the impact of individual leaders. In the making of foreign policy, awash in a sea of alliances, interdependencies, cultural identities, and public opinion, leadership might seem to be a small consideration. But individual leaders do matter, and often the foreign policies of states reflect the views and personalities of powerful people in the foreign policy process. At times these individuals play such a dominant role that certain state foreign policies actually become synonymous with the leader. We might speak, for example, of the Gaullist interests, the Maoist initiatives, or the Nehru philosophy. These, it can be argued, are more than just convenient labels masking more important influences on foreign policy. Rather, they genuinely reflect the imprint of individuals on the foreign policy of states.

Scholars investigating the role of individuals in foreign policy have suggested that leadership tends to be more or less important depending on the nature of the situation or on the nature of the individuals themselves. As indicated in Chapter 1, what an individual leader is like tends to be more significant in shaping a state's foreign policy "when the situation is ambiguous, uncertain, and complex, and when the leader is involved in the actual decision making rather than delegating his or her authority to advisers." There has also been a tendency among foreign policy scholars to assume that individual leaders are more important in the developing world than in industrial countries.[6] The logic here is that strong institutions and democratic traditions effectively constrain the whims of particular individual leaders. As these are more in evidence among the industrial countries of the world, the hand of leadership should leave a less visible imprint on these countries' foreign policies. To some extent, the countries we examine bear both of these notions out—with important exceptions.

Leadership in Developing and Industrial Countries. Turning first to the question of whether leadership is more important in developing as opposed to industrial countries, we find the evidence mixed. In Iran, as Hoyt notes in Chapter 10, "the mechanisms that Iran uses to pursue its goal of regional dominance seem to vary according to the worldview of the country's dominant figure." From the shah to Khomeini, dominant leaders have largely formulated significant Iranian foreign policy. The shah excluded many societal groups from the political process. Khomeini, too, instituted a fairly hierarchical and exclusive foreign policy system. In China, a very hierarchical regime, individual leaders play an important part in the formulation of foreign policy. As Ripley argues in Chapter 6, "[a]lthough quite different in their personalities and ideological commitments, both Mao and Deng played a dominant role in foreign policy making."

In Nigeria individual leaders have had a particularly strong influence over foreign policy. Olufemi A. Babarinde and Stephen Wright point out in Chapter 11 that during the First Republic Tafawa Balewa pushed the country into adopting a variety of conservative policies and that "a radical shift in Nigerian foreign policy in 1975–1976 can be easily attributed to the ousting of the more conservative Yakubu Gowon (a Christian from the Middle Belt) by the more dynamic and radical Murtala Muhammed (a northern Muslim)." Moreover, there seems to be little doubt that Ibrahim Babangida and Sani Abacha each left a visible imprint on the foreign policy of Nigeria during the 1990s. Still, Nigeria has increasingly felt the influence of a variety of domestic actors on its foreign policy—from retired generals to academics. Although these influences are arguably small and variable, they do serve to remind us that many different sources of foreign policy exist, even in developing countries.

Germany does not necessarily conform to expectations based on level of development alone. As Jeffrey S. Lantis argues in Chapter 4, "Even foreign ministers, such as [Hans-Dietrich] Genscher and [Joschka] Fischer . . . have been significant leaders in foreign policy debates, and their styles and beliefs have affected German foreign policy." Lantis goes on to say that despite low support among the public, "German leaders were nevertheless committed to building a consensus to ratify and implement the Treaty on European Union." Thus, despite having strong institutions and a stable democracy, individuals and their characteristics have managed to influence German foreign policy.

In France, a democracy, the strong power afforded the president in the Fifth Republic arguably circumvents the potential influence of many other societal actors. Indeed, the Fifth Republic was constructed by, and is virtually synonymous with, de Gaulle. As Kramer indicates in Chapter 3, de Gaulle's international activism was extensive, and, unconstrained by weak domestic institutions, he was able to pursue a vigorous and extensive foreign policy agenda. Under de Gaulle, for example, France ignored its ascribed role as a middle power, developing a nuclear arsenal, actively using its seat on the United Nations Security Council, centralizing its importance in European affairs, and maintaining a dominant role in Africa. De Gaulle effectively illustrates the significant role a leader can play, thereby lending support to theories of foreign policy focusing on individual leadership.

The Effects of Leaders. When a leader does have an effect on foreign policy, we must consider the individual's experiences, beliefs, and leadership styles that he or she brings to the foreign policy making process in order to understand the nature of that effect. Both India and Brazil offer compelling examples of individual leadership and the impact of leaders' qualities on foreign policy. We can see the effect of the very different personalities and beliefs of Nehru and his daughter Indira Gandhi on various foreign policies adopted by India. In Brazil,

President Fernando Henrique Cardoso provides an interesting insight into the role of leaders and their personal characteristics as they influence foreign policy. In examining these three individuals, we can begin to assess the relationship between characteristics of leaders and foreign policy.

In Chapter 8 Pavri highlights the contrast between Nehru and Indira Gandhi. She comments that Nehru leaned toward building a consensus and offering conciliatory gestures. Despite a gradual shift away from his early idealism, Pavri notes, his orientation toward socialism and working within the system to promote change prompted him "to nurture images of fraternal relations among the countries of the developing world, relations based on liberal notions of cooperation and shared values." His focus on the Non-Aligned Movement and his positive gestures toward China reflect his tendency to favor conciliation and his commitment to peaceful resolution of conflict.

Indira Gandhi, in contrast, exhibited a great deal of personal insecurity, which translated into a dominating leadership style and a penchant for enhancing her personal power. Moreover, she harbored a fundamental mistrust of regional actors and tended to view the world in very stark and conflictual ways. India's foreign policy under Indira Gandhi reflected many of these personal characteristics. Shortly after she assumed leadership India went to war with Pakistan. She also dealt quite aggressively with other regional actors, like Nepal and Bhutan, often resorting to the use of tacit threats of military action in order to gain their compliance on various issues. Moreover, her quest for personal power and her unwillingness to compromise prompted a split in the Congress Party, creating an internal cleavage that significantly shaped the process of foreign policy making for years to come. India's departure from Mohandas Gandhi's visions of peaceful engagement and nonviolence, then, might largely be explained by something as fundamental as the transition in leadership from Nehru to Indira Gandhi.

Brazil represents another interesting example of the importance of leadership. As Tollefson demonstrates in Chapter 13, Brazil's post–World War II foreign policy was highly dependent on who ruled. Shifts in U.S.-Brazilian relations corresponded to changes in leadership. President Cardoso has been particularly active and influential in foreign policy. Having served as the nation's foreign minister and finance minister, Cardoso came to power with an abundance of experience. Moreover, he personally experienced the problems of military rule in Brazil when he was forced into exile. Such experiences appear to have generated in him a strong predilection for international issues, even, as Tollefson noted, to the point of prompting the criticism that "he is too interested in foreign relations, a charge that has been rarely leveled at previous Brazilian presidents." The personal beliefs and tendencies of leaders have the greatest potential impact when the leaders are interested and involved in foreign policy. Despite his writings on dependence theory and class conflict when he was an academic, Cardoso's belief that Brazil must be cooperative in its ties to the world has affected foreign policy. Under Cardoso, Brazil has toned down its demands for permanent membership on the United Nations Security Council, expanded its ties to other countries, lessened tensions with Argentina, and embraced globalization and open economic borders, particularly in the region.

Individuals in leadership positions often face numerous and significant constraints from external and internal actors and institutions. Nevertheless, it is a human or a group of humans that actually make the choices that constitute a state's foreign policy. The chapters in this book refer to the many important decisions made by the leaders of these countries. It is clear that leaders matter at some times more than others and that at those times when leaders are important, their beliefs, perceptions, experiences, and decision-making styles can affect whether or not they recognize constraints on their states and how they respond to them.

Linkages between Internal and External Factors

A final, and more overarching, question confronting foreign policy scholars is how various factors work in combination with one another to influence foreign policy. In particular, what are the linkages between external factors and internal factors? As the chapters in this book illustrate, foreign policy is typically the result of many domestic and international factors.[7]

The relationship between internal and external factors sometimes is simply additive in nature. In other words, both types work directly and independently to influence a state's foreign policies. Both domestic and international factors exert some independent influence on Russia's foreign policy toward the Balkans, for example. Alternatively, in some cases the relationship is sequenced in that the international environment is a catalyst, presenting states opportunities or threats to which they must respond, and it is only then that domestic factors come into play, shaping states' responses.[8] In Chapter 4, Lantis argues that contemporary German foreign policy can best be understood as a response to dilemmas and opportunities in the international system, which was then moderated by internal constraints of elite and public opinion.

Or consider the role of leaders as being critical to the influence of both international and domestic forces. Leaders negotiate both the international and the domestic realms, often simultaneously being constrained by both external and internal demands. Such leaders might be characterized as playing both an international and a domestic "game," often struggling to satisfy both domestic and international audiences with their foreign policy choices.[9] In this sense, the influence of external and internal factors is mediated by individuals who are responsive to both. Russian relations with the United States over NATO expansion, the Balkan wars, and the U.S. ballistic missile defense system can be portrayed as Russian leaders negotiating with an external actor, the United States, while at the same time mobilizing and maintaining consensus at home. German and Japanese decisions to participate in United Nations peacekeeping missions in the post–Cold War era can also be seen as the result of decision makers attempting to satisfy and bargain with external pressures and internal constituencies. Israeli negotiations with the Palestinians represent another simultaneous balancing act between domestic and international demands.

Another link between internal and external factors occurs when external constraints are internalized into domestic factors. The occupation by foreign powers in Germany and Japan after their defeat in World War II meant that external actors played a significant role in setting up the democratic political systems in those states. Moreover, the nature of the military defeats themselves became part of their political culture — internalized as antimilitarism and a consensus on the priority of economics. Similarly, British occupation of the Indian subcontinent left a legacy of democratic, parliamentary rule in independent India. In many states that experienced colonialism, however, the history of external constraints produced a counterreaction at the domestic level. The desire to promote sovereignty and independence seen in the beliefs of leaders and the public in India and Mexico, for example, can be traced back to their historical experiences with interference by external powers. These beliefs, or core values, then became a domestic factor shaping subsequent foreign policy. In all of these cases, the political system itself was a product of external actors and then became an internal factor in subsequent foreign policy.

External factors also shaped the nature of the domestic landscape in France, changing the very nature of the French political system itself. As Kramer notes in Chapter 3, "In 1958, de Gaulle launched a new effort to reassert France's rank as a great power. De Gaulle and his supporters believed that this could be facilitated by domestic political reforms. They would create stable political institutions with increased power for the executive (so that national power could be leveraged in the pursuit of foreign policy)." The French leader thus responded to external conditions by molding the Fifth Republic in such a way as to challenge the distribution of power in the international system. The centralization of authority in the French political system would have long-term effects on nearly all aspects of French foreign policy making and France's relations with the world. It is interesting to note that the opposite occurred in South Africa under apartheid. There, Grundy notes in Chapter 12, instead of the political system being used as a tool for foreign policy, foreign policy was used as a means to justify the existence of the political system:

> The Cold War presented the racist government with an opportunity to use the global power struggle between communism and anticommunism as a means to weakening the domestic opponents of apartheid. By identifying its chief opposition — the African National Congress (ANC) as well as liberal whites and leftist revolutionaries — in Cold War terms and by seeking itself to be included in the anticommunist confraternity, Pretoria worked to isolate antiapartheid activists, to rationalize its antirevolutionary stance in broader, global terms, and thus to neutralize opposition from the Western world.

External factors, such as democratization pressures, world opinion on human rights issues, interdependence, and globalization, may also alter the internal structure of a domestic political system by shifting power away from the central government and into the hands of private actors such as businesses or by decentralizing policy making within the state.[10] These external pressures can also influence the interests and positions of domestic political actors.[11] China and Mexico, for example, are both struggling with the issue of becoming more interdependent with other states economically while at the same time preserving a strong tradition of autonomy and support for noninterference by other states in their domestic affairs. As China moves toward membership in the WTO, it is increasingly coming under scrutiny by various international actors interested in questions of human rights. And as it attempts to liberalize its economy, it is more and more faced with citizen demands, both political and economic. One response to such demands might be further suppression to consolidate support behind China's chosen foreign policy direction. But this could well result in international condemnation and, ironically, hinder China in realizing its foreign policy goal of WTO membership.

Mexico's choice to further its interdependence by joining NAFTA also affected Mexican internal politics. As discussed in Chapter 14, the Chiapas rebellion began on the day NAFTA went into effect. Concerned about the lack of political and economic reform and the increase in economic competition that further integration would bring to the already poor region, Zapatista leaders were able to challenge the central Mexican government's authority in the region. The uprising further linked international forces with domestic politics as human rights groups, representing a post–Cold War trend in world opinion, began monitoring the Mexican government's actions in Chiapas. The Mexican government, of course, viewed this as an intrusion into its sovereign, internal affairs.

Nigeria, too, is facing the challenge of interdependence and the effects it creates at the domestic level. As Babarinde and Wright note in Chapter 11, "the dire need for debt rescheduling and foreign investment also allowed Western governments, nongovernmental organizations (NGOs), and agencies such as the World Bank and International Monetary Fund to leverage an agenda of democratization and good governance in addition to liberal economic reforms. Such interdependency requires Nigerian domestic politics to take account of these external parameters." Thus, globalization and increased interdependence can alter the very way foreign policy decisions are made. One result of increased connections between different parts of states is that regions or provinces may establish their own foreign policies, challenging the authority of the central government. Recall how the Maharashtra regional government in India cancelled the Enron project that promised significant investment money, citing the potential for exploitation of India. Although the Maharashtra state subsequently reversed itself, it does serve to illustrate the complex linkage between the domestic and the foreign.

In the European Union, where regional integration has reached the highest stage, governments are finding that much of their authority for making foreign

policy is now moving out of their hands and into the hands of regional governments or the EU. As Kramer notes in Chapter 3,

> Vast areas of what was once French foreign policy are now European
> issues. . . . Although much cooperation in foreign policy areas is intergov-
> ernmental, it nonetheless changes the nature of foreign policy making. The
> French state is also losing power to the regions, not only to regions with-
> in France but to regions that cut across several nations. French regional and
> local governments cooperate routinely with German, Italian, and Spanish
> regional authorities. In short, as a unified Europe increasingly becomes a
> reality, the nature of foreign policy making in any nation will change in
> ways that cannot yet be imagined.

As in France, the internal mechanisms for making foreign policy are changing as a result of external processes in Britain, Germany, and the other member
states of the EU. In sum, the relationship between domestic and international
influences on foreign policy is complex. Sometimes the two sources operate independently, each pushing the state in a particular direction. At other times, however, external factors provide the right conditions for internal forces to manifest
themselves in the foreign policy process. Moreover, they may actually help to
construct or alter the domestic landscape, thereby exerting an indirect effect on
the making of foreign policy. Such complex relationships between domestic and
international factors and their influence on states' foreign policies call into question the distinction between internal factors and external factors, particularly in
the post–Cold War international system.

Conclusion: The Future of Foreign Policy
and the Study of Foreign Policy

Many argue that the world is changing in fundamental ways that have significant
implications for states, for their relationships with one another, and for the study
of foreign policy. Two issues specifically relate to foreign policy and have implications for our decision to divide the influences on foreign policy into those that
are "external" and those that are "internal" to national boundaries. These two
issues involve the ability of states to formulate foreign policy and the importance
of foreign policy.

First is the question of the strength of the state itself and whether states can
effectively conduct meaningful foreign policy. As the previous argument suggests, sovereignty may have eroded so much and states may have weakened to a
point that they can scarcely steer a course through international waters. The reasons for the weakened state are many: the rise of nonstate actors such as multinational corporations and nongovernmental organizations, democratization and
the resulting devolution of central state power to the people or to subnational
governments, the inability to control areas claimed by others in ethnic conflict,
and the transfer of policy-making authority to international and regional orga-

nizations. As Babarinde and Wright note in Chapter 11, "increasingly in the relatively strong state of Nigeria, the concept of sovereignty has something of a hollow ring, though the trappings and symbols of office (palaces, airlines, fleets of bullet-proof cars) certainly remain evident."

Second is the question of whether the issues we traditionally consider as "foreign policy" will become less important in the future. With the rise of transnational or "global" problems that require collective action, and with the rise in civil war and intrastate ethnic conflict, individual state foreign policy may become less relevant. International governmental organizations like NATO, the WTO, and the UN will likely increase in importance and the influence of individual states in world politics will decrease as problems become global in scope and collective action is required. Because global issues affect the interests of those within states, they become part of domestic policy as well. As Brian White notes in his chapter on Great Britain, a "dramatic change lies in the range of issues that now constitute the foreign policy agenda. This agenda has so blurred the boundaries between foreign policy and domestic politics that it raises the question of whether a distinctive area of British foreign policy exists any more."

These two issues — the future of the sovereign state and the decline of foreign policy as a distinct area of policy making — will certainly affect the future of foreign policy and world politics. They will also likely affect the study of foreign policy, as they call into question its very definition. Recall from Chapter 1 that the state is typically considered the primary actor in foreign policy. If the future of this actor is in question, the future of foreign policy and how it is defined are in question. Recall also that the definition of foreign policy requires a distinction between "foreign" and "domestic." Although the line between the two is often blurred, the transnational issues that dominate much of the world political agenda today may mean that any major differentiations will cease to exist.

It is because of these dramatic changes in states and their relations that the study of foreign policy is important. As noted in Chapter 1, "[F]oreign policy analysis is a distinct area of inquiry that connects the study of international relations (the way states relate to each other in international politics) with the study of domestic politics (the functioning of governments and the relationships among individuals, groups, and governments)." Thus, students of foreign policy are in a unique position to track the changes taking place within states and between states. They are also well placed to follow the complex relationships between domestic and international politics. The nature of foreign policy and its actor, the state, is certainly undergoing transformation. Understanding this transformation is the key to a systematic exploration of the future of foreign policy.

Suggestions for Further Reading

Goldmann, Kjell. "The Line in Water: International and Domestic Politics," *Cooperation and Conflict* 24 (1989): 103–116.

Hermann, Margaret G., and Joe D. Hagan, "International Decision Making: Leadership Matters," *Foreign Policy* 110 (spring 1998): 124–137.

Katzenstein, Peter J., ed. *The Culture of National Security: Norms and Identity in World Politics*. New York: Columbia University Press, 1996.

Keohane, Robert O., and Joseph S. Nye Jr. "Globalization: What's New? What's Hot? (And So What)," *Foreign Policy* 118 (spring 2000): 104–110.

Putnam, Robert D. "Diplomacy and Domestic Politics: The Logic of Two-Level Games," *International Organization* 42 (1988): 427–460.

Sassen, Saskia. *Globalization and Its Discontents*. New York: New Press, 1998.

Snyder, Glenn H. *Alliance Politics*. Ithaca: Cornell University Press, 1997.

Notes

1. For more on alliance formation and alliance behavior, see John S. Duffield, "International Regimes and Alliance Behavior: Explaining NATO Force Levels," *International Organization* 46 (1992): 819–855; Steven R. David, *Choosing Sides: Alignment and Realignment in the Third World* (Baltimore: Johns Hopkins Press, 1991); and Glenn H. Snyder, *Alliance Politics* (Ithaca: Cornell University Press, 1997).

2. For more discussion on globalization and the relationship between internal and external factors in economic interdependence, see Robert O. Keohane and Joseph S. Nye Jr., "Globalization: What's New? What's Hot? (And So What)," *Foreign Policy* 118 (spring 2000): 104–109; Saskia Sassen, *Globalization and Its Discontents* (New York: New Press, 1998); and Helen Milner, "Resisting the Protectionist Temptation: Industry and the Making of Trade Policy in France and the United States during the 1970s," *International Organization* 41 (1987): 639–666.

3. For more on the importance of role conceptions and identity concerns in foreign policy, see Thomas Risse et al., "To Euro or Not to Euro? The EMU and Identity Politics in the European Union," *European Journal of International Relations* 5 (1999): 147–187; Yosef Lapid and Friedrich Kratochwil, *The Return of Culture and Identity in IR Theory* (Boulder: Lynne Rienner, 1996); Peter J. Katzenstein, ed., *The Culture of National Security: Norms and Identity in World Politics* (New York: Columbia University Press, 1996); Michael Barnett, "Culture, Strategy, and Foreign Policy Change: Israel's Road to Oslo," *European Journal of International Relations* 5 (1999): 5–36; John S. Duffield, "Political Culture and State Behavior: Why Germany Confounds Neorealism," *International Organization* 53 (autumn 1999): 765–803; Thomas U. Berger, *Cultures of Antimilitarism: National Security in Germany and Japan* (Baltimore: Johns Hopkins University Press, 1998); Stephen G. Walker, *Role Theory and Foreign Policy Analysis* (Durham: Duke University Press, 1987); K. J. Holsti, "National Role Conceptions in the Study of Foreign Policy," *International Studies Quarterly* 14 (1970): 643–671; Glenn Chafetz, Hillel Abramson, and Suzette Grillot, "Role Theory and Foreign Policy: Belarussian and Ukrainian Compliance with the Nuclear Nonproliferation Regime," *Political Psychology* 17 (1996): 727–757.

4. For recent research on the importance of leaders in the link between the American public and U.S. foreign policy, see Robert Shapiro and Lawrence Jacobs, "Who Leads and Who Follows? U.S. Presidents, Public Opinion, and Foreign Policy," in *Decision-making in a Glass House: Mass Media, Public Opinion, and American Foreign Policy in the 21st Century,* ed. Brigitte Nacos, Robert Shapiro, and Pierangelo Isernia (Lanham, Md.: Rowman and Littlefield, 2000); and Douglas C. Foyle, *Counting the Public In: Presidents, Public Opinion, and Foreign Policy* (New York: Columbia University Press, 1999).

5. For research on regime change and foreign policy, see Joe Hagan, "Domestic Political

Regime Changes and Foreign Policy Restructuring in Western Europe: A Conceptual Framework and Initial Empirical Analysis," *Cooperation and Conflict* 24 (1989): 141–162; Joe Hagan, "Domestic Political Regime Changes and Third World Voting Realignments in the United Nations, 1946–84, *International Organization* 43 (1989): 505–541; and S. J. Andriole and G. W. Hopple, "The Process, Outcomes, and Impact of Regime Change in the Third World, 1959–81," *International Interactions* 12 (1986): 363–392.

6. For discussions of this tendency, see Baghat Korany, "Foreign Policy Decision Making and the Third World: Payoffs and Pitfalls," in *How Foreign Policy Decisions are Made in the Third World,* ed. Bahgat Korany (Boulder: Westview, 1986); Steven R. David, "Explaining Third World Realignment," *World Politics* 43 (1991): 223–256; Yaacov Vertzberger, "Bureaucratic-Organizational Politics and Information Processing in a Developing State," *International Studies Quarterly* 28 (1984): 69–95; Timothy M. Shaw and Olajide Aluko, eds., *The Political Economy of African Foreign Policy* (New York: St. Martin's Press, 1984); Jennie K. Lincoln and Elizabeth G. Ferris, eds., *The Dynamics of Latin American Foreign Policies: Challenges for the 1980s* (Boulder: Westview, 1984); and Baghat Korany and Ali E. Hillal Dessourki, eds., *The Foreign Policies of Arab States* (Boulder: Westview, 1984).

7. For a discussion of many of the possible linkages between international and domestic politics, see Kjell Goldmann, "The Line in Water: International and Domestic Politics," *Cooperation and Conflict* 24 (1989): 103–116.

8. Wolfram F. Hanrieder, "Compatibility and Consensus: A Proposal for the Conceptual Linkage of External and Internal Dimensions of Foreign Policy," *American Political Science Review* 61 (December 1967): 971–982; Charles F. Hermann, "Changing Course: When Governments Choose To Redirect Foreign Policy," *International Studies Quarterly* 34 (1990): 3–21.

9. Robert D. Putnam, "Diplomacy and Domestic Politics: The Logic of Two-Level Games," *International Organization* 42 (1988): 427–460.

10. Peter Gourevitch, "The Second Image Reversed: The International Sources of Domestic Politics," *International Organization* 32 (1978): 881–911; Lauri Karvonen and Bengt Sundelius, "Interdependence and Foreign Policy Management in Sweden and Finland," *International Studies Quarterly* 34 (1990): 211–227.

11. Helen Milner, *Resisting Protectionism* (Princeton: Princeton University Press, 1988).

INDEX